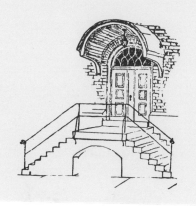

Limits to Interpretation

This book was published with the assistance of the Wisconsin Center for Pushkin Studies at the University of Wisconsin–Madison and the Frederick W. Hilles Publication Fund of Yale University.

Limits to Interpretation

The Meanings of
Anna Karenina

Vladimir E. Alexandrov

The University of Wisconsin Press

The University of Wisconsin Press
1930 Monroe Street
Madison, Wisconsin 53711

www.wisc.edu/wisconsinpress/

3 Henrietta Street
London WC2E 8LU, England

5   4   3   2   1

Printed in the United States of America

Library of Congress Cataloging-in-Publication Data
Alexandrov, Vladimir E.
Limits to interpretation : the meanings of *Anna Karenina* / Vladimir E. Alexandrov.
   p.   cm.
   Includes bibliographical references and index.
   ISBN 0-299-19540-6 (alk. paper)
    1. Tolstoy, Leo, graf, 1828–1910. Anna Karenina.   2. Hermeneutics.   I. Title.
PG3365.A63A44   2004
891.73′3—dc22   2003022202

To the memory of my grandparents

I believe that what is now called literary criticism is a form of Xeroxing. Tell me your theory and I'll tell you in advance what you'll say about any work of literature, especially those you haven't read.

Frank Lentricchia, "Last Will and Testament of an Ex-Literary Critic"

The word "understanding" is insidious. One cannot help forming the impression that it is a one-time and exhaustive act: understanding seems to imply final and unequivocal knowledge. In reality, however, it is a path into infinity; and honesty would require indicating the degree and direction of its approximation. Understanding can be imagined as a net of interpretations and translations of varying degrees of approximation. It is precisely their numbers and mutual contrastiveness that determine the level of understanding.

Yurii Lotman, *Besedy o russkoi kul'ture*

Contents

Acknowledgments   xiii
A Note on Transliteration   xiv

Introduction   3
   My Aims   3
   The Problem of Mediation in Interpretation   10
   Conceptual Mediation in Cultural and Literary Study   11

Part One. The Plurality and Limits of Interpretation

1. An Ethical Argument for Recognizing Textual Alterity   25
2. A Psychological Argument for Recognizing Textual Alterity   29
3. Alterity and Semiotics   32
4. Jakobson's "Metalingual Function" and Alterity   34
5. Hermeneutic Indices, or Guides to Textual Alterity   38
   5.1. Examples of Hermeneutic Indices   39
   5.2. Hermeneutic Indices, Predication, Simile, Metaphor   44
   5.3. Hermeneutic Indices as Guides to the Plurality and
        Limits of Interpretation   49
   5.4. Caveats about Hermeneutic Indices   50
   5.5. Are Hermeneutic Indices Inherent in Literary Works?   54

Part Two. *Anna Karenina:* A Map of Readings

6. From Theory to Practice   63
7. Early Signals   67
8. Reading Readings, and Art about Art   75
   8.1. Varieties of Texts   75
   8.2. Reading and Anna's Death   80
   8.3. Mikhailov's Paintings   83
   8.4. Mikhailov and Artistic Creation   85

Contents

8.5.	Music and the Nature of Artistic Form	88
8.6.	Form in Art and in Life	90
9.	Art and Metaphysics	92
9.1.	The Plotinian Implications of Mikhailov's "Creation"	92
9.2.	The Spiritual in Art and in Life	93
10.	The Formal Implications of the Novel's Conception of Art	95
10.1.	The Two Poles of Language and the Embodiment of Aesthetic Ambivalence	95
10.2.	Examples of Structures of Meaning	99
10.3.	Tolstoy on the Structure of *Anna Karenina*	104
11.	The Problem of Language	107
12.	Absolutism: Claims about Universal Truth and Morality	112
12.1.	The General Problem of Fictional Authority	112
12.2.	The Narrator	114
12.3.	The Narrator, Karenin's Self-Deception, and the Nature of True Faith	118
12.4.	Karenin and Echoes of Saint Paul	121
12.5.	Karenin and the "Crude Force"	123
12.6.	The Incompatibility of Saint Paul's Teachings with Human Nature	126
12.7.	Saint Paul on Marriage, Sex, and God's Work	129
13.	Relativity: Characters as Arbiters of Meaning and Value	134
13.1.	Introduction	134
13.2.	Multiple Viewpoints in Narrative	139
13.3.	Characters and Relative Time	141
13.4.	Levin	144
13.4.1.	Levin and Kitty	144
13.4.2.	Levin and His Brothers	151
13.4.3.	Levin and Others	156
13.4.4.	Levin's Faith	160
13.5.	Anna	171
13.5.1.	Anna in Moscow	171
13.5.2.	Anna's Return to St. Petersburg	174
13.5.3.	Anna and Vronsky	176
13.5.4.	Anna's Death	186
13.5.5.	Anna and Others	191
13.5.6.	Anna's Arranged Marriage to Karenin	192
13.5.7.	Anna's Moral Sense	194
13.5.8.	Anna's "Doubling"	198
13.6.	Stiva	201

	13.6.1. To Judge or Not to Judge Stiva?	208
	13.6.2. The Example of Turgenev's *Hunter's Sketches*	208
13.7.	Dolly	211
13.8.	Vronsky	215
13.9.	Kitty	226
13.10.	Karenin	228
13.11.	Minor Characters	231
14. Self and Others		233
14.1.	Understanding and Uniting with Others	233
14.2.	The Individual and the Collective	238
14.3.	Collective Coercion and the Reification of Evil	242
15. The Inner Voice and Conscience		243
15.1.	Stiva	244
15.2.	Levin	246
15.3.	Anna	250
15.4.	Kitty	252
15.5.	Vronsky	253
15.6.	Conscience, Ethics, and Relativization	254
16. Essentialism		257
16.1.	Nature and Humankind	258
16.2.	Women	259
	16.2.1. The "Woman Question"	263
	16.2.2. Women's Wisdom, Narrative Structure, and Male Insight	265
16.3.	Men	266
16.4.	Peasants	267
16.5.	Essentialism and the Problem of Freedom	270
	16.5.1. Levin	270
	16.5.2. Other Characters	274
17. Fate		276
17.1.	Anna	278
17.2.	Levin	282
17.3.	Fatidic Connections between Anna's and Levin's Plots	285
18. Literary Form, Fate, Freedom, Chance		290
Conclusion		295
Notes		301
Works Cited		334
Index		347

Acknowledgments

I am grateful to Caryl Emerson, Donna Orwin, Irina Paperno, and Robert Wechsler for reading parts of this book and for giving me their expert opinions and suggestions about a wide range of issues. I am especially indebted to David Bethea, Joseph Frank, Michael Holquist, and Hugh McLean for reading the entire manuscript. They provided me with invaluable moral support and with numerous concrete recommendations and corrections that I incorporated silently throughout the book. Had I tried to acknowledge separately every one of their points, the number of endnotes in this book would have increased significantly. I would also like to express my gratitude to the Frederick W. Hilles Publication Fund of Yale University and the Wisconsin Center for Pushkin Studies for their generous subventions.

Some parts of this book appeared in different form in *Comparative Literature, Elementa,* the *Russian Review,* and *Slavica Tergestina.* I am grateful to the editors for permission to reuse the material here (bibliographic data is in the endnotes).

A Note on Transliteration

In the endnotes to this book and whenever I quote Russian, I use the simplified Library of Congress system for transliterating the Russian alphabet. For personal names in the body of the book, I use either the transliterations that appear in Pevear and Volokhonsky's translation of *Anna Karenina* or similarly accessible forms.

Limits to Interpretation

Introduction

My Aims

This is a hybrid book that could easily have had the two parts of its title reversed. My primary aim is to propose a text-specific reading methodology, one that is tailored as much as possible to a particular work, and that is thus designed to minimize the circularity of interpretation, or the process of mediation, inherent in any act of reading. My second aim is to illustrate this method on the example of Leo Tolstoy's classic novel. The ultimate purpose of this book is to advocate a broad revision of the academic study of literature through a change in how textual interpretation, which is still the cornerstone of all literary studies, is carried out.

I conceived my approach in opposition to two trends that are widespread in the United States and that contributed to the impasse that many observers, both within and outside the academy, believe literary studies have now reached. One is an a priori reliance on various mediating ideologies drawn from such fields as philosophy, politics, race, gender and postcolonial studies, etc. Related to this is the seemingly orthogonal but actually parallel view that there is no point in talking about anything except mediation because that is all reading entails anyway. By contrast, I argue that there are compelling reasons for deferring to particular kinds of meaning that inhere in works we call literary and that there is a way to ascertain what these meanings are without regressing to notions of authorial intention or other simplifications. The second trend I oppose is the imperative that many scholars feel to produce new interpretations of works of literature. More often than not this leads to distortion, hairsplitting, and a reductive sense of the works' meanings. What I propose instead is that a work of literature be seen as a structure that can motivate a specific *range* of divergent and even contradictory interpretations of varying degrees of plausibility.

My approach might be characterized as "neoformalist" or "quasi-structuralist" and is thus consciously retrograde in the current American academic climate. I build on fundamental ideas about the relational nature of meaning in language and literature that were developed by two leading Russian thinkers of the last century—Roman Jakobson and Yurii Lotman. I also complement their ideas with arguments from reader-oriented theory, developmental and cognitive psychology, cultural anthropology, and ethics. Despite the fact that Jakobson's and Lotman's writings are now out of fashion among many American academics, I believe that there is great value in returning to them because they provide persuasive explanations of how language in literature actually works. Also especially important is that their conception of linguistic meaning can serve as a basis for a reading methodology that is both *adaptive* and *pluralistic*.[1] An approach such as this does not anticipate the conclusions it will yield and thus has the unique benefit of being in harmony with the generally liberal social and political views widespread in American academe, something that cannot be said about many of the theoretical approaches to literature that are now in vogue.

What is the proof for my claim about novelty being a scholarly preoccupation? And what possible objection could anyone have to it?

Rather than survey more examples of literary scholarship than anyone would have the patience to read, I would like to offer the following concise form of evidence—brief characterizations of new books culled from publishers' advertisements in the May 2000 issue of the journal *PMLA,* which I chose simply because this issue contains a large number of such announcements (page numbers follow the quotations): "perspectives . . . that official histories ignore," "the necessary starting point from which all future discussions . . . must proceed," "a completely new approach," "investigates . . . materials hitherto ignored" (377), "nothing in print . . . comparable to this book in scope and variety," "this revision of modernism . . . the ways in which the author seeks to rethink it out from under the limitations of," "reveals unexpected ramifications . . . readings . . . often satisfying and surprising" (379), "redefines," "rewrites," "new theories, new technologies, and new ways of thinking," "a revelatory examination" (383), "enlightening book . . . fresh . . . criticism" (387), "one of the first books" (389), "opens the path for a radical revision," "first work in any language," "first sustained analysis" (391), "an entirely new approach" (393), "the freshness of the perspectives" (399), "first book-length study," "situates the often neglected collection" (401), "fresh insights . . . a passionate call for radical change," "original and engaging ways of understanding," "provocatively argues that he is not," "to challenge existing critical notions" (403), "challenges many of the major currents in scholarship . . . an important step in redefining," "new readings," "fresh and vigorous arguments," "distinctive and fresh . . . remarkable authority and originality" (405), "contests the notion," "a major breakthrough," "fresh approach" (409), "fresh," "no other such collection" (411), "provocative," "inventive study" (413), "remarkable new look," "valuable reconsideration" (415), "highly original," "will contribute to a transformation of our thinking" (419), "subverts the stock image," "challenges existing criticism," "throwing light on some corners . . . not usually explored," "defamiliarizes . . . invites a reexamination" (423), "reassesses," "sheds new light," "a fresh perspective," "offers new insights" (425), "pathfinding book" (427), "original . . . freshest new voice," "draws on newly discovered manuscripts," "first full-scale literary biography," "first biography," "first modern edition," "a radical break with earlier interpretations," "a searching critique of . . . assumptions" (428–29), "may well mark the beginning of a revolution" (432), "a critical de-centering," "undeniably original . . . a fresh paradigm-shaker" (433), "a revolution in our readings," "provocative," "a dazzling contribution to the project of reclaiming" (435), "a compelling reassessment," "reimagines the canonical origins . . . challenges existing perceptions" (436). This list does not include descriptions of all the books advertised in this issue of the journal or of all *kinds* of books that could be called scholarly, such as editions, translations, handbooks, and so on. But there is little doubt that it illustrates a dominant trend in how literary scholarship is valued by a broad range of academic publishers and thus by the academy in general.

The defining feature of these ads is that they conceive of originality in terms of an author's *dialectical reaction* against contemporary critical approaches and traditions or, somewhat less often, against those from the recent past. (In fact, if one judges by the most common kinds of literary scholarship, the older the critical analyses of a particular work, the more likely are they to be ignored or acknowledged only very cursorily by subsequent reinterpreters.) And it is precisely in the dialectical character of scholarly publishing that the problem lies. When most scholars pursue novelty, they proceed by focusing on what they see as competing, more adequate, or overlooked interpretations of particular works; and their publications typically contain some version of the claim that other investigators have misread the works or missed something vitally important in them. Paralleling this is the widespread belief of many academics in the *progress* of critical methodologies and theoretical paradigms (which, in fact, also usually develop via dialectical reactions against past beliefs). As a result, new theoretical approaches are often automatically assumed to be not just different from but superior to preceding ones. For example, an anonymous evaluator of an article that I once submitted to a fashionable journal complained about my citing Jakobson as an attempt to "exhume" him, as if it were a truth universally acknowledged that poststructuralism (note the implied progress) had buried him forever.[2]

The typical product of this kind of fixation on exegetic originality is an analysis of some limited aspects of a work or works—obviously those that appear not to have received the same kind of attention in the past, which necessarily makes these "new" aspects swell in magnitude and importance in comparison to whatever had received the attention of earlier scholars. In turn, the new analyses serve as theses for future antithetical readings. Even when scholarly works present themselves as building on and incorporating previous studies, which happens especially often in longer publications such as books, their primary claim on the reader's attention is still that they have something new to say. Indeed, why publish or read them if this were not the case? The usual consequence of this is a limited view of any work in which the novelty is sought, because to be original means not to give full attention to what others have said about different aspects of the work, as a result of which these shrink in relative importance. This procedure loses sight of the unavoidable fact that a work of art is "broader and more vital than its interpretations," as Lotman once put it, and that "an interpretation will always be only an approximation."[3]

The problem that I have sketched here can be criticized from at least four perspectives. The first is that there certainly are genuinely innovative readings of works in the sense that they reveal something other readers had not noticed before (or, as is often the case, that relatively *few* readers had noticed earlier and that had not been sufficiently *publicized,* which is an important distinction). I do not doubt this, and I flatter myself by thinking that even I have made discoveries of this kind. But a common difficulty in this case is that the new reading is usually presented as being more perceptive, accurate, and fuller than the earlier ones, which thus tend to be pushed aside rather than reconsidered in relation to the new one; and this despite the fact that older readings may have seemed, and may still seem, equally convincing to large numbers of other readers. I acknowledge nothing unusual when I say that I too have been tempted by this kind of self-protective self-aggrandizement.

The second possible criticism of the dialectical scheme is that books and articles that synthesize previous literary scholarship are published all the time. I agree and can think of examples myself. But there are relatively few of these, especially in the field of textual exegesis as compared with literary-historical or other contextualized approaches.

The third objection is that because literary scholarship is an accumulation of knowledge, specialists will try to incorporate new readings of favorite works into an ever richer amalgam of interpretations. However, here it is necessary to distinguish between scholarly *publishing* and scholarly *reading*. It is a fact that many scholars try to keep up with their specialized fields by reading whatever is published in them, as a result of which they may *know* of various contradictory and divergent viewpoints and interpretations. They may even teach some of them to their students. However, as the blurbs from *PMLA* demonstrate, this knowledge does not necessarily translate into *publications,* which mostly celebrate innovation. And because of the amount of amour propre that most scholars invest in their publications, which are, after all, their most visible and important professional achievements, they also tend to be especially protective of the innovative views they publish. Even in less formal publications such as conference papers or in professional discussions with colleagues in corridors or over drinks, most scholars feel strongly that they need to demarcate their own positions from those of their peers, be they contemporaries or immediate predecessors. The academy provides few if any laurels for simply repeating what others have said before (at least in principle), and no one takes pleasure in being seen by peers as an epigone of some more renowned scholar whose work is evaluated as "groundbreaking" (again, at least in principle). Collaborative scholarly works by two or more individuals that consist of literary analysis are rare and do not disprove the general pattern.

The fourth perspective from which the dialectical schema can be criticized is that the emergence of new readings is, in fact, the true mode of existence of the kind of artifact that we call a literary work of art. According to this view, the meaning of any utterance depends on its context. Thus, because the cultural contexts for a literary work's reception will inevitably change through time (they can be political, economic, religious, aesthetic, scientific, etc.), so will the meanings that emerge from a work. From this perspective, the pursuit of novel interpretations is not at all problematic or reductive, and the ability of a work to show new and unexpected facets over time is a measure of its value to the members of the culture in which it exists. This view of a work as protean is, of course, also an argument against the idea that meaning inheres in a work, because the work emerges as a stimulus for readings that are primarily functions of largely impersonal extraliterary assumptions, beliefs, or associations.[4] I do not see this view as simply false, but most of what follows in this book is an extended argument against such extreme relativism and a defense of meaning as a function of particular kinds of verbal relations inherent in works we identify as literary. There is no doubt that works of literature prompt different readings by virtue of their ambiguities and lacunae and the frequently indeterminate relations among their constituent elements. However, the coherence of a work, the fact that it can be recognized as the "same" work through time, implies a minimal network of significant relations or formal links among the words that constitute it. In life, cultural contexts and semantic fields gradually shift; in literature, structure fixes words and their semantic fields into more permanent configurations.[5]

The difference between the dialectical style of exegesis that I fault and the methodology that I advocate hinges on my relative lack of concern for novelty in interpretation. Instead, I seek two things: to understand how a work can prompt a *plurality* of different interpretations *simultaneously,* without regard to whether these are "old" or "new" in the history of the work's reception; and how this configuration of readings allows one to speak about what can be called the *limits* of that work's interpretations.[6] I believe that it is not only possible but usually necessary to read a given work multifariously (although, as I will explain, I mean something quite specific by this). Doing so has the liberating effect of making one—in any event, has made me—far more open to how others read a work because one's own view of it is no longer hampered by a search for novelty. In other words, it becomes increasingly difficult to believe that the variety of readings that a work has received over time is due either to most of the readings being misguided (although the possibility of erroneous readings cannot and should not be excluded) or to the absence of an inherent configuration of meanings in the work itself (which does not mean that all meaning in a work is fixed). Another way of putting this is that I seek to examine the relations among different possible readings of a work as well as that work's ambiguities, which are actually different sides of the same coin. It is a striking fact that most experienced readers both inside and outside academe readily acknowledge that at least some and frequently a great deal of ambiguity is an important feature of enduring works of literature. But it is an equally striking paradox that this fact is usually not manifested very prominently in most academic publications, which tend to focus either on "new" textual *determinacies* that the author has unearthed or on the kinds of *predictable indeterminacies* that are functions of the critical methods deployed, like the "aporias" on which some deconstructionists used to focus (which in turn recall the "inevitable contradictions" that practitioners of Socialist Realism liked to invoke when criticizing "bourgeois" writers).

Am I not contradicting myself when I claim that I shun originality at the same time that I advocate what I believe is a different and consequently innovative sort of reading? What needs to be understood in this regard is the difference between the kind of pursuit of novelty that I find restrictive and the inclusiveness of interpretations that I hope to attain. If one abandons the paradigm of originality, one can focus on adding to, refining, or modifying the *range* of a work's different readings, but without necessarily abandoning or overturning any, most, or even some of them (although these too are all possibilities that cannot be excluded a priori). This view implies that scholars may develop new forms of general agreement about the range of interpretations that (some) works of literature can sustain (not all works are equally ambiguous or rich). However, an end to all debates about the different meanings of works is highly unlikely for numerous reasons: these include the indeterminate nature of the relations among different interpretations, the varying degrees of ambiguity that characterize individual plausible readings, the ineluctable role of the reader's involvement in constructing the meanings of a work and in judging which are plausible and to what degree, and the professional pressure to stand out from the crowd and be innovative.

All these preliminary discussions lead me to the second aim of this book, which is far easier to state: to test the reading methodology I propose on the example of *Anna Karenina*. There is no necessary connection between the method and Tolstoy's novel: I chose it because it is well known, popular, complex, and a personal favorite. In principle, the method should work for any text or utterance; but whether it does or not is best judged by what it reveals about an entire long work rather than about selected examples from various shorter ones. Although my reading of the novel takes up the larger portion of this book, I am, of course, not primarily concerned with producing my own new interpretation of *Anna Karenina* that reacts against those of earlier or contemporary readers (although some of this is inevitable because not all readings are equally plausible). What I hope to do instead is to account for the *plurality* of contradictory or simply divergent interpretations that the novel can sustain simultaneously by showing how and where different possible meanings can be generated in it. My reading of the novel is thus an attempt to "map" or to understand the relations among as many of its plausible meanings and ambiguities as possible and thus to identify what complexly inheres in it. This also implies that there are limits to interpretation and that there are meanings that fall outside the realm of plausibility.

The kind of "global" reading I seek to produce is limited, however, and does not presume to account for all of a work's different effects. Like legions of readers from around the world, I too experience the novel on an emotional and not just an analytical level. In fact, were it not for Tolstoy's remarkable ability to engage us emotionally, *Anna Karenina* would not be the great work it is. But I do not attempt to connect the kinds of affects this novel induces with the meanings it generates except occasionally and in elementary fashion. At present, there is no way to do this without invoking subjective reactions that are, paradoxically, as unverifiable as they are crucial to the experience of reading.[7]

The Problem of Mediation in Interpretation

The circularity of reading that I seek to reduce to a minimum—but not to escape, because this is impossible—can be described in several ways.[8] It can be conceived abstractly in terms of the basic conditions necessary for any communication to take place: the receiver of a message must have internalized codes in order to construct the meanings of the signs that reach him; thus, a message is necessarily always a function of the codes used to decipher it. A simpler and more obvious variant of this argument is that we already have to know a language in order to be able to understand a message communicated in it, and the message can communicate only what the resources of a given language will allow. Circularity can also be conceived as the inevitable quandary faced by anyone who wants to read something that is new to him but who of course cannot do so other than in terms of his previous mindset and experiences, whether of reading or of life. From this perspective, any reader enacts interpretations that are prefigured to varying degrees in the assumptions about existence that he brings to the task of reading. It is important to realize that these can include intentional stances as well as entirely unconscious motivations and can range from reading with a particular ideology or theory in mind to "simply" asking a question as obvious (and as difficult to answer) as, Why did Anna Karenina kill herself? Any reading is also automatically predicated on a large array of overt or unwitting beliefs regarding the act of reading itself, the ontology and value of literature, indeed, the meaning of the concept "literature," its relation to "reality" outside a work, the nature of the self and of the world, and so on. In this sense, each act of reading both forms the questions that a reader brings to a given work and then shapes the answers that he gleans from it.

By focusing on mediation as an inherent feature of and obstacle to reading, I am, in fact, raising a question about how one can read a work of literature and apprehend whatever peculiarities and distinctive features it may contain. But this in turn is a variant of a larger question—how can one get out of the confines of one's self, of one's limited and limiting knowledge and experience, and know anything that is not already familiar to some extent? Albert Einstein's remark that a given scientific theory "decides what we can observe" shows that this problem is not unique to humanistic inquiry.[9] The limitations that this problem places on human understanding can be illustrated by the fact that there is probably nothing so alien that human beings would fail to characterize and thus grasp it on some level, even if only in such abstract terms as "appealing," "frightening," or "incomprehensible." And if there were something so alien that we could say nothing about it (which possibility is put into question by the phrase that I just used to express it), then that "incomprehensible something" would probably not even register as existent. Total, radical alterity is thus probably unknowable and impossible except as some abstract concept (which fact is also confirmed by the familiar linguistic expression that I just gave it). Another way of saying this is that some degree of mediation—or some degree of "filtering" experience through familiar categories—is always inherent in any act of knowing.[10]

Conceptual Mediation in Cultural and Literary Study

The most powerful forms of mediation are probably the ones that we deploy unwittingly. Because this issue bears directly on reading, I thought it would be useful to consider some examples of conceptual mediation drawn from the discipline "cultural psychology," which is concerned with understanding the ways in which basic psychological categories vary in different cultures.[11]

Consider the phenomenon of personal names, which most of us use automatically to identify people whom we consider to be unique individuals bearing specific traits. Lotman went so far as to claim, "Perhaps the most striking manifestation of human nature is the use of personal names and the underscoring of individuality, the uniqueness of the separate personality connected with it."[12] However, investigations of psychological categories in non-Western cultures demonstrate that a conception of human nature as rooted in "individuality" and the "uniqueness of the separate personality" is a specifically contemporary Western notion that can be highly misleading when applied to many other cultures around the world. (It is, of course, reductive to speak of "the West" or of any other large geographical area without differentiating among its various constituent cultural traditions; I do so not because I think these are unimportant but for the sake of simplicity and to illustrate a principle that can and should be applied to smaller cultural entities.) A counterexample to the individualistic conception of the self is provided by Clifford Geertz in his well-known article, "'From the native's point of view': On the Nature of Anthropological Understanding" (1974), in which he describes naming practices in traditional Moroccan society:

[A] man I knew who lived in Sefrou and worked in Fez but came from the Beni Yazgha tribe settled nearby—and from the Hima lineage of the Taghut subfraction of the Wulad Ben Ydir fraction within it—was known as a Sefroui to his work fellows in Fez, a Yazghi to all of us non-Yazghis in Sefrou, an Ydiri to other Beni Yazghas around, except for those who were themselves of the Wulad Ben Ydir faction, who called him a Taghuti. As for the few other Taghutis, they called him a Himiwi.

Geertz also adds that "calling a man a Sefroui is like calling him a San Franciscan: It classifies him, but it doesn't type him; it places him without portraying him." In short, this system of nomenclature is not predicated on a conception of people as monads with portable identities and the existential freedom to define themselves as they see fit, all of which are implicated in Western conceptions of the self.[13]

The Western notion of personhood gives rise to a wide array of additional assumptions that can act as major barriers to understanding other cultures. For example, Janet E. Helms has identified a source of possible bias in how the cognitive ability of African Americans is measured by standard tests that are predicated on the Western belief that selves are distinct from each other and from their environment. The "Afrocentric" cultural view is that the person is interconnected with his or her surroundings, which may thus prompt the misleading conclusion that the test taker is "unduly" concerned with the ambiance in which the test is conducted. Similarly, the Afrocentric belief that time is marked and measured by events and customs that are socially meaningful, which reflects the relative value placed on the group rather than on the individual, may lead the test taker to try to produce a "good" answer rather than finish all the questions on time.[14]

As the last example demonstrates, conceptions of selves can underlie or merge with conceptions of time and with value judgments, which, in turn, inevitably shape existence in different ways. Hope Landrine has pursued this connection and has identified a series of far-reaching cultural implications that stem from the Western European assumption that time "flows" from past to future: "the 'past' is behind and 'backward' while the future is 'ahead' and 'forward.' . . . time is a 'valuable' natural resource that should be 'saved' and 'used wisely' rather than 'wasted.' . . . [time] should be 'managed' . . . and . . . ought to be 'stolen' for intimate purposes." According to

Landrine, these metaphors are implicated in numerous clinical concepts that play a major role in the mental health professions and that include punctuality, delay of gratification, impulsivity, laziness, goal-directedness, reality testing, orientation to time and place, and the kind of influence that the "past" can and should have on the "present." Landrine's point is that such assumptions, which are all the more coercive for being mostly unconscious, can seem profoundly "alien" to representatives of other cultures, such as those "who take it for granted—equally unwittingly—that time flows backward (things start in the present and then become the past), that the future does not exist (because it's the present when one 'arrives' there), and that time is constituted and marked not by a clock, but by their own behavior."[15]

If largely or entirely unconscious assumptions such as these can interfere with understanding the sui generis nature of basic concepts in foreign cultures, then approaching verbal artifacts from other cultures with fixed notions about literature, the self, time, value, and much else obviously also risks producing major misunderstandings. On the one hand, unexamined preconceptions could be as broad as projecting our generally postromantic conception of the "literary work of art"—with its associations of being a particular kind of written "construct" or "organic unity" that a solitary reader tries to "interpret" in order to get at what it "contains"—onto a cultural system that has an entirely different view of the status and function of linguistic composition and of how people relate to it. One example of the latter is what has been called "orature," or the kind of public oral composition that Gîtahi Gîtîtî has characterized as "the primary source of literary creativity in Africa."[16] Another is the hybrid Balinese practice of performing oral vernacular translations and paraphrases of literary works written in the archaic language Old Javanese that Mary Sabina Zurbuchen has studied. On the other hand, theoretical assumptions could be as specific as the argument that selves are constituted from the outside in via dialogic exchanges with others (Mikhail Bakhtin), or that literary works capture the circulation of social energy (Stephen Greenblatt), or that all "metanarratives" are now defunct (Jean-François Lyotard), among many others. As it happens, all three of these currently influential Western theoretical positions can be seen as differing not only from other, non-Western cultural beliefs but also from those that were foundational in premodern Europe and that persist to this day in the legacies of particular writers, such as that human beings are defined by immaterial souls, or that words ultimately derive from a divine realm, or that all natural languages around the world share the same few basic features.

Given this, is it really possible to claim in our age of heightened post-multicultural awareness that the contemporary literary theories are "right" and that these venerable beliefs are "wrong"? After all, we are not dealing with scientific progress, despite the widespread assumption among many theorists that they are on the "cutting edge." It is a fact that countless reproducible astronomical observations and space flights have disproven the Ptolemaic, geocentric view of the cosmos while simultaneously confirming Copernican heliocentrism. But what kind of "evidence" could conceivably "disprove" something like a novelist's *faith* in the reality and potency of a spiritual dimension of being, or a poet's *conviction* that he has written a sonnet expressing perfectly his complex autumnal mood? Because most contemporary literary theories are consciously predicated on specific philosophical or ideological assumptions about such issues as the nature of the self, of language, of social relations, of the possibility of meaning, etc., they can frequently be at odds with beliefs that underlie and are expressed in particular works of literature that see things differently. Within the realm of human beliefs there is no absolute ground that can be used to adjudicate what individuals choose to view as true and real.

Accepting this conclusion would seem to be essential for anyone interested in studying different cultures or the literatures of different cultures, which necessarily has to be motivated by the conviction that others around the world do not always believe the same things that we do and that there is something important to be gained from trying to understand how their beliefs differ from ours. By emphasizing cultural differences in this way, I do not mean to deny the claims about "human universals" that have been made by anthropologists, evolutionary psychologists, linguists, and others and that are clearly valid on some, perhaps relatively coarse-grained (although still very important) levels of human experience. But if there were no differences among literatures and cultures, there would be no reason to study any cultural tradition other than one's own. It follows, therefore, that the paramount task is to find a methodology of reading that does not project onto works but that enables whatever is in them to emerge.

As the above examples from cultural psychology demonstrate, it is possible to become aware of one's own mediating biases and to minimize them to the extent that one can grasp unfamiliar paradigms in other cultures. Geertz has explained that this is achieved via a process analogous to how one reads a work of literature (or, perhaps better to say, how one *should* read a work of literature). In both cases, understanding follows the "hermeneutic circle," which entails grasping how details fit the whole and the whole defines the details. In Geertz's view, this process is "as central to ethnographic interpretation, and thus to the penetration of other people's modes of thought, as it is to literary, historical, philological, psychoanalytic, biblical, or for that matter to the informal annotation of experience we call common sense."[17] Geertz's conception of understanding, which gains authority from having been tested in the field on real cultural differences, is also implicitly opposed to the two trends in academic literary criticism that I described at the outset. Because the hermeneutic circle involves understanding the way a work defines the elements that constitute it and how these elements define the work, it is neither partial nor biased (or at least only minimally biased by virtue of its reliance on the idea of "parts" and "wholes").

The high degree of self-consciousness that this discussion of mediation implies also has to be applied to the conception of reading proposed below. In other words, I will have to justify my view that meanings inhere in literary works and that it is valuable, in the sense of being morally and psychologically necessary, to understand these as fully as possible. This does not mean, however, that I see "authorial intention" as retrievable or even relevant to textual interpretation, or that a work's meaning is fully determinate, or that the reader can be factored out of the process of interpretation.[18]

The primary lesson for literary interpretation that can be drawn from cultural psychology is that any critical approach based on considerations extrinsic to a work will betray it. Even though I do not see the distinction between extrinsic and intrinsic as always simple and clear, it is still the case that the more dogmatic and universal are one's a priori theoretical and cultural assumptions, the more predictable will be the claims one makes about any work to which these are applied and the more occluded will be whatever quiddity that work may actually possess. Simply put, some ideologies cut works to their own shapes much more brutally than do others. This is the point of Lentricchia's wry formulation that I used as my first epigraph.

One obvious example of this that most American academics would not find objectionable because of its distance from us in time as well as space is "Socialist Realism" in the former Soviet Union. According to this official state artistic doctrine, all works produced under its banner were expected to embody an image of social reality in its revolutionary development. This artistic doctrine was, of course, overtly linked to the nominally Marxist social and political ideology that held sway over all aspects of life in the country. Given this, it is highly ironic that there was always superabundant evidence of the irreconcilability between the doctrine and many cultural phenomena to which it was applied (with the obvious exception of the often stillborn works that were intentionally created under its aegis). Indeed, the only way

Socialist Realism managed to maintain itself—and highly imperfectly at that—was via a ruthless police state.

As alien as Socialist Realism and the Soviet political system may seem to us, there are, in fact, numerous systems of belief in the United States, both within and outside academe, that have a similar hegemonic flavor. These ideologies function on a far smaller scale, of course, and are incomparably less pernicious in their social effects, but they resemble totalitarianism in the sense of informing all aspects of individual behavior and worldview for those who subscribe to them. Just one striking example is the movement in American law schools known as "critical race theory," which uses racial perspectives and attitudes as the touchstone for defining "reality." From this movement's point of view, an *invented* story of abuse by a member of a racial minority, even a story that is widely acknowledged to have been fabricated, is ultimately still "true" because it expresses genuine, far-reaching fears and forms of mistreatment of the minority over time.[19] Another example is various fundamentalist religious groups that strive to impose on society their scripturally based beliefs about such matters as forbidding abortions or teaching evolution in public schools.[20]

Within academe, however, there is often a curious disjunction between theory and its existential implications. There are always exceptions, of course, and it would be unfair to make this a universal claim. For example, it is well known that some proponents of such trends as "postcolonial" studies, which view literature and other forms of expression primarily in terms of how they reflect social, political, economic, cultural, and gender inequities between "First" and "Third World" countries, do, in fact, manifest their beliefs via social activism and political behavior outside the academy. But in many other cases, those who advocate particular theoretical positions do not appear to be troubled by inconsistencies between how they approach works of literature and how they deal with the relations between themselves and other people, even when the philosophical underpinnings for the two forms of activity would appear to be the same. We can see an exceptionally vivid example of this in what became known as "L'Affaire Derrida" on the pages of the *New York Review of Books* in 1993. In the context of reviewing two books about Heidegger's links to Nazism, Thomas Sheehan described a conflict that had erupted between Jacques Derrida and the editor of one of the books, Richard Wolin, over the latter's inclusion of an interview with Derrida in English translation. There is no need to go into all the details of this "affair," which include Derrida's remarkable threat of legal action against Wolin and Sheehan's speculations about the real reasons behind Derrida's umbrage. What is noteworthy is that after Sheehan's review appeared, Derrida, who has been for decades one of the leading theoreticians of linguistic impersonality and indeterminacy, felt compelled to write several letters to the *Review* to explain why he objected to having his interview appear in Wolin's book. Especially significant is that he did not refer even once to the ideas for which he is famous, such as the "free play" of signifiers or the impossibility of a single "plane of discourse." Instead, he couched his argument in the conventional ethical terms of legally *owning* the utterances in question, thus transforming himself into the "transcendental signified" of his own discourse: "Do I not have the right to protest when a text of mine is published without my authorization, in a bad translation, and in what I think is a bad book?"[21] Derrida's critique of Sheehan's and Wolin's command of French also implies that he conceived of translation not in terms of something like endlessly deferred meaning, as one might have expected based on his theoretical writings, but in terms of unequivocal adjudication via reference to universally acknowledged codes.[22] Under the circumstances, it is hardly surprising that Wolin and Sheehan recognized the discrepancies between Derrida's remarks in these letters and his well-known theoretical positions, as in Wolin's question about how Derrida can "consider himself the sole 'author' of and possessor of rights to *an interview,* which is, after all, a joint venture?"[23]

Other influential theoretical positions can also be seen as committing their proponents to beliefs and forms of behavior that would seem unforgivably narrow-minded if they were directed toward actual living interlocutors rather than texts. An example is Paul de Man's well-known essay, "The Rhetoric of Temporality," in which he argues that all Romantic depictions of symbolic perceptions, which are verbalizations of a perceived union between the self and nature, manifest an inherent contradiction that is, in fact, allegorical. On the basis of this conclusion, de Man states that it is an unwarranted "temptation" for a poet like Wordsworth to claim for himself the kind of "temporal stability" that he finds in nature.[24] In making this argument, which glides with suspect ease from the text to its author, de Man in effect juxtaposes what an impartial observer might describe as two rival truths. The first belongs to the poets on whom de Man focuses, but the second is de Man's own and derives from what he has determined, through his study of literature and philosophy, to be the inescapable deep truths about language, time, human existence, and the relations among them.[25] From de Man's perspective, the claims of the Romantic poets necessarily emerge as misguided, self-deceiving, or "blind." They are, consequently, falsehoods and not truths, even if the poets themselves appeared to believe that what they were saying was true. In any event, de

Man believes that the poets' linguistic praxis betrays their claims and that he understands this in a way they did not. Thus, in the end, de Man's procedure is analogous to *rewriting* and *correcting* a work's meaning from the reader's point of view.[26] The general pattern underlying this kind of procedure has been effectively summarized by Lentricchia in his bitter manifesto about abandoning literary studies: "Texts are not read; they are preread. All of literature is *x* and nothing but *x*, and literary study is the naming (exposure) of *x*. For *x*, read imperialism, sexism, homophobia, and so on."[27]

My aim is entirely different. I do not want to argue with dead or living writers about what is true or false. In fact, when writing about their works, I try to avoid revealing anything about my own views as much as possible, even though I realize that this is an ideal that can only be approached but not reached. Instead, I strive to understand what the writers are saying as fully and clearly as possible *in their own terms,* no matter whether I personally believe this to be false, heinous, ambiguous, contradictory, anachronistic, irrelevant to my own view of things, offensive to me and to others, or, by contrast, brilliantly perceptive and deeply moving. In my view, any analytical method that is incapable of revealing a dominant textual "truth" or meaning that is repugnant to the reader or that contradicts the reader's worldview is worthless.

To acknowledge that I seek this particular kind of "accuracy" in reading is not to claim anything original. Like the writer's perennial wish to capture as faithfully as possible the way life really is—which, in its own way, has informed movements and aesthetic systems as different as Classicism, Sentimentalism, Romanticism, Realism, Symbolism, Modernism, Postmodernism, etc.—the wish to understand as clearly as possible what works are about has underlain virtually all theoretical positions, past or present. From Matthew Arnold's search for "high seriousness," to Boris Eikhenbaum's analysis of how works are "made," to de Man's tropological deconstructions, no one has ever actively tried to *avoid* understanding what a work is "really" about or what an encounter between a work and a reader reveals about either of them, no matter how differently this aim was construed. Thus, whatever claims for novelty and utility I make on behalf of my method do not stem from my abstract aim but from how I go about realizing it.

As I hope to show via my analysis of *Anna Karenina,* "understanding" what this novel (or, by extension, any other work) says does not mean that I reify it into a rectilinear, monological message. On the contrary, I seek a maximally full range of meanings, both distinct and blurry, and without regard to the interpretive consequences that any one meaning may cause the others. In other words, I do not assume that the work will necessarily be "unified," or that characters will be "consistent," or that their behavior will demonstrate Freudian conceptions of the unconscious, or that aporias will emerge, or anything else that I personally may like or dislike. At the same time, it also bears repeating that I do not believe in the possibility of being entirely objective about this or any other work of literature; however, this is not the same as saying that all interpretations are entirely relativized. Personal likes and dislikes and other subjective responses and projections are inherent in constituting a work as one reads it but to an extent that cannot be predicted in advance of an encounter with a given work; and because the subjective cannot be subtracted from an individual's interaction with the work, there will always be an *evaluative* component to reading. Nevertheless, there is still a considerable difference between acknowledging this as an inescapable fact, and trying to work around it as much as possible by speaking about the degree to which different interpretations seem plausible, and setting out with firm ideas about what life and literature are like and being prepared to argue on behalf of these views in the face of all comers and texts. For this reason and because the border between what is "subjective" and "objective" will always vary (from reader to reader, from one work to another, and from one textual feature to the next in a particular work), I have reduced to a minimum my own evaluative remarks about Tolstoy's novel; anyone can provide their own. What I do instead is try to identify the matrix of meanings in the novel that is inevitably implicated in the value judgments that readers make about it.

Following this strategy of openness to *Anna Karenina*'s polysemy, thematic patterning, and incoherence proved to be intermittently frustrating but ultimately exhilarating and liberating. I believe it is a measure of the extent to which consistency and coherence are still seen as virtues in the world of academic literary analysis that I was troubled at times by my inability to trace consistent patterns of meaning across the entire novel. Initially, I found myself becoming attached to sequences of details that I discovered in the text and then feeling disappointed when the sequences disappeared, did not emerge elsewhere, or were contradicted by other textual details. The disappointment faded, however, when I was able to survey the kinds of fascinating complications that emerged instead. I hasten to explain that I indulge in this firsthand reminiscence not because I believe it has any inherent value or that it is unique, but because I believe it illustrates a general feature of how analytical literary scholarship is conducted. Despite the enormous influence of various forms of poststructuralism during the past several decades, and the consequent erosion of faith in coherent selves, determinate meanings, causal sequences, overarching systems, and the like, most studies produced by literary scholars still consist of relatively narrow analyses of works along particular thematic or formal axes. In other words, they betray a search for or faith in patterns that dominate and explain entire works, even though a commitment to tying up all loose ends and extracting a unified message from a work can be as reductive as any poststructuralist approach.

These considerations set the boundaries of my inquiry in the first part of this book. My aim is to suggest a reading methodology based on principles that appear to hold the least danger of prestructuring the works to which the methodology is applied and the most promise for capturing whatever is distinctive in the works themselves. Another way of stating my aim is that I want to account for the variable readings that a literary work will provoke, which thus echoes Lotman's remarks about "understanding" that I used as my second epigraph. Anyone who has examined a well-known work's reception over time cannot help being struck by the variations among readings generated by different individuals and periods. To determine which are plausible for a particular work and which are not is also what I would like to do. One practical problem that emerges in connection with this is terminological: it becomes necessary to verbalize differing degrees of ambiguity or plausibility, which is, of course, difficult to do with any accuracy. We do not possess a vocabulary that allows a refined expression of degrees of relative certainty and uncertainty in connection with literary interpretation. Nevertheless, because particular meanings are not always simply right or wrong, definitely present or absent, clear or muddled, it is important to try to articulate whenever possible the extent of each of these oppositions.

As I mentioned, my approach relies on fundamental insights by the linguist Roman Jakobson and the theoretician of literature and culture Yurii Lotman. I will have more to say about Jakobson's and Lotman's ideas in Part One of this book, but I would like to acknowledge here that I derive my conception of "literariness" from them and that this conception is central to my project. Jakobson identified the dominant characteristic of the kinds of complex utterances that we call "literary" as the "poetic function" of language, which, as he famously put it, "projects the principle of equivalence from the axis of selection into the axis of combination."[28] (For more on his "functions," see 4.) This a wonderfully efficient formulation of an idea that is both simple and profound in its implications for understanding a literary work's ontology, its relation to a cultural context, and how to interpret it. At the heart of this idea is that the words in a work we call "literary" exhibit two kinds of relations—to the world at large and to the work itself; moreover, the words and other units of meaning within such a work are related to each other via similarity that encompasses difference ("equivalence"). In Jurij Striedter's lucid exposition, a word in a literary work "refers the reader to an extraliterary reality, which it signifies." At the same time, because of the specific way that language is *arranged* in a work, each word in it also "acquires meaning for the reader through its specific function in the work." This "second direction or meaning" can be seen as "refract[ing] the first, deflecting as it were every individual statement from its orientation to a preexisting reality back to the work itself [and] only entering back into relationship to external reality via the work's overall structure. In this respect the work as a whole is the genuine carrier of meaning."[29]

My analysis of *Anna Karenina* in Part Two is an extensive illustration of this conception of how meaning is constituted in a literary work. But to make my principles entirely clear at the outset I thought it would be useful to give a brief example here. Let us consider the metaphor "the iron gates of life" to be a minimal, miniature model of a literary work in which "iron gates" and "life" are made into equivalents in Jakobson's terms (they are both similar and different). The structuralist semiotic approach would say that we understand the adjective and two nouns in the metaphor because they refer to an "extraliterary reality," while the article and preposition establish relations among these nouns and adjective according to the rules of English grammar. But the *meanings* of the metaphor, which include such ideas as that life is heavy and constricted and that opportunities in life open and close, among others, result from the specific relations of the words to each other, and these relations are unique to the *form* of this particular utterance, or how it is arranged. Were I to say "the life of iron gates," the meanings would obviously be entirely different despite the fact that all the words remain the same. The dominant characteristic of works we call literary is the multiplication of the "inner" relations among the words (as well as both smaller and larger units of language) that constitute them, with rhyme and meter being obvious examples of relations in poetry and such phenomena as repeating motifs, juxtapositions, antiphonal echoes, and "situation rhymes" (see *10.1*) appearing in prose.[30]

The tradition to which Jakobson and Lotman belong and that they were instrumental in establishing encompasses Russian Formalism, Czech Structuralism, and the Moscow-Tartu School of structuralism and semiotics. This is one of the fullest and most convincing complexes of literary and cultural theory elaborated in the twentieth century. However, in the United States and in much of Europe theoretically inclined literary scholars outside the Slavic field, as well as many within it, view this complex as having been superseded by newer ideas.[31] This view is also reflected in the critical, as compared with the simply chronological, implications of the term *poststructuralism,* even though its focus is not primarily the Russian theoretical tradition, much less the Czech, which is very little known outside Slavic circles. Because of this, an additional part of my aim in the pages that follow is to illustrate how aspects of this rich Slavic legacy can contribute valuable perspectives to current theoretical debates in the United States, as well as provide counterarguments to some of the more extreme and provocative positions that have been articulated.

Part One

The Plurality and Limits of Interpretation

There are somewhere criteria for limiting interpretation.
Umberto Eco, "Interpretation and History"

I. An Ethical Argument for Recognizing Textual Alterity

The problem of how to minimize the circularity inherent in the act of reading can be addressed from the perspective of the relations among ethics, psychology, semiotics, and linguistics.[1]

Few among us would deny the moral imperative to grasp as precisely as possible what an interlocutor is saying, no matter how seemingly foreign or bizarre it may appear at first. To do otherwise, whether through inattention or, worse yet, through a desire to use the interlocutor's remarks primarily as an example of some issue that is of special interest to the listener, is not only to risk misunderstanding but also to deny the speaker an essential measure of his or her humanity. An argument such as this presupposes the absolute value of all human beings, which, it seems safe to say, is a given in many modern liberal societies, including the United States, at least in (political) theory.[2]

However, rather than pursue the implications of this argument in the abstract, it would be more useful for my purposes to consider one of its concrete applications in a specifically academic context concerned with reading. In the epilogue to a special issue of *PMLA* on "Colonialism and the Postcolonial Condition," Satya Mohanty finds support for multiculturalism in Kant's "categorical imperative," which is a well-known eighteenth-century version of the moral argument in question: "Now, I say, man and, in general, every rational being exists as an end in himself and not merely as a means to be arbitrarily used by this or that will. In all his actions, whether they are directed toward himself or toward other rational beings, he must always be regarded at the same time as an end." Mohanty nominates Kant's ethical principle as "perhaps the most powerful philosophical ally" in contemporary polemics against the pernicious legacy of colonialism and "as the strongest basis for the multiculturalist belief that other cultures need to be approached with the presumption of equal worth."[3]

What is useful in Mohanty's version of the argument is that it lends itself to elaboration and extension of a sort that most liberal-minded individuals, such as I imagine I am addressing, should find persuasive. Thus, it does not seem too great a leap to argue that the same "presumption of equal worth" that Mohanty wants to have accorded to "other cultures" is also justified with regard to representatives from subcultures here *at home*—be they a Hmong émigrée arguing for bilingual education at a school board meeting in Texas, or an African American alderman in Chicago making a pitch for reelection on television. Indeed, the only appropriate response to either of these two speakers from someone who takes to heart the kind of argument Mohanty makes would presumably be rapt attention driven by a desire to fathom the essence of their remarks, even though one is mediated by the television format. But what if, for the sake of argument, the individual in question is a white, middle-aged, comfortably well off, tenured professor of Spanish on the West Coast who, to add another complication, has composed a detailed diary of daily life on campus? Does it make a difference if this person is a man or a woman, that the diary entries were not spoken but written, that they are subject to all the vagaries of verbal self-presentation, and that they might even be trivial? Would any of these characteristics justify an abandonment of the moral imperative? And if not, what is the justification for approaching any differently a poem or a novel written a century or two ago in Brazil, England, or Japan? A work of literature is characterized by its unique arrangement of language, by its form, and understanding a complex utterance such as this may be vastly more difficult than understanding an interlocutor standing in front of you. But the moral reason for trying to do so remains unchanged.[4]

This issue can also be approached from a somewhat different perspective. During the past several decades in the United States, we have witnessed a growing insistence on the need to pay attention to ever-smaller social groups. This process began in the 1960s with the civil rights movement and the rise of feminism, when "blacks" and "women" were recognized as having been disenfranchised by a culture and society that had privileged "whites" and "men," two categories that until then had been thought sufficient to constitute "human beings." This process continued as feminism evolved and "women" were further divided according to categories of race, ethnicity, economic status, sexual practices, and other criteria, so that the interests of poor, rural Chicanas could no longer be assumed to be identical to those of urban, lesbian blacks. Some of the same subdivisions were subsequently applied to "men"; and the imperatives of "political correctness" and "postcolonial studies" led to the creation of numerous other categories of "human beings" (e.g., "subaltern," "mestizo," "disabled"). In all cases, the reason for making the newer and ever-finer distinctions was *ethical*— the conviction that each group had not received a fair share of the attention, opportunities, power, wealth, etc., that the surrounding society and culture possessed and should redistribute.

I would argue that especially for those who think along these lines, the process of fission has not gone nearly far enough, because the trend's logical end point is not any *group* but the unique human *individual* as he or she is conceived in the Western tradition. No matter how deeply one may believe in the importance of group traits, one can always get to a level of detail where distinctions among individuals become essential (even if these are seen as "socially constructed"). Surely, someone who thinks that the experiences of first-generation Chinese American women mark them in unique and important ways would not assume that all the women in this category are simply interchangeable. And if this is so, then all individuals take precedence over all groups (which holds even if a given individual's belief is that the group to which she or he belongs is more important than she or he is!). In fact, one could argue that because individuals change over time, or are at least capable of changing over time, it is hardly just to consider even any individual as permanently determined. An ethically and cognitively more accurate conception is that individuals exist within particular valenced spatiotemporal parameters, or what Bakhtin termed "chronotopes."[5] This is one of the reasons why I am interested in a reading methodology that attempts to recognize the specificity of each text to which it is applied.

Of course, texts are not the same as people, and the relation between the hermeneutics of reading and the hermeneutics of dialogue will depend on individual cultural circumstances. Thus, letting your interlocutor see that you are bored by his heartfelt confession can be an ethical lapse in our culture, but tossing his book aside with a disparaging comment may not be, provided that he does not find out. One can also argue, however, that because language is humankind's distinguishing characteristic, all words, even if written, remain ultimately expressions of selves, notwithstanding such ideas as Roland Barthes's "death of the author." As Charles Sanders Peirce put it, "My language is the sum total of myself."[6] One can better appreciate the force of this statement by noting that the effort required to choose and arrange language in particular ways in a work of literature results in even more of the author being reflected in it (even if one takes an "intertextual" view of literature). Thus, if the author of the book we had disparaged found out that we had tossed it aside, most of us would feel that ethical considerations have become an issue in our behavior. This would hold no matter what the value of the book is, whether it is someone's sacred text, like the Book of Mormon or the Koran, or inept pulp fiction, because both involve the issue of personhood, which in our culture invokes or should invoke the categorical imperative. Indeed, even trying to imagine the author, no matter whether he is near or far, like or unlike me, inevitably evokes the idea of another person and thus moral constraints on how I may relate to his words.

Whoever doubts that such a personalized and proprietary attitude toward the written word could still be valid in our post-poststructuralist day might wish to recall the intensely visceral responses that we academics and other professional writers typically have toward obtuse, negative, or simply insufficiently reverential reactions to our work, even years after its first publication. What is the first thing most academics do when they pick up a new publication in their field? They look to see if their work has been cited and in what terms. In short, there is not very much Tolstoyan renunciation of copyrights and rejection of royalties among us. "L'Affaire Derrida" is an especially revealing example of how deeply ingrained this mixture of ethics and linguistic possessiveness actually is. To be protective of one's own utterances while simultaneously arguing that it is impossible to "own" linguistic meaning is to manifest a disturbing lack of self-consciousness if not bad faith.

I conclude, therefore, that from the perspective of the value inherent in any human being, trying to understand any utterance on its own terms, no matter how difficult this task is, how the utterance was made, who made it, or when remains a moral imperative.[7]

2. A Psychological Argument for Recognizing Textual Alterity

The ethical argument about reading can also be coordinated with one drawn from major trends in Western developmental and cognitive psychology that hinge on the ineluctable role of transactional exchanges between self and other in the process of individual maturation. Jean Piaget's highly influential theory of intellectual development from childhood to adulthood includes the fundamental idea of "accommodation," which is one of two functional invariants in his system of human knowledge and which involves the progressive modification and restructuring of this system in a way that allows the individual to assimilate new information. Although for Piaget representational thought in the young child does not depend on internalizing verbal signs from the social environment, natural language and, therefore, other selves come to play an enormously important role in the development of conceptual thinking at later stages. In its essence, the "genesis of cognition" for Piaget "is above all a constructive process."[1]

The recognition and negotiation of otherness or alterity, whether of things or other persons, also lies at the heart of Lev Vygotsky's "zone of proximal development," which the influential Soviet psychologist defined as "the discrepancy between a child's actual mental age and the level he reaches in solving problems with assistance."[2] This "zone" is thus the locus of the "loan of consciousness," in Jerome Bruner's apt phrase, that adults make to children in order to help them achieve ever higher levels of linguistic competence via incremental steps through heretofore unknown areas of knowledge and experience. Bruner, a well-known American psychologist, adapts and extends Vygotsky's ideas to a "constructivist" view of human development as a process of learning and manipulating new arrangements of already existing sign systems about the world (especially narrative art), which in their ensemble constitute what is known as "culture."[3]

Additional support for a conception of human development as depending on language and the necessary alterity of the "other" comes from the ambitious theory of a biological basis of mind that has been advanced by the Nobel laureate and neuroscientist Gerald Edelman. He posits the existence of a human capacity for what he calls "higher-order conscious-ness," which "is based on the occurrence of direct awareness in a human being who has language and a reportable subjective life" and which distin-guishes humans from other animals, who have only a lower "primary con-sciousness" that is "limited to the remembered present."[4] The crucial con-nection between selfhood, language, and other human beings emerges from Edelman's explanation that "higher-order consciousness depends on build-ing a self through affective intersubjective exchanges. These interactions—with parental figures, with grooming conspecifics, and with sexual partners—are of the same kind as those guiding semiotic exchange and language building." Edelman goes on to add that these "affectively colored exchanges through symbols initiate semantic bootstrapping," by which he means that the process of self-formation that begins with emotionally colored transactions between self and other that are then semioticized leads in turn to the process of "connecting preexisting conceptual learning to lexical learning."[5] The result of the interaction of higher-order conscious-ness with primary consciousness "is a model of a world rather than of an econiche, along with models of the past, present, and future."[6] In sum, Edelman's conception of how a distinctly human consciousness is formed is predicated on the individual's relations with others that are mediated by the same kind of process of meaning formation that underlies semiotic ex-changes in general.

Why would transactions with alterity necessarily have to undergird psychological conceptions of human development? Because, as the well-known neurologist and writer Oliver Sacks bluntly puts it, "living orga-nisms are born into a world of challenge and novelty, a world of signifi-cances, to which they must adapt or die."[7] One might have thought that this conclusion would be a self-evident truism. However, as I will illustrate below (5.5), in the current American theoretical climate it is far from trivial to recognize that for a number of leading students of the mind, alterity em-bodied in individual language use *is* real but *not* insurmountable; put more simply, difference can be overcome via language. This realization has far-reaching implications for a theory of reading, and not simply because of an abstract resemblance between reading and cognitive acts but because of the kinds of explicit claims that Piaget, Vygotsky, Bruner, and Edelman make about the linguistic bases of selfhood.

In its general shape, if not in its scientific provenance, this idea should already be quite familiar to those who know Mikhail Bakhtin. Vygotsky's, Bruner's, and Edelman's schemes in particular resemble closely Bakhtin's fundamental conception of dialogue, which lies on the borders among psychology, epistemology, and theory of language, which is predicated on a similar, mutually cocreative role of interlocutors, and which also posits a self that cannot even be conceived outside of verbal exchanges with an other.[8] For Bakhtin as for these students of mind, existential and verbal alterity are negotiated in the same way.

3. Alterity and Semiotics

There is also support for the linguistic side of the bridge that psychological theories build between self-formation and semiosis among such leading theorists of language and meaning as Ferdinand de Saussure, Charles Sanders Peirce, Roman Jakobson, and Umberto Eco. In effect, all four agree that the *minimal* condition necessary for meaning to arise is the establishment of a relation between two things, whether a signifier and a signified, a sign and its object, an expression and its content, or one sign and another.[1] Thus, if the self can be understood schematically as a reflexive system of remembered interactions between the "subject" and, at a theoretical minimum, one "object" (or other self) outside it, then the self can also be understood as a system of *meanings* that results from iterative experiences of the kind that also characterize any other kind of meaning formation.[2]

Lotman's later writings provide extensive additional support for the relations among alterity, selfhood, and meaning. One of his fundamental ideas is that thought, like meaning, can arise only as a result of relations between two different things—in this case, via an individual's recognizing alterity and attempting to translate it into whatever terms he already possesses. Following Bakhtin, Lotman also sees consciousness as being "profoundly dialogic" and posits that "in order to function actively, one consciousness requires another."[3] Thus, according to Lotman, no form of thinking "can be mono-structural and monolingual: it absolutely must incorporate heteroglot and mutually untranslatable semiotic formations."[4] Lotman's emphasis on the "untranslatability" of different languages is valuable precisely because it underscores the pivotal role of alterity in the generation of what we understand by "meaning." "Untranslatability" should not be understood as the absolute impossibility of translation, because it is obvious that if no translation between two languages were possible, then no meaning could arise between them. However, the fact that elements of foreign languages are routinely used as signs for the incomprehensible, or as "mere" decoration by individuals who cannot, in fact, translate them (as the popularity of tattoos of Oriental ideograms in the United States attests), suggests that absolute untranslatability is probably impossible. As Tzvetan Todorov put it in his study of how both Aztecs and Spaniards translated each other into familiar cultural terms, "any investigation of alterity is necessarily semiotic, and reciprocally, semiotics cannot be conceived outside the relation to the other."[5]

Following Lotman, one can make the global generalization that the conditions for the generation of meaning are everywhere congruent—within a sign, between signs, between phrases, sentences, or utterances, between larger subdivisions of a language such as dialects or jargons, between individuals, and within that phenomenon we call a conscious self. Lotman goes even farther in this great chain of semiosis, to the antipodes "below" the self and "above" an individual language, when he hypothesizes an explicit parallel between the functioning of the hemispheres of the human brain and the workings of entire cultures: "in both cases we discover *as a minimum* two fundamentally different methods of reflecting the world and of generating new information, with the result being complex mechanisms of exchange between these systems."[6] In another essay he becomes even more daring in his speculative reach when he refers to "left" and "right spins" in the "structure of matter" as being the deepest level of the symmetry/asymmetry relation (difference within similarity, or similarity encompassing difference) that is fundamental to all meaning creation.[7]

It is possible to conclude, therefore, that in our culture the moral imperative to recognize the independence of the other has a parallel in the inescapable role that the other plays in psychological conceptions of self-formation, which in turn is also paralleled by the conditions necessary for something "to mean." Thus, immorality entails a shift in attention from the other to the self and a consequent conversion of the other into an extension of the self. This resembles the kind of withdrawal into the self and denying or not registering the other that occurs in solipsism as well as in the psychological dysfunction called autism, with all of the negative associations that this entails (except that autism is obviously not volitional).

The congruence among these moral, psychological, and semiotic formulations constitutes a very weighty argument for the idea of a negotiable and surmountable alterity, whether in dialogue or reading. In the latter case, what is crucial is that each text be allowed to tell the reader what to do with it and not the other way around. And the only way to achieve this morally, psychologically, and culturally necessary goal is by doing one's best not to bring irrelevant conceptual mediations or associations to the work, which means treating it with the exquisite care one would accord an interlocutor whom one does not wish to offend, and by approaching it with the multileveled attention one would bring to a dialogic exchange that has existential consequences for both participants.

4. Jakobson's "Metalingual Function" and Alterity

Understanding one's interlocutor is of course not simply a matter of grasping the surface content of his message. As Jakobson has famously argued, any act of verbal communication can be analyzed in terms of six basic aspects, or "functions," of language that are oriented toward and tell us about the addresser, the addressee, the context, the message itself, the contact between the speakers, and the code within which the given communication is taking place.[1] Jakobson conceived of these six functions as universally true—as applicable to all languages at all times and as intrinsically present in them.[2] Moreover, because these functions have formal values in addition to semantic ones, like the grammatical categories of words in addition to their meanings, all six are relatively immune from the subjective interpretations of individual speakers.[3] Although in principle all six can be found in any given utterance, usually fewer are actually present, and one dominates. The actual significance of each function is the result of its relations with the others. From this perspective, a literary work is one in which the "poetic function"—or a focus on the message itself—*dominates* the other five but does not necessarily eliminate any of them. There are consequently degrees of "literariness," just as there can be degrees to which an utterance is dominated by any of the other functions. For example, an utterance can be concerned primarily with the nature of the contact between two speakers, with establishing a channel of communication and with keeping it open (what Jakobson calls the "phatic function"). In the United States this is often done via talking about the weather. Although the ostensible subject of such conversations is a past, present, or future meteorological event that appears to concern the interlocutors (in Jakobson's terminology this is the "context" for their utterances, or their remarks' "referential function"), the actual purpose can be primarily to initiate contact between them, perhaps as a prelude to more substantive dialogue. Given this variable manifestation of the functions, an absolutist argument that attacks the idea of "literariness" by insisting that a text has to be either "literary" or "nonliterary" is both misguided and a betrayal of Jakobson's ideas. It would be more accurate to say, for instance, that the poetic function is strongly developed in *Moby-Dick* and weakly in *Jaws* (which is dominated by other functions). Jakobson himself used the 1950s American political slogan "I like Ike," with its internal rhyme, sound repetition, and rhythm, to demonstrate the presence of the poetic function in utterances we do not consider literary.[4]

Jakobson also recognized that the specific configuration of functions in an utterance could not prevent it from being "used" for purposes having little to do with this inherent arrangement.[5] In a text such as a sonnet the multiple reflexive relations among its different levels (phonetic, metrical, lexical, syntactic) "refract" its references to the real world and thereby create a sui generis system of meanings. However, none of this will necessarily stop someone from reading the sonnet in political or some other terms. At the same time, it is essential to underscore that such a use represents, or should represent, a second phase in an interpretation, one that follows the apprehension of whatever meaning results from the inherent configuration of functions. Without this, one is not reading the sonnet but projecting an a priori meaning onto it.

Also especially important for understanding any utterance's specific meaning is what Jakobson calls the "metalingual function" of language, or "glossing," which entails translations between the linguistic codes that are implicated in an utterance. Focusing on these allows one to identify the culturally conditioned semantic fields from which the speaker selects the specific words, phrases, and attendant ideas that constitute that utterance.[6] Here are some everyday examples: "a foal is a baby horse"—translation between terminology pertaining to horses and humans; "idleness is the root of all evil"—a psychological state translated into a botanical-moral metaphor; and "the crowd spilled out like a stream overflowing its banks"—a simile equating human group behavior and a potentially catastrophic natural process. Each of these examples has specific and far-reaching implications for a particular worldview. Thus, the anthropomorphizing of horses and the equinizing of human beings in "a foal is a baby horse" is a translation between the animal and human realms that implies continuity between "nature" and "culture" as well as a particular cosmology and much else besides. As this example also demonstrates, a listener's attention to the "metalingual function" is a necessary and to some extent an automatic feature of her focus on the denotative or referential dimension of a speaker's message. Another way of putting this is that by focusing *consciously* on the codes utilized in discourse, the listener can discover at least some of the contexts that are essential for understanding the message.

(This will vary depending on whether we are dealing with oral or written discourses [see 5.5].) Furthermore, by focusing on translations between codes in an utterance, the listener discovers not only what *kind* of specific meaning is generated in it but also *how* the generation of meaning is conceived in that discourse—whether meaning is easy or difficult to determine, open or closed, limited to particular topics or not, and so on. In short, without paying attention to and using the "metalingual" dimension of discourse you simply cannot grasp fully what your interlocutor is saying.

The importance of the metalingual function in communication is also suggested by Jakobson's conclusion that it may be rooted in fundamental human mental processes. In his classic essay "Two Aspects of Language and Two Types of Aphasic Disturbances," Jakobson provides evidence from clinical studies of brain lesions that one of the polar types of aphasic impairment involves a "similarity disorder," or the affected individual's inability to select and substitute for each other words that are drawn from different semantic fields. The second polar type of aphasia is a "contiguity disorder," which involves an inability to combine smaller linguistic elements into larger (longer) ones. Intermediate types of impairment between these two poles also exist. Under normal circumstances, selection and combination are the two processes that are manifested in varying ratios in all the different kinds of utterances that human beings produce.[7] In Jakobson's terminology, the "similarity disorder" is "a loss of metalanguage," and its recurrence in clinical situations suggests that it is connected to basic mental operations or neurological structures. Metalanguage is thus an inherent feature of how we function in the world of languages that is our inescapable domain.

Additional evidence in support of this inference is Jakobson's observation that metalanguage, which can also be understood as talking about language, plays a central role in the verbal behavior of preschool children, thus demonstrating that it is essential for the acquisition of language.[8] Similarly, as anyone who has tried to learn a foreign language can confirm, second language acquisition is impossible without metalinguistic operations, which involve, among other things, trying to equate lexical items and their associations in one language with those that more or less approximate them in another.

Jakobson's analysis of the central role that the metalingual function plays in speech thus suggests that it is transferable to reading and, specifically, to literary exegesis. Other theorists such as Mikhail Bakhtin, Hans-Georg Gadamer, and Hans Robert Jauss have also argued that there is at least heuristic value in understanding the reading process as a kind of dialogic give-and-take between a speaker (the text) and a listener (the reader).[9] This follows from the fact that the reader does not simply receive utterances passively from a narrator and characters with an implied author behind them but actively responds to them in ways that prepare his reception of the still-unknown ones that follow, just as those that follow reshape ones already heard. Consequently, as Wolfgang Iser and other reader-oriented critics have argued, the kinds of expectations and recapitulations that readers manifest will affect what the text appears to state. (The extent to which the text is thought to "respond" will vary from critic to critic and work to work, and in many, although not all, cases there is a presumed asymmetry in favor of the text as the primary but not exclusive source of meaning.)[10] But even without conceiving of reading as a quasi-dialogic activity, the universality of "glossing" in language as Jakobson understood it suggests a reading methodology that will not flatten or recode the texts to which it is applied.

5. Hermeneutic Indices, or Guides to Textual Alterity

Although the reader's contribution to the act of interpreting a work of literature cannot be ignored, no reader is free to make what he wills of a given text. The primary reasons are that all literary works are structured in ways that determine their meanings (as well as their ambiguities) and that they are filled with versions of Jakobson's metalingual function. To distinguish these textual moments from the glosses that appear in quotidian utterances, I propose the term *hermeneutic indices*. These moments are *hermeneutic* because they have to do with the most basic as well as the overarching conditions of meaning formation; and they can be designated *indices* because they identify the locus, the content, and the implications of specific instances of meaning generation in the work. That metalanguage is a valid ground for interpretation follows from the fact that the abstract idea or possibility of meaning is necessarily prior to any specific meaning. Even such fundamental and seemingly a priori concepts as time, space, and causality are conceived in terms of relations and are therefore kinds of meaning.

Speaking impressionistically, one could say that hermeneutic indices are signs of a text's self-consciousness about the kinds of meanings with which it is concerned. Hermeneutic indices should thus not be personified as authorial intentions, which remain inscrutable or irrelevant in the terms of my present argument. The *minimal* formal manifestation of a hermeneutic index, as in every instance of meaning generation, is the relation between two semantic units, which, as Jakobson has shown, can be achieved in only two ways—via similarity and contiguity or paradigmatically and syntagmatically. In other words, linguistic meaning *in general* arises from the relation between semantic units that are juxtaposed or that are separated by some quantity of text. In *verbal art,* however, meanings arise from more complex, *simultaneous* relations among semantic units that are *both* contiguous *and* separated from each other (although the number and complexity of such relations will, of course, vary from work to work). As a result, a given hermeneutic index can have implications for the entire literary work in which it appears.[1]

5.1. Examples of Hermeneutic Indices

An essential caveat about hermeneutic indices is that the generation of meaning does not necessarily imply certainty, especially in literature. Some hermeneutic indices may define unequivocal meanings, but others will produce varying degrees of ambiguity. For example, to say that a sophomore is a second-year student, which is one of Jakobson's examples of the metalingual function, may not allow for much uncertainty, especially in the kind of context in which this gloss is likely to appear.[2] But if a character in a novel equates pregnancy and illness, as we will see her do in *Anna Karenina,* then there is a significant degree of indeterminacy produced by this specific juxtaposition.

Before proceeding any farther, therefore, it would be useful to consider some illustrative examples of different types of hermeneutic indices. On the level of both the narrator and the characters, we find everything from large-scale, direct commentary about the principles underlying a given fictional world to much smaller and subtler indices.

Several minimal hermeneutic indices, or those that consist of short, simple equations between two distinct semantic fields or codes, appear on the first pages of Ivan Turgenev's novel *Fathers and Sons* (1862). The narrator introduces one of the characters, Nikolai Kirsanov, and says that he owns a "fine *estate* of *two hundred souls,* or, as he began to put it after he had arranged the division of his land with the peasants and started a *'farm'* —of nearly *two thousand desiatinas* of land."[3] This statement contains two hermeneutic indices on Kirsanov's level and one on the narrator's. Kirsanov's involve two translations, from the traditional Russian term for "estate" (*imenie*) to the foreign term "farm" (*ferma*) and from "two hundred souls" (the number of adult male serfs he owns) to "two thousand desiatinas of land." Kirsanov's substitution of new terms for old ones obviously implies that he prefers the new code and its conceptual framework, which evokes the entire series of radical political ideas that characters discuss at length within the novel's fictional 1859 time frame. This includes such portentous events as the imminent liberation of the serfs in 1861, the consequent reapportionment of the land between landowners and peasants, and the anticipated social dislocations. However, the narrator's hermeneutic index works in opposition to Kirsanov's because the narrator continues to use, and thereby implicitly preserves, the old translation of "estate" into the number of male serfs on it ("two hundred souls"). This impression is also confirmed by the narrator's quotation marks around the new word "farm," which implies his ironic distance from the newer code.

A similar example appears on the novel's second page. The narrator gives a subtly ironic description of the old-fashioned practice by provincial Russian young ladies who pretend to a degree of refinement of using French equivalents for their given names. As the narrator puts it, Kirsanov's mother was "as a girl called *Agathe,* but as a general's wife *Agafokleya Kuzminishna Kirsanova*" (emphasis added). Here we again have a translation that implies two different codes. The married name is not only markedly provincial and eminently Russian (despite its Greek etymology), but also humorously Gogolian in its polysyllabic cacophony, especially when juxtaposed with the French "Agathe." The humor's function here is similar to that of the narrator's irony toward the newer code in the first example. If we were to assemble all such details throughout the novel (which number in the hundreds), they would be seen as contributing to a *polyvalent* narrative code that, among other important things, deflates the pretensions to novelty or topicality expressed by several major characters while simultaneously and subtly underscoring the timeless paradigms of human behavior. This, of course, does not mean that the narrator simply condemns the novel's radical hero, Bazarov, or that he supports the reactionaries instead. Moreover, all of the characters also project arrays of indices that the reader has to evaluate as well. In their ensemble, the hermeneutic indices in *Fathers and Sons* constitute contradictions and ambiguities as well as determinate patterns of meaning that pertain to all aspects of the novel's form and content.

An example of a more extended hermeneutic index that is also a narrator's response to a character can be found in Aleksandr Pushkin's classic novel in verse *Eugene Onegin* (1825–32). In it, the jealous young Romantic, Vladimir Lensky, wants to challenge his friend Onegin to a duel because the latter has flirted with Olga, whom Lensky loves:

"I," [Lensky] reflects, "shall be her savior.
I shall not suffer a depraver
with the fire of both sighs and compliments
to tempt a youthful heart,
nor let a despicable, venomous worm
a lily's stalklet gnaw,
nor have a flower two morns old
wither while yet half blown."

The stanza then concludes with the narrator's *translation* (and deflation) of Lensky's clichéd rhetoric into the prosaic couplet "All this, friends, meant: /

I have a pistol duel with a pal."[4] This translation constitutes a hermeneutic index. The ironic contrast between the narrator's and Lensky's codes helps to define the narrator's distance from Lensky and contributes to the construction of the complex narrative-authorial persona in the work, including his attitude toward Romanticism and much else besides.

A less obvious but still resonant hermeneutic index appears in *Crime and Punishment* (1866) when Svidrigailov commits suicide in front of a Jewish fireman, whom Fyodor Dostoevsky describes in his characteristically anti-Semitic fashion (pt. VI, chap. 6). Among the things Svidrigailov tells his hapless witness before pulling the trigger is "If they start asking you, just tell them he [i.e., Svidrigailov himself] went to America."[5] This equation between suicide and a journey to America is somewhat unexpected in the context of the novel. Nevertheless, it clearly points to Dostoevsky's negative view of the United States as a soulless and materialistic society, rather than as a land of infinite possibilities for existential self-creation, which is, of course, how vast numbers of nineteenth-century European emigrants saw it, including some other Russians.[6] The fact that the suicide and the image of a caricatured Jew are juxtaposed necessarily sets up a relation between the two that can be read as having negative implications for both. Moreover, Svidrigailov's wish that the Jewish fireman should repeat the equation if questioned by the authorities can be seen as an attempt to implicate the fireman in the negativity of the suicide itself.

A major hermeneutic index opens the prologue to Andrei Bely's *Petersburg* (1916). "What is this Russian Empire of ours?" the narrator asks and then attempts to answer the question over the course of one and a half pages via a series of ever-narrowing definitions: "This Russian Empire of ours is a geographical entity. . . . This Russian Empire of ours consists of a multitude of cities. . . . Petersburg . . . actually does belong to the Russian Empire. . . . Nevsky Prospect is a Petersburg prospect," and so on.[7] Thus, the entire prologue can be read as one long and unsuccessful attempt to define the "Russian Empire" in terms of conventional concepts and banal, logical, bureaucratic language such as that found in official government documents. The narrator not only gets bogged down in this attempt, as a result of which he literally begins to hem and haw, but also comes to the seemingly absurd conclusion that Petersburg "only appears to exist." Finally, he ends with a more esoteric definition of the city's ontology, which foreshadows the occult worldview in the novel that appears to be the only way of truly understanding any aspect of its existence.[8]

The above examples are drawn from nineteenth- and twentieth-century Russian texts, but hermeneutic indices obviously appear in all works of literature. Herman Melville's opening words in *Moby-Dick* (1851), "Call me Ishmael," constitute an index with specific generic and intertextual implications that translate the otherwise unnamed narrator into the ambiguous outcast in the biblical theodicy centering on Abraham (Genesis 16–25). A few lines farther down, the profound ambivalence that the narrator named "Ishmael" feels about his place in the order of things and about the limits of what can be known is enhanced by the subtler indexical equations he makes between the sea voyage and therapy for a physical/spiritual malaise, on the one hand, and the sea voyage and suicide, on the other. A more elaborate index suggesting the impossibility of determinate meaning is constituted by Ishmael's long series of glosses on the "whiteness" of Moby-Dick: the term acquires so many associations that it comes to mean both everything and nothing.[9] (There is some resemblance between this and the example from the prologue to Bely's *Petersburg*, except that in Bely's novel the failure of a certain kind of prosaic language to express a particular meaning is a foil for a different, symbolic conception of language that is introduced in the body of the novel.) Other kinds of hermeneutic indices in *Moby-Dick* include metaphors—Ishmael's "landsmen . . . pent up in lath and plaster—tied to counters, nailed to benches, clinched to desks"—that bear on the problematics of cognition that he broaches on the novel's first page, and a simile—Ishmael sees Manhattan "belted round by wharves as Indian isles by coral reefs"—that implies an (ironic?) equation between "nature" and "culture."[10]

In Vladimir Nabokov's *Lolita* (1955), adjectival constructions carry hermeneutic implications, as when in the beginning of his narrative Humbert addresses the "misinformed, simple, noble-winged seraphs." Among other things, this introduces and plays with the idea of determinate meaning being possible, Edgar Allan Poe's poem "Annabel Lee," and the possibility of otherworldly influences on earthly events. The couplet that Humbert quotes near the novel's end, "The moral sense in mortals is the duty / We have to pay on mortal sense of beauty," is also a hermeneutic index that links ethics and aesthetics in a way that is central to the novel's depiction of his passion for Lolita, his guilt over what he has done to her, and the metaphysical dimension that hovers behind his narrative.[11]

A different kind of hermeneutic index appears at the center of a short Nez Percé oral narrative that in its written English translation (1988) is entitled "Coyote and White-Tailed Buck." It tells how Coyote, a creator figure in other tales of this kind, wants White-Tailed Buck to become more alert than he currently is so that no one would find it easy to club him to death; as it is, even a woman could do it. After failing to scare Buck by shouting at him in various ways, Coyote decides to try another method: he points his genitals at Buck's nose until he almost touches it, as a result of which Buck gives a warning snort. Coyote is satisfied and concludes that henceforth "only a man who prepares himself, taking a sweat-bath and cleansing himself, will be able to kill you." The narrative ends with the statement that this is how white-tailed bucks became difficult to approach and how it came to be that only those who are properly prepared can kill them. Thus, central to this narrative is the causal connection between the emergence of Buck's heightened awareness and Coyote's male scent and genitalia, which implies that Buck's new awareness shares some traits with Coyote's sexuality. This correlation between the stimulus and the response is, therefore, like a physical manifestation of a translation between two different concepts. Consequently, it is tempting to infer that the narrative articulates a necessary relation between male sexuality and consciousness, or at least consciousness of the fear of death.[12] Before Coyote intervened in White-Tailed Buck's existence, women could have approached and killed Buck without alerting him, even though they presumably had not taken sweat-baths and cleansed themselves the way men have to if they want to succeed in a hunt. And even though woman figures in the narrative, there is no mention of "White-Tailed Doe" in it. More generally, therefore, the narrative makes fundamental distinctions between males and females in relation to mental states, functional roles, and, possibly, the purifying effects of (ritualistic?) sweat-baths.

My final illustration of a hermeneutic index is drawn from "The Madman" (1973), a short story by the contemporary Nigerian writer Chinua Achebe. Among the many themes that this well-known story raises, the question of what determines a person's identity is one of the most intriguing, especially because of the ways in which this question engages views that many in the West take for granted regarding the continuity and duration of selfhood. In the story, Nwibe, "a man of high standing," approaches the members of his town's "honoured hierarchy," or "_ozo_," with the request that he be admitted into their group. "When we see we shall believe," they respond to him, and the narrator explains that this "was their dignified way of telling you to think it over once again and make sure you have the means to go through with it. For _ozo_ is not a child's naming ceremony; and where is the man to hide his face who begins the _ozo_ dance and then is foot-stuck to the arena?" Noteworthy here is the implicit equation (or translation) between a man's worth and his performance during a specified event like an initiation. This emerges as more important than whatever he achieved in the past, even though past achievements were a prerequisite for his admission to initiation. A similar equation, or hermeneutic index, is at the heart of Nwibe's transformation into the story's second madman. When Nwibe chases after the story's original madman in a vain attempt to recover the garment he has stolen, he is perceived and defined by two girls as "a stark-naked madman" despite the fact that he is naked only because he has just been robbed. Thus, Nwibe's nakedness and furious behavior during his futile pursuit are all that anyone he encounters notices about him, and he is judged only on the basis of his appearance at a given moment; none of the traits that defined him earlier remain. Even the narrator appears to support the redefinition of Nwibe as a madman by referring to the thief as "the man with the cloth," as if his madness had dissipated as soon as he donned the garment he had stolen, and by calling Nwibe "the naked man." That a person's nature can change so radically and so quickly is also reflected in the occult event that other characters in the story invoke to explain Nwibe's madness. Impelled by his pursuit of the thief, Nwibe enters "irrevocably within the occult territory of the powers of the market." Thus, a person's limited and specific action also appears to open him to the power of divinities who (help to?) change him from what he had been.

5.2. Hermeneutic Indices, Predication, Simile, Metaphor

What are the general features of hermeneutic indices, and what kinds of questions do they raise?

Although Jakobson defined the metalingual function, or glossing, in terms of translation between codes, it is important to note that the distinction between a gloss and the grammatical and logical construction known as "predication" is not always sharp or clear. The dictionary definition of predication is "affirming something of another thing . . . the attachment of a predicate to a subject, ascription of a property to an individual, or assignment of something to a class."[13] Thus, the example Jakobson uses to illustrate the metalingual function (a sophomore is a second-year student) could also be seen as predication because it involves "affirming something of another thing" or "assignment of something to a class." However, this dictionary definition is so broad that it can subsume a larger variety of linguistic operations than the translation between codes that is central to Jakobson's conception. This suggests that although all hermeneutic indices are instances of predication, not all predication produces what can *usefully* be seen as hermeneutic indices; and what distinguishes them from each other is the idea of the code or semantic field.

In Jakobson's example, the term *sophomore* is a synecdoche for the world of American college life and is thus part of a particular, culturally defined cluster of terms. In order to get the maximum amount of information from the gloss one would need to exploit the term's *associations* within the code (such as "sophomoric" implying overconfident but immature, as well as "undergraduate," "major," "requirement," "academic probation," "intramural," "commons," "binge drinking," or, if we go back several decades, "food fight," "beanie," "panty raid," etc.). By contrast, if one were to *minimize* the associations of the term and to see it merely as a possible substitute for the ordinal and ordinary "second-year student," the result would be a relatively impoverished set of meanings. On the other hand, as this example also shows, whether or not something is interpreted as being part of a code or semantic field can depend on the context. Hermeneutic indices should therefore not be conceived as always standing out in a text the way that raisins can in a cake; at times they also merge with everyday grammatical and syntactical constructions. In the final analysis, the idea behind using hermeneutic indices is to systematize and make overt what is implicated in verbal understanding anyway. This is another way of saying that hermeneutic indices are *variants* of Jakobson's metalingual function, which is a universal feature of language. I say "variants" to suggest a broader conception than Jakobson's because the effect of the metalingual function can, in fact, be produced not only by translating individual words between different codes, but also by *juxtaposing* larger semantic units via a structural relationship that is like montage or metaphor.

It follows from the above that the ability to distinguish semantic fields or codes is the prerequisite for recognizing glosses or hermeneutic indices. But not all semantic fields are consistent either across boundaries between different cultures or through time in a given culture, which raises an important question about how one can hope to grasp meanings from alien or past cultures. For example, in the West, "madness" is now seen largely in the context of psychophysiological disorders and usually as something to be deplored and treated. In some other cultures, however, as well as in many loci in the premodern West, "madness" can be a sign of contact with the divine and thus a mark of distinction. (In the examples of hermeneutic indices above, this association is present to varying degrees in the works by Melville, Dostoevsky, and Achebe.) Consequently, if something in an utterance is associated with madness via translation, equation, or juxtaposition, the meaning that results will depend heavily on how one sees the behavior that is identified as "mad" in the first place or, in other words, on the semantic field in which one locates it.

This is precisely where the difference between complex literary works and simpler, everyday utterances emerges especially clearly. The meaning of the latter can depend entirely on the extralinguistic context in which they occur. But in literary works, and especially in narrative genres, virtually all aspects of the world are verbalized either implicitly or directly, including not only characters and their exchanges but thoughts, settings, physical appearance, past histories, and the like. As a result, one can frequently infer from a work itself how it conceives of semantic fields and what constitutes a noteworthy translation between them, as opposed to a simple metonymic glide within an undifferentiated field.

Support for this claim can be found in the venerable argument by the Russian Formalist Viktor Shklovsky about "defamiliarization" (ostranenie) as the distinguishing characteristic of the kind of utterances we call "literature." A writer creates defamiliarization when he describes an event, character, or setting in unfamiliar terms, which means that he eschews the semantic fields or codes that would normally (habitually) be used for such things at a given time in a given culture. One of Shklovsky's examples is Tolstoy's famous description in *War and Peace* of Natasha Rostova at the opera, which is presented as an example of pernicious and immoral urban artifice via two nonhabitual perspectives onto it. The first is that of a naïf who does not recognize theatrical and operatic conventions, the second is that of a sophisticate who uses technical musical terminology (bk. 2, pt. 5, chap. 9). Whether or not either of these is how a given reader happens to see opera anyway is far less important than recognizing how the novel defines the opera via a jarring and valenced juxtaposition of perspectives. Although Shklovsky's concept of defamiliarization reflects the earliest period of Russian Formalist theorizing, it can, in fact, be correlated with Jakobson's "poetic function" and the later Slavic structuralist and semiotic conception of verbal art (e.g., Yurii Tynianov, Jan Mukařovský, Yurii Lotman). This is because the effect of defamiliarization also arises in literary works as a result of the way literary *structure* puts words into meaningful relations with each other in a way that does not normally happen outside the work. For example, in *Eugene Onegin* Pushkin rhymes "Rossini" with the adjective *sinii*, which means "blue"; and in *Moby-Dick* Melville makes a hunt for an albino sperm whale into a symbol for the mysteries of existence.

The movement of metaphors between cultures demonstrates that telling juxtapositions of semantic fields can also transcend a given culture. Even several millennia after being coined, Homer's "wine dark sea" is still recognizable in English for its suggestive linkage of viticulture (and hence agriculture) with inebriation, feasting, ritual libations, and the alluring, perilous, necessary, natural, and divine realms of marine voyages. This kind of interpretation of a distant cultural formulation still seems plausible even though our conception of metaphor is not Homer's. Classicists have argued that before Aristotle the ancient Greeks did not distinguish between literal and metaphorical meanings, and treated images as sufficient explanations of phenomena. Thus, when a Hippocratic writer explains how the body makes stones via an image of "smelting," this image of "a process similar to smelting . . . becomes the explanation."[14] But even if the ancient Greeks did not see metaphors as figurative in the same way we do, their sense of what we call metaphors still appears to have allowed for connections among different semantic fields. Similarly, Shakespeare's metaphor in *Hamlet*, "thy commandment all alone shall live / Within the book and volume of my brain" (1.5.109–10), is also a juxtaposition of terms from different semantic fields that is intelligible to readers around the world (or at least to those whose cultures see books and brains as repositories of knowledge and memory). Even the metaphoric origin of the Russian colloquial expression "to turn someone's head" in the sense of infatuation ("vskruzhit' golovu"), which links circular movement with human anatomy, is still recognizable despite its being so familiar that it has become "worn out."

However, although there are similarities between metaphors and hermeneutic indices it would be misleading simply to equate them, because the explicit translation that characterizes indices is frequently only implicit in metaphors. The resulting difference between translation and juxtaposition is that metaphors always function "bidirectionally" and establish symmetrical relations between their two terms; moreover, the relationship of similarity does not involve judgment of either term. Thus, in the metaphor "the iron gates of life" we conclude that iron gates are like life and that life is like iron gates; similarly, in the metaphor from *Hamlet* books are like brains and brains are like books. These "expansions" of the metaphors also show why similes function in the same way. If we say that "Achilles is like a lion," this also means that a lion is like Achilles; and if "Kotik Letaev is burning as in fire," then the fire is also like his burning. However, in the example from *Eugene Onegin* the narrator's translation or recoding of Lensky's Romantic effusions introduces a *value* judgment that interdicts seeing them as a neutral and therefore a balanced equivalent of the prosaic formula. In this sense, Pushkin's hermeneutic index can be seen as *unidirectional,* even if Lensky's Romanticism still preserves some of its wistful and naive charm. Similarity in this case *does* involve judgment of one term from the perspective of the other. The examples from Turgenev function in the same way: it becomes impossible to take at face value either the liberal terminology of a country squire or the Francophone pretensions of a provincial young lady, even if both still retain some of their appeal. On the other hand, the examples of indices from Dostoevsky do seem reversible because they are characterized by juxtaposition rather than translation: thus, Svidrigailov's suicide is colored by Dostoevsky's anti-Semitic description of the fireman, who, in turn, is also tarnished by virtue of Svidrigailov's choosing him as a witness.

Significant juxtapositions such as this can take place on widely differing textual scales. For example, Tolstoy's short story "Three Deaths" describes in turn the deaths of a lady, a peasant, and a tree that is cut down to make a cross for the latter's grave. These separate stories are not linked strongly in terms of plot and appear more like elements in a cinematic montage. However, the overall story's meaning emerges from a consideration of the relations among the three episodes, and is guided by the narrator's increasing sympathy as he moves from the lady to the tree. A similar effect on a smaller scale is achieved by the celebrated scenes in chapter 8 of Flaubert's *Madame Bovary* that consist of Rodolphe's seduction of Emma intercalated with speeches at the agricultural fair. Here the juxtaposition of civic banalities with Rodolphe's clichés, which implies their equivalence despite their surface difference, is clearly to his disadvantage.

One problem with all these isolated examples is that, as the analysis of *Anna Karenina* will demonstrate, a single novel contains hundreds or thousands of hermeneutic indices. Examining one or two out of their contexts makes it impossible to do justice to their implications. On the other hand, analyzing and integrating large numbers of them proves manageable because many indices, like other constituents of verbal art, inevitably repeat. The result is that patterns of meaning emerge, and one does not have to juggle many divergent individual meanings.

At the same time, as the analysis of *Anna Karenina* will also show, hermeneutic indices in any complex narrative do not usually define unique answers to the majority of textual questions. Instead, they identify a series of varying *ranges* of meanings pertaining to different textual issues that collectively map the shape and the limits—both the terrain and the borders—of a work's possible interpretations.[15]

5.3. Hermeneutic Indices as Guides to the Plurality and Limits of Interpretation

Because the idea of "limits" is inherently problematic as well as currently unfashionable in many critical circles, it is essential to make several caveats about what hermeneutic indices can and cannot provide the reader.

A spatial simile that might be helpful is a map such as geologists produce in order to understand the configuration of bedrock below the earth's surface (although the spatial nature of a map has obvious limitations when applied to a temporal form such as narrative). Individual outcroppings wherever they appear in a given area are examined to determine the kind of bedrock and the spatial orientation of its characteristic structures (the strike and dip of bedding, foliations, etc.); this can be seen as analogous to identifying and analyzing individual hermeneutic indices. Data gleaned from outcroppings are noted on a topographic map of the area and are then integrated by the investigator to produce the most likely configurations of what exists below the earth's surface; this is analogous to the procedures of the reader, who attempts to understand the relations among indices as well as their collective implications for the meanings in a work. Thus, although data from individual outcroppings can be quite specific in what they indicate (some can also be unclear or multivalent), there will not necessarily be a unique way to integrate all of them into a complete picture of what actually exists beneath the earth's surface. (This will vary depending on the kind of geological terrain one is dealing with.) Another way of putting this is that there will be areas of the geologic map about which the investigator will be more certain because the relations among the data there are clearer, while other areas will be ambiguous in the sense of supporting a series of possibly conflicting constructions. This is like the range of diverging or even conflicting interpretations of particular textual issues that assemblages of hermeneutic indices can support, all of which need to be described if one is to account for a work's range or limits of interpretation. And in a way similar to the geologist's deducing from data in outcroppings the likeliest dominant features of the local geology as a whole, the process of fashioning a "map" of readings entails correlating individual indices in accordance with relational and hierarchical criteria, such as narrative levels, that are relevant to the particular text at hand. The result in both cases is the construction of a background/foreground structure of relations that allows individual details to be assigned meanings. In either case, a meaningless jumble is impossible because of the inherent and constitutive laws that are a function of each phenomenon's existence. Thus, there will be limits to the range of possible interpretations that can apply to a given area, which also means that some interpretations will be implausible or interdicted. The coherence of any work—some degree of which is necessary for it to be recognizable as a work—also leads inevitably to a core of relative certainty regarding some of the work's concerns as well as to areas that are ambiguous to varying degrees. To describe both is the goal of the reading methodology that interests me.

But as with any real map, the question of scale is paramount here as well. The kind of map that I propose to draw in the second part of this book cannot be imagined as exhaustive in the sense of showing every meaning in the novel. There are several reasons for this. One is that meaning is partially dependent on the reader, as a result of which no complex work, whether large or small, can have a single totalizing reading. Another is that because meanings are permutations of relations among textual elements, no one reader could possibly recognize all of them in a work of any length and complexity; limitations of consciousness and memory will inevitably interfere. There also have to be practical limits to the scope of an exegesis such as this that are dictated by the exigencies of publishing and by the kinds of demands that can be placed on the reader's interest and attention. Finally, in the same way that one does not need to record every last feature in all the outcroppings in a given area in order to produce a geological map, it is not necessary to examine every hermeneutic index to infer the general distribution of the plausible readings that a work can support.

5.4. Caveats about Hermeneutic Indices

One important consideration to bear in mind about these textual moments is that they are not hermeneutic can openers that allow one simply to extract a work's unmediated message. They are also decidedly not master keys to authorial intentions. Rather, they can be thought of as an array of vectors within the text that point to ways of understanding the text and can vary from exemplary models, to negative examples, to false leads, to ambiguous hybrids of all three. It is worth recalling Jakobson's claim that metalanguage is inherent in discourse, which means that listeners automatically use the glosses in their interlocutors' remarks to orient themselves within the resulting meanings. By contrast, analyzing a work of literature via its hermeneutic indices is carried out consciously, systematically, and warily in order to minimize projection and to maximize the apprehension of possible meanings, no matter how seemingly eccentric or discordant.

The array of interpretive vectors in a work can be broad or narrow, "open" or "closed," to adapt Eco's terminology, depending on the work in question. Moreover, these vectors, like anything else in a text, need to be weighed and evaluated via Dilthey's inevitable "hermeneutic circle," according to which one understands a detail via its relation to the whole and the whole in terms of the details. As the references above to theories of meaning are meant to indicate, there is, in fact, no way to escape the kind of relational constraint on meaning that is implied by the hermeneutic circle. This remains true no matter what one's relevant field of reference may be—a single work, a dialogic exchange, or a particular culture. Individual hermeneutic indices can thus also be mono- or polyvalent, simple or difficult to interpret. However, despite not only the *possibility* but the *probability* that identifying and analyzing some hermeneutic moments in some works can yield ambiguous results, one cannot neglect even these if one places any value on understanding a given work. Thus, the limits or perimeter of the resulting interpretive "map" can be sharp, fuzzy, or elusively gradational; but even in the latter case, there will always be some readings that fall outside what the text can support.

A second consideration is that although the function of hermeneutic indices is to guide the reader in determining the immanent meanings of a given work, those meanings will always be *partial* because they are the result of relations among the work's determinacies and its indeterminacies, which only a given reader can "fill in." The reader's role as the text's cocreator has been theorized extensively by Roman Ingarden, Felix Vodička, and Wolfgang Iser, among others, and can be highly variable. But even if individual indices in particular works can yield widely divergent interpretations, the phenomenon of a hermeneutic index can still be seen as the necessary *complement* to the textual "gaps" that Iser identifies as the primary motivators of the reader's construction of textual meaning. "Gaps" raise questions about how to constitute meaning; hermeneutic indices are moments when meaning is actually constituted.[16]

The potential variation in how an indeterminacy will be incorporated into a structure of meaning, or whether an indeterminacy will even be recognized as one, may depend entirely on the reader's background. For example, whether or not two juxtaposed details in a text signify something specific can depend on whether or not the reader has the knowledge or imagination necessary to recognize a relation between the two. This can be illustrated via the parodic or subtextual evocation of one work by another. Ivan Turgenev's short story "Raspberry Water" ("Malinovaia voda," 1848), from the famous collection *A Hunter's Sketches (Zapiski okhotnika),* focuses on a pathetic rural character named Stepushka who bears unmistakable traces of, and is described in a narrative style clearly recalling, Akakii Aka-kievich from Nikolai Gogol's classic story "The Overcoat" ("Shinel'," 1842). However, Turgenev does not signal his debt to Gogol, as a result of which only the reader who recalls the earlier work on the basis of details in "Raspberry Water" will be able to read accurately the hermeneutic indices that define Stepushka, in the sense of understanding how they evoke a complex literary antecedent. Just one example is the list of relaxing pas-times in which Akakii Akakievich did *not* indulge after work, which is the hidden model for the list of things that Stepushka does *not* do on holidays: "he did not show up at the tables and barrels that had been set out, did not bow, did not approach his master to kiss his hand, did not drink a glass to his master's health in one swallow."[17] Thus, if one does not recognize Gogol's presence behind the scenes, Stepushka could be read as a purely pathetic character or, if one does, as Turgenev's reduction of Gogol's com-plex and rhetorically charged grotesque to pathos, which is quite a differ-ent interpretation. The hidden allusions to Gogol are the kind of "sub-merged" semantic field that may very well escape recognition during an analysis that relies only on hermeneutic indices and other purely "intrin-sic" criteria. However, I do not see this as a weakness of the reading meth-odology that I advocate, which can be seen as a necessary first phase, or ground, for subsequent work. I am not at all opposed to scholarship that focuses on cultural contexts or allusions in literary works. What I insist on is that such interpretive data be correlated with the array of potential read-ings that inheres in a work and that determines the ultimate meanings of the extrinsic cultural traces in it.

A third feature of hermeneutic indices is that they can have a direct connection to questions of literary value, but only because these are usu-ally tied to the meanings that readers find in literature. On the one hand, Lotman has argued that the density and complexity of the meanings com-municated via all the resources of organized literary language contribute decisively to a work's impact; "beauty is information," as he put it.[18] In-deed, one of the primary reasons why we consider some works compel-lingly "deep" is that they juxtapose far-reaching ideas without resolving the differences among them in any simple fashion, which draws the reader into prolonged and pleasurable thinking and musing about them. On the other hand, the same ideas can be evaluated antithetically by different readers, which means that, ultimately, meaning and value can be sepa-rated, at least to some extent. Thus, Dostoevsky, who is widely revered by countless readers around the world precisely for his "depth," can strike other readers—including major figures such as Tolstoy, Chekhov, and Nabokov—as naive and seriously flawed.

A fourth consideration bearing on hermeneutic indices is the difference between writing and orality. In Lotman's formulation, "that which is unknown to any speaker of a particular language is included in a written communication, while that which is unknown to a specific speaker is included in an oral one. For this reason, written speech is much more detailed."[19] Lotman also stresses that oral speech is part of a syncretic communicative act that, in addition to other features of language such as intonation and speech volume, includes appearance, facial mimicry, gestures, clothing, etc. As a result, the organization of oral speech bears some resemblance to a cinematic sign system, and "written speech is the result of the translation of this multi-planar system into the structure of a purely verbal text."[20] Because the entire world in a literary work is verbalized, the difference between oral as opposed to written speech from the point of view of hermeneutic indices is more quantitative than qualitative. Literary works will usually contain more indices, as well as indices that apply to a larger range of phenomena, because they consist not only of dialogues but of verbalizations of the contexts for dialogic exchanges, such as settings, physical appearance, and so on, all of which obviously bear on the work's meanings. These indices pertaining to contexts inevitably help to delimit and define the dialogic interactions among the characters, which affects the nature of the "map" of possible readings that results.

Finally, it is important to underscore again that attention to hermeneutic indices in a work cannot free one entirely from bringing to it various assumptions, or aspects of historically conditioned cultural codes, that are the ground for the encounter between text and self or, indeed, that are the ground for *concepts* like "text" and "self"—such as believing that novels or poems are meant to be read as if they were true in some sense, that they contain narrators, individual characters, settings, extractable meanings, etc. I am, of course, also implicated in this kind of mediation by virtue of relying on thinkers such as Jakobson, Lotman, and the others. However, as I have argued, not all mediations are equal, and the criterion for choosing among them is ultimately ethical: *that mediation is best that mediates least.* Consequently, my justification for relying on the above individuals is that their conception of language and texts suggests a reading methodology that reduces mediation to what can be likened to an *asymptotic minimum.* And this default position is the best that one can hope for, because there are no absolutes in the practice of literary interpretation.

Focus on hermeneutic indices thus offers the possibility of an *adaptive* and *text-specific* reading strategy, one that can, in principle, "require" any kind of interpretation from any perspective, be it Freudian, "ecocritical," religious, or epistemologically skeptical. Although relevant to any kind of literary work, hermeneutic indices are especially illuminating in a "many-voiced" genre like the novel because they help to capture the variety of meanings usually present in such works.

The light that hermeneutic indices shed on a work's interpretive limits has the additional benefit of illuminating the history of the work's reception. Having a "map" of potential readings of a work helps one understand what motivated specific, narrower readings as well as the consequent debates among their partisans. And although this was not my intention when I first conceived of hermeneutic indices, producing a map of potential readings also provides a criterion for *evaluating* a work's critical reception in the sense of distinguishing between readings that are plausible and those that are not. This is the focus of some of my endnotes in the second part of this book.

5.5. Are Hermeneutic Indices Inherent in Literary Works?

My claims about hermeneutic indices involve a question that has received much attention in the English-speaking world during recent decades: What is *in* the text as opposed to what the reader *brings* to it? I would like to conclude, therefore, by considering two debates about this question that took place between Wolfgang Iser and Stanley Fish, and Umberto Eco and Richard Rorty, with additional comments by Jonathan Culler. Both are instructive and representative examples of the kinds of arguments that have been adduced.[21] Here too Jakobson and Lotman have seminal arguments to contribute.

Despite the differences in participants, the debates are congruent, with Fish and Rorty advocating what became known as the "neopragmatist" conception of reading. This assumes that readers cannot know anything determinate in a work and that it is specious to talk of anything really being *in* a work, because all readers do is deploy various reading strategies that either serve their needs or reflect assumptions widespread in the social collective to which they belong.[22] Iser and Eco are far from being representatives of the same theoretical movement, even though both have written much about the relation between the reader and the text. Nevertheless, in terms of the above debate they overlap to the extent that both see texts as exerting definite constraints on readers' interpretations. Iser's phenomenology of reading assumes a dynamic relation between textual determinacies and in-determinacies that readers negotiate, while Eco claims the existence of an "*intentio operis*" that cannot be neglected by readers who would construe a work's meaning.[23]

Although this opposition between the two pairs of critics may be fundamental, it is not, in fact, insurmountable. First of all, we can take as a given that the primary semiotic universe within which we function is that of natural languages. Because there appears to be no way to escape the mediating agency of language, we then have to agree that there is probably nothing like a brute translinguistic ground that can be known directly (which is different from saying that this ground does not exist; it probably does, but we cannot cognize or verbalize it in an immediate way). And because language is a social phenomenon, it also follows that what we do with language when we read or speak is to a considerable extent a function of conventions elaborated by others.

Nevertheless, there is nothing that prevents us from analyzing phenomena *within* language and from bracketing the question of unmediated knowledge of anything beyond language. Even if a given language mediates one's relation to whatever the language is applied to, within that all-encompassing field of mediation there are particular features that can still be identified, analyzed, and understood in the terms of that mediating field. (Many everyday utterances are dominated by what Jakobson calls the "referential function," which entails allusions to the world of things, events, and concepts within which the speaker exists. But because this function is still obviously manifested in language, it also cannot provide an escape from the mediating field.) Among such analyzable linguistic phenomena are the relations among language's constituent elements. Grammar is one category of relations. Jakobson's six invariant functions constitute another, so that the difference between the metalingual and poetic functions is the difference between *kinds* of relations among elements of language. Moreover, as I mentioned, whatever can be identified as a form of linguistic ordering in utterances that we call literary can also be found to varying degrees in all other forms of language use; the difference is one of quantity, not quality.

Consequently, there is no reason to invoke unknowable "essences" when dealing with structures of meaning in works we call "literary." What we have in them is merely thickenings or concentrations of relations that can be found throughout language, although these are precisely the kinds of thickenings that allow one to distinguish between *Anna Karenina* and a newspaper article about a socialite's marital difficulties (and, at their best, these thickenings are the products of genius). *Anna Karenina* is like this newspaper article in that it refers to a world of individuals, customs, places, events, and the like. But these are placed into a matrix of relations that make them echo each other, repeatedly and complexly, and thus produce multiple additional meanings that draw the reader into receding labyrinths of thought. By contrast, the newspaper article will eschew this kind of matrix almost entirely in its attempt to report the simple who, what, when, where, why, and how of events, and any speculation about meanings beyond this will be largely a result of the reader's own intelligence, knowledge, imagination, or ingenuity. In other words, both the determinacy and polyvalence of artistic discourses are facts, but these are not *in essence* different from what we find in everyday uses of language. Thus, the quiddity of a literary work is accessible in the same terms as those that apply to the reader's mundane use of language, and the work is not merely the function of the individual reader's projections.

Bearing these considerations in mind, I would like to return to Fish's critique of Iser, which is that Iser's "gaps are not built into the text, but appear (or do not appear) as a consequence of particular interpretive strategies, [thus] there is no distinction between what the text gives and what the reader supplies; he supplies *everything*."[24] In short, Fish is arguing that if readers cannot have unmediated access to a textual essence, then everything is so mediated that it is not worth talking about anything except for the process of mediation itself, which, in turn, is a kind of social determinism that a given exegete cannot escape.

There are several counterarguments that can be made against this position. First of all, as I argued above, the fact that language is a form of mediation does not prevent one from speaking about the kinds of relations that can be identified within its field, which range from those that are ambiguous to those that are fixed. Second, Fish's procedure with regard to Iser is undermined by his own claims, because Fish has had no difficulty in grasping what he believes is the "essence" of Iser's argument despite the fact that Fish's reading is predicated on his own specific conclusions about the nature of language, interpretive strategies, the difference between life and art, and so on. Thus, as far as Fish is concerned, he *can* discern the alien truth in what others say, which means that he is not merely enacting ideational projections sanctioned by his interpretive community. Indeed, if it were otherwise, no change in readings or readers would be possible.[25] Third, as my discussion of the role of alterity in ethics, developmental psychology, and semiotics was meant to demonstrate, there are compelling arguments in favor of the view that the individual's dependence on making another's language his own is *the* defining condition of being human and alive.

Foreign language acquisition suggests a related argument. As we have seen, Jakobson explained that learning one's first language obviously implies that one is capable of metalingual operations and that one simply cannot learn additional languages without this aptitude.[26] Lotman echoes this view (as well as Bakhtin) when he argues that no form of thought can be "monostructural" or "monolingual" and that "consciousness without communication is impossible. In this sense, one can say that dialogue precedes language and gives birth to it."[27] It follows, therefore, that anyone who has learned another language, including Fish, must be capable of recognizing and negotiating alterity, because the mechanism for doing so is the same as that in all language acquisition—relating the new to the old via translation.[28]

The same principle undergirds all disciplines that are predicated on the conviction that an outsider can learn an alien culture's system of signs and meanings. As I mentioned, Geertz draws direct parallels between how one goes about understanding alien cultures and how one reads texts. But we do not have to turn to anthropological fieldwork to find evidence in support of his claim. An example of a well-established discipline in American academe that routinely bridges these procedures and that, in fact, cannot do otherwise is classical philology, especially the branch that seeks to determine the original meanings of words. For example, Ruth Padel has found that "[ancient] Greek tragedy describes what happens inside human beings daemonically and biologically, in ways that read to us like metaphor. But [ancient Greek] daemonology and biology are very different from ours, and play a role in Greek ideas about the self that matches little of our experience."[29] Padel engages this problem by inferring what meanings key words appear to have in specific textual contexts and then builds up the ranges of meanings to which these words allude. One of Padel's examples is *phrenes,* which she interprets as being a term for the internal organs where most Greeks at the end of the fifth century B.C. located thinking, perception, and feeling. When trying to understand what *phrenes* originally meant, Padel is careful not to prejudge their physical, intellectual, and metaphysical qualities. Thus, *phrenes* emerge as both receiving and expressing emotion as well as practical ideas and knowledge; they are both mobile and containers; individuals have *phrenes* and are in them; *phrenes* flow with emotions that behave like liquids, etc.[30] This process of interpretation is, of course, the process of the hermeneutic circle, and the result is a sense of ancient Greek "psychology" that is quite unlike ours. But despite its otherness, we can still know it.

It is useful to bear this example in mind when we turn to Rorty's argument against Eco, which is, like Fish's against Iser, determinedly antiessentialist. Rorty rejects the idea that "the text can tell you something about what *it* wants, rather than simply providing stimuli which make it relatively hard or relatively easy to convince yourself or others of what you were initially inclined to say about it."[31] However, Rorty does recognize the moral argument based on Kant that sees texts as if they were "honorary persons" (which is an especially felicitous phrase, in my view), and although he says that he does not accept the argument fully, he concludes, nevertheless, that it can still be relevant for "distinguishing between knowing what you want to get out of a person or thing or text in advance and hoping that the person or thing or text will help you want something different—that he or she or it will help you change your purposes, and thus to change your life."[32] With this remark, Rorty cracks the door to a critique of his position, for how can something stimulate change if all one does is project one's preoccupations onto it? In fact, Rorty throws the door open to a negotiable alterity when he goes on to speak in passionate and ethically charged terms about the "great love or . . . great loathing" that certain "first-rate" works can induce. Even though he insists that this is not in response to the kind of textual "*intentio* or . . . internal structure" that Eco posits, the fact remains that the significant works in Rorty's canon—he mentions Heidegger and Derrida specifically—embody something new that he has clearly learned from them and that makes him single them out for special praise.[33] Given this, is it too simple a question to ask how the internal structure of Heidegger's arguments in German and of Derrida's in French can be separated from what makes Rorty celebrate them?

An inevitable corollary to the question about what is *in* the text as compared with what the reader brings *to* it is the matter of the *context* into which a reader places a work in order to make sense of it. Culler broaches this topic in his response to Eco in the above debate when he distinguishes between "understanding" a text and "*overstanding*" it, which "consists of pursuing questions that the text does not pose to its model reader." Culler's conclusion is that "many of the most interesting forms of modern criticism ask not what the work has in mind but what it forgets, not what it says but what it takes for granted."[34] However, a persuasive counterargument is that one cannot actually carry out the procedure Culler advocates unless one already has a good idea of what a work "has in mind" or "what it says," which in fact begs the very question that I am attempting to answer here. In other words, if one does not know which way the grain of a text runs, and if determining its direction is far from simple, Culler's call for reading against the grain risks becoming an invitation to read *randomly* (which is presumably not what he intends). Thus, if one wants to grasp what a work "forgets" or "takes for granted" and does not want simply to invent what these could be, one has to deal with the linguistic structures that determine meanings, including hermeneutic indices.

In light of my arguments above, which implicate the reading of literary works in human negotiations of linguistic alterity that have much more at stake than does reading considered by itself, there seems to be no alternative but to privilege any text over any exegete's beliefs, even with all the ambiguities and pitfalls that this may entail. Indeed, as Lotman eloquently argued in essays he wrote during the latter part of his life, human beings are what they are only because they do their best to surmount the differences among them through linguistic means, both in person and via writing. And although these attempts at understanding can never fully succeed, in their novelty the "imperfect" results that arise constitute nothing less than the primum mobile of culture.[35]

Part Two

Anna Karenina: A Map of Readings

α
it seemed that she understood everything
                    (182, II.21)
she saw, or it seemed to her that she saw
                    (263, III.8)
it seemed to him that he had always seen it
                    (279, III.13)
it seemed to him that there had never been
                    (321, III.24)
it seemed to her that she understood everything
                    (462, V.2)

ω
Yes, the one obvious, unquestionable manifestation of the Deity is the
laws of the good disclosed to the world by revelation, which I feel in
myself

                                                    (815, VIII.19)

6. From Theory to Practice

Before turning to the opening of *Anna Karenina,* I would like to clarify the relation between the methodology I advocate and the results I claim for it by explaining briefly the procedure I followed to produce the map of possible readings (see also *5.3*). A seamless transition from theory to praxis probably requires more self-consciousness and self-control than most investigators are likely to possess; and much theory is based on abstraction that leaves out some of the fine-grained specifics that make individual works of literature what they are. It is to be expected, therefore, that at least some dehiscence will occur between any methodology and its results. Nevertheless, awareness of this problem may help to mitigate it, especially in the case of a methodology that is inherently adaptive and that is based on linguistic phenomena inherent in discourse.

I started by reading through the novel several times and marking in the margins all of the textual moments that fit the criteria of hermeneutic indices *(5, 5.1, 5.2);* these numbered roughly 1,600. I transferred references to these moments onto index cards, noted their implications for the novel's array of meanings, and then sorted the cards by the categories that appeared to emerge from the novel itself, that is, the narrator, characters, structure, plots, themes, scenes, recurring imagery, and so on. Finally, I arranged these categories into a sequence that begins with the implications of the novel's opening lines and pages, which are especially important because they shape the reader's expectations with regard to the remainder of the text, and then goes on to the novel's portrayal of reading, perceiving art, and construing meaning in general, all of which have a bearing on the reader's attempt to understand the novel in its own terms. The length of my discussions of various other topics tends to be a function of the extent to which the novel emphasizes them. Thus, I analyze the relations among characters in some detail because this is what the novel is mostly about. At all stages I adjusted the meanings of individual indices when new or different connections among them seemed to warrant it.

My procedure thus flows naturally from my methodological commitment to suppressing as much as possible all a priori projections onto the novel and to grasping how meanings emerge in it from the bottom up. This procedure is actually the only way to deal with a large amount of variegated data of any kind if one believes in trying to understand its defining characteristics.

My focus on the textual moments I call "hermeneutic indices" also grows out of the general task I set myself. As my examples above show *(5.1)*, hermeneutic indices are especially telling instances of meaning creation because they reveal something about the frames of reference that underlie the text (which obviously implies that they are not *all* the instances of meaning creation in a text). They are among the most important elementary units on the most basic textual level out of which the higher, more complex textual meanings are composed, and their importance is a function of the *larger* quantity of information they reveal by virtue of pointing *beyond* themselves to the semantic fields they imply (via the juxtaposition or translation that defines them). Thus, as we will see, the equation in *Anna Karenina*'s first line between *family happiness* and *resemblance* is far more revealing of some of the novel's larger meanings than is the characterization of Stiva shortly thereafter as having a *body* that is *full* and *well tended*, because the first involves the unexpected juxtaposition of two semantic fields, while the second does not.

But despite the explanatory power of hermeneutic indices, it is important to remember that they are merely variants of Jakobson's "metalingual function" in the sense of being *comparable* to the overt kinds of recoding or glossing that he identifies *(4)*. Consequently, by focusing on hermeneutic indices I do not claim that I have discovered an unknown feature of language; instead, I advocate a systematic exploitation of a feature of language that has been neglected in textual interpretation. Moreover, given that glosses are inherent in utterances, we cannot expect hermeneutic indices always to stand out in the text as if they were either heterogeneous elements in it or potential knots of evidence waiting for some belief to illuminate their true nature (such as the cigars or father-son quarrels that used to emerge as predictable symbols in the light of vulgar Freudianism, or the descriptions of white or upper-class family life that are now often seen as racist or elitist). My concern with understanding how meaning arises also leads me to rein in the temptation to discuss fictional characters and their worlds as real beyond the text, which is a form of interpretive drift that is discernible in other critical studies and that is a testimonial to Tolstoy's artistry even if it is a manifestation of unwarranted readerly projection. My mapping project is limited to understanding the matrix of meanings that can give rise to such extensions.

Finding and using hermeneutic indices requires painstaking, slow reading and a kind of blank openness to the implied, far-reaching cultural resonances found in certain kinds of linguistic structures. This is not a claim for complete objectivity but a method for increasing the probability of neither missing something important in a work nor overemphasizing something that is minor; polyvalence and ambiguity are inherent in the method and the results. I seek to work in the middle space between the impossible goal of complete objectivity and the chaos of unconstrained interpretation. The large number of questions that I raise at times in response to particular indices is the consequence of this openness, as are the narrower conclusions that I also make. In short, my focus on hermeneutic indices, like my way of integrating them into categories, is a kind of inescapable or "default" procedure that is dictated by my methodological commitment to trying to see how the text itself generates its various meanings. Given the few simple premises on which I rely—respect for individuals and the ways in which their utterances are structured—there is no other way to read.

Incidentally, to avoid redundancy in the map of readings I do not use the term *hermeneutic index* each time I discuss one; neither do I explain each time what it is about a given textual moment that makes it a hermeneutic index. But I would not have focused on these moments were they not especially telling in the way and for reasons I describe *(5)*. I would be happy to explain my choices to any reader who may not understand or who remains unconvinced.

The form in which I present my findings is also meant to reflect my methodological assumptions. Because meaning is relational, I chose to divide this book into a system of numbered sections with limited foci (rather than into broader chapters) because these make it simpler to signal cross-references among parts of the map. This is supplemented by a detailed index to the entire book that further increases the number of fine-grained cross-references and that makes it easy to locate any particular topic of interest.

I invite other students and admirers of the novel to amend the resulting map of possible readings. My hypothesis is that well-intentioned scholars who agree with the few basic principles outlined in Part One—which I cannot see escaping in our time and culture—can reach a consensus about *Anna Karenina*'s meanings in terms of *areas* and *degrees* of both *certainty* and *uncertainty*. This kind of reading is especially necessary today because of the shockingly narrow view of Tolstoy that some scholars have recently advocated and that surprising numbers of others appear to have accepted (samples appear in the notes to Part Two). In keeping with my goal of understanding the novel more broadly, I map not only the "new" interpretations that I may have "discovered" (which would be falling into the dialectic that I fault in my introduction) but also follow interpretations wherever they may lead, which means on occasion retracing well-trodden paths left by earlier investigators. This is a form of "consensus," and is thus partial confirmation of the possibility of a map of readings. However, in the interest of efficiency, space, and clarity, and because I resist traditional conceptions of originality in literary scholarship, I will not footnote every critical commonplace to show who had expressed it earlier, but will attempt to give a sampling of the kinds of observations others have made.

7. Early Signals

What is most striking about the beginning of the novel is that it opens not with Tolstoy's own words but (apparently) with God's, as quoted by Saint Paul: "Vengeance is mine; I will repay."[1] Any epigraph functions as a potent hermeneutic index because of its primacy and because its relation to the body of the text is like a metaphoric montage; and depending on whether it is a précis of what is coming, a clue about part of it, an ironic contrast, or a hybrid of all of these, it can be "open" or "closed" to a broad range of interpretations. In the case of *Anna Karenina,* given that Tolstoy chose not to indicate the epigraph's source in Romans 12:19, and Boris Eikhenbaum's suggestion that Tolstoy got an early version of the epigraph not directly from the Bible but via Schopenhauer, the number of possible interpretations increases even more.[2]

Could Tolstoy have been alluding to some Schopenhauerian rather than Pauline conception of vengeance? Does the fact that Tolstoy truncated the biblical verse by eliminating its opening phrase, "For it is written," which is a pointed allusion to an antecedent in Deuteronomy 32:35 (with an echo in Leviticus 19:18), imply a preference for orality and a suppression of the idea of writing and/or of the Old Testament? Does the elimination of the final phrase of the verse, "saith the Lord," imply that Tolstoy could have been leaving room for himself instead of God as the manipulative authority behind the lives of his fictional creatures? This is a broad range of questions, but it is not unlimited, and readers will feel compelled to look in all the implied directions as they continue through the text.[3]

Additional questions arise when the epigraph is considered in its immediate biblical context, assuming that it is valid to bring this context to bear on the epigraph and on the body of the novel. The warrant for doing so would appear to be threefold: the reactive nature of vengeance, which requires understanding the transgression that justifies it; the fact that the epigraph is a syntactic fragment, which cannot help evoking the "virtual" passages that precede and follow it; and the additional references to Saint Paul's teachings in the novel, including his central theme of charitable

Christian love, which emerges in connection with Karenin and, even more importantly, with Levin at the novel's conclusion.

In the verses that surround the epigraph, Saint Paul teaches two things: that human beings should try to behave with loving charity toward each other (Romans 12:10–18) and that there is a kind of cosmic balance sheet according to which evildoers will inevitably be punished by God (12:19–21). In the pivotal verse 19, human beings are specifically enjoined from acting toward each other in terms of an "eye for an eye" causality: "Dearly beloved, avenge not yourselves, but *rather* give place unto wrath: for it is written, Vengeance *is* mine; I will repay, saith the Lord." Thus, the kind of retributive causality that tempts human beings is the prerogative of God alone. But this does not mean that human charity is separate from or unrelated to divine vengeance: "Therefore if thine enemy hunger, feed him; if he thirst, give him drink: for in so doing thou shalt heap coals of fire on his head" (Romans 12:20). Biblical scholars acknowledge that the latter part of this verse is "difficult" but have interpreted it as alluding to "a certain Egyptian ritual, [in which] a basin of burning charcoal carried on the head was a token of penitence."[4] A conventional metaphoric interpretation is that the enemy will burn with shame for his misbehavior. Thus, turning the other cheek emerges as being subsumed in an all-embracing divine plan from which there is no escape: even when you treat with kindness those who do you ill, which would seem to break the causal chain inherent in vengeance, the effect of your behavior is still to cause evildoers the necessary pain (fire) of recognizing that they have sinned. This is apparently how Saint Paul sees good overcoming evil, the point with which he concludes the twelfth chapter (verse 21). In chapter 13, he expands the theme of individual subordination to authority that is implied in his description of God's retributive plan by including obedience to every form of secular and social power.[5]

These passages consequently announce the existence not only of a divine law but also of an inescapable divine presence in all human affairs. This is obviously a highly structured and hierarchical conception of existence: it provides guidance for smooth, indeed ameliorative human relations (one should yield selflessly to the other), but, if humans fail to be good, it posits a kind of "safety net" in the form of God's punishment, which will either force wrongdoers to change or will hurt them to show that they have erred.[6]

However, the passages are ambivalent with regard to human freedom. On the one hand, Saint Paul's urging human beings to make moral choices implies that they are free. On the other, the fact that charitable treatment of an enemy will cause him to feel penitent makes the seemingly free act of human charity into part of a divine design that does not allow those who choose evil to escape unpunished.

Other important questions also remain unclear: how, when, and where is God's punishment meted out? As Saint Paul's words suggest, not everyone actually treats evil with goodness—that is an ideal for which humankind must strive. So perhaps those who act cruelly toward evildoers are also unwitting agents of God's punishment because the result of their cruelty is the evildoers' pain. But what if innocents are made to suffer at the hands of evildoers? How does this fit the divine retributive scheme (to paraphrase Ivan Karamazov's famous formulation of this question)? And does it make a difference if punishment is an *internal* torment that is *like* coals heaped on the evildoer's head? Does God wreak vengeance on all evildoers or only on some of them? And what could it mean about the nature of God's world if some may perhaps escape punishment? We also need to consider that in these verses and, indeed, throughout this entire chapter Saint Paul's focus is on human behavior on earth. Consequently, although we cannot eliminate the possibility that God's vengeance will be manifested after death in the punishments of hell, this is not the likeliest implication of the epigraph.

All these possibilities are clearly relevant to a novel named after an adulteress and need to be examined in detail. However, it is worth noting even at this early stage that the novel hardly presents a simple illustration of the issues raised by Saint Paul's teachings. Anna is the novel's primary sinner and is tormented internally and ostracized publicly. But as numerous readers have asked since the novel was first published, what about her brother Stiva, who is a chronic adulterer, although not a home breaker like Anna, and who remains irrepressibly happy and successful at the novel's end?[7] Indeed, there are no textual indications suggesting that he will suffer even after it ends. Perhaps the key difference between Anna and Stiva is that she ruins and abandons her family, whereas he "merely" undermines his family's moral and financial well-being.[8] Another difference is that Anna seeks to hurt Vronsky for what she believes is his growing indifference toward her and by doing so encroaches on the divine prerogative for vengeance.[9] By contrast, Stiva is tolerant of others' foibles, and his response to offenses such as insults is to forget and joke about them, as in the incident with Bolgarinov (VII.17). But if Anna's vengeance against Vronsky is the cause of her own punishment, what is Karenin's punishment for his vengeful thoughts about Anna shortly after he learns of her adultery and for his refusal later to grant her a divorce? Are his (temporary) misery and ridicule and his professional failure commensurable with Anna's death? And what about Princess Betsy and others in her circle? She too is an adulteress, but this does not result in any punishment that we ever witness, even though her intentional ostracism of Anna can be seen as part of the punishment that *is* meted out to *Anna.* Another possibility is that Anna suffers and commits suicide because she cannot overcome her *own* sense of guilt, whereas Stiva feels guilty only rarely and much more shallowly. This would appear to make character into destiny, which also raises questions about ethics and the relation of the human and the divine. Without even considering any of the other characters or issues in the novel, this brief glance shows that the relation between the epigraph and the body of the text is polyvalent and defines a major and possibly a permanent indeterminacy.[10] Whether or not this needs to be seen in negative terms, however, is best considered in light of the novel's conclusion, which, like *War and Peace,* acknowledges God's inscrutability from the limited human perspective.

The relation between the epigraph and the novel's famous first sentence seems to be simpler because both proclaim what appear to be unequivocal and universal laws.[11] On one level, Tolstoy's announcement that "All happy families resemble one another; each unhappy family is unhappy in its own way" can thus be seen as a kind of secular parallel to the Pauline epigraph. Furthermore, via its apodictic nature, and through simple physical contiguity that produces an effect like montage, Tolstoy's sentence is also colored by the quotation from Saint Paul. In short, we are left with the impression that there may be a connection between the role of God in judging human beings and the nature of the human condition that is Tolstoy's focus, but without knowing what this connection actually is. And because first impressions in literature are probably even more important than those in life, the question of the relation between the human and the divine starts to loom over the novel from the very start.

The first sentence also comprises a veritable quiver of hermeneutic indices that point the reader toward a specific array of expectations.[12] There is an obvious focus and value placed on the *family* as a fundamental unit (Tolstoy does not write, "All happy *people* resemble one another"), which, on an abstract level, implies a concern with interconnectedness, not separation, and with complexes of relations among men, women, and children and not just between any individuals and the world or God (see also *14.1*). In other words, human values (the presence or absence of happiness) are defined in terms of family clusters in a kind of triangular relationship that includes (an implied, if not necessarily intelligible) God: the individual is a part of a family, and God (somehow) rules over all.[13] Similarly, resemblance is elevated, whereas uniqueness and all its cognates—originality, individuality, existential self-creation, anything exceptional—are implicitly devalued by being marked as "unhappy."[14] The "tone" of the sentence (what Jakobson would call its "emotive function") is one of certainty couched in epigrammatic form, which implies that its speaker not only believes in the *possibility* of universal truths but *knows* what they are, or at least *believes* that he knows, which is a crucial difference. Another wrinkle in this sentence is that it does not say anything about the relative *numbers* of happy and unhappy families. So it is unclear how much happiness there is in the world. Perhaps it is rare.[15]

The novel's next sentence represents a further narrowing of the focus but in the same apodictic mode: we move from Divine Law, to Universal Family Law, to what could be called the Law of the Oblonsky Household, which paradoxically claims disorder in comparison to the preceding two: "All was confusion in the Oblonskys' house."[16] Given what has just been said in the novel's first sentence, we can infer that whatever is happening to the Oblonskys is somehow unique. Why? Because their being "upset" means that they are "unhappy," and "each unhappy family is unhappy in its *own* way" (emphasis added). However, it is worth noting immediately that developments later in the novel do not quite bear this out. Anna and Karenin's family will become unhappy in a way *similar* to Stiva and Dolly's and for the same reason—the adultery of one of the partners. Moreover, one of the reasons why Anna and Vronsky's attempt to create a simulacrum of a family fails is Anna's (probably unfounded) fears about Vronsky's fidelity. A related, receding causal chain is the irregular upbringing that Vronsky and Anna received: his mother had numerous affairs, and we know hardly anything about Anna's youth except that she was manipulated into marriage by an aunt (see *13.5.6*). In short, despite the narrator's claims about happy families, which *are* borne out by parallels among the Shcherbatskys, Lvovs, Levins, and a wealthy peasant's family that Levin visits (323–25, III.25), there are also patterns of similarity to family *unhappiness*.[17]

The structure of the novel's second paragraph can be read as supporting this conclusion as well. Punctuating the description of disorder in the Oblonsky household are eight repetitions in some fifteen lines of the word *dom*, which means "house" or "home" in Russian, and of the derivative noun *domochadtsy*, or "members of a household." These repetitions function as a semantic and acoustic refrain and centripetal organizing principle within a description of centrifugal disharmony.[18] The two opposing tendencies, which appear on contiguous but not identical textual levels (sound and meaning in one case, meaning alone in the other) imply that the paragraph's surface message may contain a contradictory countermessage as well. Perhaps this also has retroactive implications for the sequence of "laws" with which the novel begins. If we go backward through the text, the countermessage about the Oblonsky household can be correlated with the interpretation that the "law" of family life may not, in fact, be universal the way the narrator claims. And if this is the case, then it seems plausible to infer that the law of divine retribution may not apply to all human beings, as the vastly different fates of Anna, Stiva, and the others also suggest.

The narrator's portrayal of the Oblonsky household is also inconsistent. After describing how all is "upset" in it, the narrator specifies that everyone "felt that there was no sense in their living together and that people who meet accidentally at any inn have more connection with each other than they" (1, I.1). But when Stiva's faithful valet, Matvei, comes in to dress him, it is clear that they understand each other perfectly and that the servant remains not only loyal but also fond of his master (4–5, I.2). Even more striking is the narrator's contradictory remark that although Stiva was "roundly guilty before his wife and felt it himself, *almost everyone in the house,* even the nanny, Darya Alexandrovna's *chief friend, was on his side*" (5, I.2, emphasis added). The nanny, Matryona Filimonovna, acknowledges that "everything in the house has gone topsy-turvy" (6, I.2), which echoes the narrator's earlier "confusion." But this does not eliminate the oddity that the narrator would give two irreconcilable readings of the household in short succession (i.e., all are alienated from each other versus almost all are on Stiva's side), especially given the inevitable importance and weight of the novel's opening passages for setting aspects of the novel's tone and themes.

Can it be that this discrepancy is merely a slip on Tolstoy's part, like the temporal "errors" that have been discovered in the text?[19] (See *13.3.*) Or is the discrepancy evidence of the novel's a priori skepticism regarding all laws and generalizations? Neither of these possibilities can be disproven unequivocally, although neither is very likely for two reasons: the first is the resemblance between the nanny's contradictory viewpoint and the *relativization of perception* that is widespread throughout the novel (and that I will discuss in detail below [see *13*]); the second is the narrator's proclamation of laws and generalizations at different points throughout the novel. As a result, what may seem to be a slip or inconsistency in one textual location can be seen as part of a larger *pattern,* which means that it is not accidental but part of the novel's overall design and meaning (a remark that I intend to be entirely agnostic with regard to whether or not any of this was Tolstoy's intention, which is possible but unknowable).[20] We may be inclined to dismiss what seems to be a unique event as accidental (although there are also styles of reading that focus precisely on this, such as deconstructive and psychoanalytic ones), but we cannot dismiss consistent inconsistency.[21]

How is relativized perception manifested in the continuation of the scene? When the narrator speaks the Law of the Oblonsky Household, he does so from his own superior perspective, but when he describes the householders' actual relations via free indirect discourse, he "descends," as it were, into the consciousnesses of several minor characters who, with the exception of Matryona Filimonovna, are not even named or specified. Given this, we can infer that perhaps everyone sides with Stiva not because they have pondered the moral implications of his adultery, which may be the narrator's concern and what informs *his* perception of disorder, but simply because they, like almost everyone who meets Stiva, have been won over by his geniality and easy charm (a supposition that *is* confirmed amply throughout the novel). This implies that a personal reaction to something may be more important than any kind of impersonal (abstract, general) perspective onto it—in short, that the self may be the primary arbiter of meaning and value. This has the virtue of spontaneity and of being instinctual and therefore "natural." But as Anna's case demonstrates most vividly in this novel, instinct can put an individual at serious odds with morality.[22]

As this sampling of the novel's opening lines and pages shows, there appears to be a repeated tension in them between laws and generalizations that the narrator announces, on the one hand, and the way characters behave and are portrayed, on the other. Do these contradictions mean that the laws and generalizations could simply be invalid and that at heart Tolstoy was a skeptical "fox" who believed in many different things rather than a "hedgehog" who believed in one overarching truth, to paraphrase Isaiah Berlin's famous, influential, and ultimately misleading formulation? In one form or another, this critical view has persisted from the 1860s to our day.[23] Berlin's argument, which focuses largely on *War and Peace* and reflects his own militantly secular philosophical skepticism, implies that Tolstoy was blind to a fundamental inconsistency in his thought and his art: his genius for capturing the details and variety of life was at odds with his inability to create convincing, all-encompassing religio-philosophical schemes.

Although there is some truth to Berlin's claim, it has, unfortunately, been spread too broadly by others and used to homogenize the great works of Tolstoy's middle period. *Anna Karenina* is far more internally divided than *War and Peace*. Moreover, the nature of the "divisions" in *Anna Karenina* is much more complex than formulas like Berlin's would suggest, and a choice between the poles of a simple binary opposition does not do justice to the interweavings of the novel's affirmations and ambiguities. Berlin's approach also does not take sufficient account of the "literariness" of Tolstoy's novels. The structural holism of *War and Peace* and *Anna Karenina*—the number of finely nuanced echoes or relations among characters, scenes, situations, and other details—is developed so extensively that it simply cannot be divorced from the thematic inconsistencies in the novels. Also misleading is the methodological move popular among some of Berlin's followers of projecting from Tolstoy's life to his works or vice versa, which on the level of textual detail that interests me is an imponderable connection.

Thus, rather than claim that Tolstoy or, to be precise, his narrator in *Anna Karenina* believes in individual truths rather than general ones, I would argue that he believes *both* in the laws he announces *and* in the human behavior he portrays, even if the "fit" or relation between them is difficult or impossible to ascertain. As I have already mentioned, the novel ends on a similarly paradoxical note—with Levin realizing that it is futile for a limited human being to try to understand the divine order of things beyond the simple commandment to do good unto others. Levin's behavior toward his coachman and his wife is a concrete illustration that he is caught between two truths that even exemplary human beings like him (in Tolstoy's hierarchy in this novel) can reconcile only partially and with difficulty. This is quite different from claiming that Levin, like Tolstoy, professed one thing and actually believed another. Anton Chekhov may have been thinking of issues like this when he commented that Tolstoy did not so much solve problems in *Anna Karenina* as pose them correctly.[24]

8. Reading Readings, and Art about Art

I would like to shift now from the novel's early signals to hermeneutic indices that deal with the interpretation of verbal texts and other kinds of semiotic constructs, as distinct from "realia" such as characters' remarks to each other, their appearance, behavior, thoughts, emotions, or the spaces they inhabit. In other words, I want to examine scenes when characters are shown to be reading words or trying to make sense of other types of communication such as paintings or music. Because these exegetic moments deal with artifacts like the novel *Anna Karenina* itself, it is worth exploring the possibility that the acts of interpretation depicted *in* the novel are relevant for understanding something *about* the novel—such as its form, its status as a text, and, more broadly, how it conceives of the generation of meaning.[1]

8.1. Varieties of Texts

The first act of reading appears on the novel's second page when Stiva recalls how Dolly intercepted his note to a former governess that reveals that they have been having an affair. Even though the narrator participates in the characterization of this note as "revealing everything" (otkryvsheiu vse), thus indicating that its message is unequivocal, Dolly acts as though she cannot fully understand it and turns to Stiva to ask what it means. In other words, in her distraught state she is willing to rely on Stiva's mediating reaction, on whatever context or code (or lies) he may bring to an utterance that she hopes does not have the fixed meaning it appears to have. Unfortunately for Stiva, his reaction causes Dolly to break with him. But, as the narrator explains, had Stiva acted differently, he might have succeeded in redefining the note in a way that would have accorded with Dolly's attempt to deny its import. Her act of reading thus emerges as relativized because it is a function of her own wishes. This raises a small but important question about the extent to which determinate verbal meaning is possible in this novel and thus about the efficacy of the novel's didacticism, which is sounded as early as its first sentence. Dolly's experience is also significant because it is early evidence of continuity between the way characters interpret verbal meaning and how they view each other (see *13*).

This pattern continues as the novel unfolds. Later the same morning Stiva reads a series of everyday texts as he goes through his usual routine. The first is a telegram from Anna, announcing her arrival on the following day. "Thank God," says Matvei, the faithful valet, when Stiva tells him the news, which indicates that the servant understands the message the same way as his master does—in terms of Anna's promise to help patch up Stiva's marriage (5, I.2). But Dolly's response to the telegram is quite different. After Matvei shows it to her at Stiva's request, she informs Stiva that she is leaving and that he can do whatever he wants when Anna arrives. Stiva then turns to his morning mail, which includes a letter from a merchant who is preparing to buy a forest on Dolly's estate (6, I.3). When this sale takes place later in the novel, we learn that Stiva is quite carefree about it and is delighted with the money he receives, even though Levin insists that Stiva has allowed himself to be fleeced by the merchant. However, during the morning in question, Stiva's attitude to the letter is controlled entirely by his falling out with Dolly: the letter pains him because it mixes financial considerations into his attempt to mend his relations with her. A similar relativization of meaning characterizes Stiva's reading of his liberal newspaper. We are told that he originally chose to subscribe to it because its views accorded well with his personality, or so he imagines (7, I.3). But this morning, although Stiva can still read successfully between its lines, he finds that it does not give him the pleasure he usually receives—once again because of his damaged relations with Dolly.

There are comparable moments later in the novel as well. For example, Anna gets a note from Karenin that she understands but that sidesteps her confession as if she had never made it, which recalls Dolly's wishful reaction to Stiva's note to the governess (292, III.16); Karenin seeks Countess Lydia Ivanovna's help in figuring out how to understand a note from Anna and how to respond to it (518–19, V.25); and the countess's note to Anna hurts Anna deeply despite the fact that the countess had concealed this hidden aim of the note from herself (520, V.25). When Vronsky is at the provincial elections, he knows what Anna's note to him will say even before he reads it. But this seemingly perfect communication turns out to be one-sided, because a letter that Vronsky sent Anna had not yet reached her, and her note's contradictions actually alienate him further from her, which is not at all what she intended by sending it (665, VI.31). Misunderstandings and confusion also characterize Anna and Vronsky's exchanges of notes and telegrams before she dies; for example, "She did not realize that his telegram was a reply to her telegram and that he had not yet received her note" (761, VII.29). The minor character Golenishchev, whom Anna and Vronsky meet in Italy, has a related problem. Shortly after he appears in the novel, he is depicted as arguing against imaginary opponents in anticipation of their possible misunderstanding of a treatise that he has not even written yet (462, V.7). A more ambiguous example is Anna "reading, reading one book after another" when Vronsky is away at the provincial elections (666, VI.32). We are not given any details about how she reads, but the context implies that the activity may be little more than a way to fill the time that weighs on her: "She was sitting in the drawing room, under a lamp, with a new book by Taine, reading and listening to the noise of the wind outside."

Questions about Anna's relation to writing emerge even in connection with a children's book she writes herself (695, VII.9). For one thing, Stiva's praise for it may be as self-indulgent and superficial as all his other value judgments. For another, the association he makes between the book and Anna's taking in an English girl as a kind of foster daughter evokes an ironic contrast with Anna's inability to love her own daughter by Vronsky, which in turn makes one wonder how well she can execute the task of writing for children. An ancillary motif that may also cast a small shadow on the book is that Anna's charity toward the girl's family may be her (unwitting?) compensation for Vronsky's cavalier attitude toward paying the salary of the girl's father, Cord (303, III.19), who worked as a horse trainer for him and who took to drink. Of course, it is also possible that Anna is simply being kind to the Englishman's destitute family.[2]

It is important to note that there are also counterexamples of successful readings in *Anna Karenina*, although these are less numerous and less prominent. Levin and Kitty's ability to decipher each other's encoded messages is a striking instance of perfect, indeed transcendent communication (that is never achieved again by them or anyone else).[3] Later, Kitty obviously understands Levin's diaries when he gives them to her as a written confession about his lack of faith and past sexual misdeeds; however, her weeping is not the reaction he expected and can be interpreted as a reading that diverges at least somewhat from his intention (408, IV.17). In a similar vein, Levin also understands, although he refuses to accept, the philosophers he reads. (His attempt to recode Schopenhauer's *will* as *love* [788, VIII.9] recalls the opportunity Dolly offers Stiva to reinterpret the intercepted note.)

Other instances of "successful" readings are alluded to throughout the novel but are not described in any detail. These appear as part of the texture of daily existence and include the bureaucratic papers that are central to Stiva's and Karenin's work, Karenin's habit of reading whatever is in fashion, Levin's reading what Sviyazhsky recommends, Countess Lydia Ivanovna's numerous notes to various friends, and the like. But although references to such moments are fairly common, the relative lack of attention they receive allows them to slip into the background.

What determines if a written message succeeds or fails to communicate? Most of the failures noted above occur in connection with simple communications that are variants of the characters' everyday behavior and that reflect their enclosure within their own personalities (see *13*). Is it possible, therefore, that more complex writings fare differently? On the basis of scenes when characters engage complex works of art, the answer would appear to be "no."

The first such instance is the passage about Anna reading an English novel during her train ride to St. Petersburg after her visit to Moscow (100–101, I.29). Whatever else one could say about this rich scene, it does not suggest that Anna is a good reader in the sense of getting out of the text something that seems related to its patent meaning. In fact, although she is described as understanding what she reads after not being able to focus on it initially, we are also told that she finds it "unpleasant" to have "to follow the reflection of other people's lives. She wanted too much to live herself." As a result, Anna does not so much enter into or grasp the fictional characters' lives as try to *usurp* them by projecting herself into the work: "When she read about the heroine of the novel taking care of a sick man, she wanted to walk with inaudible steps round the sick man's room; when she read about a Member of Parliament making a speech, she wanted to make that speech" (100, I.29). Then, when the hero is on the verge of winning his goals of an estate and a baronetcy (which the narrator defines ironically as "his English happiness"), Anna suddenly feels that he must be ashamed and that she "feels ashamed of the same thing." She searches for a cause for her feeling and tentatively correlates it with Vronsky but in a way she cannot fully comprehend or accept. It is not clear if Anna projects her shame onto the novel or if there is something in the novel that motivates it. But in either case, the ethical questions that are triggered in Anna are short-lived, because for the time being she is able to ignore them.[4]

Thus, the model of reading that Anna enacts in this scene can be thought of as either interpretation or *mis*interpretation. (In connection with this it is also unclear, and does not matter very much, if the novel Anna tries to read is meant to be good or bad.) This ambivalence undermines the possibility of reading and writing works of art for didactic purposes or even simply in terms of determinate meanings. Why? Because Anna's reactions, especially her sense of shame, do not seem to have much to do with the novel she is holding. Whatever may be in the book is eclipsed by the strength of her feelings about Vronsky, which the narrator underscores by repeating the words "shame" and "shameful" (styd, stydnogo) seven times in ten lines and by describing Anna's "inner voice" as saying "Warm, very warm, hot!" when her thoughts turn to Vronsky. Even if we interpret Anna's being flooded by shameful feelings and her evasion of them as a *negative* example for the reader of *Anna Karenina* (an illustration of how *not* to read this novel), her behavior still constitutes a pessimistic image of the possibility that a text will be understood or will affect the reader in any predictable way.[5]

An additional dimension of this interpretation is suggested by Liza Merkalova's calling Anna a "real heroine from a novel" (297, III.17). This is a metaliterary hermeneutic index that creates a *mis-en-abîme* because it reminds the reader of the fictionality of a character who may be misreading a text about other fictional characters. One wonders if this can be the novel's projection of the possibility, or perhaps even the probability, that both Anna and *Anna Karenina* will be either misread or read very differently by their different readers (which means that the novel will transmit only a relativized meaning). The ambiguous image of Anna reading the book of her own life at the moment of her death adds to these reflexive implications (see *8.2*).

Near the end of the novel, we see Koznyshev confront the same problem from the opposite perspective, that of the author rather than the reader, when he publishes a scholarly book on which he has worked for a number of years. Despite his great hopes for the book, which deals with Russian and European forms of government, it is first greeted by deafening silence. Then one scathing review appears that is apparently motivated by the reviewer's personal animus against Koznyshev (770, VIII.1). Whether or not the book is good or bad and whether or not the reviewer is right or wrong do not change the fact that the incident again dramatizes the likelihood of misreading and misinterpretation in a way that may reflect back onto *Anna Karenina* (see *8.2*). Because Koznyshev's book is very different from the novel that Anna reads on the train and from Tolstoy's novel about her, one can also argue that it has little or nothing to do with her death and implies instead such things as the sterility of Koznyshev's overly rational and verbal pursuits and the suspect nature of his new enthusiasm for the "Slavic question." But because Koznyshev is so completely a creature of words and of print, his book's failure is still noteworthy in these terms as well.

8.2. Reading and Anna's Death

Another important aspect of the story of Koznyshev's book is its location in the novel. It opens part VIII and thus follows immediately after Anna's suicide, which closes part VII. These two events might seem to be unrelated because they are dissimilar, but their contiguity foregrounds the images of books and reading that are central to both. The famous last sentence about Anna's death refers to the candle by which "she had been reading that book [of her life?] filled with anxieties, deceptions, grief and evil" and that "lit up for her all that had once been in darkness" before going out forever. This is a polyvalent image whose meaning is a function of the various possible connections that can be made between it and other relevant details in the novel. One is that Anna's final experience echoes Nikolai's death, which Levin sees in terms of the widespread religious and Romantic belief that death brings understanding impossible in life. Tolstoy's descriptions of Prince Andrei's death in *War and Peace* and of "The Death of Ivan Ilich" are different variations on this theme. But if we conclude that the juxtaposition of Anna's death with the reception of Koznyshev's book has implications for her final act of figurative reading, then it is possible that the textual "illumination" she experiences at the moment of death may be as erroneous as the reading his book receives (and thus as limited as many of the perceptions she makes in life [see *13.5.4*]). Even in death, therefore, or at a moment near death, understanding something like the alterity of a text may not be possible.

A different possible interpretation of the juxtaposition is that it *contrasts* the failure of Koznyshev's book with the success of Anna's illumination. But this is unlikely given the status that written words—and, by extension, books—usually have in the novel, especially in comparison to their antithesis. The most striking example of the latter is the scene between Levin and Kitty at Stiva's dinner party. Although they use a written code, it is entirely private as well as transparent because they are already in complete *nonverbal* harmony with each other (see *14.1*). By contrast, Anna's final "understanding" occurs via reading a book, a purely verbal form of communication, which, if one chooses to push the interpretation this far, is impersonal, mediate, and by implication the product of urban technology (assuming for the sake of argument that the book she reads is not something like her own handwritten diary). None of these traits of printed books agrees with the values advanced in *Anna Karenina,* in which Tolstoy demotes verbal communication in favor of feeling and instinct, promotes the personal and immediate over the abstract, and celebrates manual labor over technological innovation. From this perspective, therefore, Anna's final act of reading may imply error, not insight, and rather than the book of life, she may be reading the book of her death—of all that went wrong and that brought her to suicide.

Even if Anna's final act of reading is not erroneous, whatever she gets out of it can be interpreted as simply redundant. The narrator characterizes what Anna reads as "filled with anxieties, deceptions, grief, and evil," which, although an accurate description or summary of the final part of her life, is how she has been seeing things anyway. The narrator's characterization can also be understood more broadly as Anna's reinterpretation of her *entire* life from the vantage point of her troubled mental state during her *final* days and hours. But if this is the case, then Anna is still seeing things from a very limited and personal perspective, one that does not, in fact, account for the "bright past joys" that she recollects several moments and lines earlier. In sum, the difficulty of deciding whether or not Anna achieves insight before her death suggests that the relation between her final scene and the episode of Koznyshev's book is based more on difference than on similarity. (However, the presence of both similarities and differences between the two, even if on different levels of meaning, does suggest the utility of describing the relation between them as "metaphoric," which bears on the question of the novel's holism and form [see *10.1, 10.2*].)

The candle by which Anna reads the book can also be related to different antecedent details in the novel that allow it to be interpreted in opposite ways—as shedding genuine illumination or the ambiguous light of partial vision.[6] One possibility is that Anna's candle recalls the flame that flickers into life when Levin's son is born (in this context, there is a kind of antiphonal logic to Anna's candle going out when she dies): "in the deft hands of Lizaveta Petrovna, like a small flame over a lamp [ogonek nad svetil'nikom], wavered the life of a human being who had never existed before and who, with the same right, with the same importance for itself, would live and produce its own kind" (716, VII.15). A "candle" is not exactly the same as an "icon lamp," which is the likeliest translation of *svetil'nik,* and there is no reference to reading in connection with the birth of Levin's son. On the contrary, and as one might expect, the most important communication in the scene takes place without language via vision and visceral screaming, as in the baby's "bold, brazen cry, not intent on

understanding anything" (716, VII.15). Nevertheless, if one chooses to relate Anna's candle to these images, then it can be interpreted as partaking
of their metaphysical implications and thus implying some kind of existence after death: perhaps Anna's soul disappears into the same realm out
of which the child's appears (see *9.2*). It is equally possible, however, that
any relation between Anna's candle and the baby's flame is based primarily
on *contrast;* and from this perspective, Anna's death may be final. We can
also trace a slight but suggestive echo between the baby's demanding and
self-indulgent cry, which the narrator clearly approves, and Anna's comparable need to satisfy her emotional wants, no matter what the moral cost.
On the other hand, Anna is an adult who may be seen as responsible for
her actions, whereas the baby is not. It does not seem possible to make a
final choice among these echoing alternatives.

A different antecedent is the candle that is extinguished and relit during Anna's last night before her suicide. She takes her "usual dose of
opium" when she goes to bed and thinks that she could easily avenge herself on Vronsky for how she believes he has been treating her by drinking
the entire container. Suddenly, the candle by her bed goes out, and such
terror of death seizes her that for a long time she cannot understand where
she is or what has happened to her. This event can be read as Anna's symbolic death, and its correlation with her thoughts of vengeful suicide inevitably recalls the novel's epigraph. If we pursue this connection, it is possible to infer that her "death" may be divine punishment for her wish for
vengeance, which in turn stems from her sense of personal injury or from
her ego. This interpretation is supported by the way in which Anna's attitude and emotions change together with the illumination in the rest of this
scene: when she succeeds in lighting another candle, she feels a renewed
sense of life and a flood of love for Vronsky. The entire sequence of images
can thus be seen as built on two contrasting series of equations (or hermeneutic indices) that are traditional in many of the world's major religions,
including Christianity: Darkness = Ego/Vengeance/Suicide = Death; and
Light = Love for Another = Life. However, although Anna is granted this
symbolic or prophetic lesson, she fails to learn from it. When she goes to
look at Vronsky asleep, she cannot shed the impression that he would not
reciprocate her love were he to wake up; and for whatever reason, she cannot forget herself enough to love him unrequitedly. She returns to bed,
takes another dose of opium, and spends a troubled night before awakening to the nightmare of the little old man working iron and speaking
French. These events appear to determine her subsequent actions and
therefore lend themselves to being interpreted as sealing her fate (see *17.1*).

When Anna finally sees Vronsky the following morning, he is speaking to a young woman in a carriage, and she concludes the worst: "The fog that had covered everything in her soul suddenly cleared. Yesterday's feelings wrung her aching heart with a new pain. She could not understand now how she could have lowered herself so far as to spend a whole day with him in his house" (753, VII.26). After a bitter exchange, Vronsky leaves, and Anna's thoughts return to the darkness that terrified her when the candle went out, which is now melded with recollections of her nightmare.

Nothing in this complex sequence of events suggests that Anna is justified in her belief that she has achieved privileged insight into her situation or that "The fog . . . suddenly cleared," as she thinks. We do not have a stable, external perspective showing us Vronsky's "true" expression and attitude toward her, but we do have mercurial changes in Anna's view of things caused by her unbalanced emotional state, presumably due in part to the influence of two doses of a potent narcotic. Thus, if we choose to relate the play of light and darkness in this sequence—whereby one candle goes out, another is lit, and fog dissipates—to the scene of Anna reading by candlelight at the moment of her death, then the "anxieties, deceptions, grief, and evil" about which she reads may be as personal and limited, or as true and as false, as anything else she sees.[7] (For more on Anna's death, see *13.5.4* and *17.1*.)

8.3. Mikhailov's Paintings

A similar conclusion about the difficulty of communication is suggested by the passages dealing with the painter Mikhailov in Italy. Anna, Vronsky, and Golenishchev visit Mikhailov's studio to see his masterwork in progress, *Pilate's Admonition,* which is centrally concerned with two issues—the representation of the divine in human form and the relation between divine and human judgment. The painting thus raises questions that are also implied by the novel's epigraph.[8] At first, Mikhailov is greatly interested in his visitors' opinions and is delighted that they recognize even an iota of what he sees in his painting (473–74, V.11). But then he changes his mind and decides that his visitors' remarks are actually trivial and no different from millions of others that could also have been made. When Anna and the others leave and Mikhailov looks at the painting himself from his own masterful viewpoint, he sees things in it that no one else had and is convinced of its great perfection (476, V.12). This scene thus presents the perception and interpretation of a work of art as relativized to the extreme. It also suggests that via his work the artist communicates primarily with himself or, as Mikhailov thinks of it, with the dimension of being that is the source of the vision he embodies in his art. (Although we are also privy to Mikhailov's thoughts, we cannot really share Mikhailov's self-confidence, because no detailed reasons for it are given.) And if we choose to apply this interpretation to the novel *Anna Karenina,* we again arrive at the pessimistic conclusion that there is unlikely to be any agreement about determinate artistic meaning even if the artist has successfully captured a spiritual experience of his own. In turn, this suggests the difficulty if not the impossibility of communicating a spiritual reality via an artistic medium (and perhaps via any "language," including Saint Paul's).

But maybe this is because Mikhailov is not much of an artist? Or maybe the discussion of Mikhailov's painting is irrelevant to the aesthetics that undergird *Anna Karenina*? In fact, there are two textual details suggesting that he is a peer of Tolstoy himself and that his art is, in a sense, coterminous with Tolstoy's own. One is Mikhailov's portrait of Anna. The narrator validates it as consummate; it shows Vronsky something that he had not seen in Anna (477, V.13); and it even mesmerizes Levin (all of which also shows that in certain cases art *can* communicate its message [see below]). In other words, as a result of the way the novel is plotted, Mikhailov's portrait is implicitly equated with Tolstoy's own "portrait" of Anna, namely, the one presented throughout *Anna Karenina*.[9] Moreover, because Mikhailov's portrait shows Vronsky something about Anna's "sweetest inner expression," it augments the redemptive dimension of how she is portrayed in the novel.

The second detail is the narrator's description of Kitty's reaction to Anna at the ball in Moscow. Kitty understands that the effect of Anna's appearance depends on her toilette being invisible: "it was just a *frame,* and only she was seen" (79, I.22, emphasis added). Thus, the way Tolstoy "paints" this scene by evoking conventions of pictorial representation in it anticipates the two painted portraits of Anna that we see later. (The other one is in Karenin's study and is by an unnamed "famous painter" [284, III.14]. There is also Vronsky's unfinished portrait, but it says more about him than about his subject [see below].)[10] And if the verbal and pictorial portrayals of Anna are related, we have to consider the possibility that Tolstoy may have granted Mikhailov at least some of his own views on the creation and perception of art.

The reflexive consequence of this possibility is that just as Mikhailov's portrait communicates something essential about Anna to a variety of viewers, so will the novel about her. This obviously contradicts the indications that the meaning of art is relativized. Similarly, the fact that Vronsky and Anna are charmed by Mikhailov's painting of boys fishing indicates that art can be interpreted in a way that is not random, overly personal, or solipsistic (although it may be noteworthy that Mikhailov had entirely forgotten about this painting and did not even like looking at it any longer [475–76, V.12]). This also contradicts the relativization of perception implied by other correlations of details. Is there a way to resolve this discrepancy? One could argue, for example, that the complexity of Mikhailov's painting of Christ before Pilate explains the diversity of interpretations it motivates in comparison to the relative simplicity of the portrait of a charming and attractive woman, or of two small boys engaged in a quiet pastime. After all, Matthew 27, which Mikhailov cites as his inspiration, is one of the seminal texts of the entire Christian tradition and has probably given rise to as much complex interpretation and commentary as any novel ever written. However, as we saw in such cases as Stiva's and Dolly's reading everyday communications, the verbal simplicity of a message hardly guarantees that it will be interpreted in the same way by different people or even by the same person at different times. The same conclusion is suggested by Karenin's reaction to the portrait of Anna hanging in his study, which is, in fact, the first one mentioned in the novel. The narrator characterizes it as "beautifully executed," and it is safe to infer that Karenin originally saw it this way as well. But when he looked at it after Anna confessed her affair to him, he "gave such a start that his lips trembled and produced a 'brr', and he turned away" (284, III.14). Karenin's reaction is clearly a function of his attitude at the given moment and thus may not be relevant for understanding the difference between simple and complex pictorial subjects. In the long run, however, such distinctions are probably irresolvable, because the novel does not take an unequivocal stand on them and because there seems to be no end to the receding vistas of details and correlations that can be adduced on behalf of either alternative. (On the other hand, Tolstoy's turn in *What Is Art?* [1897] and during the latter part of his life toward simple and moral art that was accessible to the masses may be related to the uncertain presentation of different kinds of art in *Anna Karenina*.)[11]

8.4. Mikhailov and Artistic Creation

In addition to dealing with the *perception* of works of art, the chapters about Mikhailov also contain an important description of the process by which art is *created*. We are told in some detail about his sketch of an enraged man that has been stained with candle wax or grease. Especially noteworthy is that although the stains were a chance event, Mikhailov sees them as giving the man a new pose (469, V.10). Moreover, he also works another "chance" detail that he happens to recall into the revised drawing—the face of a merchant from whom he buys cigars.

What does this genesis of the sketch mean? Is it Tolstoy's acknowledgment of the role of the unforeseen and the contingent in art and in life? The continuation of the passage suggests otherwise.

Mikhailov's sense of the absolute "rightness" and "correctness" of the resulting sketch is communicated in part via his hermeneutic index that defines the sketch as preexisting his attempt to create it, as something that is concealed by layers of dross that have to be removed in order for its true nature to become visible. (He sees his painting, *Pilate's Admonition,* in the same way.) In other words, he recognizes a relation between the sketch and the candle wax stain that leads him to see the sketch as tending toward an a priori perfection (see also *9.1*). Another way of saying this is that he perceives things *relationally,* and what happens by chance causes the modification of the drawing in such a way that the new element is incorporated seamlessly into the old to form a new totality. Thus, even if the event was accidental in life, it is *not* preserved as such in art, where it is digested, as it were, by relationalism that reconfigures the sketch. This conclusion would seem to have implications for the formal texture of *Anna Karenina,* in which details also exist in networks of relations that define the details' meanings (see *10*).[12]

The privacy of the experience underlying art is another theme that emerges from the narrator's discussion of Mikhailov's creativity, which he contrasts with Vronsky's dilettantism:

[Vronsky] understood all kinds [of art] and could be inspired by one or another; but he could not imagine that one could be utterly ignorant of all the kinds of painting *and be inspired directly by what was in one's soul,* unconcerned whether what one painted belonged to any particular kind. Since he did not know that, and *was inspired not directly by life but indirectly by life already embodied in art,* he became inspired very quickly and easily, and arrived as quickly and easily at making what he painted look very much like the kind of art he wanted to imitate. (465–66, V.8, emphasis added)

The italicized passages constitute a revealing two-part hermeneutic index in which the narrator defines true inspiration in terms of "what was in one's own soul" and in terms of "life." Because these two elements can be seen as the poles of all human experience, the narrator's formulation might seem to be entirely unobjectionable. On closer inspection, however, a problem emerges because the narrator does not specify the nature of the *relation* between the two elements. The simplest way to interpret his statement is that he implicitly equates the artist's internal life with life itself. But this is a radical and anarchistic claim, because if "life" is what people make of it by internalizing it, then internal life takes precedence over what lies in the world outside. In fact, the narrator faults Vronsky for being an epigone in the sense that he is *unable* to see the world in his own terms; he can see it only in terms mediated by others' perceptions.[13] Another way of putting this is that Vronsky is faulted for being able to see existence only as others see it, which means in terms of communicated, shared categories and values rather than private, solitary ones. (This also distinguishes Vronsky, who is largely a creature of collective values throughout the novel [see *13.8*], from Levin, who is usually seen as an eccentric [see *13.4*].) The difference between Mikhailov and Vronsky in this regard is that Mikhailov, who is the one real artist in the novel, is concerned with issues of artistic precedent and genre *only* to the extent that his work transcends them. Indeed, he values his own painting, *Pilate's Admonition,* precisely because it is unlike anything anyone has painted before. (One could also say that Vronsky's imitation of others' artistic styles is a *parodic echo* of Mikhailov's attempt to capture in his paintings what he sees as a preexisting ideal.) But when the privacy of experience inherent in the creation of true art is considered in the context of the novel's relativization of artistic perception, the result is again a distinctly skeptical view of the possibility of determinate communication. (For more on Mikhailov's "creation," see *9.1*.)

A different pessimistic perspective on the relation between conventions and artistic communication is suggested by Levin during his visit to Anna. Among the things they discuss are paintings, and he remarks that because the French had pushed conventions in pictorial art to a greater extent than anyone else, they see their return to realism as especially meritorious. Anna is delighted with this idea and broadens it to include writers such as Zola and Daudet; then she adds: "But perhaps it always happens that people first build their *conceptions* out of invented, conventionalized figures, but then—once all the *combinaisons* are finished—the invented figures become boring, and they begin to devise more natural and correct figures" (698, VII.10). Anna's statement can be taken as implying either the triumph of something like "realism," or a process of literary evolution in which the primary motor of change is a desire to replace conventions that have become ineffective with new means of expression that appear to allow a more adequate or "truer" portrayal of "reality" (a view that would be developed extensively by Russian Formalists and structuralists, including Jakobson).[14]

One cannot help wondering if any of this applies to *Anna Karenina* itself. Were we to assume that it does, then the consequence would be two irreconcilable readings. The first might be that this novel is an effective means of communication because it has created "more natural and correct figures." But if we do not assume that "realism" is the end point of the process that Anna describes, then in principle the process is endless. As a result, the second reading might be that this novel doubts the ability of its own techniques to communicate effectively either with a jaded contemporary public or with subsequent generations of readers. (The novel's "anxiety" about this possibility is related to but not identical with its actual literary-historical innovations and fate.) The process that Anna describes may thus be at odds with Mikhailov's view of artistic conventions, which he disparages in favor of a seemingly unmediated apprehension of a personal vision. Anna's evolutionary scheme can also be interpreted as undermining Mikhailov's view because inspiration has to be embodied in some form of expression, and the latter necessarily has to be conventional to some extent in order to be intelligible; thus, in time, these conventions will wear out, and the vision they embody will fade. Similarly, the idea of impermanence in the evolutionary scheme can be seen as paralleling the ways characters abandon firm stances, such as when Kitty gives up trying to emulate Varenka or Karenin drifts away from the charitable love he discovers when he believes that Anna is dying (see *13.9, 13.10*).

8.5. Music and the Nature of Artistic Form

Another meta-aesthetic scene in the novel that suggests the same conclusion about the relational nature of artistic form that we find in Mikhailov's painting is Levin's attending a concert of contemporary music, including a "fantasia" entitled *King Lear on the Heath* (684, VII.5).[15] The similarities extend to the behavior of the audience, which recalls the variety of (mis)perceptions that Mikhailov takes for granted: "the ladies in hats, who had carefully tied ribbons over their ears especially for the concert, . . . all the faces, either unoccupied by anything or occupied by interests quite other than music" (684–85, VII.5). Most of this audience will not "get" the music, but neither will Levin, even though he avoids "meeting musical connoisseurs and talkers" and stands with "lowered eyes, listening."

Despite the effort he makes, Levin's dominant reaction is annoyance with the composer's seeming whims: the sounds of the piece appear to him to be "totally unexpected, and in no way prepared for." Similarly, the emotions evoked by the music alternate without any rhyme or reason, "like a madman's feelings." Levin turns to a friend, Pestsov, for his reaction, who reminds him that the music cannot be understood without an accompanying text from Shakespeare's *King Lear.* But Levin is not satisfied with this explanation and argues for the segregation of the arts, each of which has its proper domain. Thus, according to him, the attempt of the "Wagnerian" trend in music to incorporate the other arts is as wrongheaded as poetry's attempt to describe facial features, which is the task of painting. By contrast, Pestsov likes the piece, insists that all arts are one, and defends the principle of the *Gesamtkunstwerk.*

This discussion touches on a variety of topics that are also broached elsewhere in the novel, but who is right? Levin is, of course, the much more important character and is the beneficiary of the narrator's relatively parsimonious approval throughout the work, which inevitably colors our response to his views. Significant as well is that Levin's brief remarks about artistic domains are in harmony with what we actually see in *Anna Karenina* itself: Tolstoy does not, in fact, spend a great deal of time describing the "objective" physical appearance of people and things (assuming that Levin's view of "poetry's" proper domain applies to other verbal forms like the novel), but, instead, describes the internal states of characters as they interact with each other and their world—what has been called his famous "dialectic of the soul."[16] For example, because of Anna's effect on Kitty, Vronsky, Karenin, Levin, and others, we know something about her eyes, hair, ample body, charm, energy, and "beauty" in general. But we would still be hard-pressed to picture her as (relatively) clearly as we can, say, Grushenka or Katerina Ivanovna in Dostoevsky's *The Brothers Karamazov,* or any of the characters in Turgenev's *Fathers and Sons,* whose physical appearance and spiritual makeup are described in some detail from the authoritative perspective of the narrator.

This helps to justify applying Levin's conclusions to *Anna Karenina* as a hermeneutic guide. His fundamental point is that good art is characterized by a functional interrelationship among its constituent elements. In other words, it is the internal coherence that makes a work good. It is not sufficient for interrelationships to exist between a given text and some ancillary one on which it depends (as between the music Levin hears and the Shakespearean text) or, by extension, between the work and a "reality" that acts as a kind of necessary explanation or crutch for it. This is, of course, not to say that "reality" is irrelevant to art. Levin's thoughts at the concert about the emotions evoked by the piece make it clear that he does not see even a relatively "abstract" work of classical music as independent of "reality"; however, its *internal structure* is more important than its *referential nature*. In short, individual elements in a work of art acquire their most important meaning via their networks of relations with other details (see also *10*). In Mikhailov's case we saw this from the point of view of artistic *production;* in Levin's case we come to the same conclusion from the point of view of artistic *reception*. A corollary of this view is that freedom and contingency of textual elements in narrative—especially in great narratives, which are the products of exceptional artistic craftsmanship—is something like an oxymoron (see *18*). Finally, the similarity between Mikhailov's practice and Levin's perceptions also extends to the kind of holism that Levin seeks in his life and that Stiva criticizes as unrealistic (42, I.11).

8.6. Form in Art and in Life

The importance of the conclusion about freedom being at odds with artistic form is that it suggests a fundamental difference between life and art: any "disorder" that may occur in life—assuming for the moment that we can neglect the patterning in human existence implied by fate, characterological determinism, essentialism, social roles, etc.—is inappropriate in art (see *9.2*).[17] The way the narrator first introduces us to Mikhailov epitomizes this opposition. The artist is annoyed with how his wife handles their bill to the landlady and takes refuge in his drawing because "[h]e never worked so ardently and successfully as when his life was going badly" (469, V.10). One of Levin's own experiences earlier in the novel both personalizes this opposition and confirms it. During a visit by Koznyshev to Levin's estate, the half-brothers debate the usefulness of various innovations such as schools for peasants and the like. Levin argues about this from the perspective of his own personal utility (see *13.4.2*). Moreover, Levin does so in a way that displeases Koznyshev not only because of Levin's ideological position but also because of the *form* his argumentation takes: Koznyshev "did not like contradictions, especially the sort that kept jumping from one thing to another and introduced new arguments without any connection, so that it was impossible to know which to answer" (244, III.3). Levin's style of arguing comes from the heart, not the head, and although he realizes that Koznyshev will triumph in the actual debate, Levin continues to believe that he is right. Levin lives his "arguments" rather than developing them according to artificial intellectual rules the way Kozny-shev does. At the concert, however, Levin is annoyed by a musical structure that is very like that of his own argument with his half-brother.

If we pursue the connection between the two scenes, then this similarity can be interpreted in several different ways: as indicating that the integration of details into a structure of relations is central in art even if it is not in life; as suggesting that Levin's ideas about rural innovations are as confused as the musical piece he hears and that his brother is right; or as pointing to Levin's inconsistency, which allows him at different times to act in one way and speak in another. The choice among these alternatives is not arbitrary, however, because there is ample evidence in the novel that Koznyshev's views on various matters are flawed. And the resemblance between Levin's judgments at the concert and other discussions of art in the novel implies that his views on art are not random. In fact, the difference between art and life that emerges from this comparison of the two scenes may be implicated in the novel's uncertainty about the possibility that art's message can reach an addressee.

Levin's response to the music is additional evidence for this. Although he appears to be an assiduous auditor of the composition, he is also a rebellious and unsuccessful one. He refuses to suspend disbelief sufficiently to allow the hybrid musical genre to work on him as it does on his acquaintance Pestsov. In the work's own terms, which Levin rejects out of hand, he fails to "read" it. Thus, despite the fact that the narrator seems to share Levin's distaste for the new music, Levin's resistance to hearing it adds to the sense that *Anna Karenina* projects a degree of skepticism (but not certainty—witness Pestsov) about the possibility of any work's being understood, including itself. This possibility, of course, coexists (asymmetrically) with its opposite, as is demonstrated by Mikhailov's—and Tolstoy's—efforts at self-expression in the face of mistaken or partial understanding.

9. Art and Metaphysics

9.1. The Plotinian Implications of Mikhailov's "Creation"

A comment that Vronsky makes about "technique" when viewing Mikhailov's painting triggers a series of reflections in Mikhailov's mind that have additional important implications for the novel's worldview (474, V.11). Mikhailov infers that Vronsky, like many others, believes in the possibility of painting well without any regard to what is being depicted. By contrast, Mikhailov sees the technical mastery in a painting as indistinguishable from its subject matter; more simply, he sees form as inseparable from content. This conclusion has to be considered together with Mikhailov's reaction to the wax-stained sketch, which is characterized by a new and "correct" unity that emerges out of a seemingly chance event. Crucial to understanding the significance of this detail is Mikhailov's sense that in "creating" his sketch he is, in fact, only removing layers of obstructing material: "in making these corrections [in the sketch], he did not alter the figure, but only cast off what concealed the figure. It was as if he removed the wrappings [pokrovy] that kept it from being fully seen" (470, V.10). He sees his other works in the same way: "He knew that great attention and care were needed to remove a wrapping [pokrov] without harming the work itself, and to remove all the wrappings [pokrovy]" (474, V.11).

This seemingly paradoxical conception of creating something that already exists can be reconciled within a Plotinian or Neoplatonic aesthetic, according to which the ideal form of the work of art preexists the artist in an ideal realm, and the artist's efforts are directed toward manifesting the work of art in the material world.[1] Thus, the artist does not create ex nihilo or by chance but reveals or transcribes something from a transcendent or noumenal realm. This conclusion does not sit completely comfortably with the role of chance in providing elements that are then integrated into a larger artistic whole (unless one moves to the view that the world in the novel is ruled entirely by providential or fatidic forces), but, nevertheless, it is suggested by the novel.

Are there additional connections between Mikhailov's conception of art and *Anna Karenina*? On the level of relations among textual details, the reader's experience with the novel is, inevitably, very like Mikhailov's with his sketch, because both find connectivity, if not unity, in diversity. Indeed, the debates among this novel's interpreters usually center on whether or not particular relations or connections among disparate details are convincing, but all who read the novel make connections all the time. This has also been the case with every other novel ever written, of course, and is ultimately the consequence of the culturally conditioned expectations about reading that are part of our culture, which is that texts are presumed to be meaningful or, in other words, that they consist of relations.[2] However, the Plotinian aspect of Mikhailov's aesthetic cannot be readily applied to *Anna Karenina*. There is no evidence in it, beyond the implicit "equation" of Mikhailov's and Tolstoy's "portraits" of Anna, to suggest that just as Mikhailov taps or reveals a noumenal realm during the process of creation, so did Tolstoy when he worked on the novel.[3]

9.2. The Spiritual in Art and in Life

As we have seen, the passages about Mikhailov's paintings can be read as advancing antithetical conceptions of art and of life. But there are also parallels between Mikhailov's aesthetics and Levin's experiences that imply the opposite. A key detail is Kitty's appearance when she is on the verge of going into labor. Levin looks at her and is "struck by what was now being bared before him, when all the wrappings were suddenly removed [vse pokrovy byli sniaty] and the very core of her soul shone in her eyes" (707–8, VII.13; my translation here attempts to preserve the lexical echoes in Tolstoy's text). This image recalls the narrator's description of Mikhailov when he is working on his sketch of the enraged man: "he did not alter the figure, but only cast off what concealed the figure. It was as if he removed the wrappings [snimal s nee te pokrovy] that kept it from being fully seen" (470, V.10). The metaphysical implications in both scenes seem comparable because Levin sees Kitty as transfigured by contact with the transmundane in a way that is "above his understanding" (708, VII.13).[4] (This is also echoed in how Vronsky perceives Karenin when Karenin forgives Anna on her sickbed: "He did not understand Alexei Alexandrovich's feelings. But he felt that this was something lofty and even inaccessible to him in his world-view" [415, IV.17]; there are very few moments in the novel when a character appears to glimpse a truth that is normally beyond his ken and sphere of interests.) Because Levin's perception is colored by his unique love for Kitty, it is unlikely that anyone else could see her in the way that he does (and, in fact, the reactions of others in her family to the birth are entirely conventional). Consequently, Levin's perception of Kitty is also as private, as real for him, as inaccessible to others, and as metaphysically charged as is Mikhailov's of *Pilate's Admonition.*

This impression is augmented by Levin's reaction as Kitty's labor progresses. Despite being an "unbeliever," he is so overwhelmed by what happens that he begins to pray. In the narrator's words, all of Levin's previous religious doubts "flew off his soul like dust" (kak prakh sletelo s ego dushi; 709, VII.13). Because this image of a soul being revealed appears in the narrator's discourse and is similar to how Levin sees Kitty's soul and how Mikhailov conceives of his art, it strengthens the case for the existence of a metaphysical reality that can touch individuals but that exists independently of them. Thus, although one of the conclusions suggested by the parallels between Mikhailov and Levin is that private and ultimately incommunicable interpretations and perceptions occur in life as in art, another is that life and true art may be rooted in a higher reality that at least some individuals are vouchsafed to glimpse during certain kinds of liminal experiences.

Mikhailov's disdainful attitude toward Vronsky's attempt to paint Anna's portrait has similar implications. The narrator communicates Mikhailov's annoyance with Vronsky's dilettantism via the contrast between someone who loves a real woman and someone who caresses a big wax doll that he has made for himself (478–79, V.13). Given the context of this passage, the reference to "wax" may perhaps be seen as an ironic evocation of the candle wax stains on Mikhailov's sketch and its Neoplatonic implications, which are glaringly absent from Vronsky's dabbling. In addition, the inauthenticity of Vronsky's attempt to paint Anna is contrasted not only with Mikhailov's own wonderful portrait but also, because of the links discussed above, with Levin's perception of Kitty's soul and with his baring his own soul under her influence. If we decide to pursue this sequence of associations one step farther, we can conclude that the image of the wax doll bears not only on Vronsky's artistic dilettantism but also on the nature of his relations with Anna in general, which emerge as inauthentic in comparison with Kitty and Levin's, despite Anna and Vronsky's genuine passion for each other (i.e., Kitty's and Levin's souls are bared, but Vronsky's portrait of Anna remains unfinished and reveals nothing; by stark comparison, Mikhailov's shows even Vronsky something about Anna's soul that he had not known). As we will see, it is possible to reach this same conclusion via other exegetic paths.

10. The Formal Implications of the Novel's Conception of Art

10.1. The Two Poles of Language and the Embodiment of Aesthetic Ambivalence

The scenes in the novel dealing with different kinds of art imply an ambivalent aesthetic because they present a relational conception of artistic meaning and form while simultaneously raising doubts about the ability of art to communicate that meaning. As we have seen, this conclusion is suggested by two different aspects of the novel—how artistic structure is characterized in it and how characters react divergently to particular works of art as well as to other kinds of utterances (see also *13.2*).

But in addition to being *described* within the novel in a way that seems applicable to it, is this ambivalence also *embodied* in the novel itself? And how could this kind of aesthetic self-consciousness be created in *Anna Karenina* if we do not have interpretations of the novel included within it (a problem that is addressed, if not entirely solved, in *War and Peace* by the narrator's comments about writing history in the "digressions" and epilogues)? The answer to this question appears to lie in the combination of the novel's structure and narrative style—in how the "parallel" plots alternate while the narrator remains silent about how they relate to each other. This presents the reader with the opportunity to infer larger meanings and the need to question them at the same time.[1]

We can better understand how this works by examining more closely some structural issues in the scenes about Mikhailov's painting and the concert that Levin attends. Although both present a relational conception of artistic meaning, they differ in the extent to which each conceives of relation in terms of contiguity as compared with similarity. Roman Jakobson famously described these alternatives as the *metonymic* and *metaphoric* (or *syntagmatic* and *paradigmatic*) "poles" or "axes" of language. (They can also be correlated with Joseph Frank's distinctions between *temporal* and *spatial* form in the arts.)[2] According to Jakobson, both types of relations are inherent in all languages as well as in art, although they appear in widely differing ratios in different works, genres, periods, and kinds of art. In general, narratives such as the novel are dominated by metonymic relations among their constituent elements, or are "forwarded essentially by contiguity," whereas poetry, and especially the lyric, is dominated by metaphor, or "the principle of similarity." However, as Jakobson's designation "poles" implies, the actual ways that meaningful relations are constituted in particular works can be and usually are hybrids of these two end types rather than pure versions of either one.

For example, Mikhailov adds the effects of the candle wax stain and the chin of the cigar merchant to his original sketch of an angry man only some time after he makes the initial drawing. In Jakobson's terms, there is a linear or "metonymic" relation among these elements—and in the narrative about them—that reflects the temporal and causal contiguity involved. But there is also spatial contiguity in the relation between the stains on the paper and the original drawing that causes Mikhailov to see the original differently, and this relation can be interpreted in two ways. If we assume that he sees the stains as causing a kind of optical distortion of the drawing (due to the layering of stains "over" the original sketch or their position in relation to it), the relationship can be understood as metonymic. But if we assume that he may have seen something like "anger" or a partially anthropomorphic shape in the stains, then their relationship to the drawing could be metaphoric as well.

Mikhailov's process of artistic creation is further described as removing layers of wrappings, which implies an asymptotic, or metonymic and temporal, approach to the work's ideal form. However, there is also a spatial and metaphoric dimension to Mikhailov's procedure (and the narrative about it) because he introduces the merchant's chin into the sketch from some "distance." The merchant was not a direct model for the sketch, but Mikhailov uses his chin because he happens to remember it the way he does all faces and recognizes that something about it "fits" the sketch. In other words, the merchant's chin is both similar to and different from the one in the sketch, which is the distinguishing characteristic of metaphor.

The relation between the sketch and its ideal form (assuming that it has one) can be seen as both metaphoric and metonymic, depending on which "draft" of the sketch one has in mind. A rough sketch may have only a distant, metaphoric relation to its ideal; but successive "drafts" of the sketch change only slightly one from the next and approach the ideal metonymically. Similarly, the overall composition of the sketch, the way the parts of the angry man's body relate to each other and to the space around them, can be seen as both spatial and thus metaphoric; but the parts of his body and the space around it also relate to each other via contiguity and are apprehended in time, or metonymically.

The coexistence of both kinds of relations can be seen more clearly in Mikhailov's chef d'oeuvre, *Pilate's Admonition,* which is described in greater detail. At its center is the metaphoric relation between Christ and Pilate as embodiments of divine and worldly truth and authority. But the painting also contains a short narrative about their meeting that is placed within a context of additional metonymic elements based on spatial contiguity, such as the relation of human figures to each other and to the background. It is, of course, pointless to speculate in more detail about a fictional painting (despite its possible echoes of the real painting, *Christ Shown to the People* [1858] by A. A. Ivanov),[3] but it is not unreasonable to assume that in canvasses of this type there may also be metaphoric relations among such things as the shapes and the placement of people and natural objects.

The same metaphoric and metonymic relations are central to the concert Levin attends, even though music is a temporal rather than a spatial art and he experiences rather than produces it. Levin complains about the absence of any sequential development in the composition he hears, which thereby confirms the primary importance of linear or metonymic (contiguous) relations in a temporal artistic form *(8.5).* (Because Levin complains only about the absence of motivated transitions *between* different segments of the composition, we can infer that metonymic relations between smaller units of music, and metaphoric relations of recapitulation and variation among them, may actually exist *within* the individual segments that he hears.)

Conversely but consistently, Levin also rejects relying on a libretto that supposedly "explains" the composition. This attack on "program music" is a denial of a metaphoric link between music and language. In fact, as we have seen, Levin's entire conception of the segregation of the arts is implicitly antisynaesthetic and thus antimetaphorical on this level. But at the same time, Levin's rejection of a relation between "parallel" texts from different arts implies the acceptance of a relation between parallel texts of the *same* kind. This would seem to apply especially well to the two dominant plots in *Anna Karenina* (Anna-Vronsky and Kitty-Levin), which are largely independent of each other in terms of causal links (although they are importantly and multifariously connected in other ways).

As all these examples illustrate, works of art are characterized by a dense network of metonymic and metaphoric relations among their constituent elements, and the same textual elements can often be involved in both kinds of relations. This is also the idea behind the "poetic function" (see the introduction and *4*).[4] How do these two kinds of meaning formation operate in the rest of *Anna Karenina?*

The linear, metonymic development of the major plotlines is usually straightforward. However, the segmentation and alternation of individual plots results in several temporal lacunae or periods of "dead" time in characters' lives about which we learn little or nothing. Even when the narrator or a character briefly recapitulates what happened, the reader is still left with the task of bridging the gap between plot segments by projecting the characters' prior and subsequent behavior into the lacunae (see also *13.3*). Examples of such lacunae in the Anna-Vronsky plot are the nine months that pass between Vronsky's first mild success in his pursuit of Anna and his actual seduction of her. The months between the August day during which Vronsky arranges his financial matters and the week during the winter that he spends showing the sights to a foreign prince pass without notice. Apart from learning that Anna and Vronsky visited Venice, Rome, and Naples, that they avoid certain kinds of social situations, and that they are getting bored, the reader knows little else about the three months prior to their arrival in the small Italian city where they meet Mikhailov. Relatively little specific information is provided about the six-month period that Anna and Vronsky spend on his estate before Dolly's visit. In Kitty's case, a comparable gap occurs during the two months between the ball and the medical examination; all we know about her is that she was miserable. In Levin's life there are two such periods—the first is his trip abroad, the second is the hiatus between the scenes of the Levins on their estate and their move to Moscow for Kitty's confinement. These kinds of lacunae occur in many novels, and there is no reason to expect that every moment in a character's life will be narrated in the same detail. But Anna's and Vronsky's periods of "dead time" are longer and more frequent than Kitty's and Levin's, which is in harmony with how Anna's and Vronsky's lives accelerate and are marked negatively in comparison to Kitty's and Levin's (see also *13.3* and *17*).

The metaphoric links among different plot segments are a more complicated matter. Usually these are manifestations of some form of similarity and difference between paired elements within the same fictional category—such as the behavior of two characters, their internal lives, or their situations. (R. F. Christian aptly called the latter "situation rhymes.")[5] Like metonymic relations, metaphoric ones exist on every textual level and every page, but there is a major difference between the two. Because metonymic relations are expressions of contiguity, they rely on relatively fixed ways of relating two things—via temporal succession, spatial proximity, or physical and/or psychological causality; in other words, they express the a priori conditions of existence that most readers would accept as givens. Thus, even if we cannot explain briefly or clearly why Anna commits suicide, we assume, of course, that there are psychological reasons that motivated her (no matter how we conceive of "psychology"). By contrast, metaphors rely on more ambiguous relations of similarity and difference between things that are not contiguous, and their evaluation can depend to a considerable degree on individual judgment and cultural conventions. This is why hermeneutic indices that attempt to glean principles of interpretation from the novel itself are an essential exegetic tool, even if they are not a magical sesame for all the novel's mysteries.

It will not always be possible to distinguish clearly metonymic relations from metaphoric ones, and it is not always the case that metonymic relations are transparent and fixed while metaphoric ones are opaque and indeterminate. Nevertheless, because the narrator in *Anna Karenina* does not define the relations of the novel's plotlines to each other, and because these relations cannot be based on anything like the relative certainty of the contiguity that structures individual plotlines, the reader of the novel is left with both an imperative and a quandary that are different sides of the same coin: to relate elements from the separate plots but without explicit guidance about how to do this and what the relations mean. This task is particularly urgent at chapter boundaries, when the narrative shifts from one plotline to another and the reader feels compelled to understand the reason for the resulting juxtaposition (as, for example, in the transition from Karenin's ultimatum to Anna to preserve their status quo [the end of III.23] to the night that Levin spends on a haystack [the beginning of III.24], which contrasts artificiality with a sylvan setting and compares two approaches to family happiness).

10.2. Examples of Structures of Meaning

It is worth examining several "parallels" between different plots to illustrate how they function as generators of meaning that is polyvalent within relatively circumscribed borders, or that is both plural and limited.

Consider Kitty's inadvertent role as potential home breaker at the German spa when the consumptive Russian artist, Petrov, develops a crush on her to such an extent that his wife becomes jealous (226–27, II.33). There are numerous variants of this "triangular" situation, both large and small, elsewhere in the novel—from the central one of Vronsky's role in Anna's

life, to Vasenka Veslovsky's attempted flirtation with Kitty, to Stiva's repeated adultery, to Dolly's brief fantasy about having an affair, to Levin's
momentary succumbing to Anna's wiles when he visits her, to the two
young officers in Vronsky's regiment who pursue a functionary's wife on a
drunken lark, and so on.[6]

But what does it mean that the situation in which Kitty finds herself recalls a series of others in different ways and to varying degrees? Is it merely
a fact of contemporary Russian mores, like going to the theater or getting
married in church? This seems rather unlikely, because *Anna Karenina* is
too obviously structured to be simply an encyclopedia of upper-class life.
On the other hand, the repetition of emotional situations from character
to character necessarily implies something like the universality of certain
human propensities or traits (see also *16*). An obvious distinction between
Kitty's accidental involvement with Petrov and Vronsky's intentional seduction of Anna is that Kitty ends the "affair" as soon as she learns of it. Is
the point, therefore, that, with regard to Petrov, Kitty paradoxically assumes Anna's role at the ball when Anna more or less inadvertently attracts
Vronsky and draws him away from Kitty? And if so, how can we fail to conclude that the ways of the heart are inscrutable and that one cannot predict
how or where love will bloom (which may be a variant of the personal
"take" on things that dominates characters throughout the book)? Does
this not tend to exonerate Vronsky, Anna, or Stiva? In turn, is this not a
negative comment on the kind of dispassionate and selfless charity that Varenka practices, which seems admirable on the one hand but sterile on the
other? Or, by contrast, is the temporary and partial parallel between Kitty
and Anna not a warning about the moral consequences that can follow on
the heels of innocent, albeit wandering, affections? Does the fact that Dolly
and Levin also recoil from their short-lived "straying" serve as an additional
example to those who do not? But how does this possibility relate to Kitty's
self-indulgent reaction when she discovers the effect she has had on Petrov,
which is to give up any attempt to be a "ministering angel" like Varenka
and to return to what she sees as her own unchangeable nature, thus complicating any moral generalizations about her or the situation she is in?

Can another possibility be that Kitty's unwitting involvement in another's passion is a sign of hidden forces that bind individuals together and
that structure characters' lives? This does not seem as plausible as that the
artist's infatuation with Kitty is really about a dying man's grasping at
straws. Is the link, therefore, more to Nikolai Levin and the special affection that he develops for Kitty later in the novel when he is on his deathbed?
(He is, in fact, present at the spa, but Kitty avoids him at this time because

she is repulsed by his behavior and his connection with her memories of spurning Konstantin Levin's proposal [216, II.30].) And what would be the point of this last parallel? To underscore the obvious poignancy of loss through death? Or could it foreshadow the novel's theme of birth balancing death via a metaphysical connection between the two, as may be implied when Kitty discovers her pregnancy just after Nikolai dies?

In fact, my answer to most of these questions is "yes," albeit with different degrees of conviction and hesitation, as I have tried to suggest. There is at least some textual evidence for each alternative, and they are all interrelated even if they are not always reconcilable. Thus, to eliminate even one would be to betray and impoverish the novel by narrowing the range of its themes and disrupting the branching networks of its "situation rhymes." Rather than being a bewildering range of choices, however, the array of possibilities, which comprises permutations among a limited set of terms, can be seen as evidence of the novel's richness and depth, even if these cannot be readily packaged in summaries or generalizations.

Another series of plot parallels can be traced among the scenes describing how Levin, Anna, and Vronsky return to their homes from Moscow. The sequential description of each return and the inevitable typological similarities among individuals reentering familiar spaces, relations, and frames of mind after absences are reason enough for considering the similarities and differences among them. But there is additional evidence suggesting the pointed nature of the comparisons and the need to bear them in mind throughout the novel. The first two returns are linked by such details as Levin discovering to his annoyance that his instructions were ignored and that the buckwheat was burned in the new kiln (94, I.26) and Anna being upset by how her instructions for altering three dresses had not been followed by the dressmaker (110, I.33). Some of the pairs of terms that characterize the contrast between these two returns are value-laden: food versus fashion, country versus city, perhaps seriousness versus frivolity. But both returns are also characterized by the inevitable contrast between will versus inertia, the ideal versus the real, and the personal versus the collective, and are thus constitutive of the way things are in Tolstoy's world. Vronsky is the odd man out in this sense and does not return to discover any disappointments on the level of mundane reality, presumably because of his carefree bachelor life. Instead, he laughs when his friends spill coffee onto an expensive carpet (114, I.34), which underscores the wastefulness and triviality of his concerns by comparison with Levin's and even Anna's.

Linking their returns also underscores such things as Levin's comfort at home following his fiasco with Kitty and his wish to reestablish on his estate the image of organic family wholeness and happiness that he remembers from childhood (which may be foreshadowed via his pleasure at the birth of a prize calf). This contrasts with Anna's awkwardness and mixed feelings about her husband and her slight disappointment with her son (who may stand in a kind of ironically metaphoric relation to Levin's calf), which suggests that Levin's hope for future family happiness in the country is the positive version of what Anna is experiencing in a negative form in the imperial capital. The contrast may also be related to the "timelessness" of Levin's aspirations, which focus on re-creating the past life of his parents, in comparison to the "rootlessness" of Anna's life: she did not know genuine family life as a young woman, was manipulated into her tepid marriage (see *13.5.6*), and embarks on an affair that disrupts all of her familial and personal ties. Because the relation between Levin's and Anna's returns home involves not only contrast but also some similarity (which is why it can be thought of as "metaphoric"), an additional, more tentative possibility is that some of Anna's disappointments may eventually become Levin's, which is in fact implied by the (relative) distance Levin feels from Kitty when he discovers his faith at the novel's conclusion.

Smaller plot parallels are especially good examples of "situation rhymes." After Kitty rejects Levin, Tolstoy staggers the narratives about them so that we follow Kitty's plot for several days until she attends the disastrous ball and only then return to Levin at the moment when he leaves Kitty's house following his failed proposal (84, I.24). The effect of this shift back in time is that what had been one plotline is now (temporarily) split into two parts that have a metaphoric relation to each other: we are presented with two sets of dashed hopes of two attractive characters who have become confused about their affections, who react to their failures very differently, but who will eventually claim that they were destined for each other *(17.2)*. An even smaller example is Levin looking at Kitty when Vronsky first appears (50, I.14) and Betsy glancing at Vronsky and reading his expression when she knows that Anna is about to enter the room (137, II.7), which is one of many vivid illustrations of the theme of mediation that can be seen in the novel.

There are also plot parallels that are so definite that they may reflect authorial intentionality. One is Vronsky's affair with Anna and the horse race when he makes a mistake and inadvertently breaks Frou-Frou's back. Among the details that have prompted many readers to link the two are the energy and tenderness that characterize Anna and the horse (61, I.18; 182, II.21); the repetition of the words describing Vronsky as he stands over Anna when they have consummated their affair, which is likened to murder—"Pale, his lower jaw trembling" (149, II.11), and Vronsky standing over the dying horse—"pale, his lower jaw trembling" (200, II.25); and, of course, the tragic ends of Anna and Frou-Frou.[7] However, are we to conclude that because Vronsky openly blames himself for a grievous mistake he made during the race he is equally guilty of seducing Anna and causing her death? Although Vronsky is described as the murderer in the scene of Anna's "fall," the scene progresses with Anna emerging not only as his victim but also as his "accomplice," an impression that is confirmed by how their affair develops. Thus, although the race emphasizes Vronsky's error and, by implication, Anna's relative passivity, it would be an unwarranted reduction of the complexity of their motivations simply to blame him for everything; on the other hand, had he not pursued Anna assiduously for a year, no affair would have developed.[8]

Another meaning that can be gleaned from the parallel has to do with time. If one has noticed the relative slippage of time between the Anna-Vronsky and Kitty-Levin plotlines, then it is possible to see the parallel between the affair and the horse race as underscoring the speed with which Anna and Vronsky move through their lives in comparison to Levin and Kitty (see *13.3*). Because the novel's "objective" references to temporal indicators such as months and times of the year cannot be made into functions of the characters' own psyches without transforming the entire novel into a freewheeling modernist experiment, we have to conclude that by living in different temporal frames the characters are caught in something they do not control, like a fatidic medium, or a marked authorial attitude, which may be the other side of the same coin (see *10.3*). But if Anna and Vronsky are caught in a temporal flow that hastens them toward disaster, then the issue of their volition and thus their blame becomes moot. A different interpretation that preserves both volition and determinism is also possible, however: as Anna's sudden haste to leave Moscow on the morning after the ball suggests (97, I.28), she and Vronsky are caught by the temporal flow when they first *conceive* of sin. This issue may not be resolvable, because there is evidence that Anna's fatalism also predates her meeting Vronsky (see *17.1, 17.3*).

The parallel between the affair and the race cannot be reduced to any one of the meanings essayed above. Moreover, none of these meanings is the exclusive result of the parallel alone, because each meaning is also an extension of themes that emerge clearly elsewhere in the novel. The difficulty of collapsing ranges of meanings into a single meaning is the source

of uncertainty, but this uncertainty is *productive* because it is itself condu-
cive to the generation of meanings within the established thematic array.
In short, the metaphoric parallels among plot elements help to define *controlled ambiguities,* whose function is to make the reader resurrect and try
to rethink characters and situations from other parts of the novel. (The impossibility of reconciling these ranges of meanings resembles the ambiguity that characters produce via their differing reactions to whatever they
encounter [see *13*].) From this point of view, because the rethinking is
channeled by the text, the novel emerges as a kind of "generator" for stimulating reflection along particular thematic lines that usually cannot be resolved into anything narrower or more limited.[9]

In addition to the specific meanings that are produced by localized parallels like the ones above, we also have to consider the fact that the novel as
a whole is structured as several large parallel plots. Perhaps the dominant
impression these "mega"-parallels produce is one of limitations to the
range of human experience. As the countless localized parallels suggest,
there is a common, finite matrix of motivations, interests, and situations
within which characters function, as a result of which life is not a field of
unstructured, infinite potential. This is, in fact, what makes the plot parallels possible in the first place. (However, the number of permutations of
relations is so large that the impossibility of recognizing them all or keeping them all in mind may produce the impression of infinite possibilities.)
In subsequent sections, I examine several possible causes for these limitations, including conscience *(15),* essentialism *(16),* and fate *(17).*[10]

10.3. Tolstoy on the Structure of *Anna Karenina*

Even if there are excellent reasons for not automatically privileging an
author's readings of his own works, it is still intriguing and illuminating to
see what Tolstoy thought about the form of *Anna Karenina* and how this
relates to what the novel itself expresses. His comments appear in oft-cited
letters to friends who were perplexed by or who misunderstood the way
the novel is put together.

Here is what Sergei Rachinsky wrote to Tolstoy on 8 January 1878:

Two words about *Anna Karenina*—this is indubitably your best work. . . . [But
there is] a basic deficiency in the construction of the whole novel. The book lacks
architecture. Two themes not connected in any way develop side by side, and they

develop magnificently. How I enjoyed the acquaintance of Levin and Anna Karenina. You must agree that this is one of the best episodes of the novel. Here the opportunity presented itself to tie together all the threads of the story and to provide a unified conclusion. But you did not want this.

Tolstoy's famous response twenty days later was unequivocal:

Your opinion about *Anna Karenina* seems wrong to me. On the contrary, I take pride in the architecture. The vaults are thrown up in such a way that one cannot notice where the keystone is. That is what I tried to do more than anything else. The unity in the structure is created *not by action* and *not by relationships (acquaintance) between characters,* but by an *inner* unity.[11]

In other words, the novel's structural design is subtler than one dependent on "metonymic" relations such as physical or psychic causality (plot), consanguinity, friendship, antipathy (relationships among characters), and the like. Tolstoy had, in fact, already suggested what this "inner continuity" may be in another well-known letter to Nikolai Strakhov from 23 and 26 April 1876:

In everything, in almost everything that I have written, I was guided by the need to gather ideas linked among themselves in order to express myself. But each idea expressed separately in words loses its meaning, becomes terribly debased when it is taken alone, out of the linking in which it is found. The linking itself is based not on an idea (I think) but on something else, and to express the essence of that linking in any way directly by words is impossible; but it is possible indirectly, with words describing images, actions, situations. . . . [The kind of literary critics we need now] are people who would show the meaninglessness of searching for ideas in a work of art, and who would constantly guide readers through that *endless labyrinth of connections* that is the essence of art, and toward the laws that serve as the basis for these linkages.[12]

What emerges most clearly from this passage is Tolstoy's definition of literary art not in terms of its content but in terms of its construction — its relations or "linkages" among constituent elements. He does not specify what these linkages are or what kind of linkages can be communicated indirectly through descriptions of "images, actions, situations." But if we conflate this remark with his later one to Rachinsky, we can infer that Tolstoy is referring to linkages that are not determined by contiguity alone. This leaves open the possibility that Tolstoy may be alluding to what we (following Jakobson) would call the "metaphoric" linkages among textual elements. This is, in fact, the only other kind of relation that can underlie verbal meaning, which arises either from contiguous relations and/or from distal ones. Indeed, "labyrinth of connections" is an excellent metaphor for the kind of network of relations implied by Jakobson's "poetic function," which presupposes the maximal development of "linkages" among all elements in a text.

However, it is also important to note that calling all noncontiguous links "metaphoric" creates a relative sense of certainty that Tolstoy does not express: he acknowledges that he cannot pin down the "something else" on which linkages are based. Nevertheless, the fact that linkages among "images, actions, situations" have to be motivated by some sort of *similarity,* and that "images, actions, situations" are also *different kinds* of phenomena, suggests that they can plausibly be seen as constituting metaphoric relations.[13]

Another conclusion to be drawn from both letters is that Tolstoy did not want to make too obvious the linkages that constitute the architectonics of *Anna Karenina.* Perhaps this is related to the narrator's silence about plot parallels, how they are meant to function, and what they signify. In the continuation of his letter to Rachinsky, Tolstoy urges him to look for the "unity" (sviaz') that he had missed and expresses certainty that he will find it. The interest of this remark is that it confirms Tolstoy's conviction regarding the importance and communicability of his central structural *principle,* but without necessarily predicting what its consequent "message" will be.

11. The Problem of Language

In addition to writing, spoken language is also subjected to self-conscious scrutiny in the novel. There are frequent instances when nonverbal communication proves to be far more effective than what characters say to each other, as in the narrator's judgment of Varenka's inopportune comment about mushrooms during the scene with Koznyshev: "It would have been better for Varenka to remain silent" (564, VI.5). There are also passages when the narrator and the characters grapple with the unreliability of language as such. The main problem they face is that, rather than leading toward understanding and truth, language often functions as a screen that separates the self from the truth. As has long been noted by many readers, these are characteristic features of Tolstoy's fiction in general.[1]

On a number of occasions, the narrator and characters sense that the relations among signifiers, signifieds, and their referents are inadequate or misleading, either in general or with regard to particular experiences. The first example appears very early, in the novel's fourth paragraph. Stiva wakes up from a dream that he finds amusing and delightful, but even though he recalls some of its surrealistic elements, he concludes that "one can't say it in words, or even put it into waking thoughts." Were this not the beginning of a long novel, Stiva's comment would be a commonplace. But under the circumstances, because all the other major characters also fail to express what is most important to them, it is a hermeneutic index that implies the existence of powerful but mute liminal experiences and a world in which mystery plays a central role. The narrator reverses the tables on Stiva later in the novel when he ridicules the position that Stiva yearns to win because of the high salary it pays: "member of the commission of the United Agency for Mutual Credit Balance of the Southern Railway Lines and Banking Institutions" (719, VII.17; the convolution is even stronger in Russian: "mesto chlena komissii ot soedinennogo agenstva kreditno-vzaimnogo balansa iuzhno zheleznykh dorog i bankovykh uchrezhdenii").[2] The prolix "Gogolian" absurdity of the name is underscored by Prince Shcherbatsky, whose offhand remark shows that it is a signifier attached more to the satisfaction of Stiva's personal needs than to a specific position in a genuine business enterprise: "He's now getting a post as member of the committee of the commission and whatever else, I don't remember. Only there's nothing to do there—what, Dolly, it's not a secret!—and the salary's eight thousand" (808, VIII.16).

Of all the characters, Karenin is most thoroughly trapped in a veil of words that prevents him from grasping the nature of life. This is in part a consequence of his paper-oriented, bureaucratic existence, which automatically keeps him at several removes from the actual events that are his purported interests. As a result, when he is confronted by Anna's adultery, he cannot link the old vocabulary constituting his life with the new realia that she introduces into it: "now, though his conviction that jealousy was a shameful feeling and that one ought to have trust [in one's wife] was not destroyed, he felt that he stood face to face with something illogical and senseless, and he did not know what to do" (142, II.8). In fact, Karenin fails when he attempts to carry out the fundamental semiotic process of understanding alterity by translating it into familiar terms: "To put himself in thought and feeling into another being was a mental act alien to Alexei Alexandrovich. He regarded this mental act as harmful and dangerous fantasizing" (144, II.8). The only way in which Karenin can escape from the vicious circle of undecidability that the narrator invokes and relate the new events to himself is by preparing a speech for Anna that is built around a subset of his familiar assortment of (empty) signifiers: "public opinion," "propriety," "religion," "marriage," etc. (144, II.8). Most significantly, Karenin uses language in a way that even alienates him from his own being. As the narrator explains, Karenin talks with Anna "involuntarily in his habitual tone, which was a mockery of those who would talk that way seriously. And in that tone it was impossible to say what needed to be said to her" (149, II.10; see also 104, I.30).[3] The consequence of Karenin's linguistic trait can be inferred from the location of the narrator's comment about it, which is immediately preceding the lines of ellipses that mark Anna's actual "fall."

Levin's attitude toward language is antithetical to Karenin's and obviously reflects the differences in their lives and many of their values. From Levin's perspective, the kind of abstract vocabulary that defines Karenin's world is entirely false and misleading. For example, when Levin reads various nonmaterialistic philosophers, he concludes that words such as *"spirit, will, freedom, substance"* are a "verbal trap"; the italics in the Russian text imply a metalingual focus on these words as *signs* (788, VIII.9). And when he finally discovers his God and law of goodness, he couples his conception of truth with a denigration of reason and language; in fact, he anticipates that he will not be able to *tell* Kitty what he has discovered.

The same belief that language cannot grasp what is essential appears in the description of Levin's drive through the countryside with Koznyshev, who rhapsodizes about what he sees. By contrast, "Levin did not like talking or hearing about the beauty of nature. For him words took away the beauty of what he saw" (241, III.2). This implies that Levin believes he can perceive nature directly, which underscores how isolated he is in his own world: not only does he not want to speak about nature, there are no adequate words to communicate his perceptions (assuming, for the sake of argument, that these are not tainted by language). A variant of this situation appears in connection with Kitty when she is briefly in thrall to Mme Stahl's religiosity. Prince Shcherbatsky characterizes her as a "Pietist," and Kitty is "frightened by the fact that what she valued so highly in Mme Stahl had a name" (229, II.34). This implies that Kitty would have preferred appealingly vague sentiments to the prosaic determinacy of a sign. The narrator reverses this relation when he provides the first, highly "defamiliarized" glimpse of Mme Stahl, whom he describes as follows: "a bathchair in which something lay, dressed in something grey and blue, propped on pillows under an umbrella" (230, II.34). In this sentence, the precision of the signifier "Mme Stahl" is counterbalanced by the intentionally ironic vagueness of its signified and referent ("something lay . . ."). This foreshadows not only Prince Shcherbatsky's disparaging remarks but also Kitty's disillusionment with the entire project of self-improvement that is inspired by Varenka from Mme Stahl's entourage.

Levin also associates excessive verbalism and empty language with the artificiality of city life and opposes it to physical labor in the country as an absolute value. This emerges in the restaurant scene with Stiva, when the waiter translates the Russian names of everyday dishes into menu French (34, I.10) and when Levin comments that city dwellers eat such things as oysters in order to delay satiating hunger, whereas country dwellers try to eat as quickly as possible in order to get back to work. (He makes a similar point about city dwellers growing their fingernails so long that they cannot work with their hands the way country dwellers do [35–36, I.10].) Stiva's attitude toward language in this scene is a neat variation on the theme of artificiality and shows him to be the consummate urban denizen. Although French names are actually the norm in the "artificial" setting of the restaurant in question, Stiva perversely chooses to use Russian names for the dishes he orders, as a result of which he creates a second and more refined layer of artificiality.[4] (By contrast, in jaded society circles Princess Miagky's simple and sensible talk produces the impression of a "most witty joke" [135, II.6].) Similar evaluations appear when Levin is living in Moscow during Kitty's confinement and remarks that he spends entire days talking in ways that he would never have done in the country and that this, together with only eating, drinking, and not doing any work, has begun to make him feel "befuddled" (*on oshalel* [703, VII.11]). Levin also dislikes using foreign words in Russian (350, III.32), presumably because of the additional layer of mediation they add and because they counter his gravitation toward Russian essentialism (see *16.5.1*).

When Anna first commits adultery, she cannot conceive of the words that would do justice to her feelings of "shame, joy, and horror" (a description that illustrates the paradox at the heart of Tolstoy's perennial attempts to communicate the limitations of language via language). Even on the second and third day after her "fall," she still cannot find the words or formulate the thoughts that would allow her to think through all that was in her soul (150, II.11). Anna's sense of semiotic disorientation is also communicated in this scene via the reference to her "spiritual nakedness" (149, II.11), which shows that the consequence of her entry into a world of new significances is that she is stripped of her familiar values and semantic garb (which also echoes the complex theme of clothing elsewhere in the novel [e.g., see *18*]). Another aspect of Anna's relation to language is that she loses control of it. When she tells Vronsky during an early stage of his pursuit that she "forbade" him to speak of his love, she realizes that by using this word she "acknowledged having certain rights over him and was thereby encouraging him to speak of love" (139, II.7). In other words, the signifier she uses is not attached to the signified that she expects, and it turns against her or at least against that part of her consciousness that struggles to resist her attraction to Vronsky.

Some elements of this kind of linguistic slippage can also be seen in the deracinated signifiers Anna employs. When she exclaims in her despair "My God! My God!" the narrator stresses that neither word actually means anything to her because she could seek comfort in religion only at the price of giving up the one thing that gives her life any meaning, namely, Vronsky (288, III.15). Signifiers that have a very loose relation to signifieds characterize the kind of causerie that typifies Princess Betsy's stylish set, especially the choice new circle within it that is called, "in imitation of an imitation of something, . . . *Les sept merveilles du monde*" (294, III.17; see also *16.1*). A similar illusion of meaningfulness characterizes aspects of Vronsky's world, such as his impression that most of his friends abroad understand his relations with Anna "in the right way" (469, V.7). The narrator comments that if either Vronsky or the others were asked to explain what they meant by the phrase "in the right way," they would be hard-pressed to do so. Vronsky and Golenishchev also use the word "talent" similarly. As Mikhailov understands very well, it is actually a shorthand reference to their vague delusions rather than the denotation of an artist's actual gift (477, V.12).

The effect of this kind of linguistic skepticism and indeterminacy is threefold. First of all, characters such as Stiva, Karenin, and Princess Betsy emerge as the butts of the implied author's irony (and even humor). Second, the inclusion of Levin and Anna, who carry most of the novel's thematic weight, contributes to the impression that the novel is "insecure" or "anxious" about its mission, which is, in simplest terms, to communicate. Finally, the varieties of linguistic skepticism also leave the field open to nonverbal ways of communicating and of grasping truth—like seeing, feeling, and intuition—that are dramatized especially vividly in scenes of liminal experiences such as Nikolai dying, Kitty giving birth, and Levin discovering his faith. However, although these moments are described as if they were windows onto eternity, the fact that we are told about seemingly transcendent experiences via a medium that repeatedly questions itself of course implicates these experiences in the questioning as well. This is not to say that the privileged insights are simply undermined and negated by linguistic indeterminacy. Tolstoy clearly marks positively both his favorite characters and their most important experiences, but in a way that does not fully coordinate his message with his medium.

12. Absolutism: Claims about Universal Truth and Morality

12.1. The General Problem of Fictional Authority

Where in *Anna Karenina,* other than the epigraph, is the claim made for an absolute and transcendent ethical norm? Before trying to answer this question, it is worth considering how seriously such claims can even be taken in a work of fiction.

A novelistic character's perception or judgment is usually presented as an individual point of view and thus subject to all the vagaries of personality, bias, and misperception that are commonly assumed to accompany individuality in our culture (errare humanum est). Consequently, the individual viewpoint is always open to question unless it is confirmed by something else in the work, such as the experiences of other important characters, which would suggest that they reflect dominant features of the novel's fictional world, or by the narrator, assuming that he is sufficiently omniscient, consistent, and plausible to be judged reliable. In short, the validity and verisimilitude of a given character's or narrator's views are measured primarily by the criterion of the work's *internal consistency*.[1] Another way of putting this is that the narrator's remarks will be accepted as the truth about a given fictional world or as reliable depictions of events in it only if the actions and views of characters do not contradict them.

Whether or not the narrator's and characters' views are true in the sense of fitting the reader's understanding of things in the "real" world is an important but secondary consideration with regard to deciding if something is meant to be true within a fictional work. The distance between what readers see as true in their own worlds and what they are willing to accept as the truth of fiction can be quite large. Thus, a man's transformation into a beetle ("The Metamorphosis," Franz Kafka), or a bronze statue's coming to life (*Petersburg,* Andrei Bely), or a woman's ascension into the sky (*One Hundred Years of Solitude,* Gabriel García Márquez) are all readily accepted by many readers as "true" in this sense. Similarly, Pierre's meeting with Davout in *War and Peace,* during which Pierre exchanges a look with the

French marshal that the narrator characterizes as having "saved him from death" and showed them both that "they are brothers" (vol. 4, pt. 1, chap. 10), must be understood as an event that actually occurred in the sui generis world of that novel for the simple reason that it is presented as real by the narrator and not undermined by Pierre, Davout, or any other character. Some readers may not believe that such looks are possible, and the exceptionally credulous might have to be told that the event never actually occurred because Pierre is an invented character while Davout was an historical personage. But it would be an egregious misunderstanding or misrepresentation of the fictional world in which both characters coexist to claim that Pierre imagined or hallucinated the life-saving look or that it is unimportant in the novel's hierarchy of meaning. Another example is the willingness of many readers to take at face value Father Zosima's elevated spiritual position in *Brothers Karamazov*, which is acknowledged by most of the major, positive characters in the novel. It matters little if one does not personally believe in God, dislikes Zosima's spirituality, or finds his monastic quietism unacceptable in the face of the social and political inequities widespread in late-nineteenth-century imperial Russia. The fact that Dostoevsky modeled Zosima in part on an actual monk, Paissy Velichkovsky, and an important Russian Orthodox spiritual tradition, and that Zosima happens therefore to be literally verisimilar, is something that most readers do not know or even care about when they are persuaded that Zosima functions as a kind of living saint in the novel.[2] Zosima's status is of course also not undermined by the fact that he occupies only one position in a series of complexly structured dialogic exchanges with Ivan and other characters. These are oppositional, but they are not inconsistent; and the essential role that Zosima plays in the relational meanings that emerge from the dialogues is the warrant of his fictional "reality."

Fictional authority in *Anna Karenina* is different from these examples because it is largely dualistic, but without being either dialogic or inconsistent. On the one hand, Tolstoy's typical practice is to portray characters as existing in private worlds that are reflections of their own mental states. In other words, there is relatively little or no "outside" in the novel's world that is independent of a given "inside." Even when characters are very close to each other, such as the happily married Levin and Kitty, we still see them when they are acting primarily in accordance with their own personal values and characters *(13)*. They are thus always alone on some fundamental level of emotional and mental life and incapable of sharing with others everything that is important for them. Moreover, the narrator is often complicit in such relativization, either by confirming it or by not undermining it, although there are also some exceptions when he speaks up to contradict characters.

On the other hand, the narrator and some of the characters also make remarks that purport to be expressions of universal and transcendent truths. It does not seem possible to resolve this difference by accepting as valid only the personal truths or only the universal truths.[3] There are too many examples of each pole in the novel for either one to be dispensable. Neither does it appear that the two kinds of truth cancel each other, nor that they can be synthesized readily at some higher level of abstraction (even though one kind of not entirely satisfactory synthesis may be possible). Instead, these two kinds of truth can be seen as divergent textual vectors that define the boundaries of a variegated field within which one can discern with differing degrees of certainty *several* possible conceptions of what truth may be for human beings. This is, of course, itself a kind of truth, which means that the novel is *not* open to just *any* kind of truth. To characterize these possibilities and to consider the implications of their co-existence is my goal in the pages that follow.

12.2. The Narrator

Throughout the novel, the narrator makes ethically unambiguous judgments of some of the characters and their actions that thus echo the tenor, albeit not always the substance, of the epigraph and the novel's first two sentences. (For more on the narrator, see *12.3, 12.7, 13.1,* and *16.*) For example, he defines Vronsky's behavior toward Kitty when he visits her house as "the luring of a young lady without the intention of marriage" and as "one of the bad actions common among brilliant young men such as himself" (57, I.16). Later, the narrator intrudes into Vronsky's self-satisfied musings about Anna and characterizes him as devoting "his life to involving her in adultery at all costs" (128, II.4), thus eschewing, in a defamiliarized way, the euphemisms of a high-society romantic "affair." The narrator also condemns Anna and Vronsky when he describes how her son, Seryozha, functions as a moral compass for them because he shows how far they had strayed in moral terms (186, II.22). However, in this case the narrator's condemnation is somewhat diminished by his likening the two lovers to a mariner who watches the divergence between his actual course and the correct one but is "powerless to stop." From one perspective, the lovers emerge as at least partially *passive* victims of their passion; from another, the narrator also implies that they may be *actively* deceiving themselves:

"they knew but did not want to know" (186, II.22). Later, when Anna and Vronsky meet Golenishchev in Italy, the narrator damns Anna via his sarcastic description of how Golenishchev flatters himself by thinking that he understands Anna when in fact she cannot understand herself how she could be happy after making her husband miserable, abandoning him and her son, and losing her good name (461, V.7). In an elaborate simile, the narrator states that Anna's feeling of revulsion toward Karenin is caused by her recollection of the "evil" she had done him and is like the reaction of a "drowning man" who pushes away another in order to survive (463–64, V.8; this simile can also be seen as foreshadowing Anna's death). Earlier, the narrator had characterized Karenin's attempt to ignore Anna's infidelity as "madness" (201, II.26), and his belief that he had sympathized with cuckolds in the past as "not true" (279–80, III.13). One of the narrator's loudest pronouncements is his condemnation of Levin's despairing, materialistic conclusion about human existence being a brief and pointless event in an indifferent cosmos. He labels Levin's view "a tormenting untruth" (789, VIII.9), which, of course, implies that he approves of the faith that Levin will discover soon thereafter and, by extension, of the other "spiritual" insights that Levin has elsewhere in the novel.[4]

The narrator is frequently very negative about aspects of contemporary public life, such as when he ironizes at the expense of the power and pretense of medical science and the famous doctor who had been invited by the Shcherbatskys to cure what is actually Kitty's broken heart (117–20, II.1; see also 203, II.26). In similar fashion, when describing Karenin's bureaucratic initiative on behalf of indigenous peoples, the narrator lambasts government agencies for imagining they can understand or control human events through the accumulation of second- or thirdhand data (370, IV.6). Karenin's thinking about numerous cases of divorce that have taken place in the highest social circles leads the narrator to redefine the practice as a husband's "yielding up" or "selling" an unfaithful wife (281, III.13), which further tarnishes the elite layers of society. (There is little doubt that this description is the narrator's, both because its straightforward terminology is of a piece with his other "defamiliarized" descriptions and because Karenin himself is incapable of such a direct, nonbureaucratic view of the situation.) The narrator is also openly sarcastic about the new form of commercialism that has appeared in Moscow and St. Petersburg to which Stiva wants to attach himself: "This post, like all such posts, called for such vast knowledge and energy as could hardly be united in one person. And since the person in whom all these qualities could be united did not exist, it would be better in any case if the post were occupied by an honest man rather than a dishonest one" (719–20, VII.17). In keeping with his frequently disparaging asides about various forms of depravity widespread in high society, especially in St. Petersburg, the narrator is scathing about the character and methods of those who embrace the Serbian war (771, VIII.1). The result of these kinds of comments is that much of urban culture, and especially its highest levels surrounding the imperial court, is condemned for superficiality, vanity, immorality, and hypocrisy (see also *14.3*).

The narrator's strong opinions are not always negative, however. He seems to share Kitty's pain at Vronsky's indifference toward her at the ball and, in a rare instance of anticipating a character's distant future, describes the "tormenting shame" she feels as persisting years later (80, I.23). In a scene witnessed by no one else, his likening a crestfallen Kitty at the ball to a butterfly implies tender admiration for the young woman's fragility (82, I.23). Later, the narrator describes the coming of spring in the country in a long, carefully structured passage that betrays not only close observation and knowledge of nature but also genuine visceral pleasure in the process. References to Easter and to other holidays in the post-Paschal Russian Orthodox Church calendar give nature's rebirth a spiritual and human dimension that culminates in the scene of Levin's joyous response to the season (152–53, II.12; see also *16.1*). It is a striking paradox, however, that the narrator's masterful description, which on some level must parallel Levin's perceptions, attitudes, and experiences, would also probably be rejected by Levin because he does not like verbal descriptions of nature (see *11*).

Narrative humor is another obvious method that Tolstoy uses to color aspects of his fictional world, even though this is not a widespread or dominant technique. For example, the narrator uses gentle irony when he describes Dolly's initial difficulties in the country, where she goes to stay with her children. (This includes a "terrible bull who bellowed and therefore probably would also charge" [260–61, III.7].) These are overcome with the help of a "club" that Matryona Filimonovna, the nanny, establishes with some of the locals. The light humor here serves to foreground such themes as Stiva's irresponsibility, Dolly's combined determination and helplessness, the contrast between how city dwellers see the country (including Stiva and Koznyshev) as compared to those who live and work there (Levin and the peasants). A similar humorous moment is the narrator's description of how Agafya Mikhailovna, Levin's old housekeeper, "stared gloomily at the raspberry jam, wishing with all her heart" that it would not cook properly because she is being forced to prepare it according to Kitty's family method rather than her own (554, VI.2). We are made to smile here at the old retainer's resistance to change, which is both inevitable and ultimately welcomed by her, and which is part of the overarching "family" theme. The kindly old beekeeper's concern with giving Dolly's son more bread in the scene when Levin and his father-in-law are debating the Balkan war with Koznyshev and Katavasov (806, VIII.15) is a gentle, humorous dig at the rhetoric of those in favor of the war and accords with Levin's typically personalized view of it. Humor in its sarcastic variant is more obvious and widespread and includes the descriptions of Vasenka Veslovsky's misadventures at Levin's (e.g., VI.9), Levin at the provincial elections (VI.26 ff.), and the scenes with Landau (VII.22). In all such cases the humor serves to further tarnish the subjects to whom it is applied.

At times the narrator employs value-laden symbolism that conveys his judgments less directly. Just before Levin happens to glimpse Kitty in the carriage on her way to spend the summer in the country with Dolly, which shatters his fantasy about marrying a peasant woman and resurrects his love for Kitty, the narrator notes that the "bleak moment" has come that "usually precedes dawn, the full victory of light over darkness" (277, III.12). This strongly marked image is echoed in the language characterizing Kitty's appearance moments later: she is "bright" (svetlaia); the joy of seeing him "lit up her face" (osvetila ee litso); and she concentrates for him "all the light and meaning of life" (ves' svet i smysl zhizni; 277, III.12). An additional dimension of the narrator's symbolism is a possible parodic echo between this light imagery and the Russian term for "high society," which is *svet* or, literally, "light" and which is, of course, anything but positive in the novel's hierarchy. By contrast, it is also possible that the symbolic light imagery anticipates Kitty's appearance after she has given birth: "her eyes, bright to begin with [vzgliad ee i tak svetlyi], brightened still more [svetlel] as he approached her" (717, VII.16). The flame that flickers into existence with the baby's birth may also be related to the author's light symbolism.

In a related vein, the narrator also makes occasional pronouncements about universal truths of human behavior that recall the "laws" he announces in the novel's opening lines, thus reminding the reader of the possibility that human existence and behavior are fixed in essential ways. This is, of course, in keeping with the nineteenth-century European novel's general tendency to focus on the way that particular characters and events illuminate larger truths, be they social, moral, psychological, and so on. But it is striking that in *Anna Karenina* each supposed "universal" is usually countered or complicated by some other claim or event. For example, when Stiva frets over how he reacted when Dolly confronted him with his note to the governess, we are told that, "as often happens," he regrets not the event but how he responded to his wife; the narrator also explains that what had happened to him is "what happens to people" when they are suddenly caught in something shameful (2, I.1). The paradox of this "truism" is that it posits duplicitous behavior as an automatic psychological defense mechanism, which thus raises questions about the possibility of ethical behavior in general. Another example is how Countess Nordston's fondness for Kitty is manifested in her wish that Kitty be married to Vronsky, who fits Nordston's own ideal; this is, according to the narrator, what married women "always" want for their younger unmarried women friends (49, I.14). However, this generalization does not prevent Kitty from subsequently being able to convince Countess Nordston that Levin is in fact her ideal suitor, even though the countess continues to dislike Levin.

Later in the novel, the narrator draws an explicit parallel between the crystallization of water when it freezes and how social relations always form in predictable ways at places such as the spa where the Shcherbatskys arrive (214, II.30). This generalization certainly accords with the narrator's description of the family's behavior. But because it evokes a law of nature it also ironically foreshadows Kitty's amoral rejection of Varenka as a role model and her decision to resume her role as a privileged family's sheltered daughter, all of which reconfirms the novel's theme of character being destiny. Here is one final example that would seem trivial if it were isolated but that resonates with the others. After describing Dolly's difficulties in arranging her life in the country, the narrator says that the Oblonsky household had one unnoticed but essential person in it who was able to fix everything, "as in all family houses" (261, III.7). A striking exception to this is the Karenin household, where Anna's newborn daughter might have died from lack of care were it not for Karenin's suddenly taking an interest in her (419, IV.19).

12.3. The Narrator, Karenin's Self–Deception, and the Nature of True Faith

How the narrator understands religious faith emerges from his sweeping condemnation of the new Evangelical Christianity in vogue among some members of St. Petersburg society. They are "totally lacking in depth of imagination, in that inner capacity owing to which the notions evoked by the imagination become so real that they demand to be brought into correspondence with other notions and with reality" (glubiny voobrazheniia, toi dushevnoi sposobnosti, blagodaria kotoroi predstavleniia, vyzyvaemye voobrazheniem, stanoviatsia tak deistvitel'ny, chto trebuiut sootvetstviia s drugimi predstavleniiami i s deistvitel'nost'iu). Karenin was introduced to the movement by Countess Lydia Ivanovna, and like its other members sees nothing "impossible or incongruous in the notion that death, which existed for unbelievers, did not exist for him, and that since he possessed the fullest faith, of the measure of which he himself was the judge, there was no sin in his soul and he already experienced full salvation here on earth" (511, V.22).

The narrator's remarks constitute a major hermeneutic index that defines true faith as the ability to correlate the products of one's imagination—"notions," "ideas," or "representations," all of which are possible translations of the Russian *predstavleniia*—with other notions, ideas, or representations and with reality.[5] (The emphasis on "correlation" in these remarks also suggests a parallel between the structure of religious faith and artistic structure [see *8.6*].) However, the narrator's formulation lends itself to diametrically opposed interpretations because it is not clear what he means by bringing "*notions . . .* into correspondence with other *notions* and with reality." Either he is referring to different ideas in a *single* mind or to different ideas arising in *different* minds: the former implies idealism or solipsism (because correlating different ideas in the same mind does not necessarily entail seeing external "reality" from a perspective other than one's own), while the latter denotes realism (because the "triangular" relationship between at least two different minds and the world outside them does allow an individual's ideas to be verified from a perspective other than his own). The faith that yields insight into religious truth can thus depend either on a process confined to a single mind or on a process of empirical verification.

These different alternatives shed very different light on the nature of religious faith and reenact the opposition between absolutized and relativized perspectives that recur throughout the novel. It is therefore especially noteworthy that in the continuation of his critique of Karenin and the Evangelicals the narrator appears to tilt toward a "solipsistic" or "idealistic" interpretation of faith, which means that he shifts to the individual or relativized pole of truth and value that is usually the domain of characters in the novel. This can be inferred from how the narrator faults Karenin for his facile conclusions that death and sin do not exist for him even though both exist for nonbelievers and that he is himself the judge of the fullness of his own faith. The last point might seem to imply that faith has to be judged by someone else. But in the continuation of the passage, the narrator describes Karenin's present feelings about his faith as a measure of its falsity and contrasts these with his earlier feelings as a measure of its truthfulness:

"Alexei Alexandrovich vaguely sensed the levity and erroneousness of this notion of his faith, and he knew that when . . . he had given himself to his spontaneous feeling, he had experienced greater happiness" (511, V.22). That a personal perspective is inescapable in such experiences also emerges very strongly in the narrator's final remarks about how psychologically important it was for Karenin to deceive himself: "it was so necessary for him in his humiliation to possess at least an invented loftiness . . . that he clung to his salvation as if it were salvation indeed." The net effect of this rich and complex series of passages about Karenin's faith is that his error is identified, criticized, and *excused,* all at the same time. This suggests a remarkably tolerant, or resigned, attitude on the narrator's part as he discriminates between his own insights and the limitations of his characters.

Is there anyone in the novel who embodies the narrator's conception of faith and thereby bridges at least part of the distance that separates the narrator from Karenin and the other characters? The most striking example is Levin at the end of the novel when he decides that he has discovered the same true faith shared by millions of others even though he also realizes that he will not be able fully to manifest or even communicate it (see also *13.4.4*). In many ways, Levin's religious journey is the opposite of Karenin's or Countess Lydia Ivanovna's. Levin is more thoughtful, self-aware, and sensitive than they are and shows much more humility than they are capable of when he assumes that there will always be mysteries that human beings cannot understand. He also does not even begin to approach the conclusion that he is without sin; quite the opposite, he is always painfully aware of his own fallibility. In other words, Levin can be seen as interconnecting all these ideas or as correlating them in a way that implies he possesses the "depth of imagination" that the narrator makes into the essential criterion of true faith.

Nevertheless, as we have seen, one of the ways of reading the narrator's critique of Karenin is that an external measure of some sort—the outside world and/or ideas originating in other minds—is necessary to verify and anchor religious faith (and, perhaps, any ideas with existential implications). By this standard Levin's success is less certain although still possible. He does read widely, refers to a variety of religions, is struck by a peasant's comments about what constitutes a just life, and believes he understands the faith of those near and dear to him. All this suggests that he is able to grasp the ideas of others. However, he simultaneously rejects virtually all that he reads and abandons trying to understand a number of central aspects of Christianity and the tenets of other religions. Levin also typically interacts with others around him primarily in terms of his own interests, as when he interprets one peasant's casual quotation from another peasant in a way that triggers his religious awakening. All this raises doubts about the degree to which his convictions differ from Karenin's in the end. (There are other reasons to question his faith as well [see *13.4.4*].)

The only way to resolve this difference would seem to be the (somewhat shaky) process of *internal* self-verification suggested by the narrator's description of Karenin's vague sense that there is something frivolous and false in his new faith in comparison to the joy he experienced when he spontaneously and unthinkingly surrendered to his faith at Anna's sickbed. This implies that the purity and strength of the individual's inner feelings—whether pertaining to falsehood or to goodness—may themselves constitute the gauge by which the validity of those feelings can be measured. Karenin's relatively short-lived experiences at Anna's sickbed and during the days that follow do resemble Levin's religious feelings at the end of the novel and thus mutually buttress each other (a conclusion that also shows how the reader's involvement in the process of "correlating" textual data yields a sense of a fictional work's verisimilitude and validity). But even if these privileged feelings, which can also be understood as manifestations of conscience (see *15*), appear to carry their validity within them, they still diverge from the narrator's criterion of "correspondence . . . with reality." Furthermore, the narrator's acquiescence in Karenin's necessary self-deception also undermines, although it does not eliminate, the potential validity of any other religious intuitions that Karenin had. And given this, can we think of Levin, or of anyone else who trusts in his own faith, as entirely free of self-deception?

12.4. Karenin and Echoes of Saint Paul

Prior to his "conversion" by the countess, Karenin undergoes a complex spiritual trajectory from automatically repeating religious pieties, to an unconscious desire that Anna meet with "retribution" for her crime (282, III.13), to heartfelt forgiveness of her, and finally to his sense that something is thwarting his free expression of love. By virtue of their subject matter, all these phases serve to remind the reader of the novel's epigraph and its biblical context as a potentially authoritative moral touchstone and concise theodicy. This impression is augmented in the case of the above phrase about "retribution," because in the original Russian it contains near-palindromic echoes of the sound orchestration in the novel's epigraph as well as a rhyme: "Mne otmSHCH[enie], i AZ VOZ-DaM" — "poluCHila

VOZ-MeZDie ZA svoe prestupl[enie]." Given Karenin's largely unappealing character, it is somewhat paradoxical and curious that he would be the primary vehicle in *Anna Karenina* for these and other Pauline associations, unless this fact is itself taken as a comment about the teachings in question (see *12.6*). (Other possible allusions to the epigraph can also be detected whenever "vengeance" is invoked, as in Koznyshev's formulaic response to old Countess Vronsky that "it is not for us to judge" when she condemns Anna for destroying her son's life [778, VIII.4]; there are additional examples like this as well.) But the actual meaning of the allusions to Saint Paul are far from simple because of the specific contexts in which they occur.

The most striking instance appears in the scene between Karenin and Anna when both think she is dying. Contrary to his expectations, "the joyful feeling of love and forgiveness of his enemies filled his soul," which of course recalls the core teaching of Romans 12. Karenin is then described as kneeling with "his *head* on the crook of her arm, which *burned* him like *fire* through her jacket, [and] sobbed like a child. She embraced his balding *head*" (413, IV.17, emphasis added). The italicized words in this passage could be read as a veiled allusion to the "difficult" part of Romans 12:20 that describes a ritual act of penitence. (The possibility that this scene evokes Saint Paul's grudging allowance in 1 Corinthians 7:9 that it is "better to marry than to burn" seems less likely, because it does not fit well either Karenin's or Anna's situation.) In other words, it is possible to interpret this scene as Karenin's enactment or embodiment of a specific *image* in Paul's teaching and not just its general *message:* Karenin acts lovingly toward those who hurt him, forgives them, and simultaneously expresses contrition for any wrongs he may have done them. However, given the logic of the exchange described by Saint Paul in verse 20, where it is the charitable behavior of the innocent party that makes the guilty feel the "fire," one could also say that it should have been *Anna* who feels the fire on *her* head. One could argue, of course, that because Anna is ill and febrile and because she feels very guilty toward her husband at this moment, she is, in fact, suffering the "fire" of penitence. But if one follows this interpretation, one has to conclude that because Karenin did not cause her illness and fever via his forgiveness, the parallel with Romans breaks down after all (unless one chooses to see Karenin as *sharing* Anna's feverish torment).

Or is Karenin's inability to give Anna the kind of love she finds with Vronsky evidence of Karenin's guilt before her, even if it is a function of Karenin's fixed character? And what about Vronsky? Beyond having a look of "suffering and shame" in this scene, he is not associated with the fire imagery, although he is crushed by Karenin's magnanimity, which transcends his understanding. This will lead to Vronsky's suicide attempt, which can be seen as a kind of penitence, but one that would obviously be difficult to reconcile with the Christian message of Saint Paul's Epistle. Finally, it is also quite possible that the association of "head" and "fire" is merely a co-incidence and that the entire passage is simply an evocation of basic Christian teachings, such as those found throughout the New Testament and not only in Romans. All of these alternatives remain plausible, and it is doubtful that there is any way to decide among them. But perhaps it is not necessary to choose, for the simple reason that all the possibilities evoke the same ethical norm, which thus continues to hover over the novel.

Judging by the tone with which the narrator describes Karenin's spiritual rebirth at Anna's sickbed and Vronsky's and Anna's initial reactions to it (415–16, IV.18), the change in Karenin is clearly meant to be taken as a genuine embodiment of the Christian ideal in its pure form. But this is a transcendent moment that does not last, and soon Karenin's recollection of how he forgave Anna "burned his heart with shame and remorse" (520, V.25).[6] Why would this be the case? Judging by other moments in the novel that are somewhat analogous, such as Kitty's giving up her ideal of becoming a ministering angel like Varenka, or Levin resigning himself to behaving as he always has after he discovers his new faith, it seems to be in the nature of things in Tolstoy's world for individuals to fall away from the ideals that attract them. But what is it about Karenin in particular that makes him unable to live the Christian ideal?

12.5. Karenin and the "Crude Force"

The narrator invokes at least two reasons why Karenin's spiritual rebirth does not last. The first is Karenin's feeling that external pressure of some sort is forcing him out of the charitable state of mind he had discovered by Anna's sickbed: "He felt that, besides the good spiritual force that guided his soul, there was another force, crude and equally powerful, if not more so, that guided his life, and that this force would not give him the humble peace he desired. He felt that everybody looked at him with questioning surprise, not understanding him and expecting something from him. In particular, he felt the precariousness and unnaturalness of his relations with his wife" (419, IV.19). This passage implies that the "force" in question may be more than the curiosity, distaste, ridicule, and opprobrium of others, as if it were a transcendent antithesis to the positive spiritual force that Karenin experienced and whose efficacy even Vronsky confirms via his awed reaction. (By contrast, Levin feels a beneficent "external force" at different points in his life [see also *17.2*].) Through this opposition, the force thus acquires a touch of the transmundane, of metaphysical evil. But does this force exist outside Karenin's consciousness? The answer appears to be both "yes" and "no."

On the one hand, Karenin cannot fail to notice that Anna's dislike for him resurfaces when she recovers. Anna actually reverses the Pauline edict to love one's enemies when she admits to Betsy that she has "heard that women love people even for their vices . . . but I hate him for his virtues" (427, IV.21). (Anna's reversal is so pointed and so clearly motivated by her situation that it makes one wonder if it might not be due more to the fundamental impracticality of the edict than to her own moral weakness [see *12.6*].) Karenin also notices that his acquaintances, especially the women, can barely suppress their malicious joy when they see him (420, IV.19). Their reaction is very probably "real" because it is similar to the joy Karenin saw in his lawyer's eyes, which the narrator had described as having an existence independent of Karenin's mind (367, IV.5). Karenin's expectation that society will force him "to do what was bad but seemed to them the proper thing" (425, IV.20) is confirmed when Stiva tries to persuade him to grant Anna a divorce by taking the blame for her adultery upon himself, which Karenin interprets as an expression of "that powerful, crude force which guided his life and to which he had to submit" (432, IV.22). Finally, the narrator comments openly that members of society judge Karenin and laugh at him (515, V.24).[7]

On the other hand, there is evidence that Karenin's "crude force" may also be a name for his own feelings of insecurity and unhappiness that he projects onto those around him. For example, the old nurse's "displeased" tone leads Karenin to think that in her "*simple* words . . . [he] seemed to hear a *hint* at his situation" (421, IV.19, emphasis added); Princess Betsy's footman replies to him, as the narrator puts it, "with what *seemed* to Alexei Alexandrovich like a smile" (420, IV.19, emphasis added); and in the wet nurse's contemptuous smile at the idea that she might not have enough milk, Karenin "also *detected* mockery of his situation" (421, IV.19, emphasis added). Given such moments, which are of course familiar human reactions from someone who has experienced a traumatic event, it becomes difficult to distinguish which instances of "crude force" are real and which are imagined by Karenin; and doubts about the existence of some cannot but make others ambiguous as well.

The narrator provides an additional reason for wondering about the extent to which a real external force prevents Karenin from maintaining his charitable feelings. We are told that almost simultaneously with Anna's leaving him, his career comes to a halt: "Whether it was the confrontation with Stremov, or the misfortune with his wife, or simply that Alexei Alexandrovich had reached the limit destined for him, it became obvious to everyone that year that his official career had ended" (515, V.24). Karenin is unaware that the end has come but cannot help noticing the "sea of hostility and mockery that surrounded him," as the narrator puts it (517, V.24). This reaction by others to Karenin's bureaucratic failure resembles the reaction that his marital problems elicited, which leaves open the possibility that Karenin may have confused the two different reactions, especially given the chronological correlation between them, and the fact that he always defined his bureaucratic labors in moral terms. Moreover, the possibility that Karenin had "reached the limit destined for him" may be an allusion to how his sterile and pedantic personality inhibited his creative reach. And if Karenin's personality was one of the reasons for his career's end, then his blaming a "crude force" may be his self-serving rationalization, or misunderstanding, of his reemerging dominant character traits that had been briefly eclipsed by moments of genuine compassion. Karenin's "crude force" may thus not be transmundane and may be transpersonal only to the extent that it reflects the reactions of other members of society to his unattractive person and character when his marriage and career are failing.

If the "crude force" is a reification of Karenin's personal and professional problems, it is important to note also how its significance, and the analogous experiences that other characters have, are relativized. Countess Lydia Ivanovna forms a strong sentimental and even romantic attachment to Karenin precisely when he feels that everyone has turned against him, which suggests the "force" he fears is not in fact ubiquitous. Levin resembles Karenin to the extent that he also appears odd to most of those in his social set and in turn feels awkward around them much of the time. But Levin's dominant reaction to the disapproval he elicits is simply to ignore and avoid others as much as possible, with the exception of a few friends and family, which he does quite successfully and more or less happily. This is of course relatively easy for Levin to do because he chooses to live in the country and not to get involved in various initiatives with other landowners; but this fact also confirms that different characters manifest different values when confronting analogous problems. In comparison to Levin, Anna and Vronsky resemble Karenin in being far more seriously at odds with society. Vronsky is criticized and Anna is ostracized for having allowed their affair to assume its extreme form, and Anna is further condemned by her own sense of guilt. However, neither identifies these problems as a quasi-occult force or reifies them into one (although Anna does experience "doubling" [see *13.5.8*] and may be enmeshed in a fatidic pattern [see *17*]). As a result, the "crude force" may be restricted to Karenin's world alone, which, however, does not make it any less real for him (see also *14.3*).[8]

Considering such different reactions from Anna and Karenin also raises a basic question: why should he be exposed to a similar kind of societal judgment as his wife if he is not to blame for anything? He is really "guilty" only of having a tepid personality that could not satisfy Anna. Perhaps some look askance at him largely because he is cold, dry, humorless, unimaginative, and physically unattractive. Others presumably take envious pleasure in seeing the fall of a prominent figure in society and the government. His opponents in the bureaucracy strive to undermine him because of his attack on their plans. Or is he ridiculed because of the streak of inherent frivolous cruelty in the jaded social set, which thrives on gossip and superficial relations? Is this because the urban, civilized world is fallen? Or is his fall a manifestation of an inscrutable divine vengeance? This would seem unlikely as well as unfair, because he has not so much done wrong to others as manifested the character traits he has always had. Perhaps in the end Karenin's "crude force" is a term for the inherently abrasive relations among human beings, as in Schopenhauer's concept of the "will," which grinds down any more charitable motivations.

12.6. The Incompatibility of Saint Paul's Teachings with Human Nature

The second major reason why Karenin is incapable of maintaining his attitude of Christian charity is that pride quickly insinuates itself into it and perverts it. When, in an attempt to be faithful to the ideal of turning the other cheek, Karenin temporarily yields to Stiva's entreaty about granting Anna a divorce, which would require Karenin to assume all the blame in connection with it, he no longer feels simple humility: "He felt grieved; he felt ashamed. But along with grief and shame he experienced joy and tenderness before the loftiness of his humility" (432, IV.22). In other words, his egoless "good" act automatically elicits its opposite in him—an egotistical satisfaction. This is a telling development for several reasons. It again underscores the relativity of values and perceptions in the novel's world: what a character believes in, and what a character *does* with an existing belief system, is a function of that character's personality, which puts its indelible stamp on everything. In turn, this also raises fundamental questions about the extent to which something like the teaching in Romans can, in fact, be embodied by human beings (although it is worth recalling that although Saint Paul instructs people to "live peaceably with all men," he recognizes that this will not be easy and adds: "If it be possible, as much as lieth in you" [Romans 12:18]). Karenin is certainly not an "everyman" in *Anna Karenina,* which probably does not have one, but if he cannot embrace the teaching in its pure form for any length of time, then perhaps others cannot either. This conclusion is also suggested by Anna's inability to overcome her revulsion toward Karenin despite his forgiveness and her feeling of guilt. The problematic nature of Levin's discovery of faith at the novel's end and his resigned acceptance of his irascibility lend additional support to these reservations. Consequently, the evocation of the Pauline teachings surrounding the novel's epigraph in connection with Karenin not only reminds the reader of them but also underscores the *distance* between the teachings and the behavior of characters in the novel who are attracted to different aspects of the teachings with varying degrees of intensity and conviction.

A similar conclusion is suggested by Karenin's musing about the relation between his charitable behavior and his suffering at the hands of others. As the narrator explains, "He simply could not reconcile his recent forgiveness, his tenderness, his love for his sick wife and another man's child, with what there was now—that is, when he, as if in reward for it all, found himself alone, disgraced, derided, needed by none and despised by all" (505, V.21). Even more pointedly, on the next page Karenin realizes that people hate him *because* "he was shamefully and repulsively unhappy." Each of Karenin's thoughts is a complex hermeneutic index that again evokes the Pauline doctrine only to raise questions about it: in both cases, Karenin's actions and states of mind are equated with what *are not* appropriate or equivalent responses from others within the Pauline moral code.

Is Karenin wrong to expect from others something more akin to his own behavior toward Anna? Is this a sign of his weakness, because his expectation is too closely linked to human rather than divine conceptions of causality and justice? Should he have endured being despised, suppressed his sense of self, and continued to behave charitably? Is not a Christian who suffers in this world supposed to be recompensed only in the next (a possibility that is broached in the novel in connection with Countess Lydia Ivanovna's facile faith and when Levin decides that it is unknowable)? Or is there something wrong with the teaching itself, in the sense that it asks too much of human beings?

In trying to navigate these alternatives, the reader also has to consider the constant stumbling block of Karenin's prosaic and phlegmatic personality. Tolstoy's conception and portrayal of character is such that there is no easy way to factor out Karenin's dominant traits from an evaluation of the Christian ideal that he tries to enact, even though this kind of "depersonalized" behavior is exactly what Saint Paul advocates. For example, after Anna admits to him that she is having an affair, Karenin formulates a plan that will attain two goals—maintain the appearance of propriety that he values and simultaneously punish Anna by thwarting the affair's further progress. The narrator then underscores that only after Karenin gets to this point does he realize that his actions could also be understood as conforming to religious teaching, and that earlier he had not sought guidance in religion (282, III.13; on the other hand, see also Karenin's earlier appeal to religion when he admonishes Anna [147, II.9]).

The only way that one can "tell the dancer from the dance" in this case is if Saint Paul's teachings are articulated in the novel in a pure form, and this is not the case (not even in the truncated epigraph). Even during the extraordinary moment when he forgives Anna, Karenin is described as finally yielding to a feeling that he had suppressed throughout his life (418, IV.19). His act of forgiveness thus seems to have been in him potentially all along. But is this a latent divine spark or a culturally determined value? Are these different? Or is there some new dimension to the experience that comes from outside him and that he briefly embraces? Karenin is a stickler for bureaucratic rules and regulations but is otherwise a weak man. Does this mean that he is too weak to embody the Christian ideal in its purest form for any length of time even though that ideal also privileges meekness and weakness? So it would seem. The only person with whom he establishes what might appear to be reciprocally loving relations is Countess Lydia Ivanovna, but her role is tarnished by the narrator's sarcastic portrayal of her shallow religiosity, selfishness, and hypocrisy, by the fact that she has a crush on Karenin that blinds her to what others find unattractive in him, and by her falling under the sway of the charlatan Landau.

Levin is another character who strives to embody Saint Paul's teaching. But although he is far stronger than Karenin in terms of will, intelligence, and richness of emotional life, in the end he resigns himself to never being able to act consistently toward others in accordance with the universal law of goodness that he feels he has discovered. This is a consequence of his sense of his own and of humankind's distance from the divine (which is a marked difference from Karenin's self-confidence in his new Evangelical faith). But although Levin may believe that the law of goodness is inviolate, can the reader do so as well simply on the strength of Levin's faith in it and without seeing him realize it in practice? Indeed, it is notable how some of

Levin's behavior as a landlord, in which he is motivated largely by a personal hierarchy of values that is tempered by generally charitable behavior, diverges from the ideal that is implied in Romans. Although Levin does help his peasants on occasion when they are in need, he also sells them hay during a time of shortage, even when he feels sorry for them; and he does not forgive a worker who leaves his job because his father had died, and actually docks the man's pay (791, VIII.10). It is not selfless love for the other or any law of universal goodness that motivates Levin in cases such as these but the pragmatics of being a squire who wants to hold on to the family estate.

A similar but more extreme case in point is Anna's state of mind while she is on her fateful way to the train station, which Tolstoy renders via his celebrated "stream of consciousness." Among the many things she darkens with her anguished gaze is a beggar woman with a child who, Anna assumes, must believe that people pity her. This encounter of course evokes the topos of Christian charity, but Anna's reaction to the beggars is antithetical. She formulates a question in her mind that constitutes her (direct, albeit unwitting, and quasi-Schopenhauerian) challenge to Saint Paul's teaching about charitable behavior: "Aren't we all thrown into the world only in order to hate each other and so to torment ourselves and others" (764, VII.30). A few pages later she again concludes that "we're all created in order to suffer, and that we all know it and keep thinking up ways of deceiving ourselves" (766, VII.31). Thus, at the moment when Anna feels the greatest need for help of any kind and might be expected to be especially open to feelings of compassion, she is shown to turn directly away from the ethical code that is supposed to provide succor to those like herself. Does she fail the code, or is the code incommensurate with her personality and extreme suffering?

12.7. Saint Paul on Marriage, Sex, and God's Work

Another important complex of Saint Paul's teachings is evoked by Karenin's quotation from 1 Corinthians 7:32–33: "He that is married careth for the things that are of the world, how he may please his wife, he that is unmarried careth for the things that belong to the Lord, how he may please the Lord" (516, V.24; Karenin actually reverses the two parts of the sentence).[9] The context for this passage includes Saint Paul's grudging admission that it is "better to marry than to burn" with sexual lust (7:9) and his commandments regarding sexual behavior. Adultery is of course forbidden, and divorce is condemned—but with the additional qualification that if a woman leaves her husband, she should not remarry or should return to him.[10] If Anna is judged by these biblical teachings alone, then she is clearly guilty. But the fact that Karenin is the vehicle for introducing the teachings into the novel raises questions about their validity and relevance. This inference is supported by the way Karenin tries to use Saint Paul to justify his bureaucratic labors, which he imagines "serve the Lord" even better now that Anna has left but which the narrator ridicules (516, V.24). The absurdity of Karenin's alluding to Saint Paul in this context is further underscored when, shortly after quoting the verses about marriage, Karenin is struck by a particularly robust chamberlain's calves at a court reception, which he makes into his own hermeneutic index confirming that "all is evil in the world" (516, V.24).

Earlier in the novel Karenin had also evoked the general tenor of Saint Paul's teaching in 1 Corinthians when he admonished Anna about the nature of marriage: "it is my duty to you, to myself, and to God, to point out your duties to you. Our lives are bound together, and bound not by men but by God. Only a crime can break this bond, and a crime of that sort draws down a heavy punishment" (147, II.9). Although on this occasion Karenin's remark is not undermined by his own weakness or facile beliefs, it is put into question by the circumstances surrounding his marriage to Anna. We are told that this was the result of possibly cynical manipulation by Anna's aunt, who coerced the wavering Karenin by claiming that he had compromised Anna (507, V.21; see *13.5.6*). Given this, what is the relation between divine involvement in the marriage bond to which Karenin alludes, following Saint Paul, and the actual way in which Karenin and Anna's marriage came about? Are we to assume that the aunt's ability to compromise Karenin reflects a divine sanction (and that, by extension, other aspects of the social world are similarly determined)? This seems rather unlikely, although there is a fateful dimension to Anna's life *(17.1)*. Karenin's Pauline remark also reevokes the question of how, and how consistently, punishment is meted out to those who break the divinely sanctioned marriage bond.

The unappealing use to which Karenin puts his energies when he embraces the argument that the unmarried are better able to please God makes one wonder how or even if this ideal is relevant to the rest of the novel. In fact, it does not seem to fit the behavior of any of the characters, none of whom is interested in a spiritual life dedicated primarily to God. And if there is not a single character who assumes this radical stance, then there does not seem to be any reason for inferring that the reader is supposed to either (especially given the additional complications stemming from the novel's uncertainty about determinate meaning). Levin, who bears the bulk of the narrator's approval, wants nothing more when he is single than to get married, to the extent of even toying with marrying a peasant girl. All his agricultural endeavors are directed primarily toward maintaining and enhancing an estate appropriate for starting a family. It is true that he is much concerned with behaving morally, that he regrets his past sexual experiences, and that he is pleased with himself for having resisted unspecified sexual temptations during the winter following his rejection by Kitty (151–52, II.12). However, he never thinks of marriage as a second-best palliative for lust, and nothing detracts from his desire for a family. The same could be said about Kitty and Dolly, who also live for their families, or about their parents, or the minor character Lvov (their brother-in-law), for whom marriage and especially children are the ultimate raison d'être, to the extent that he returns to Russia from a post abroad for the benefit of his children's upbringing (681–82, VII.4). The one character in the novel who might seem to be an embodiment of Christian selflessness is Mlle Varenka. It is therefore especially noteworthy that Kitty's flirtation with imitating Mlle Varenka's charitable behavior at the spa in Germany ends with Kitty's rejecting it because it goes against her own nature. Moreover, Varenka's behavior could be interpreted as being at least as much a result of her docile character and dependent social position as of her commitment to Christian virtue.[11] In fact, her near betrothal to Koznyshev demonstrates her eagerness to exchange her life of serving others for marriage and a family of her own. Vronsky is the only major unmarried character in the novel, and Stiva often behaves as if he were. One could interpret both as rather harsh parodies of the idea that freedom from marriage allows one to do God's work.

As for Saint Paul's general distaste for sex and carnality, we can discern a strong whiff of it in a number of places in *Anna Karenina,* such as the episode of Levin showing Kitty his diaries, which chronicle his sexual past and make her weep, and in the narrator's characterization of their honeymoon as "the most difficult and humiliating time of their life," "ugly, shameful," and "unhealthy" (483, V.14). Levin's relations with Kitty achieve a stable, noneroticized state only some time after they are married. But Tolstoy does not erase passion altogether from their lives, as is suggested by the surreptitious kiss they exchange when Kitty demonstrates why Koznyshev's courtship of Varenka failed (566, VI.5).[12] In a related vein, the narrator's remarkable hermeneutic index equating Vronsky's first sexual possession of Anna with murder, and the repeated emphasis on Anna's "body" as humiliated, dead, and dismembered, can be seen as echoing Saint Paul's emphasis on human "bodies" being "members of," or belonging to, Christ, and on fornication as a sin against one's "own body" (1 Corinthians 6:15, 6:20, 6:18; it of course also foreshadows how Vronsky will see Anna's corpse [780, VIII.5]). Given the gravity of this hermeneutic index and the length at which the narrator dwells on it, it has to be reckoned as one of the weightier condemnations of Anna and Vronsky's adultery, even though this is far from being the novel's final word on their passion or, as we have seen, on the role of Pauline teachings in human existence.[13]

A smaller evocation of Saint Paul's sexual attitudes is suggested by Vronsky's gruffness toward and Yashvin's sneering at two officers in their regiment (175–76, II.19). This can be interpreted as reflecting Saint Paul's condemnation of homosexuality (1 Corinthians 6:9), especially given the fact that the narrator marks both as physically unattractive, thus denigrating them even more in the reader's eyes. Yashvin's epithet for the two, "the inseparables" (vot nerazluchnye), is later repeated by Karenin in his description of Anna and Betsy as "the inseparables" (ne stanu razluchat' nerazluchnykh; 205, II.27), which serves to further tarnish both women morally, but without implying any "unnatural" sexual relations between them (even though Anna later describes Betsy as the most depraved woman she knows).

The novel diverges from Saint Paul in its treatment of the sexual transgressions of characters like Stiva and Princess Betsy and her circle. The former in particular seems immune from any criticism, except for Dolly's unhappiness (which she appears largely to forgive him, even if she does not forget his straying), his own very short-lived and specific pangs of guilt at the novel's beginning, and an occasional twinge of conscience that he quickly overcomes or forgets (although, as I will suggest below, these twinges are important in the context of similar experiences that other characters have [see *15*]).

Another departure from Saint Paul, who would just as soon have everyone abstain from sex altogether if this were only possible, is the kind of value that the novel places on children as the reason for marriage. This is one of the prime motivations in Levin and Kitty's marriage and is the bedrock of Dolly's existence. Indeed, it underlies Dolly's shock and incredulity when Anna tells her about the contraceptive measures she employs to prevent having any more of Vronsky's children (637, VI.23). It is only in Tolstoy's "Kreutzer Sonata" (1889) and some other later works that the extreme position on procreation articulated by Saint Paul (as well as Saint Matthew and others in the New Testament) finds fuller fictional embodiment.

It is also quite remarkable that even the narrator appears capable of abandoning his own moral scruples under the influence of a female character's appeal. The most striking example of this is, of course, the narrator's portrayal of Anna's beauty and charm at different points in the novel, even after he had described her "fall" in the grotesque terms of a murder and of a corpse that must be cut up and disposed of. One could argue, however, that at worst Anna is a morally ambivalent character, that her passion and love for Vronsky are genuine and thus exonerate her, at least somewhat, and that her anguish over what she has done to herself and to her family also redeems her, at least to some extent. Thus the narrator's positive portrayal of Anna is not necessarily a sign of his own moral ambivalence. But the matter is quite different in the case of Liza Merkalova, one of the society beauties at Princess Betsy's whom Anna finds especially attractive. It would seem that Liza's behavior is more than questionable in terms of the morality of the narrator, who openly calls her "perverted" and signals her erotic aura by describing two admirers who follow her everywhere. However, in a passage where it is impossible to distinguish between Anna's and the narrator's perceptions, which suggests, for lack of evidence to the contrary, that their perceptions merge here, Liza is described as having "something in her that was higher than her surroundings—there was the brilliance of a diamond of the first water amidst glass" (300, III.18). At this point nothing except this (minor) character's beauty and charm seems to matter to the narrator, whose reaction in this regard is of a piece with some of his descriptions of Anna as well and relies on aesthetic rather than ethical criteria. In this, he recalls the kind of "amoral" relativization that we saw in the reactions of Stiva's servant and the nanny toward him even when everyone recognized that he was guilty before Dolly.[14]

13. Relativity: Characters as Arbiters of Meaning and Value

13.1. Introduction

In the world of *Anna Karenina* it matters a great deal who is perceiving, interpreting, or evaluating something and even what an individual's emotional or mental state is at any moment. Different points of view are of course a dominant feature of the novel in general, and several mutually complementary explanations have been given for this. Lotman invokes semiotics and information theory when he argues that literary works must be heterogeneous in order to maintain their primary cultural function as repositories and generators of meaning. In novels, this necessary heterogeneity is typically achieved via differences among characters' points of view, as a result of which authorial "truth" is a "supratextual construct" comprising the "intersection of all the points of view." The novel thus implies that reality cannot be exhausted from any one perspective.[1] Similarly, Striedter suggests that the "multiple interpretability" necessary for a work to survive through time was achieved by the Realist novel through "the multiplication of psychological and narrative perspectives." This development was a compensation for the Realist dismantling of the Classical and Romantic reliance on metaphor and symbol, and for the plurality of interpretation that flowed from these tropes.[2] Both of these explanations can also be correlated with Ian Watt's well-known argument in *The Rise of the Novel* that the emergence of the novel as a dominant genre can be explained by the rise of middle-class individualism and values in eighteenth-century England. Georg Lukács, in his classic *Theory of the Novel*, comes to a related conclusion when he contrasts the novel to the organic holism of the epic: "a new perspective of life is reached [in the novel] on an entirely new basis—that of the indissoluble connection between the relative independence of the parts and their attachment to the whole. But the parts, despite their attachment, can never lose their inexorable, abstract self-dependence; and their relationship to the totality, although it approximates as closely as possible to an organic one, is nevertheless not a true-born organic relationship but a conceptual one which is abolished again and again."[3] Thus, according to Lukács, fragmentation of meaning is inherent in the novel, which is the characteristic genre of an alienated age.

What distinguishes *Anna Karenina* from many other nineteenth-century novels is the higher-than-usual ratio of passages presenting the viewpoints of characters to those giving the viewpoint of the narrator. This is a striking, albeit still *relative* departure from Tolstoy's own practice in *War and Peace,* in which narrative commentary is far more widespread and swells to the dimension of the essaylike "digressions" on the practice and philosophy of historiography, especially in part 2 of the epilogue. The dominance of a narrative voice that colors the events and characters it describes is also an important feature of other well-known nineteenth-century novels such as Stendhal's *The Red and the Black* (1830), Balzac's *Père Goriot* (1835), Dickens's *Bleak House* (1853), Turgenev's *Fathers and Sons* (1862), and Hardy's *The Mayor of Casterbridge* (1886). In this regard, *Anna Karenina* is perhaps comparable only to *Madame Bovary* (1857), which is marked by Flaubert's famous desire to achieve what he termed "impersonality": "The artist in his work must be like God in his creation — invisible and all-powerful: he must be everywhere felt, but never seen."[4] Compare this to Tolstoy's description of how he worked on the scene of Levin's confession and conversation with the priest on the eve of his wedding: "I changed this part of the story four times, and it still seemed to me that one could tell on whose side I was. But I've noticed that any work or story produces an impression only when it's impossible to tell with whom the author sympathizes. And so it was necessary to write everything in such a way that this wouldn't be noticeable."[5] Other examples of Tolstoy's "impersonal" narration would presumably include scenes such as the *relatively* neutral descriptions of the railroad station in Moscow when Anna's train arrives (59–60, I.17) and of the setting for Vronsky's race (196, II.25), both of which are steeped in knowledgeable details but are relatively uninflected except for a general tone of agitation and anticipation (compare with *12.2*). At the same time, it is important to underscore that such scenes obviously remain highly meaningful in a *relational* sense. The train station acquires significance because it is the place of Anna's first encounter with Vronsky and because it suggests the implacable social transformations of railroads and the physical power of trains (both synecdoches of modern civilization).[6] And the atmosphere of the race contrasts with calmer sylvan settings such as Levin's estate and thus invokes the theme of relative time in the novel (see *13.3*), the contrast between nature and urban artifice, and related themes.

In the Russian context, *Anna Karenina* also occupies a unique position in relation to Dostoevsky's novels. Bakhtin has famously argued that Dostoevsky grants his characters *relative* freedom from authorial control, which translates into the self-effacing role of his narrators and the extensive dialogic relations among his characters, who seem to be speaking their own minds even when what they say or think is modified by present or imagined interlocutors.[7] By comparison, what is noteworthy about *Anna Karenina* is how *antidialogic* this novel is in Bakhtinian terms—how much it is concerned with portraying characters locked into individual perspectives that are modified very little, if at all, via verbal exchanges with others.[8]

A widespread conversational trajectory between two characters in *Anna Karenina* is an enthusiastic beginning that sets up the parameters of the exchange, followed by a failure of the two minds to meet, and concluding with a cessation of communication as the characters withdraw into mulling over their private concerns without any further regard to who is in front of them. We see this happen repeatedly between well-intentioned pairs such as Levin and Stiva, Levin and Koznyshev, Levin and Dolly, Levin and Sviyazhsky, Anna and Vronsky, Dolly and Karenin, etc.[9]

This depiction of dialogue does not make *Anna Karenina* any less "artistically" composed, of course, or any less "realistic" than Dostoevsky's works, which might seem to follow from Bakhtin's privileging dialogic relations among characters as the distinguishing characteristic of the novel and of ideal human relations in general. On the contrary, and as we have seen, *Anna Karenina* contains an extraordinarily developed "labyrinth of connections" that links textual elements both large and small, contiguous and distant, and that is an expression of the artistic ordering Jakobson called the "poetic function." In my view, Bakhtin's dialogicity can be best seen as a particular *kind* of relational meaning in language, one that can be subsumed under Jakobson's more general and more ample category.[10]

Recognizing the antidialogic nature of *Anna Karenina* leads to an unexpected conclusion about Tolstoy's reputation as one of the greatest, perhaps the greatest, of the "realist" novelists. Literary "realism" is a notoriously slippery concept to pin down, for some very good reasons.[11] But if we assume that it has something to do with the idea that "objects of sense perception or cognition exist independently of the mind" and that it is concerned with "fidelity . . . to nature or real life and to accurate representation without idealization," then it is possible to argue that there is a strong streak of "idealism" in the worldview that emerges from *Anna Karenina*. Tolstoy's *relative* emphasis on how characters see things, and the *relative* self-effacement of the narrator in the novel, produce the impression that "the essential nature of reality lies in consciousness" and not outside it.[12] Another way of saying this is that the world in which a given character exists may very well be real and may impinge on the character's psyche, but the only way it can be known is through that character's perspective, which will inevitably color the world in particular ways.[13]

There is an overt discussion of a related issue early in *Anna Karenina* itself. Levin drops in on his half-brother, Koznyshev, when he is in the middle of debating a "fashionable question," as the narrator puts it, with a professor of philosophy: "is there a borderline between psychological and physiological phenomena in human activity, and where does it lie?" (23–24, I.7). Tolstoy portrays the professor satirically: he is a wizened, yellow little man, with a narrow forehead and mind, all of which inevitably colors his position in the debate, which is that an individual's representation of the external world is entirely a product of sensory data. The satirical effect is enhanced by the professor's invocation, in support of his materialistic stance, of authorities with the comical names "Wurst, Knaust, and Pripasov," which are German and Russian for "Sausage, Stingy, and Provisions."[14] By contrast, Koznyshev rejects this view and implies that there is more to human consciousness than what is supplied by sensory data. This also appears to be Levin's position; he asks if being can be independent of material embodiment or, in other words, if consciousness can survive death. The fact that Levin raises this point shortly after the professor defends his materialistic position suggests that Levin may also not see things in a materialistic way (which thus anticipates his discovery of faith in God at the end of the novel *[13.4.4, 15.2]* as well as the novel's essentialism *[16]*). Although this debate is not concluded, it does reflect the way in which characters' predispositions, or subjectivities, play the primary role in shaping their interactions with others and with the world throughout the novel.

This feature of the novel is noteworthy for several important reasons. From the point of view of narrative technique, it is related to what could be called the "touchstone effect," whereby characters whom the narrator marks positively or negatively then make evaluations of others. The result is that the reader's opinions are guided without the narrator's overt involvement, on the principle that the reader will probably like whomever or whatever a positive character likes and dislike what the character dislikes.

The novel's "idealism" also bears on Tolstoy's overt preoccupation with ethics, the role of the divine in human affairs, and overarching truths regarding the human condition. This is because a major indeterminacy opens up between the characters' consistently relativized acts of meaning creation and the occasional insistence by the narrator (and several characters) on a divinely sanctioned, universal ethical code that supposedly rules over all human relations. One way in which these *could* be related in the novel, which does not mean that this is how they necessarily *are* related, is through a total determinism that makes all human actions the manifestations of divine will. Another, opposite way to relate them is by seeing the narrator's viewpoint as no more privileged than that of the characters. Thus the narrator's judgments and beliefs are as private as all the others, and reflect neither unmediated access to higher truth nor a commitment to symmetrical dialogic relations and all they imply.

As I will demonstrate at some length below, characters throughout *Anna Karenina* usually construct meanings or make interpretations that are largely private, in the sense that they stem from personal codes, values, temporary moods, and characterological predispositions. Surveying a catalog of such instances in the novel suggests that the most important events in the lives of characters usually occur in ways and on levels that are inaccessible to others.[15] There are important exceptions to this, of course, especially in the early phases of the novel's two central love plots. But in the later phases of the same plots characters are again portrayed as isolated within themselves to varying degrees. This is due in part to Tolstoy's narrative emphasis—his practice of focusing in detail on moments when characters are caught up in their private worlds and of only summarizing or alluding to harmonious relations among them (for the latter, see *14.1*). Thus, isolation is on center stage, while connection is relegated to the novel's wings.

An analogy for the relations among characters is semiotics. Because the way they see each other and their worlds is a function of their internal states, what they perceive is defined through relations within the system that they constitute at any given moment. This is like the meaning of a sign being dependent on the system into which it is introduced and of which it becomes a part by virtue of syntax and structure. An example of this is the way "oysters" come to be charged with at least two special meanings in the novel because of how differently Stiva and Levin see them during their dinner together (35–36, I.10); these overlap to some extent with "dictionary" definitions of the mollusk but are certainly not identical to it.

The sheer number of relativized moments produces the impression that most collective action or agreement, be it between individuals or among members of families and other groupings, occurs through a kind of inertia or partial commitment that leaves the deeper levels of the participants' psyches relatively uninvolved rather than through successfully coordinated and fully conscious effort (see *14.2*). As I will argue below, this appears to be true even in the case of Levin and Kitty, who achieve the highest level of family happiness among all the major characters in the novel. Despite their genuine dedication to each other, in the end Levin knows that he cannot share with Kitty what is most important for him.[16] Indeed, the novel concludes with a major hermeneutic index when Levin defines religious truth as something personal and fundamentally incommunicable.

13.2. Multiple Viewpoints in Narrative

Before proceeding, it is necessary to consider another way of understanding the novel's perspectivalism. As Lotman has suggested, there are two major consequences to encountering different and irreconcilable points of view in a given work. One is that the array of subjective perspectives serves as the data out of which the reader can fashion an image of reality, which is the "invariant," or common ground, for all the separate perspectives. Lotman describes the structure of Mikhail Lermontov's novel *The Hero of Our Time* (1840) in this way and concludes that the different angles from which Pechorin, its protagonist, is viewed by other characters as well as by himself (in his journal) can be combined to produce a psychologically "realistic" portrait of him and of his milieu. Each individual perspective is inevitably limited, but at the same time each contributes another facet to the composite truth. (This is also how a number of critics see characters in *Anna Karenina*.)[17] The second situation that Lotman describes, which he finds in Ludwig Tieck's comedies and some of Luigi Pirandello's plays, entails a multiplicity of perspectives that cannot be reconciled and that imply the absence of an objective reality. He recognizes that hybrids of these two extreme types exist as well.[18]

Tieck's and Pirandello's works are quite different from *Anna Karenina,* but the type of model they exemplify according to Lotman seems to me to be more relevant than Lermontov's novel. One major reason is that *Anna Karenina* does not provide any unambiguous examples of the integration of disparate perspectives into a unity that the reader could use as a model for fashioning a holistic vision of existence. In other words, there are no unequivocal hermeneutic indices that imply anything like the idea that "reality" is the sum of different overlapping perspectives. Neither is there an obvious need to infer that this is the case. On the contrary, as we have already seen, the narrator makes occasional apodictic remarks that purport to identify large general truths but that are rarely if ever supported by the details of the world he narrates.

This is not to say that the reader fails to draw any conclusions about the world in *Anna Karenina*. For example, when Karenin learns of Anna's adultery, he initially rationalizes an elaborate attempt to preserve the illusion of normalcy in their lives rather than undertake any action to change them (282–83, III.13). After giving us Karenin's cogitations in considerable detail, the narrator shifts to Anna, who fervently wants to change her untenable position, which she sees as consummately false and dishonest (287, III.15). It is of course obvious to the reader that Karenin's plan will horrify Anna, which is, in fact, what happens a few pages later (293, III.16). In their ensemble, these scenes allow the reader to make inferences about Karenin's blindness with regard to Anna, about Anna's dependence on Karenin for any solution to her quandary, about the tragic mismatch of their characters, and similar matters. But this does not tell us anything about the core nature of the world in the novel beyond the fact that it comprises irreconcilable viewpoints.

Another reason why *The Hero of Our Time* is an inappropriate model for *Anna Karenina* is that Lermontov's novel focuses on one intriguing (Romantic) character, which necessarily implies that trying to understand him is a worthy and achievable goal, and which helps to structure an integrated view of the world with Pechorin at its center. By contrast, *Anna Karenina*'s numerous characters and plotlines create a multiplicity of perspectives. This complicates seeing any character as a psychic unity, because any character in a novel is always the paradigmatic accumulation of individual meanings that result from his or her interactions with others, and these meanings are rarely congruent. Even when characters from the different plotlines meet on occasion, in the end they still inhabit largely different worlds and have little in common with each other on the level of their *lives*. The overarching *thematic* meanings that emerge from comparing and contrasting characters and their actions in different plotlines are, of course, another matter. The parallel plot structure of the novel encourages the reader to see multiple stories and consequently multiple worlds in it, but each of those worlds acquires its meaning by virtue of its juxtapositions with the others.

One could argue that the presence of numerous echoes among details in *Anna Karenina* (its "labyrinth of connections"), together with the absence of any other obvious principle of integration in it—be it an all-seeing and consistent narrator, a character, a plot, a conception of human psychology, a belief, or an ideology—is *itself* an image of "reality." But this is an inherently ambivalent conception because it shows centrifugal and centripetal tendencies operating simultaneously on different textual levels: the widespread resonances among details, or the novel's artistic structure, imply that the world in the novel may be unified on some deeper or higher level, while the lack of thematic coherence suggests the opposite. This ambivalence also creates a dilemma. The general kind of artistic structuring present in *Anna Karenina* is an inherent feature of the prose genre we call "the novel," while the thematic inconsistency we find in it is specific to it alone. (This remains true even if the degree of artistic structuring varies among different novels and the relational nature of artistic structure is openly thematized within this one.) Nevertheless, to choose one alternative over another would be reductive. I will return to this problem in more detail below (see *18*).

13.3. Characters and Relative Time

The most unusual indication that characters live in worlds isolated from each other is that time moves differently for them. This curious but important feature of the novel was first pointed out by Nabokov's character Pnin in the novel of the same name, who says that this "is the best example of relativity in literature that is known to me," and was later confirmed by Nabokov himself in his lectures on *Anna Karenina,* which were published posthumously. In an earlier study, I examined, reconfirmed, and extended Nabokov's findings, but, rather than send the reader to the article in question, I thought it would be both useful and simpler to repeat some of its salient points here.[19]

As I mentioned *(10.2),* Tolstoy staggers the two major plotlines early in the novel so that we go from Anna leaving the ball where Kitty is crushed to a description of Levin leaving the Shcherbatskys after Kitty rejects him (83–84, I.23–24; see also "dead time," *10.1*). This can be considered a flashback, because the rejection happened several days before the ball, and the flashback's function is to create a "situation rhyme" between the two scenes. But this flashback can also be read as an instance of temporal *slippage,* because Levin's plotline is independent of Anna's (and Vronsky's) and falls behind it. Details such as Anna's haste to leave Moscow support this interpretation: although she is already ahead of Levin, she speeds up even more (97, I.28).

This pattern continues later in the novel as well. When Anna and Vronsky consummate their affair, we are told that this had been Vronsky's desire "for almost a year" (149, II.11). Two pages later, however, when we return to Levin we learn that although "three months passed," he had not grown indifferent to his grief over Kitty's rejection (151, II.12). Thus, at this point, the Levin plotline is nine months behind that of Anna and Vronsky.

Another temporal node is related to the horse race. We learn that the time of the race is just before July 15, which is when Karenin gives Anna household money (200, 202, II.26). But after the race is described, we shift to Soden in Germany and Prince Shcherbatsky's return from a side trip in "June" (228, II.34). So Kitty's time seems to lag behind Anna's, just as Levin's had. Moreover, when we return to Vronsky, who is putting his financial affairs in order on the *day after* the races, we are told it is a clear "August" day (302, III.19, 313, III.22). Thus, Vronsky again leaps ahead in relation to Kitty and Levin.

At the end of part III, we can infer that Levin leaves for Europe during the first week in October (III.32). But at the beginning of part IV, Vronsky's story is picked up in the "middle of winter," as we are told in connection with his hosting a foreign prince (353, IV.1), which means that Vronsky is again ahead of Levin. That winter is also when we see the dinner at the Oblonskys, and it is possible to calculate when it must have taken place. On the day after the dinner, Kitty and Levin are betrothed, and Karenin returns to St. Petersburg, where Anna is near death after giving birth to her daughter. Shortly thereafter, Vronsky attempts suicide. We are told that Anna's daughter became ill at the "end of February" (419, IV.19) and that this was two months after the child's birth (418, IV.19). Thus, the Oblonsky dinner must have occurred around the end of December because Karenin leaves the dinner right after the child is born. A month after their child's illness, or, in other words, three months after the birth and the dinner, Anna and Vronsky leave for Italy (435, IV.23). By contrast, Levin and Kitty's wedding takes place six weeks, or one and a half months, after the dinner at the Oblonskys' (453, V.4; 437, V.1), which means that at this time Anna and Vronsky are one and a half months ahead of Kitty and Levin.

We next shift to Anna and Vronsky in Italy, where they have been for three months; that is, their story jumps to four and a half months ahead of the time when we last saw Kitty and Levin. We have to assume, of course, that Kitty and Levin's life together has been going on all this time as well. But when the story does shift back to them, we are told that they had been married only three months (479, V.14) and are therefore still one and a half months behind Anna and Vronsky. Even though the two main plots intersect when Anna and Levin finally meet following her return from Italy, the times between the plots are still not reconciled permanently, and additional examples of temporal slippage can be found in parts VI and VII of the novel.

Why would time flow in a "relative" way for these two pairs of characters? An answer is suggested by two major scenes that are marked by different experiences of time and that are emblematic of the characters' lives—Vronsky's horse race and Levin's mowing with his peasants.

Readers have long noted that Vronsky's fatal accident with Frou-Frou can be read as an allegory of his affair with Anna (see *10.2*). Like Anna's departure from Moscow, Vronsky's preparations for the race, as well as the race itself, are marked by his having to hurry. After a meeting with Anna he looks at his watch and leaves "hastily" in order to get to the track on time. He then drives some distance, looks at his watch, and realizes that he is "late" (191, II.23). Because he runs an errand on the way he has to "gallop" to the track (192, II.23). Under these circumstances, it is ironic that Vronsky changes "unhurriedly" and believes that he never hurries or loses his self-control, especially because shortly thereafter he asks his English stableman, "Am I late?" (192, II.24), and finds that he does not have time to fully check the man's saddling (194, II.24). The actual race goes well until Vronsky inexplicably makes a mistake related to time that is the opposite of his headlong rush: he fails "to keep up with the horse's movement" and lowers himself onto the saddle, as a result of which he breaks the horse's back (199, II.25). This lack of synchrony between Vronsky and the horse can be read as a lack of coordination between him and Anna. In these terms, it is not Vronsky's rushing that kills Anna but his inability to catch up with her as she rushes ahead of him. (The scene of Anna and Vronsky on the same train from Moscow to St. Petersburg, even though they meet only at a stop in a symbolic snowstorm, also implies rushing through time, because trains are associated with modernity and speed.)

The opposite experience of time characterizes various peak events in Levin's life, especially the great mowing scenes: "The longer Levin mowed, the more often he felt those moments of oblivion. . . . These were the most blissful moments. . . . Levin did not notice how the time passed. If he had been asked how long he had been mowing, he would have said half an hour—yet it was nearly dinner-time" (252–53, III.5). Levin also feels that he has fallen out of the normal flow of time on the eve of his betrothal (IV.15) as well as during his son's birth (VII.14). In fact, a desire to recapture a timeless past characterizes Levin's entire life plan, which is to reproduce on his estate the family life that he recalls from his own childhood. Koznyshev unwittingly echoes this when he tells Kitty that she and Levin are "enjoying quiet happiness far from all the currents in your quiet backwater" (781, VIII.6).

The result of juxtaposing these famous scenes with the evidence of temporal slippage is that Vronsky and Anna appear to be rushing through life toward the end of their time, which is death, whereas Levin and Kitty linger in slow time, which is life. What may have seemed to be merely mistakes in the novel's plotting can thus be interpreted as the shape of the novelistic world.[20]

Did Tolstoy intentionally create the various temporal slips discussed above? This is an unanswerable question. I have found no evidence that he tinkered with temporal indicators in the novel's drafts in order to create consistent "slippage," and it is perilous to speculate about an author's unconscious motivations. Nevertheless, it seems plausible to hypothesize that the way time functions as a reward or punishment in *Anna Karenina* may reflect Tolstoy's attitude toward the two pairs of characters.

Many years after completing the novel Tolstoy would make a related point in his preface to a Russian translation of Guy de Maupassant (1894). In the context of criticizing naive views of what creates artistic unity, he comments that "the cement that binds a work of art into a single whole, and that therefore produces the illusion of reflecting life, is not the unity of characters or situations, but the unity of the author's original *moral attitude* toward his subject."[21] This idea may be irrelevant to *Anna Karenina* because it reflects Tolstoy's later frame of mind and interests, following his spiritual, artistic, and personal crises of the late 1870s and early 1880s. The temporal disjunction between the novel's two major plotlines is also not exactly evidence of the work's unity on this level. But a subtle binary system of punishment and reward linked to time does constitute a coherent value system, one, moreover, that echoes and connects with other overt signs of the author's or narrator's approval and disapproval, including the epigraph and the possibly fatidic and vengeful patterns of existence (see *17*). As usual, however, none of this appears to apply to Stiva or Princess Betsy, which means that relative time alone cannot be the key to the novel's ethics.

13.4. Levin

13.4.1. Levin and Kitty

Central to Levin's existence is his relation to Kitty, and it is striking that his views of her are presented as being so private that they are virtually incommunicable.[22] This begins with his attitude toward the entire Shcherbatsky family, all the members of which, "especially the female side, seemed to him covered by some mysterious poetic veil [*zavesoi*]" (21, I.6). This image is echoed later, and Levin is granted a glimpse behind the veil, as it were, when he has his vision of Kitty during childbirth: "all the wrappings were suddenly removed and the very core of her soul shone in her eyes" (707–8, VII.13, my literal translation; needless to say, no one else sees Kitty in this way). The mysteriousness of the Shcherbatsky sisters for Levin is also communicated by the narrator in semiotic terms when he lists their daily activities as if they were signifiers without signifieds: "Why these three young ladies had to speak French and English on alternate days; why at certain hours they took turns playing the piano . . . why all these teachers of French literature, music, drawing, and dancing came there . . . all this and much more that went on in their mysterious world he did not understand; but he knew that everything that went on there was beautiful, and he was in love precisely with the mysteriousness of it all" (21–22, I.6).

All this might seem to be quite normal for a character who lost both parents at an early age and who is drawn to a harmonious and attractive family with three pretty daughters. It is noteworthy, however, that the narrator intervenes at strategic points to underscore the uniqueness of Levin's viewpoint (one could almost call it his "solipsism") but without offering anything like an alternative or a corrective to how Levin should be seeing things or how things really are (and there is no one else who does this either). When Levin goes to see Kitty at the ice-skating rink, he recognizes that she is there "by the joy and fear that overwhelmed his heart"; the narrator then adds: "There seemed to be nothing very special in her dress, nor in her pose; but for Levin she was as easy to recognize in that crowd as a rose among nettles" (28, I.9). This is a remark that also puts the reader in the position of having to accept Levin's perception of Kitty, but without any real possibility of constructing a different, more accurate, or "realistic" view of her. It might seem tempting to interpret the remark that Kitty "was more beautiful than [Levin] had imagined her" as indicating that she exists independently of his perceptions. But the narrator's description of Levin's thoughts culminates with the effect her smile has on him: it makes him recall feelings from his "early childhood" (29, I.9). This makes his view of Kitty even more private, because she becomes a function of his own past and of his association with "slow" time in the novel. None of this is to say that other characters in the novel do not find Kitty attractive. Plenty of men do—from Vronsky, who is charmed by her freshness; to unnamed young men at society balls who make her first season a greater success than either of her sisters enjoyed; to Vasenka Veslovsky, who attempts to flirt with her. But through all these interactions Kitty remains a rather abstract "pretty young lady" that the reader would be hard-pressed to define more precisely.

Another way of saying this is that Levin's Kitty is his alone no matter what his frame of mind might be. When, not long after the scene at the skating rink, Kitty rejects Levin's proposal of marriage, it comes as no surprise that his view of her sours and that he starts thinking "how alien and distant from him she had become!" (48, I.13). This feeling persists for some time, to the extent that he even briefly entertains the thought of marrying a peasant girl when he is in the throes of his involvement with the agricultural work of his estate. But all of this changes again the moment he happens to see Kitty at dawn on a country road.

Toward the end of Stiva's dinner party Levin achieves a singular rapport with Kitty that culminates in their betrothal. But his connection with her leaves him oddly trapped in his own exuberant psychic state and thus effectively isolated from the other guests. Earlier that evening, Kitty urges Levin not to think ill of Turovtsyn, whom Levin had just called "worthless" (390, IV.11). Levin immediately embraces the correction and inflates it into the general principle "I'll never think badly of people again!" (391, IV.11). But rather than assume a nonjudgmental and more open attitude toward others, Levin turns his attention inward and focuses on his new mood and resolution at the expense of any interactions with the other guests: "He was not the least bit interested in what he said himself, *still less in what they said,* and desired only one thing—that they and everyone should be nice and agreeable" (395, IV.13, emphasis added).

Levin then goes even farther and elevates his antidialogic behavior to a general hermeneutic principle. He concludes that there is no point in two individuals arguing about anything, because the only way that one can convince the other is if both already have the same tastes or if one manages to acquire the other's. The explicit denigration of language and reason in this formulation, and the implicit elevation of private feelings and the individual human psyche, are illustrated by the fact that Kitty (alone) is able to grasp Levin's "poorly expressed thought" immediately and to rephrase it in a way that is "laconic and clear, almost wordless" (396, IV.13).

The importance of this scene for the interpretation of *Anna Karenina* as a whole is that "value" emerges as a *relative* concept: two individuals will evaluate the same thing in the same way only if they both happen, or come, to like it. But if this is so, what happens to value judgments rooted in transpersonal criteria? Can ethics be understood simply as the name given to the negotiation of difference between two or more viewpoints that are rooted in emotion rather than language, with the possibility that if the moods of the individuals change, so will their moral evaluations? This does not sit at all comfortably with the overarching moral claims that also appear in the novel.

Shortly after the dinner we have the famous passage about Levin and Kitty's cryptographic avowals with chalk on baize. These are made possible by an emotional, psychological, and/or spiritual harmony of such sensitivity that it could as well be mystical or telepathic, which makes it into a variant of the principle that Levin and Kitty had just formulated—agreement is a function of a priori sympathy. The scene with chalk also captures graphically the two characters' isolation from the other guests, none of whom could possibly decipher the codes they use, as Prince Shcherbatsky's question to them implies—"Playing *secrétaire?*" Even the reader is excluded from understanding what Kitty and Levin write until they decode it; and the final stage of their communication is actually only summarized for the reader rather than being given directly (398, IV.13). Nevertheless, despite the anarchical conception of language implied in this scene, it is still marked positively.

Levin's isolation from others continues for the next fourteen hours (the time he has to wait until he can ask officially for Kitty's hand), despite his paradoxical urge "to be with and talk to someone" (398, IV.14). Although he would have been happy to spend the evening with Stiva, because he believes that Stiva understands his euphoric state, Levin resents Dolly's hint at congratulating him because "*She could not understand* how lofty and *inaccessible* to her it all was, and she should not have dared to *mention* it" (398, IV.14, emphasis added). Levin next attaches himself to his halfbrother, Koznyshev, who is on his way to a meeting, but then actually tries to thwart physically Koznyshev's attempt to say something congratulatory, because it was "such a simple, such a low phrase, so out of harmony with his feeling" (399, IV.14).

Levin's internal self-sufficiency—or blindness to everything except his own joy—is such that at the meeting he finds everything wonderful and everyone full of kindness and loving feelings toward himself. It is significant that in this instance the narrator takes pains to underscore, via both gentle irony and humor at Levin's expense, the divergence between Levin's reactions and what actually takes place, as when he describes the secretary reading minutes that "he evidently did not understand himself" but that Levin interprets as showing that he is "a sweet, kind, and nice man. . . . It could be seen from the way he became confused and embarrassed as he read the minutes." Levin also *redefines* the debates he hears in a way that denies them any inherent value or interest: he "saw clearly that neither those allotted sums nor the pipes existed" (400, IV.14). Throughout this scene, the narrator's remarks show that Levin was being far too generous in his views (which says a lot about his character), but since he does not realize this, the difference between his views and "reality" is, of course, lost on him. Our position in relation to what occurs in this scene is ambiguous: on the one hand, we can see through Levin's amorous haze to the contentious nature of the meeting; on the other, Levin's euphoria is amusing, touching, and attractive, especially in comparison to the apparently petty behavior he misperceives.

After the meeting, Levin goes to visit the Sviyazhskys, whom he sees as especially sweet and sensitive toward him. In fact, as the narrator explains, Levin "was boring them terribly," and Sviyazhsky has no idea what had gotten into him. Levin also projects his charitable and loving feelings without any differentiation onto a servant in his hotel who, in the narrator's sarcastic description, was "obviously infected by Levin's rapture, just as people get infected by yawning" (401, IV.14); a somber gambler; and a concatenation of children, pigeons, and freshly baked rolls that he happens to glimpse on the street. The narrator characterizes the latter epiphanic event as something that Levin "afterwards never saw again" (403, IV.15), which underscores not only its uniqueness but also Levin's later isolation from part of his own past.[23]

The radical privacy of Levin's vision of the world is such that the narrator later characterizes it as a "state of madness" leading Levin to imagine that "he and his happiness constituted the chief and only goal of all that existed" (437, V.1). In a related vein, Levin is also moved to overinterpret everything, as when the Shcherbatsky doorman asks him to leave his hat, and Levin concludes, "that must have meant something" (404, IV.15). (Can this instance of Tolstoyan humor be a warning to the reader as well?) In this regard, Levin's joy is a striking contrast to Anna's despair just before her suicide, when she sees everyone and everything in the darkest and most conflicted terms. In both cases, the reader is likely to conclude that things could not really be quite as positive or as negative as each character sees them (even though in Anna's case the narrator does not intrude with "objective" descriptions the way he does with Levin). But given the reality of each character's frame of mind or the convincing palpability of the causes of their emotions, it also seems reductive to claim that each is simply wrong.

Although Levin is in love with Kitty and not with humankind in general, can the fact that he projects his loving attitude onto all and sundry be read in terms of the Pauline edict to behave kindly toward everyone, including evildoers? In other words, is it possible that Levin is a kind of fictional test of an ideal form of Christian behavior? If so, then the only plausible conclusion is new doubt about the compatibility of Saint Paul's teachings with Tolstoy's conception of human nature (see also *12.6*). By projecting only loving kindness, Levin does manage to engender similar positive feelings in several characters. But for the most part he cannot see others as they really are (assuming for the sake of argument that this may be possible in the novel, which is not at all clear) and cannot respond to their real needs. Thus, if anything, his behavior is a *parody* of Saint Paul's teachings and undermines them. This conclusion also raises questions about Levin's resolve in the novel's final pages to embrace the "law of goodness" that he believes is God's lesson to humankind. Moreover, his inability to act on this belief echoes his de facto isolation from everyone on the eve of his betrothal.

An additional facet of Levin's self-centered bliss is his passivity. He leaves it to others to make all the arrangements for his marriage, "knowing that it would all be wonderful" (437, V.1). This too could be read as a parody of Saint Paul, because it forestalls any possibility of social amelioration through active love, which is one of the implied aims of his teaching. Levin's happy resignation also foreshadows his later claim that his marriage to Kitty is "predestined" (see *17.2*), which is at odds with the freedom implicit in ethical behavior. No reader of *War and Peace* can forget the emphasis Tolstoy placed on "wise passivity" as a distinguishing characteristic of several important characters who live in harmony with providential design, including Kutuzov, Princess Marya, Platon Karataev, and, at times, Pierre.

On the eve of the wedding, Levin continues to see Kitty exclusively in personal terms, so that although "[e]veryone said she had been looking very poorly over the last few days . . . Levin did not find it so" (449, V.4). Now, this might seem to be a completely normal and familiar state of affairs for a man who is in love with his fiancée. But just when the reader may be tempted to understand Levin's reaction as no more than that, the narrator destabilizes this conclusion. During the ceremony, Levin is struck by the depth of some of the words the priest reads, looks into Kitty's eyes, and "by the look in those eyes . . . concludes that she understood [the words] as he did." Then the narrator adds: "But that was not true [nepravda]; she had almost no understanding of the words of the service and did not even listen during the betrothal." Kitty focuses instead on the vast change occurring in her life and on her "total, insuperable indifference to her entire past: to things, to habits, to people who had loved and still loved her, to her mother, who was upset by her indifference" (452–53, V.4). Kitty's "indifference," which troubles her, is of course the other side of her new love for Levin, which eclipses everything that had been important for her previously. But another implication of the passage is that despite Levin and Kitty's love for each other, and despite his feeling genuinely united to her via the ritual of marriage, he is also still unaware of what the event means to her on an essential level of her being and continues to view her in his own terms.

Nevertheless, the narrator describes the strength of the union between Kitty and Levin in terms suggesting that their individual psychic states may reflect a spiritual dimension of existence. When Levin quarrels with Kitty a few months after their wedding, he experiences a painful sense of "being split" that shows him "not only that she was close to him, but that he no longer knew where she ended and he began" (482, V.14). In addition to indicating that individual isolation is obviously not absolute, this passage also evokes Aristophanes' "myth of the androgyne" in Plato's *Symposium,* a text to which Levin himself refers during his dinner with Stiva (42, I.11).[24] In the context of the entire dialogue, Aristophanes' story of the two halves of an individual seeking each other in order to reconstitute a primal wholeness can be interpreted as a variant of the metaphysical longing that characterizes love in the *Symposium* in general. Tolstoy's description of how Kitty approaches Levin when he arrives to ask for her hand evokes these Platonic associations as well: "there came the sound of quick, quick, light steps over the parquet, and his happiness, his life, he himself—better than his own self, that which he had sought and desired for so long—was quickly approaching him. She did not walk but by some invisible force rushed towards him" (404, IV.15). Levin's sense of "being split" can also be associated with additional aspects of the novel's Platonism (see *9.1, 17*). (As we have already seen, Levin's perception of Kitty when she gives birth is intensely private and resembles a mystical experience *[9.2]*.)

However, what Tolstoy grants Levin with one hand he takes away with the other. Several months after the wedding, Levin feels both "flooded with the bright light of happiness" and annoyed with his "shameful, pampered, Capuan" existence (483, 485, V.15).[25] He blames the latter on Kitty, or, as he puts it, on her "upbringing." He thinks that she has no real interest in his work and is concerned only with her clothes and her embroidery. In one of his universalizing statements, the narrator acknowledges that such scapegoating is a common human practice but then still intrudes to correct Levin:

he did not yet understand that she was preparing for the period of activity which was to come for her, when she would be at one and the same time the wife of her husband, the mistress of the house, and would bear, nurse and raise her children. He did not understand that she knew it intuitively and, while preparing for this awesome task, did not reproach herself for the moments of insouciance and the happiness of love that she enjoyed now, while cheerfully building her future nest. (486, V.15)

Levin's blindness is again paradoxical, because he may be part of what he does not see. In the same way that his bliss on the eve of the wedding leads him to a passivity that may be a form of inadvertent wisdom about the forces that rule over humankind, Kitty's seemingly self-centered ignoring of everything but her moments of "insouciance" and "love" turns out to be part of a vast, instinctual, natural pattern of behavior culminating, ideally, in happy family life. Moreover, the impersonal nature of her behavior, which arises out of her spontaneously, implies female essentialism, a topic to which I will return *(16)*.

The final mention of Levin's relations to Kitty is in the novel's last paragraph, where he imagines how his life will be changed forever because of the new faith that he has discovered. This important passage can be approached from various perspectives (see *13.4.4*). For the present, suffice it to note that at this crucial juncture in his life Levin becomes fully conscious of the extent to which his relativized perceptions of the world characterize even his dealings with Kitty, the person who is closest of all to him: "there will be the same wall between my soul's holy of holies and other people, *even my wife*, I'll accuse her in the same way of my own fear and then regret it" (817, VIII.19, emphasis added).[26]

13.4.2. Levin and His Brothers

To a greater extent than with Kitty, Levin's isolating and self-centered perceptions punctuate and at times dominate his relations with all the other characters in the novel.[27] When Kitty rejects his offer of marriage, he feels unhappy with himself and, as if to compensate, latches onto the idea of visiting his brother Nikolai, whom he has not seen for three years (see also *15.2*). At first, Levin is struck by the difference between how his brother actually appears and how he had imagined him (86, I.24), which suggests that on a basic level he is capable of seeing people directly or at least with reduced mediation. But then his past impressions of Nikolai's difficult character flood back; and when Nikolai starts to describe a new venture he has begun, Levin "was almost not listening." Even as he feels more and more sorry for his brother, Levin is still "unable to make himself listen to what his brother was telling him about the association" (88, I.25). Nevertheless, a form of deeper understanding may be intercalated with this inattention. As the narrator explains, Levin interprets Nikolai's venture as "only an anchor" that his brother hopes will save him from "despising himself"; perhaps Levin's interpretation is correct, but we cannot be sure.

Other moments of shared understanding occur between the brothers during this meeting as well, but the dominant mood is distance. Levin agrees with Nikolai's criticisms of social institutions but still finds them "disagreeable . . . coming from his brother's mouth" (91, I.25). Levin seeks out Nikolai in the first place because he feels guilty for having neglected him, because he values the rare quality of his brother's misunderstood "heart," and because he believes that despite all his mistakes, Nikolai always wanted "to be good." (At the same time, and paradoxically, Levin thinks of his brother as trapped in his own personality, which makes Nikolai's views inevitably relativized: "He was not to blame for having been born with an irrepressible character and a mind somehow constrained.") Because of this, Levin wants to "tell him everything . . . [to] make him tell everything . . . [and to] show him that I love him and therefore understand him" (85, I.24). In light of these desires, Levin's inability to relate to his brother in terms of the latter's *actual, current* interests and needs is a betrayal of Levin's own ethical imperative and a sign of his impotence before Nikolai's mortal illness, which is what actually defines him in the deepest sense in the scenes in question.[28]

Later in the novel, Nikolai reacts to Levin in a similar way, thus completing the symmetry of the brothers' alienation. When Levin describes his activities on his estate, Nikolai listens without enthusiasm because he is "obviously . . . not interested" (347, III.31). He also simply rejects Levin's ideas, which he "deliberately" confuses with communism, as the narrator characterizes it (350, III.32). Although we are told that *in principle* the two brothers could understand each other perfectly and even wordlessly because they are so familiar with each other, the only thing they *actually* think of is "Nikolai's illness and closeness to death," which, in fact, prevents them from speaking frankly about anything (347, III.31).

The brothers' isolation from each other culminates in the scenes of Nikolai's death. There is no rapprochement between them: all that Levin or anyone else wants is for Nikolai to finally die; by contrast, the dying man alone does "not express this feeling" (502, V.20). And when Nikolai does die, Levin is left pondering the impenetrable mystery of what has happened to him. At this point, Kitty's role in Levin's life becomes crucial, because her presence by his side is the only thing that saves him from despair. But although she instills a need to live and to love in him, it is paradoxical (albeit consistent with the novel's theme of alienation) that her effect on Levin is juxtaposed with his discovering that she is pregnant, which "before his eyes" is another mystery "equally unfathomed." Thus, Levin's communion with his wife is also simultaneously incomprehension on an especially basic level of existence (505, V.20).

Levin's relations with his half-brother, Sergei Koznyshev, are no different. We first meet him when Levin comes to Moscow and looks forward to asking the older man's advice about marrying Kitty. But he never gets a chance to discuss this central issue in his life. First, a conversation that Koznyshev is having with a visiting professor about the relation between consciousness and sensory data interferes. Even when Levin asks a question about this topic from the perspective of his growing concern with ultimate philosophical issues, he is rebuffed by both (see *13.1*). His immediate reaction is to stop listening to what they are talking about, despite the fact that the subject interests him (and is relevant to the novel's other themes). When Levin is finally alone with Koznyshev, the latter asks him about his farming, but Levin realizes that this does not really interest his older brother and that the question was "only a concession to him." This further constrains Levin, as a result of which he does not even mention what really concerns him: "He felt that his brother would not look upon it as he would have wished" (25, I.7). Instead, Koznyshev raises his own pet topic—the *zemstvo*, which is a new form of rural administration. Levin's reaction to this completes the symmetry of isolation that characterizes the deeper relations between these two brothers (who maintain appropriate filial relations on more superficial levels of behavior): Levin responds that he does not know how the *zemstvo* in his district is progressing and that he simply cannot bring himself to participate in it, which upsets Koznyshev (26, I.8). The scene ends when both are distracted by their discussion of Nikolai's reappearance, but, typically, their reactions to him also differ considerably.

The next time they meet is in the country, when Koznyshev comes to spend some time on Levin's estate. Levin is very pleased by the visit, but, "despite his love and respect for Sergei Ivanovich, [he] felt awkward in the country with his brother" (237, III.1). The reason is their vastly different attitudes toward rural life and the peasantry. Levin views both in a flexible and multidimensional manner, whereas Koznyshev sees them in terms of a value-laden, binary contrast with urban life. The narrator then launches into a somewhat paradoxical analysis of the relations between the two men. He describes the genuine affection that links them and the admiration each has for some of the other's character traits. But he also focuses on how they see each other as lacking something essential, which, in fact, proves to be nothing less than the dominant trait in each personality. Thus, Koznyshev thinks Levin has a good heart but that his mind is "subject to momentary impressions and therefore filled with contradictions" (238, III.1). And although Levin admires Koznyshev as an intellectual with lofty ideals and a social conscience, he sees these not as "a virtue but, on the contrary, a lack of something . . . a lack of life force" (239, III.1).

The issue here is not that Tolstoy has created characters who are relatives and have mixed feelings about each other. There is obviously no reason to expect all fictional characters to have purely monochromatic relations (although these are certainly possible and can be found even in Tolstoy). Rather, it is that these two characters' personalities are conceived in such a way that they *cannot* get out of their own perspectives no matter what anyone says to them. During his visit, Koznyshev again raises the topic of the district's administration and berates Levin for not being involved in it. Levin is so uninterested in the entire matter that "he hardly entered into what his brother was saying," and shifts his attention to trying to make out something he notices in the distance, a reaction that Koznyshev registers and that obviously irritates him (243, III.3). Levin refocuses on Koznyshev only when the latter accuses him of having insufficient "self-esteem." Why would this remark cut Levin to the quick? Because it touches on Levin's dominant motivation in everything that he does. As he proclaims heatedly, "I think that the motive force of all our actions is, after all, personal happiness" (245, III.3). Tolstoy has Levin repeat this idea forcefully and in response to every argument that Koznyshev uses two more times in the span of one page: "I will always defend with all my might those rights that . . . touch on my interests"; "I think . . . that no activity can be solid unless it's based on personal interest" (246, III.3).

These are very significant claims in the world of this novel. They bear not only on the main issue of personal happiness that undergirds the novel's other main plotline—Anna's search for love with Vronsky—but also on the entire issue of ethics and divinely sanctioned and enforced morality. In this scene with Levin, Koznyshev argues consistently from the position of a universal ethical imperative, according to which one must want for others what one considers good for oneself. This is in basic accord with the Christian teaching implied by the novel's epigraph and echoes its secularized variant in the Kantian categorical imperative (see *1*). But none of this has any significant effect on Levin, who is marked positively in the novel, whereas Koznyshev is tarnished by an effete sterility.

Levin's views are also a striking contrast to Tolstoy's own involvement while working on *Anna Karenina* with writing primers, engaging in polemics on educational policy, teaching, and establishing schools for peasants.[29] Even when Koznyshev objects that it was not personal interest that moved people to work for the emancipation of the serfs, Levin insists, "There *was* a personal interest. We wanted to throw off the yoke that oppressed us and all good people" (245, III.3, emphasis added). Thus Levin is willing to see himself as supporting a moral principle shared by others, but only via a kind of centripetal process: the principle has to be rooted in himself, and only then does he apply it to anyone else. Although he feels that he has been intellectually bested during the argument with his half-brother, Levin senses that Koznyshev might also not have understood him fully. Levin speculates that this might have occurred because he had not been sufficiently clear or, what is even more telling, because his brother *could not* or *did not want to* understand him. Most important, however, is Levin's final reaction to the discussion and its aftermath: "But he did not go deeper into these thoughts and, without objecting to his brother, began thinking about a completely different matter, a personal one for him" (247, III.3). This proves to be the pleasure he takes in mowing with the peasants, his newly discovered *Arbeitskur* for anger or irritation.

Later in the novel, Levin differs from his brother on two additional matters. He is quite incapable of understanding the procedures or the ostensible significance of the noblemen's provincial elections, which Koznyshev and many others think are a highly significant event and which the narrator describes in a tone of nearly Gogolian satire (e.g., 649, VI.27; 651, VI.28). The varied reactions of characters in these scenes to the results of the elections, which the reader is also hard-pressed to understand in any consistent way because of the "defamiliarized" style of narration that Tolstoy employs and that is linked to Levin's viewpoint, help to buttress Levin's own disorientation. Furthermore, despite the fact that there are parties and cliques at the elections and that several ballots are cast and results obtained, all of which implies that groups of individuals can achieve shared goals, most of this "harmony" takes place on the margins of the scenes, out of Levin's direct field of vision, whose confused and incomprehending perspective dominates (see *14*).

Similarly, near the novel's end, Levin rejects the Pan-Slavist movement onto which Koznyshev has begun to lavish his energies and does so for the same reason that is always paramount for him: he personally does not feel any enthusiasm for the movement, even though his half-brother presents it as having widespread popular support. Levin also typically concludes that not only will it be impossible for him to persuade his brother or their mutual friend, Katavasov, that they are misguided in their enthusiasm, "still less did he find it possible for himself to agree with them" (809, VIII.16). This theme culminates in a statement that can only be designated as solipsistic:

"And all those considerations about the meaning of the Slavic element in world history seemed so insignificant to him compared with what was happening in his soul that he instantly forgot it all and was transported into the same mood he had been in that morning" (813, VIII.18).[30]

13.4.3. Levin and Others

Levin's relations with other important characters are similar. His friendship with Stiva dates from their early youth, and he seeks out Stiva on the eve of proposing to Kitty for his advice and moral support. Their dinner at a restaurant begins on a note of warm companionship. But when Levin mentions Kitty, Stiva introduces the matter of Vronsky's competition and then shifts to his own dalliances. Thus, although Stiva wishes Levin well and tries to advise him, the discussion does not go the way Levin would have liked. Levin's reaction is typical: he "sighed and gave no answer. He was thinking of his own things and not listening to Oblonsky" (42, I.11). For his part, Stiva knows well "this extreme estrangement instead of closeness that may come after dinner" and also knows how to rectify it by quickly calling for the bill.[31]

Some months later, Stiva visits Levin when he comes to the country to sell some of his wife's property. Levin is delighted to have his company, and the narrator describes briefly how Levin pours out his various thoughts, reactions, and plans to Stiva, all of which have accumulated during his solitary life on his estate. We are also told that Levin values especially highly Stiva's ability to understand everything on the basis of a hint, as well as his delicacy and tact in not raising the painful subject of Kitty. But this genuine harmony between the two is also short-lived. When Levin asks Stiva how his affairs are going, Stiva "understand[s] Levin's question in his own way" and starts to speak of his illicit affairs. He tries to share with Levin his enthusiasm for the "Ossianic" type of woman and for the endless variety of female types, but "Levin listened silently and . . . was simply unable to get inside his friend's soul and understand his feelings" (162, II.14). Following this, we witness detailed scenes of Levin's annoyance with Stiva's sale of a forest to the merchant Ryabinin and Levin's implicitly insulting description of Stiva's style of life and method of gaining a livelihood.

Stiva's reaction to Levin is comparably one-sided. He in effect ignores the *meaning* of what Levin says and focuses instead on his *vehemence* as an appealing and entertaining form of liveliness. There is no permanent damage, of course, and the scenes conclude with the comment that Levin comes to regret his behavior and seeks to reestablish harmonious relations with his old friend (173, II.17). Nevertheless, even though Stiva will later play a decisive role in bringing Kitty and Levin together, will help with arrangements for the wedding, and will be Levin's best man, on a deeper level the two remain distant from each other because, as we have been told at the beginning of the novel, "in his heart" each "despised" the other's life and thought that "the life he led was the only real life, and the one his friend led was a mere illusion" (17, I.5).

Some of Levin's judgments along these lines appear to be the products of his mood or hidden aim during a given argument, which relativizes them even more. In a conversation with Stiva when he comes to visit, Levin attempts to determine the proper correlation between wealth and labor, something that clearly bears on how each sees his own livelihood. Levin is annoyed by Stiva's praise for a very rich "railway magnate" and claims that "any acquisition that does not correspond to the labor expended is dishonest." But when Stiva presses the matter and asks who is to determine the correspondence, Levin feels that he is unable "to draw a clear line between honest and dishonest" (587, VI.11). The actual reason behind Levin's argument is revealed by the narrator: it is the "secret antagonism" between Levin and Stiva regarding "whose life was set up better" because they are now married to sisters (588, VI.11).

Stiva's entire visit is marred by the fact that he brings Vasenka Veslovsky with him rather than the old Prince Shcherbatsky, which disappoints Levin, and by Veslovsky's flirtatious attitude toward Kitty, which makes Levin jealous. The result is a characteristic mood shift: "Levin, who a minute ago had been in the merriest spirits, now looked darkly at everyone and did not like anything" (569, VI.6). One may ask, So what? Surely this is a familiar and plausible reaction of the kind that any reader of the novel would also have experienced in some form. Yes, of course. But Levin elevates his spontaneous and personal reactions to a fixed principle, which, were it applied by others in similar ways, would undermine any social unit larger than the family and lead to anarchy. This is the direct implication of Levin's behavior after returning from the hunt, when he unceremoniously throws Vasenka off the estate. Dolly is shocked at the thought that Levin would even consider behaving so rudely; Stiva and Princess Shcherbatsky are indignant when he does; and Levin also feels that he is completely ridiculous, guilty, and disgraced according to the norms of polite society. Nevertheless, he persists in seeing himself as the sole arbiter of all value and meaning and, in response to asking "himself how he would act another time," replies that "he would do exactly the same thing" (604, VI.15).

Levin's moral absolutism from his own perspective is absolute moral relativism from an outside point of view.

Another example of Levin's moral relativism that results from a shift in his point of view appears in the description of his visit to Dolly's estate. When he first sees her surrounded by her children, she seems to him an embodiment of the future family happiness that he yearns for himself (266, III.9). But after she touches on his unsuccessful courtship of Kitty, a reminiscence that Levin still finds painful, his mood changes, and everything in Dolly's household, including how she is raising her children, now seems unappealingly artificial (271, III.10). Is the reader to conclude that Levin's new reaction is only a temporary delusion? One could indeed argue that this is the case, given that Dolly and her children are apparently welcome to spend considerable time living on his estate after he marries Kitty. But in the context of Levin's numerous other mood shifts and consequent reevaluations of attitudes, as well as his principled defense of the personal nature of value, it is also difficult to dismiss his negative view of Dolly's life simply as an aberration.

In fact, one could argue that Levin's negative reaction to Dolly's requiring her children to speak French in this scene reflects one of the novel's major preoccupations, which is to pillory the artificiality and falsehood of modern urban culture. In this particular instance, therefore, Levin's seemingly idiosyncratic reaction can be seen as part of a supraindividual theme, which raises the possibility that there may be an overarching system of meaning in the novel that incorporates the seemingly anarchic tendencies of individuals. However, another, antithetical interpretation is also possible, which returns us to Levin's mood change being a purely personal event. The narrator tells us something about Dolly that Levin does not even suspect: she had thought through the situation he finds objectionable some "twenty times" and had concluded that she has no choice but to teach her children French in a way that risks introducing insincerity into their lives. Dolly is generally marked positively in the novel, and her decision is a pragmatic concession to the demands of contemporary aristocratic culture. This makes it difficult to judge her in simple moral terms, such as seeing all urban life as artificial.

When he is living in Moscow during Kitty's confinement, Levin meets the celebrated thinker "Petr Ivanovich Metrov." At first, both are interested in each other's ideas, but soon after they actually start to converse, it turns out that no dialogue (in any sense, including Bakhtin's), indeed, no communication, between them is possible. When Metrov asks a question that implies his own position on a matter, Levin ignores it in order to finish explaining his own thought. Metrov then interrupts, and, "not letting Levin finish his thought, . . . began explaining to him the particularity of his own theory. . . . What the particularity of his theory was Levin did not understand, because he did not bother to understand" (679, VII.3). Levin then elevates this specific experience into another general principle: "It was now clear to him that, while Metrov's thought might be important, his own thoughts were also important; these thoughts might be clarified and lead to something *only if each of them worked separately in his chosen way, and nothing could come of communicating these thoughts to each other*" (681, VII.3, emphasis added; note the a priori antidialogic argument).

Levin's idea can be interpreted in antithetical ways. His emphasis on solitary effort and silence rather than even Bakhtinian "monologism" suggests a worldview that is solipsistic and anarchical. However, his remark that solitary effort can "lead to something" leaves open a small loophole for the possibility that seemingly disjointed efforts may turn out to be orchestrated in some mysterious way that precludes chaos. In short, private effort may be an unwitting part of a larger design. This idea is also implied by the epigraph and by the references to fate in the novel (see *17;* this is also a fundamental feature of the worldview in *War and Peace*).

Levin's view of his estate seems as changeable as his view of people. When he abandons the idea of marrying a peasant girl and decides that he loves only Kitty, he also suddenly develops a "loathing" for farming and loses "all interest" in it. Part of the reason appears to be the book he is writing, which helps him to realize, as the narrator describes it, that all his efforts are contrary to the natural inclinations of the peasants. But although this might seem to be an objective reason, the narrator suggests that Levin's newly soured outlook may actually have more to do with his subjective state: "Despite excellent crops, there had never been, *or at least it seemed to him that there had never been,* so many failures and so much animosity between him and the muzhiks as that year" (321, III.24, emphasis added). The same relativization emerges at greater length in the passages that follow, in which, on the one hand, the narrator lists all the things in which Levin should take pleasure: "The herds of improved cows, the same as Pava, the earth all ploughed and fertilized, the nine equal fields planted round with willows, the three hundred acres of deeply ploughed-under dung, the seed drills, and so on." On the other hand, Levin cannot take pleasure in these achievements because they are the result of his attempt to force his ideas and methods onto a resisting peasantry. He concludes that as a result of the ensuing struggle, "beautiful machines, beautiful cattle and soil were ruined for nothing . . . energy [was] completely wasted . . . the goal of his energy was a most unworthy one" (321, III.24).

Which of these two descriptions of Levin's estate is correct? It seems unreasonable to interpret the list of achievements in which Levin should take pleasure as a purely hypothetical "wish list," because we are told that Levin would not have minded these achievements if only they had been the result of his labor alone or that of like-minded friends. This clearly supports the idea that his struggle with the peasants led to the achievements, which returns us to the crux of the problem—are things going well or badly on the estate? There does not seem to be any way to resolve this issue without taking a particular viewpoint into account, which is another way of saying that Levin's evaluation of the estate's status is entirely relativized.

13.4.4. Levin's Faith

The relation between personal and collective truths is also central to the novel's concluding chapters, which consist largely of an uneasy juxtaposition of moral certainty and extreme relativism that echoes a number of important moments earlier in the text. Because Levin's discovery of his faith functions as a coda to the entire work, it is worth examining these pages in some detail (see also *15.2*).

Levin experiences a personal crisis when his brother Nikolai dies. He tries to view this event through the lens of the materialistic and scientific concepts that replaced the religious faith of his youth but discovers that he is completely powerless to understand death or the purpose of life in general (785–86, VIII.8). As the narrator puts it, via a major hermeneutic index that ridicules Levin's attempt to deal with the ultimate questions from a nonreligious point of view, "He was in the position of a man looking for food in a toymaker's or a gunsmith's shop" (786, VIII.8).

Levin's honesty with regard to himself leads him onto the horns of a dilemma. He is greatly troubled by the fact that although most of the people in his circle have also replaced religious faith with scientism, they are apparently not bothered in the least by this in the way that he is. At the same time, Levin is also struck by the fact that all the people he likes and who are close to him are believers: his father-in-law, his brother-in-law, his half-brother, his wife, "all the women," and "ninety-nine hundredths of all the Russian people" (787, VIII.8). Levin himself embodies these irreconcilable views in a way that underscores the inescapability of relativism. He recalls that he prayed during Kitty's labor and that he was a believer at the time, but subsequently he could not return to the same state of mind and could not find room for faith in his life. He concludes that he has experienced two distinct truths and cannot choose between them:

> He could not admit that he had known the truth then and was now mistaken, because as soon as he began to think calmly about it, the whole thing fell to pieces; nor could he admit that he had been mistaken then, because he cherished his state of soul of that time, and by admitting that it had been due to weakness he would have profaned those moments. He was in painful discord with himself and strained all the forces of his soul to get out of it. (787, VIII.8)[32]

All of Levin's attempts to find answers to this quandary in nonmaterialist philosophers from Plato and Schopenhauer to the Russian religious thinker Aleksei Khomiakov come to nothing, and he is left with the despairing, materialist self-image of being merely an ephemeral "bubble" in the vastness of time, matter, and space (788, VIII.9). In fact, Levin's quandary is so acute that he comes close to suicide several times (789, VIII.9). (This is also a "situation rhyme" with Anna and Vronsky, of course, even though Levin's motivation is different from theirs.)

This is the context in which the narrator makes one of his loudest intrusions into the text to correct what he labels as his character's mistake. He describes Levin's conclusion as "a tormenting untruth, but it was the sole, the latest result of age-long labours of human thought in that direction" (789, VIII.9). Following this, however, the narrator gradually merges his consciousness with Levin's in a way that makes it difficult to tell where one begins and the other ends. This is important, because there is rhetorical continuity among the three different syntactic units that constitute the passage: the narrator's condemnation of Levin's "bubble" image, the judgment that this image is not merely false but the "cruel mockery of some evil power," and the conclusion that the way to escape this power is through suicide (788–89, VIII.9). Given what the narrator says later in the text, it is highly unlikely that he is advocating suicide here rather than simply following Levin's destructive thought processes. Because these are labeled as erroneous, it is also unlikely that a reified evil is active in the world. In fact, several pages later, after Levin's spiritual peripety has begun, his idea that life may be "the wicked mockery of some devil" is presented as a false view that he overcomes together with his thoughts of suicide (796–97, VIII.12). However, Levin's later comment that the way philosophers try to understand the meaning of life is "strange and unnatural to [man]" leaves open the possibility that they are subject to some kind of negative influence that is extraneous or alien to human beings (798, VIII.13). The close identification of the narrator's voice with Levin's erroneous thoughts also suggests a degree of familiarity if not complicity with them. This lends a degree of narrative support to Levin's ambivalence.

Levin resolves the opposition between reason and faith by embracing the latter. This is in keeping with the novel's overall emphasis on the self as the arbiter of meaning and value. Levin neither changes how he lives nor learns something new from someone else, although the catalyst for his spiritual rebirth is a chance comment made by one peasant about another, a tellingly named "Platon" who "lives for his soul" and "remembers God" (794, VIII.11). (This recalls Platon Karataev in *War and Peace,* of course, but with the important difference that no mentor figure appears on the pages of *Anna Karenina* to provide unequivocal spiritual guidance through word and example; the remark by Levin's Platon also echoes Saint Paul in Romans 8:5: "For they that are after the flesh do mind the things of the flesh; but they that are after the Spirit, the things of the Spirit.") Instead, Levin suddenly recognizes and accepts an unwavering, ingrained, nonrational essence in himself that he now believes has been his unacknowledged primary characterological motivation throughout his life: the peasant's remark causes "vague but important thoughts [to] burst *from some locked-up place* . . . blinding him with their light" and "thoughts which *had never ceased to occupy him*" to unite "into one" (794–95, VIII.11–12, emphasis added). As a result, Levin sheds the erroneous thoughts that had misled him and "discovers" that he has returned to his true self.[33] (There are resonant parallels here with the "unwrapping" that Mikhailov carries out in his art, with Kitty's related appearance during labor, and with the essentialist claims that the narrator and Levin make about women and peasants. There is also an echo of the equivocal candle that illuminates Anna's life and then goes out when she dies [see *8.2, 9.1, 9.2, 16.2, 16.4*].)

Levin realizes what his true self actually is when he focuses on how his life is determined by the various obligations he has as a landlord and family man.[34] He understands that when he acts in the capacities required of him and *does not think* about the implications of what he is doing or about whatever has *no personal connection* to him, everything goes well in practical terms. He also "constantly [feels] in his soul the presence of an infallible judge" who tells him what is good and what is bad (791, VIII.10). Whether or not this can really be called "ethics" is questionable, however, because Levin's behavior is entirely unreflecting. He himself has no idea if his actions are good or bad and, in fact, even avoids talking or thinking about this.

That Levin's behavior may actually be *amoral* is also suggested earlier in the novel in the scene when Agafya Mikhailovna, his housekeeper, asks why he concerns himself with the peasants so much. In response, Levin insists that he is concerned only with his own interests. The paradoxical connection between this moment and Levin's discovery of faith is implied by the similarity between what Agafya Mikhailovna says, "It's a known fact, a man had best think of his own soul" (345, III.30), and the remark of the peasant who speaks of the exemplary Platon: "He lives for the soul. He remembers God."[35] The only hint that Levin may have any personal volition, which would seem to be the necessary ground for genuinely ethical behavior, is that he *senses* immediately if he has acted in some way that he should not have, which implies that he may have been free to err (791, VIII.10). But since he eschews reflecting about how he should act, his retroactive sense of error can also be interpreted as indicating that he is not so much free to *choose* his behavior as simply to *understand* it according to ethical criteria that he does *not control.* All of this constitutes a highly problematic echo of the idea of divine judgment that is implied by the novel's epigraph or of Anna's behavior.

However, the range of Levin's actions seems to be so circumscribed that his freedom to act badly can also be seen as moot. In fact, he cannot even "imagine" the kind of "beastly being" he would be if he were not motivated by the unwitting faith and knowledge of right and wrong that he has within him (797, VIII.12). Kitty's remarks about Levin confirm his impression of himself. When he is in the midst of his crisis, she sees that he is troubled by his lack of faith. But she dismisses it, because she believes that she knows what he is really like, which means that she is both deeply attached to him and paradoxically distant from the despair that defines him at this moment: "What kind of unbeliever is he? With his heart, with that fear of upsetting anyone, even a child! Everything for others, nothing for himself" (785, VIII.7).

The accuracy of Kitty's judgment can be evaluated in opposite and irreconcilable ways. In light of such different aspects of Levin's behavior as his recent suicidal urges, his insistence that he alone must decide what is good, and his willingness to be severe toward peasants when the needs of his estate warrant it, Kitty's view of him could be seen as an idealizing projection that misses more than it illuminates (like Anna's view of Vronsky [see *13.5.3*]). From this point of view, Levin's "goodness" is illusory. But Kitty's judgment can also be interpreted as prescient because it anticipates Levin's imminent discovery of faith and reflects the sense of moral compulsion he feels in all his actions as well as his earlier inclination toward spiritual issues. The only way to combine the two views would be to conclude that Levin's faith may be self-deluding, which, as I will suggest, is a plausible interpretation for other reasons as well.

In any event, Kitty's intuition regarding Levin's faith can also be correlated with the sense he has of being influenced by some sort of spiritual powers, which can be taken as implying an additional limit on his freedom. At one point he stops thinking and "was as if only listening to the mysterious voices that spoke joyfully and anxiously about something among themselves." However, the implication of this remark changes immediately when he asks, "Can this be faith?" because this question in effect translates the voices from outside him into his own psyche, which is the only place that an individual's faith can, in fact, reside (800, VIII.13; see the similar reference to how Levin "never ceased joyfully *sensing* the fullness of his heart" [812, VIII.18, emphasis added]). This uncertainty about the actual locus of Levin's faith echoes the narrator's earlier critique of Karenin's and Countess Lydia Ivanovna's facile beliefs, with which it contrasts as well (see below and *12.3*), and also resurrects the entire vexed issue of the relation between universal and private truths.

The essence of the faith Levin rediscovers is a belief in God and in the law of goodness, by which he means acting charitably toward others without the expectation of personal gain or reward. Central to Levin's conception is that the knowledge of this law is not verbal, discursive, or rational (which parallels the novel's frequent positive evaluation of nonverbal communication and intuition) and that it is shared by millions of others (795, VIII.12). Knowledge of the law of goodness also appears to be characterized by determinism, which creates a paradoxical dissonance with its ethical content. In fact, Levin's successful resolution of his spiritual crisis can be seen as his replacing one form of determinism with another of a very different sort. When he repeats in his mind the scientific beliefs that he has abandoned, he refers to "an infinite development and struggle," which evokes Darwinian ideas (796, VIII.12). This is replaced by a knowledge that Levin characterizes as having been "given to me as it is to everyone, *given* because I could not take it from anywhere" (797, VIII.12). Levin thus identifies himself as one of a multitude of human beings who have been shaped by a providential gift—knowledge of "that power which not only gave me life in the past but is giving me life now." However, he also introduces a discordant note into his worldview when he concludes this statement by saying, "*I have freed myself* from deception, I have recognized the master" (796, VIII.12, emphasis added; my literal translation of "*Ia osvobodilsia* ot obmana, ia uznal khoziaina"). This is a somewhat ambivalent conception of the relation between the human and the divine, because although Levin still acknowledges a higher authority, his shift to an active voice introduces the possibility of *human* agency, which is at odds with his acquiescence to divine Providence in the rest of this passage. It seems plausible to correlate this shift in tone with Levin's tendency to rely on himself as the arbiter of value and meaning throughout the novel. As a result, the nature of his new faith becomes somewhat suspect, because it is possible to doubt the extent to which it has a basis in anything outside his own mind.[36]

Nevertheless, the dominant tone of this passage is still Levin's deference to divine authority. This conclusion is reinforced by the narrator's juxtaposition of Levin's thoughts with a description of how he lies on the ground and bends blades of grass to control and assist the movements of an insect (796, VIII.12). Here Tolstoy can be seen as rewriting in a positive key the idea expressed by the Earl of Gloucester in *King Lear* (4.1.36): "As flies to wanton boys, are we to th' gods, / They kill us for their sport." Unlike Shakespeare's gods, Tolstoy's God may be as beneficent toward human beings as Levin is to the insect. (At the same time, the fact that the bug flies away rather than follow the path arranged for it by Levin can be interpreted—if one wants to go that far—as an expression of individual volition, which again casts an ironic light on Levin's theodicy; so does Anna's fate, of course.) Similarly, the peasant beekeeper who responds to Levin's question about the justice of the war in the Balkans by saying that the tsar thinks for all his subjects is articulating a passive deference to a higher secular authority that is congruent with Levin's (807, VIII.15). Levin also finds support for his attitude in the Russian historical past by recalling how the ancient Slav tribes summoned the Varangians to rule over them (810, VIII.16).

Another problematic feature of Levin's faith is his certainty that it is shared by millions of other believers. Given the rarity of deep communion among individuals in *Anna Karenina*, one cannot help wondering how he knows. Among those who supposedly believe as he does, Levin mentions "sages and holy fools, children and old men" as well as "peasant[s] . . . Lvov . . . Kitty . . . beggars and tsars," all of whom "understand one and the same thing with certainty" (799–800, VIII.13). The reader is asked simply to accept this, because although Lvov's and Kitty's beliefs are mentioned in the novel, we do not know the details of their faith. By contrast, Karenin's and Countess Lydia Ivanovna's beliefs are discussed in detail and, with the exception of the relatively short period when Karenin forgives Anna and Vronsky, come up very short in the narrator's estimation. Levin's claim about the faith of peasants is also questionable, assuming that it should be measured by his criterion of the law of goodness, and even though a peasant's remark is the catalyst for his own spiritual rebirth. The peasants are quite prepared to cheat Levin when they can (273, III.11). They also respond initially to his new cooperative plans for his estate with taciturn distrust, not Christian charity or the law of goodness (339–41, III.29). Later, matters on the estate appear to go better, but not because the reader has been shown anything in the peasants' beliefs or behavior that supports Levin's conclusion about their faith. Consequently, we are left with Levin's personal if not solipsistic view of the matter. And what of Vronsky, Anna, Stiva, Koznyshev, Nikolai, Yashvin, Betsy, and most of the other characters for whom religious questions are matters of occasional social ritual or merely turns of phrase, as far as we can tell from what we see of them? Levin's reference to "tsars" is especially unconvincing, because even if he uses the term figuratively, the one glimpse of a member of the imperial family that we get in *Anna Karenina* is in connection with the openly licentious atmosphere surrounding Princess Betsy and Sappho Stolz (299, III.18). All we see of individuals close to the throne, such as Countess Lydia Ivanovna and Vronsky's older brother, who is well received at court despite his drunken and dissolute life (193, II.24), also hardly sheds a positive light on it.

Levin's reasons for suddenly believing in God also recall the narrator's critique of Karenin's faith. In effect, each character believes that God's truth lies in his heart and that he can determine the strength of his faith by himself. Levin is marked positively, of course, so the reader may be willing to suspend disbelief with regard to his faith more readily than for Karenin. But even if the relation between their faiths is ironic, it is hard to differentiate Karenin's complacency from Levin's certainty.[37] Perhaps what distinguishes their faiths is the difference between Levin's and Karenin's probity, intelligence, and sensitivity. Or perhaps Levin's ecstatic embrace of his faith redeems him in a way that Karenin's phlegmatic sentimentalism does not. Similarly, Koznyshev and Varenka are marked negatively by their relative lack of passion. As Saint John the Divine announces in Revelation 3:16: "So then because thou art lukewarm, and neither cold nor hot, I will spew thee out of my mouth."

However, if this is the case, then what does it say about how universally accessible true faith is? If an individual's character determines whether or not he will embrace faith in a pure or corrupt form, which recapitulates the novel's insistence on the self as arbiter of meaning and value, then what happens to the salvific and redemptive message of Saint Paul and Christianity in general? And what happens to freedom if character determines faith?

Levin's mentioning children among those who believe as he does causes even more problems because of the way he uses children in an elaborate simile to defend radical perspectivalism in matters of faith. He begins with a recollection of how Dolly's children misbehaved by playing with their food and how they responded to her rebukes with sullen distrust because all they felt was regret over not being able to continue an enjoyable pastime. Levin then proceeds to draw a remarkable equation—or hermeneutic index—between these children and the efforts that he and philosophers have made to understand the meaning of life through reason. He concludes that the misbehavior of children is like the erroneous thought processes of adults because both are in a sense "spoiled." The children know that their mother's scolding is merely a facet of her overarching love, and adults fall into error because they are "spiritually sated" in a beneficent and divinely sanctioned world (799, VIII.13). This leads Levin to the even more remarkable conclusion that there is no sin or error in his own misguided rationalism: "and even less than children scolded by their mother for their childish pranks do I feel that my childish refusal to let well enough alone is not to my credit" (799, VIII.13). (The Russian is actually somewhat unclear because of a double negative that also allows a reading opposite to the above: "i eshche menee, chem deti, kotorykh mat' branit za ikh detskie shalosti, ia chuvstvuiu, chto moi detskie popytki s zhiru besit'sia ne zachityvaiutsia mne," which means, literally, "even less than children who are rebuked for their childish mischief by their mother do I feel that my childish attempts to kick because I am filled do not count against me.") In other words, just as children cannot be held responsible for misbehaving, so cannot adults.

Levin had, in fact, partially anticipated this conclusion earlier in the novel when he dismissed Dolly's worries about two of her children's "vile inclinations," which were apparently some sort of sexual exploration carried out in the raspberry bushes, as simply a "prank" (601, VI.15). Because the imagery in these scenes is also echoed elsewhere in the novel, Levin's relativization of sin spreads as well. For example, in the scene of the horse race, the narrator equates Karenin's empty loquacity at a time when his wife's involvement with Vronsky should be absorbing all of his attention with the behavior of "a child who has hurt himself [and] jumps about in order to move his muscles and stifle the pain" (208, II.28). In light of Levin's later dismissals of adult error as meaningless childish behavior, what might otherwise be called Karenin's ignorance of life and misunderstanding of his wife are virtually excused. This is quite different from Levin's great admiration for the concern his brother-in-law, Lvov, shows for raising his children morally (683, VII.4).

Levin's subsequent comments reconfirm his revaluation of "sin" and show that it is not limited to the realm of philosophical error. He raises and immediately dismisses traditional religious explanations for the existence of evil and the expiation of sin: "The devil and sin? And how am I to explain evil? . . . The Redeemer? . . . But I know nothing, nothing, and can know nothing but what I've been told along with everybody else" (799, VIII.13, ellipses in original). That Levin sees these matters as imponderable leads him to the surprising conclusion that they are also irrelevant to his faith, which hinges exclusively on "faith in God, in the good, as the sole purpose of man" (799, VIII.13). A potential problem in Levin's argument is that without a sense of "evil" there is no way of deciding what is "good," because each term is meaningless without its opposite. A possible way out of this problem is to assume that because Levin has already identified "evil" with scientific and rational approaches to existence, his dismissal of thoughts about "the devil and sin" is simply his pleading ignorance about *ultimate* causes. This is supported by the narrator's description several pages earlier of how Levin overcame the false idea that life may be "the wicked mockery of some devil" (796–97, VIII.12). However, as we have seen in connection with what Levin says about children, other aspects of Levin's conception of sin relativize it to such an extent that it cannot be correlated with the novel's core moral concerns as they are expressed via the epigraph, Anna's agonizing about her adultery, and Levin's own preoccupation with moral behavior in earlier parts of the novel.

Levin relativizes his faith even more strikingly via a series of perceptions of the sky that are intentionally "naive" in a way that recalls his earlier simile linking adults to children. He begins by insisting that he is more justified in seeing the sky as a "round vault" than as the infinite space his scientific knowledge tells him it is simply because that is how he sees it (800, VIII.13). He then denies the relevance of another fact he knows perfectly well—that the earth moves in relation to the stars and not the other way around. (This recalls the illogical faith in immortality that an actual child, Seryozha Karenin, reveals when he devises the following syllogism: "Enoch had not died, which meant that not everyone died" [526, V.27].) By relativizing perception in this way, Levin anachronistically conflates two notions—Ptolemaic geocentrism and what could be called proto-Einsteinian relativity. However, his point is that this relativized human perspective is essential to truth because it provides the stable coordinates that astronomers need to understand the heavens accurately, and that this is like the belief in goodness that is the anchor of his faith (816, VIII.19). (Levin's simile is also a striking *reversal* of Tolstoy's argument in the final lines of *War and Peace,* where he urges us to believe that just as we cannot feel the earth move we are subject to a necessity of which we are not conscious.) Levin's conclusion—or hermeneutic index—is surprising, because he draws a parallel between the root of his *faith* and the necessary and unavoidable *falsehood* that underlies astronomical observation. But how can the latter not cast doubt on the former, even if the rational basis of astronomy is irrelevant to the revelation that leads to faith?[38]

How can even a heuristic lie lead to truth? One possible way is suggested earlier by Levin himself when he argues that the basis of faith cannot lie in reason because, in effect, earthly folly is heaven's sense and vice versa. Thus, by extension, what may appear to be an absurdity or a falsehood *here* could be a truth *there*. This idea has a long pedigree in Russian Orthodoxy and religious culture (*iurodstvo*, or "holy foolishness") as well as in the West (see, for example, 1 Corinthians 1:25, 27: "the foolishness of God is wiser than men; and the weakness of God is stronger than men"; "God hath chosen the foolish things of the world to confound the wise"). But Levin does not seem able to stick to this formula and simply to embrace the "irrational" or the "absurd," because he keeps returning to what "makes sense."

For example, despite his dismissal of reason in matters of faith, Levin appears to be troubled by the issue of verifiability. He invokes once more all those who supposedly share "that understanding of the good which always has been and will be the same for everyone, and which is revealed to me by Christianity and can always be verified in my soul" (816, VIII.19). Levin uses this continuum between countless unnamed others and his own soul as if it were empirical evidence in support of his claims, even though the existence of this continuum is based in his own intuition. Moreover, in keeping with his denigration of reason, Levin paradoxically couples this "verification" with a refusal to consider the one form of evidence that might have been able to support his intuition—whether or not other faiths have access to the same truths as Christianity (815–16, VIII.19). But perhaps we should understand Levin's continuum not as his reliance on a form of empirical evidence but as his faith in something like the mystical body of all believers. The problem with this interpretation is that Levin himself rejects it after reading the Russian religious thinker Aleksei Khomiakov, who is well known precisely for the idea of *sobornost'* (conciliarism), or that the church is a collective entity capable of comprehending divine truths that are inaccessible to the individual (788, VIII.9).

The uniquely personal nature of Levin's discovery is further underscored by the final passages in the novel, which describe his realization that he cannot explain what he has learned even to his beloved Kitty, or reveal it via actions to her or anyone else. It is possible, of course, that Levin's pessimism about Kitty reflects how he views her and is not an accurate perception of her openness to things spiritual. For example, at Nikolai's deathbed,

Kitty refers to the possibility that he may yet recover, even though the doctor gives him only three more days to live: "'Anything can happen,' she added, with the special, somewhat sly expression she usually had on her face when she talked about religion" (498, V.19). Whether or not Kitty would have understood Levin's new faith remains unknowable. But the question is also moot, because Levin will not speak with Kitty; as he puts it, he will be unable to remove the "wall" between the inner sanctum of his soul and his wife and will continue to blame Kitty for his own fears and to regret doing so (817, VIII.19). Nevertheless, as he phrases it in the novel's final sentence, he feels that henceforth his life is "not only not meaningless, as it was before, but has the unquestionable meaning of the good which it is in my power to put into it!" Levin's separation of faith from expression or praxis gives his beliefs a strangely quasi-Gnostic flavor. This obviously differs markedly from Saint Paul's teachings about charitable acts and their relation to divine retribution, which are fundamentally causal in how they link human beings and God.

Is it possible that the paradoxes, inconsistencies, and unanswered questions that circle around this description of Levin's faith could have escaped Tolstoy's notice or control?[39] Although it is unlikely that this question can be answered unequivocally, there is one sequence of passages near the end of the novel that can be interpreted as evidence for some distance between Levin and his creator. Indeed, this may be the only place where the difference between the implied author and his character can be identified with any degree of certainty on the basis of the novel itself. (Differences such as Levin's opposition to educating the peasants, which Tolstoy favored and practiced, are another matter, because evidence for them comes from outside the work.) Levin has been digesting and testing his new faith in the fields when he is summoned home because guests have arrived. As he is driving the cart, he resolves that henceforth all his relations will be different with everyone—no more alienation from his brother, quarrels with Kitty, and so on. A moment later, however, Levin's workman, who is sitting next to him, touches one of the reins to avoid a stump, and Levin flares up: "Kindly do not touch me and do not instruct me!" he blurts out with annoyance (801, VIII.14). Levin immediately regrets his reaction and concludes sadly that it was unrealistic of him to expect that he could change as quickly as he had imagined. Moreover, as soon as Levin meets his half-brother, who has come to visit, he feels awkward around him and, after exchanging a few words, feels the same cool relations that had always existed between them return once again (802, VIII.14). In short, these scenes are constructed in such a way that Levin is made to confront the delusional nature of some of his expectations.

Another way of putting this is that the author has fashioned a series of moments in which the character learns something that the author already knows. Under the circumstances, it does Levin credit that he understands at least some of the practical limitations and consequences of his beliefs. But this leaves open the question whether or not the gaps and paradoxes in Levin's beliefs are suggestions that the author has also outstripped the character with regard to other aspects of his faith. And if this is the case, then, by analogy with the moments we have been allowed to witness, Levin's faith may face additional and possibly more serious disillusionments than the ones he accepts on the novel's final page. It may also be that, as in *War and Peace*, what we have in Levin's case is a character inevitably falling away into the realm of personality and private interests after having glimpsed a divine totality, like Prince Andrei after seeing the sky at Austerlitz or like Pierre after his encounter with Platon, when he becomes involved in a proto–Decembrist movement.[40]

13.5. Anna

13.5.1. Anna in Moscow

It is hardly surprising that Anna exists in a world of her own, because shortly after the novel begins she becomes obsessed with one chief thing more completely than any other character.[41]

We first see Anna through Vronsky's eyes at the Moscow train station, with the narrator describing her via free indirect discourse. As a result, the reader shares Vronsky's impression that Anna embodies a highly attractive vitality: "It was as if a surplus of something so overflowed her being that it expressed itself beyond her will" (61, I.18). In addition to identifying part of what makes Anna appealing, this characterization also implies an asymmetrical relationship between the self and what lies outside it, or between projection and receptivity. In other words, it implies that Anna may so irradiate the world with what fills her that she sees things only in her own terms and not in someone else's or "objectively."[42]

Shortly after arriving, Anna also makes a major claim about the nature of existence when she calls the death of the railway worker a "bad omen" (65, I.18). This is one of the most important hermeneutic indices in the novel, which, however, can be understood in antithetical ways. If Anna interprets the death correctly as foreshadowing her own, then the implication is that chance does not exist, that the world is structured in a determinate way, and that some hidden agency rules over everything. (This possibility does not necessarily contradict the description of Anna as overflowing with a "surplus of something," because her character can also be understood as determined.) From this point of view, Anna's claim echoes the overarching meaning of the novel's epigraph (see 7). But it is also possible to interpret Anna's remark about an omen as her *projection* onto the world rather than her *insight* into it, especially because Stiva immediately responds with the dismissive "What nonsense!" Which alternative is correct or more plausible cannot be determined from this scene alone.[43]

When Anna arrives at the Oblonskys her behavior is also contradictory. On the one hand, her sympathy for Dolly during their conversation appears genuine, and she remembers the kinds of details about Dolly's children that cannot help winning a mother over. All of this suggests that Anna is capable of entering into another's frame of mind, at least at times and to some extent. But the most important things Anna says to Dolly can be interpreted, with varying degrees of certainty, as either her own inaccurate (or, better, private) perceptions of Stiva, as tactical dissimulations about him, as outright lies, or even as veiled or unconscious remarks about herself.

When Dolly claims that despite his infidelity Stiva is "happy and content," Anna objects, "He's pitiful, he's overcome with remorse" (68, I.19). On this occasion, we can infer that Anna is, at most, only partially right. We have already seen Stiva's predominantly ebullient and carefree demeanor in a series of earlier scenes: with his valet when he rises; at his office; at the skating rink, which he enters looking "merrily triumphant" and where he looks crestfallen only when he answers his mother-in-law's questions about Dolly's health (32, I.9); in the restaurant with Levin; and at the train station before and not long after the death of the worker. We also know that the reason for Stiva's being upset during the meeting with Dolly the previous morning was not remorse over his adultery but regret about having been *caught,* which caused Dolly the unnecessary pain of knowing what he had been up to and which led to awkward scenes at home. In fact, when Stiva is at the restaurant with Levin, which precedes Anna's arrival in Moscow, he shows no intention of giving up his philandering (and does not throughout the rest of the novel). It is all the more striking, therefore, that during their conversation Anna tries to persuade Dolly that Stiva's transgression "can't" happen again, although she adds the telling qualification "as I understand it . . ." (70, I.19, ellipses in original).

Anna also attempts to sway Dolly by explaining which aspects of Stiva's supposed remorse she personally found moving. However, the narrator quickly intrudes with a pointed parenthetical comment that can be read as undercutting the sincerity of Anna's explanation: "(and here Anna *guessed* [ugadala] what might move Dolly most of all)" (69, I.19, emphasis added). In other words, Anna's choice of what to tell Dolly at a crucial moment during their tête-à-tête may have been guided more by tactical and rhetorical considerations—the aim of which is to patch things up between Stiva and Dolly at any cost—than by a desire to help Dolly face squarely the "reality" of her situation or her husband's true nature.[44] However, it is also possible to read "guessed" in a different way—as meaning that Anna *divined* what was most important for Dolly because of her compassion for her; in fact, we are told that Anna shows "[u]nfeigned concern" for Dolly (68, I.19) and that "her heart responded directly to every word, to every expression on her sister-in-law's face" (69, I.19). Neither of these alternatives can be eliminated entirely, and they are not necessarily irreconcilable. However, the "tactical" motivation may have been the more dominant if we consider Anna's retroactive judgment of Dolly later in the novel once she returns to St. Petersburg.

Before examining this, it is worth considering another possibility— that, despite her claims to the contrary, Anna simply did not understand her brother's character very well and what she tells Dolly about him is the truth as far as she knows or imagines it. After all, we do not actually witness Stiva unburdening himself to Anna when they drive to his home from the train station, so we do not know what he told her. (When Anna returns to St. Petersburg, however, we do hear her tell Karenin "of the pity she had felt, first for her brother, then for Dolly" [110, I.33].) However, the description of how Anna finally sends Stiva into Dolly's room to ask for forgiveness suggests that Anna's judgment may be motivated by a specific agenda and not just by her limited understanding of the Oblonskys' situation: she does so "winking merrily, making a cross over him, and indicating the door with her eyes. 'Go, and God help you'" (72, I.20). The sign of the cross is a familiar, everyday gesture that a Russian Orthodox believer would use to invoke divine protection or a blessing for someone. However, in this case, nothing about Anna or the specific situation in which she makes the sign warrants interpreting it as anything more than an expression along the lines of "good luck!" The reference to God is similar and can be taken as a colloquialism that does not necessarily denote faith. Anna's winking is another matter and can be interpreted in two ways. The simplest is to assume that it is just another sign of encouragement. But it could also imply that Anna may view the Oblonskys' problem somewhat less than seriously; furthermore, by being yoked together with the sign of the cross, the winking casts a somewhat ironic light on it. This is surprising, given what we had just been shown of Anna's sympathy for Dolly. And even if the winking is Anna's gesture of solidarity *with Stiva* and is meant by Anna to be in harmony with his generally lighthearted attitude toward things, then it still implies that Anna may have been less than honest in how she described Stiva's contrition to Dolly.

13.5.2. Anna's Return to St. Petersburg

We hear what appears to be Anna's final judgment of the Oblonskys' problems when she returns home and tells Countess Lydia Ivanovna: "it was not as important as we thought. . . . Generally, my *belle-soeur* is too headstrong" (108, I.32). Anna's belittling of Dolly's feelings and of Stiva's infidelity is unexpected and cannot be reconciled readily with her behavior toward Dolly, unless Anna was simply being impulsive or benevolently hypocritical. However, Anna's remarks to Countess Lydia can be taken as supporting her (conspiratorial?) wink to Stiva. And lest the reader conclude that the peremptory tone of Anna's statement may reflect her wish to forestall any further discussion of a private matter with the countess, whom she is beginning to dislike, it is worth noting that the countess is described as "interrupting" Anna's report about her trip, which implies that Anna may have been willing to continue her description of it.

Another, more likely, and far-reaching possibility is that Anna's dismissal of the Oblonskys' problem is partially or even largely about herself and her mixed feelings toward Vronsky. Why? Because when Anna returns home and reimmerses herself in her familiar domestic routine, she discovers that the "sense of groundless shame she had experienced during the journey" to St. Petersburg, due obviously to her fascination with Vronsky's pursuit of her, "disappeared completely . . . [and] she again felt herself firm and irreproachable" (109, I.32; see *8.1* for Anna's reading on the train and *17.1* for the train's stop during the snowstorm). The fact that shortly thereafter Anna repeats to herself that she does not feel ashamed of anything and that Vronsky's behavior was unimportant (110, I.33) of course reconfirms his effect on her by her attempt to deny it.

The possibility that Anna transfers her own fears about Vronsky to her conclusion about Stiva and Dolly again returns us to the view that on a fundamental level Anna's judgment of others is inescapably private (even if, in this case, her nascent guilt creates a link between her and the universal ethical parameters implied in the epigraph and by some of the narrator's remarks). A similar example is the narrator's description of the recurvate nature of Anna's judgment of Karenin on the eve of the horse race: she "hold[s] him guilty for everything bad she could find in him and forgiv[es] him nothing, *on account of the terrible fault for which she stood guilty before him*" (189, II.23, emphasis added).[45] The seemingly automatic nature of this transference also implies that Anna is caught in an ethical web that may be part of "the way things are" in this novel's world. As I will discuss below, this suggests another far-reaching possibility that is invoked a number of times in the novel—that the link between human and transcendent realms lies in the person's conscience (see *15*).

Additional reasons supporting the hypothesis that Anna's view of others actually reflects her own (largely unconscious) self-conception can be found in how she sees her husband at the train station in St. Petersburg. She is shocked by his ears, as if they had changed while she was gone, and has an unpleasant feeling about him, "as if she had expected him to look different." The narrator then identifies what has, in fact, changed—Anna's "feeling of dissatisfaction *with herself*. . . . This was an old, familiar feeling, similar to that state of pretence she experienced in her relations with her husband; but previously she had not noticed it, while now she was clearly and painfully aware of it" (104, I.30, emphasis added). The implied duration of this "pretence" suggests that it stems from the flawed circumstances under which the two were married years before, circumstances that neither of them, and especially Anna, ever overcame entirely (see *13.5.6*). But if we infer that Anna's view of her husband has changed because of her new fixation on Vronsky, are we therefore justified in concluding that Karenin is still the same as he always has been? In short, is Anna now deluded about him? Despite the apparent logic of this possible conclusion, it is not supported by the novel. Indeed, the narrator presents Anna's new view of Karenin as perhaps even *more* accurate than her (unspecified) old one because the new one is *fuller*. She is now more conscious of her range of feelings toward him, including disappointment, which allows her to see new or at least different things in him. Another way of saying this is that the husband Anna sees upon her return to St. Petersburg is still fully and uniquely her own.

This continues to be the case later as well, when Anna's perception of Karenin undergoes several major changes following his spiritual rebirth at her sickbed: she moves from grateful acknowledgment of his "saintliness," to resentment, to hatred. Are these views progressively more wrong or more accurate? As far as Anna is concerned, she sees the truth in each case, and the narrator does not contradict her. Indeed, Anna's judgment of Karenin over time is like the motion of any two objects in space: it is always relative, because there is no third, fixed reference point outside them in relation to which their motion can be measured. And if we consider the other characters, all we have is additional relative perceptions of Anna and Karenin from different perspectives. As we have seen, the narrator does not hesitate to judge Karenin harshly in connection with such matters as his religiosity or his bureaucratic efforts, but he usually keeps this separate from Karenin's relations with Anna (see *12.2*).

Following Anna's disillusionment with her husband at the train station, we see her similar reactions to other aspects of her familiar world. "And the son, just like the husband, produced in Anna a feeling akin to disappointment. She had imagined him better than he was in reality. She had to descend into reality to enjoy him as he was." Although Anna quickly realizes that "he was charming even as he was" and receives "almost a physical pleasure" from his nearness, the fact that she also experiences a "moral solace" from him ("nravstvennoe uspokoenie"; 107, I.32), implies that her relation to her son also undergoes a change as a consequence of the effect that Vronsky had on her and that she tries to deny. In other words, we are shown how the boy's "nature" *shifts* a bit under his mother's wandering gaze; but what that nature may "really" be like in this case is not an issue. This is echoed a few lines later when Countess Lydia Ivanovna arrives, and we learn that although Anna was fond of her, "today she saw her as if for the first time with all her shortcomings" (108, I.32). Anna's reaction to the countess's influential social circle is the same: "on her return from Moscow, . . . [it] became unbearable to her. It seemed to her that both she and all the others were pretending" (127, II.4). The echo between this "pretending" and the "pretence" that troubles Anna in relation to her husband suggests a link between the two and indicates yet again the extent to which her world is a function of her mind.

13.5.3. Anna and Vronsky

That Anna would view Vronsky from a unique perspective of course follows from the burgeoning relationship between them. However, as with Levin, the narrator at times intrudes into descriptions of Anna's reactions in a way that overdetermines their privacy as well as their partiality (in both senses of the word) and thereby calls attention to them. An example is Vronsky's unexpected visit to Stiva's house in the evening following the Oblonskys' reconciliation. Anna and Vronsky glimpse each other very briefly, but this is enough for each to experience a moment of strong emotion. The narrator then goes out of his way to underscore how "strange"

Vronsky's visit seems to everyone by repeating the word five times in two pages; for example, "There was nothing either extraordinary or *strange* in a man calling at his friend's house at half-past nine to find out the details of a dinner that was being planned and not coming in; but they all thought it *strange*. To Anna especially it seemed *strange* and not right" (76, I.21, emphasis added; see also 75, I.21). What is the point of this repeated hermeneutic index? Kitty interprets Vronsky's behavior personally because she thinks (incorrectly, as it happens) that he is looking for her. Anna experiences a mixture of pleasure and fear, while Vronsky seems to feel fear and embarrassment, Stiva is perplexed, and we are not told what Dolly thinks but can infer that she too finds Vronsky's visit "strange." Thus, although on one level there is divergence in how the characters read the event, on another they are clearly unanimous in judging it as out of the ordinary. The narrator's attempt to distance himself from their interpretations by saying that "[t]here was nothing either extraordinary or strange" about Vronsky's visit creates a curiously dissonant note and seems intentionally disingenuous (even if disguised as a reference to social conventions), especially given the role that Vronsky will come to play in the novel. Perhaps at this moment the narrator can also be seen as enacting the kind of relativized perception that typifies the behavior of the characters (see *13.1*) or as engaging in an atypical instance of misdirecting the reader. Be that as it may, the narrator's comments constitute a seemingly unintentional hermeneutic index regarding the portentousness of Vronsky's role in the lives of all the assembled characters, albeit to varying degrees, of course. Most noteworthy, perhaps, is that Anna's private perception of Vronsky turns out to be silently supported by all the others. Thus, in this case, what may have seemed like her solipsistic "authoring" of her life appears to reflect something like a deeper, fateful layer of meaning in the novel's world (perhaps the same one signaled by her reference to a bad omen at the train station).[46]

Another instance of the narrator's intrusion into a portrayal of Anna's perceptions occurs when she tells Vronsky she is pregnant. Anna watches him intently to see how he takes the news, then concludes that he "understands all the significance of this event." However, the narrator contradicts her: "she was mistaken in thinking that he understood the significance of the news as she, a woman, understood it" (188, II.22). Following this, Vronsky is described as feeling an intensified "loathing" for someone: this may be Anna's son or, more exactly, Vronsky himself *because* of the son's role as a moral compass showing him how far he and Anna have strayed. (Vronsky first experiences an imprecisely focused "loathing" in the boy's presence several pages earlier [186, II.22].) The narrator's comment also posits an "essentialist" gap between the lovers, who see the "same" event in ways that are incommensurable (i.e., "as she, a *woman,* understood it"). To be sure, communication between them does take place: Vronsky senses Anna's physical agitation and grasps the momentous implications of her pregnancy. But the continuation of the scene demonstrates that the two characters' deepest thoughts and emotions run parallel to each other and do not intersect. Vronsky wants to act decisively and to end "the lie" they are living, whereas Anna evades the frank discussion he seeks. As a result, Vronsky feels so alienated from Anna that it seems to him as if another woman takes her place during such moments and rebuffs him (189, II.23). Vronsky cannot understand during this scene, and he will never understand during the course of the entire novel, that Anna's horror at the prospect of losing her son because of what she has done causes her to try "to calm herself with false reasonings and words" (190, II.24). Near the end of this chapter, the boy's sudden appearance interrupts Anna's impassioned speech to Vronsky about how happy she is, thus *structurally,* on the level of action and plot, echoing the son's role in her consciousness as an impediment to candor or to full communication with Vronsky.

Although at times the narrator undermines Anna's view of Vronsky, he does not provide a "corrected" perception of what Vronsky is "really" like in terms relevant to Anna's own viewpoint. (He does occasionally provide *his own* sarcastic perspective on Vronsky, as when he describes how Vronsky periodically brings his financial affairs into order [III.19].) For example, after Vronsky accidentally runs into Karenin at the entrance to the latter's house, the narrator generalizes about how Anna was again "bringing together her imaginary idea of him (an incomparably better one, impossible in reality) with him as he was" (357, IV.2). We can try to imagine in what ways Vronsky differs from what Anna thinks he is, but since the narrator's generalization is vague, no anchor for his judgment emerges, and all the reader can infer is that Anna cannot get out of her projections.[47] Moreover, Vronsky's unintended encounter with Karenin is freighted with motifs and coincidences that can be read as fatidic *(17.3).* This suggests an additional, extreme, and rather less plausible interpretation of why individual perceptions play a larger role in the novel than a single reality accessible to all. If the characters' actions reflect the patterns of which they are a part or of the forces that act on them, then a common reality would not be the primary field for what characters experience. The "patterns" or "forces" that impinge on the characters need not be transmundane, however, because characterological determinism can be seen as fateful as well.

It is paradoxical that once Anna's affair with Vronsky actually begins and she is drawn, or rushes, progressively deeper into it, descriptions of her private perceptions and of her differences and distance from Vronsky occupy more of the narrator's attention and, consequently, more textual space than do portrayals of the lovers' physical or emotional closeness. Their love, passion, and spiritual attraction are obviously central to the novel's concerns, but they are usually only alluded to in passing or take place in the wings rather than on center stage. One possible way to account for this is Victorian sexual taboos. Another is suggested by the history of love stories in European literature in general, which is that it is more entertaining to tell and to hear unhappy stories than happy ones.[48] What militates against this interpretation, however, is that the description of the adulterous lovers is contrasted with that of the newlyweds, Levin and Kitty, who are clearly meant to represent the novel's positive pole (although, as we have seen, the narrator also dwells at greater length on their differences than on their harmonious relations).

At one point, Tolstoy has Anna make a remark that provides a plausible explanation not only for her own behavior throughout the novel but also for that of all the other main characters, which suggests that here we encounter one of the work's thematic dominants. Amid the thoughts that rush through Anna's mind after she confesses her affair to Karenin is the following: "I've realized that I can no longer deceive myself, that I am alive, that *I am not to blame if God has made me so that I must love and live*" (292, III.16, emphasis added). This is a polyvalent hermeneutic index. Anna can be understood as contradicting the novel's epigraph, because she makes God responsible for her actions (unless we assume that the epigraph implies a deterministic world in which all human actions are part of a divine design, which is possible but which goes against the grain of the moral exhortations Saint Paul makes throughout Romans). By denying the possibility of free choice, Anna can also be seen as positing a psychological determinism that explains why she behaves as she does; by extension, her remark implies that others may be similarly determined (all of which also contradicts Saint Paul and the emphasis on human freedom in most forms of Christianity). However, the context for Anna's remark also suggests that she may be rationalizing her guilt or seeking to avoid personal responsibility for her adultery by invoking a specious determinism that she invents herself (although this still indicates the inescapability of the personal perspective in her life).[49] Whether or not Anna's claim is true can be ascertained only by continuing to examine whatever evidence the novel provides about her that bears on this issue.

Another sign of a division within Anna is the discrepancy between her contradictory views of relativization and her own behavior. For example, early in the novel, when Karenin refuses to alter his severe judgment of Stiva because he is a relative, we read that Anna "knew this feature in her husband and liked it" (111, I.33). This detail is all the more exceptional since it is a defense of an absolutist perspective in the middle of Anna's decidedly "defamiliarized" and highly personal views of Karenin following her return from Moscow. A contrasting example is the remark Anna makes after Vronsky begins to pursue her through various St. Petersburg salons: "if there are as many minds as there are men, then there are as many kinds of love as there are hearts" (138, II.7). On the one hand, this claim echoes the easygoing tolerance that characterizes Stiva's and Princess Betsy's libertine attitude toward love and that might seem to apply to Anna too, now that she has embarked on her affair. But on the other hand, Anna does not actually embody this laissez-faire stance in her own behavior because she yearns for a "conventional" life with Vronsky and suffers when she cannot have it. Her remark also contradicts the novel's first sentence, in which the narrator makes his absolutist generalization about all happy families being alike. However, the narrator is not always consistent himself, as we have seen, and on at least one occasion appears to support Anna's remark about "many kinds of love." This happens when he sanctions, via free indirect discourse, her admiration for the attractively dissolute Liza Merkalov (300, III.17), which suggests that her seductive appearance and manner somehow obviate questions of morality (see *12.7*).

The scene of Liza Merkalov in Princess Betsy's salon contains additional arguments in defense of perspectivalism that echo Anna's behavior. Betsy herself tells Anna: "You see, one and the same thing can be looked at tragically and be made into a torment, or can be looked at simply and even gaily. Perhaps you're inclined to look at things too tragically" (298, III.17). A short while later, Stremov, one of Betsy's other guests, says to Anna and Liza: "to keep things from being boring, you mustn't think they'll be boring," to which Anna replies, "I'd be very glad if I had said that, because it's not only intelligent, but also true" (301, III.18). Betsy's and Stremov's remarks deal with very different kinds of experience (the first alludes to Anna's affair with Vronsky, while the second is merely salon causerie), but both imply that individuals construct their own lives and worlds. Despite the congruence of this view with what Anna had said herself about different kinds of hearts and loves, there is also a dose of irony in it at her and Betsy's expense. When Anna's affair becomes a public scandal, Betsy will join in ostracizing her, thus effectively demonstrating that Anna's world is *not* completely a function of her conscious wishes and efforts and that Betsy herself adheres to the conventions of all the other members of her set.[50]

A salient instance of relativization, which is especially important because it functions as a rare instance of *meta*relativization in the novel, appears in the description of how Anna and Vronsky respond differently to the same day, shortly after the horse race: "That same clear and cold August day which had had such a hopeless effect on Anna, to him seemed stirringly invigorating and refreshed his face and neck" (313, III.22). Vronsky takes pleasure in his physical well-being and looks forward to his rendezvous with Anna, whereas she is at a loss about how to disentangle herself from her husband. These differing reactions, and the narrator's silence about the discrepancy, are familiar examples of Tolstoy's practice throughout the novel. However, after describing what Vronsky enjoys seeing on his drive, the narrator adds the following: "Everything was as beautiful as a pretty landscape just finished and coated with varnish" (313, III.22). This comment can be read as reflecting either Vronsky's or the narrator's perspective, or both. In any event, the allusion to painting establishes a link with the important chapters about the painter Mikhailov in Italy *(8.3, 8.4)*. One of the most prominent themes in them is that perceptions of pictorial art are often unpredictably relativized, which is a conclusion that can be correlated with other forms of expression in *Anna Karenina* and applied to the novel itself. Moreover, the chapters about Mikhailov also describe Vronsky's banal tastes in art and his own unsuccessful attempts to paint. Thus, juxtaposing the "landscape" that Vronsky sees on his drive with the openly meta-aesthetic chapters about Mikhailov reinforces the idea that the way characters perceive life is similar to how they perceive art, with both activities marked by a perspectivalism that can segue into such different forms as incommunicability and amorality.

A major gauge of the distance separating Anna and Vronsky, even during the peak moments of their affair, is her son, Seryozha. Relatively few pages are devoted to him, but the narrator's elevation of the boy to the status of a moral compass for the lovers obviously recalls the emphasis in the novel's opening lines on the importance and value of family life. The most profound expression of the different significance the child has for Anna and Vronsky appears when they return to Russia: "For Anna one of the objects of the trip to Russia was to see her son. Since the day she left Italy, the thought of seeing him had not ceased to excite her. And the closer she came to Petersburg, the greater became the joy and significance of this meeting for her" (530, V.29). This is hardly a surprising reaction from a mother, even one who had managed to forget about her son for periods of time (464, V.8). However, Anna's initial request for a meeting with Seryo-zha is answered by silence from Karenin and Countess Lydia Ivanovna, which causes Anna especially profound grief "because it was solitary. She could not and did not want to share it with Vronsky. She knew that for him, though he was the chief cause of her unhappiness, the question of her meet-ing her son would be a most unimportant thing. She knew that he would never be able to understand all the depth of her suffering" (531, V.29). In other words, Anna's perception of her son remains entirely private.[51]

By this stage in their affair, the friction between Anna and Vronsky has come to define their relationship more than either passion or occasional expressions of tenderness. Tolstoy renders the ebb and flow of Anna's thoughts and emotions with great subtlety, but it is striking how they all point to her inability to escape the constraints of her mind and her unique vision. In a particularly poignant scene a few pages after Anna's rumina-tions about Vronsky's indifference to Seryozha, Anna has trouble removing a photograph of her son from an album, and, in an action with obvious al-legorical significance of which she seems unaware, she finally succeeds by pushing the picture out with one of Vronsky taken in Italy. Conflicting feelings arise within her: she suddenly remembers "who had been the cause of her present grief," which is, of course, another instance of her inescap-ably private view of Vronsky; however, the sight of Vronsky's photograph also awakens an "unexpected surge of love" for him. (Anna's ambivalence about her time with Vronsky is also indicated by the hermeneutic charac-terization "unpardonably happy" [neprostitel'no shchastliva] that she uses for herself in Italy [463, V.8].) Moved by this feeling, Anna turns to Vron-sky in her imagination, but then suddenly accuses him of leaving her alone in her anguish. At this point, the narrator intrudes to correct her, because "she herself had concealed from him everything to do with her son," which again underscores the privacy of her outlook. Moments later, Anna sends for Vronsky because she yearns for his consolation and words of love, but the servant tells her that he has a visitor and cannot come alone. Anna im-mediately assumes that Vronsky is avoiding her and has stopped loving her, and then proceeds to "go over" all the events of the last few days in a way that confirms her fears (539, V.31).

Anna's predisposition toward conflict with Vronsky because of his sup-posed insensitivity toward her becomes self-perpetuating and leads to more friction and thwarted communication. For example, although she invites Yashvin to dine in order to please Vronsky, for which he is grateful, she is "offended" when Vronsky refers to "how painful our life here is for me, too," and quickly walks away from him, presumably because she sees herself as the primary victim and infers that he is blaming her (541, V.31). Later, they are again out of synchrony: Anna "seemed not to notice Vronsky's concerned and questioning expression" when she returns home, whereas he is now "troubled and alarmed" by her "quickness and grace," the very traits that had "so delighted him" earlier (541, V.32). (A similar reversal occurs a few pages later, when Vronsky is reminded of the impression she had made on him at the ball in Moscow, except that now her beauty both "attracts" and "offends" him [546, V.33].) After behaving in an unusually defiant and provocative way, Anna looks at Vronsky with an expression "the meaning of which he could not fathom" (542, V.32). When Vronsky questions her, she responds in a way that implies her willful incomprehension: "*It was as if* she did not understand the meaning of his words" (emphasis added). The narrator then enters the scene to underscore the distance between them by describing Vronsky's attempt to try to "wake her up, in the same way that her husband had once spoken to her" (542, V.32). The damning irony in this hermeneutic index hinges on the evocation of the a priori alienation between Anna and her husband that originates in their courtship and marriage (*13.5.6;* the reference to awakening may also be an echo of Anna's "insights" before she dies *[8.2]* and the dreams that she and Vronsky share *[17.1]*). When Vronsky tries to reassure Anna about his love, "[s]he did not hear the words but saw the coldness of his eyes" (543, V.32). He is also struck by her "deliberate refusal to understand her position" and by his own inability to explain to her what is most important for him at this point—that it would be highly inappropriate for her to go to the theater (543, V.33).

Similar moments occur throughout the rest of the novel. When Dolly comes to visit Anna at Vronsky's country estate, the two women fail to have the heart-to-heart talk both anticipated. Anna takes medicine containing a significant amount of morphine, which, by calming and cheering her, further isolates her from her surroundings. She then returns to her bedroom, where Vronsky looks into her eyes inquiringly because he wants to know what passed between her and Dolly, whose visit was important for them both. But Anna, "understanding that look differently, smiled at him" (641, VI.24). As the reader can infer, Anna's concern at this moment is largely unrelated to Vronsky's—she cares only about the physical effect that her beauty continues to have on him. Later, when Vronsky protests that he would give his entire life for her, Anna is described as "not listening to him." The one thing that Anna *does* understand clearly in this scene is the "cold, angry look" that contradicts Vronsky's "tender words," a look she never forgets (668, VI.32).

With the deterioration in their relations, Anna progresses from not listening to Vronsky to imputing alien motives and words to him in a way that functions as a negative analogue of the attractive vitality she exudes the first time we see her. In both cases, what is "inside" her cannot help but overwhelm whatever is "outside." Thinking that his love for her has diminished and "[h]aving as yet no object for her jealousy, she was looking for one . . . and sought pretexts for indignation in everything" (740, VII.23). When Vronsky speaks of his plans for "you and for the children to come," Anna hears only the reference to "children" and accuses him of not thinking of her (747, VII.25). After a particularly bitter quarrel, Anna recalled "all the cruel words he had said, [and] also invented the words he obviously had wished to say and might have said to her . . . and she could not forgive him for them, as if he had actually said them to her" (751, VII.26).

Vronsky's reference to children and Anna's reaction to it have a prehistory, both in her relations with him and in some of the novel's most important themes. The narrator explains that Vronsky's wish to have more children has been a source of irritation for Anna because she interprets it as meaning that he no longer values her beauty (748, VII.25). The implicit equation that Anna makes between having children and being unattractive also evokes Stiva's philandering, which, we have been told, was motivated largely by Dolly's having lost her looks by the age of thirty-three in the process of giving birth to "five living and two dead children" (3, I.2). This specific association is also repeated in one of the most unusual hermeneutic indices in the novel, which appears in Anna's remark to Dolly during her visit to Vronsky's estate. After dumbfounding Dolly with the revelation that she uses contraceptive measures (something that is, in fact, implied in the text via a line of ellipses rather than spelled out), Anna says that she has two choices before her—to be "a friend, a companion" to Vronsky or "to become pregnant, meaning ill" (637, VI.23). The way in which Anna redefines pregnancy as illness, and the extremes to which she goes in order to avoid it, are obviously antithetical to everything that Dolly stands for, even though Dolly had also briefly entertained related thoughts and made a comparable equation herself before rejecting it unequivocally (606–7, VI.16; 637, VI.23). It is all the more noteworthy, therefore, that after Nikolai's death the narrator uses the same hermeneutic index when he informs us that Kitty's "illness was pregnancy" (505, V.20), which makes it impossible to condemn Anna's redefinition as entirely perverse. (There is also some resemblance between the narrator's hermeneutic index and the notion of "morning sickness" that was used in British English as early as 1879, according to the *OED,* except that this condition is conceived as explicitly diurnal and transient.) Anna's remarks thus establish a (weak) link with her brother and his values, and suggest that their being siblings may explain certain similar aspects of their behavior, although we actually know nothing about whatever childhood they may have had together. (We can even trace faintly the theme of *implied* contraception in Stiva's relations with his paramours.) In turn, the theme of the Oblonsky family returns us to the narrator's programmatic first sentence and the value it places on family life. Although there are different ways of reading the narrator's remarks (see *7*), Anna's not wanting any more children puts her at odds with his overt message (as well as with the senior Shcherbatskys, the Lvovs, and Levin and Kitty, in addition to Dolly).

The chain of associations between Anna's deteriorating relationship with Vronsky and major themes from the beginning of the novel does not stop here. Immediately after Vronsky's exasperated explanation that he *was* thinking of her when he referred to children, Anna, who was "not listening to his words," gazes instead "with horror at the cold and cruel *judge* who looked out of his eyes, taunting her" (748, VII.25, emphasis added). The significance of this detail lies in Anna's seeing or defining Vronsky in terms that recall the novel's epigraph about divine judgment. Can this mean that God somehow acts through Vronsky? Perhaps. From one perspective, the immediate context for Anna's perception makes it clear that she is to some indeterminable degree projecting her "paranoia" onto Vronsky. Given what we know of him, it is unlikely that he would act toward her as hatefully as she believes, even though we have no way of being sure about this in this specific instance. It is possible, therefore, that all she sees in Vronsky is her own guilty conscience, insecurity, and unhappiness. From another perspective, however, he obviously *is* a major element in the suffering she experiences as a consequence of her various transgressions; moreover, his patience with her has begun to fray. Thus, if the epigraph is understood as implying that divine vengeance is meted out (unwittingly) by other human beings, Vronsky can be seen as part of that process. These two possibilities can also be put together, which results in the following schema: the "outside" judge that Anna sees in Vronsky is a function of the "inside" state that she projects onto the world; and her "inside" state of guilt is her *conscience*, which is the locus of the contact between the human and the divine. This schema is both supported and undermined by related moments in the novel (see *15*).

Anna's imagining the hurtful words that Vronsky *could* say to her progresses with painful logic to her imagining that he undertakes hurtful *actions*. When she sees him smile after receiving a package from the young Princess Sorokin, Anna initially infers that this is a sign that he wants to abandon her and marry the princess. All the information at the reader's disposal indicates that Anna's fears are unfounded (although Vronsky's need for an occupation and companionship in addition to Anna's does constitute a form of withdrawal from her, as she realizes). But the way in which the narrator chooses to describe Anna's conclusion, which, in typical fashion, he gives via free indirect discourse, lends it considerable weight and persuasiveness in the reader's imagination: "The fog that had covered everything in her soul suddenly cleared. Yesterday's feelings wrung her aching heart with a new pain. She could not understand now how she could have lowered herself so far as to spend a whole day with him in his house" (753, VII.26). By this point in the novel, Anna has already thought of suicide, and the strength of her delusion about Vronsky's designs on Princess Sorokin is concomitant with her despairing state.

However, some ten pages later, on her fateful journey to the train station, Anna changes her mind and admits to herself she knows perfectly well that Vronsky "would not deceive me, that he doesn't have any intentions towards Princess Sorokin, that he is not in love with Kitty, that he will not be unfaithful to me" (763, VII.30). She realizes instead that their relations are irremediably damaged because Vronsky's love for her has cooled, while hers—like her possessiveness, which he also resists—has grown in intensity.[52] In effect, Anna *recodes* her initial delusion into something more plausible; but her clearer view of Vronsky cannot change her conclusion that he is slipping away. On this occasion, the narrator uses a different image for her sudden insight: "She saw it clearly in that piercing light which now revealed to her the meaning of life and of people's relations" (763, VII.30).

13.5.4. Anna's Death

The narrator's correlated images of "fog that . . . cleared" and "piercing light," and their connection with Anna's (mis)perceptions of Vronsky, anticipate the imagery associated with Anna's final moments, when she decides to "punish him and be rid of everybody and of myself" and is twice granted insight into what may be the higher truth of her own existence (for additional discussions of Anna's death, see *8.2* and *17.1*). Before throwing herself under the railway car, she makes the sign of the cross, "and suddenly the darkness that covered everything for her broke and life rose up before her momentarily with all its bright past joys" (768, VII.31). This description stands out because it acts as a kind of supplement (or corrective?) to Anna's unremittingly negative perceptions of everyone and everything moments earlier, during the "stream of consciousness" passages describing her trip to the train station. Can it be that the sign of the cross she makes over herself is an (authorial) ironic echo of the sign she makes over Stiva when she sends him in to Dolly at the beginning of the novel, an event that also stemmed from an adulterous relationship? This possibility is supported by the narrator's description of the gesture as "habitual" but is undermined by the gesture's awakening memories of childhood and girlhood, two periods in life that are always marked positively in the novel; the specific contexts for the two gestures are also incommensurable.

Anna's actual death is rendered via an image that appears to imply that she achieves maximal insight at the final moment: "the candle by the light of which she had been reading that book filled with anxieties, deceptions, grief and evil, flared up brighter than ever, *lit up for her all that had once been in darkness*, sputtered, grew dim, and went out for ever" (768, VII.31, emphasis added). In fact, however, this passage is deeply ambiguous. We do not know if Anna sees anything beyond the limits of her own consciousness, any more than Levin does when he convinces himself that he has discovered God, but this remains a possibility. The narrator's not telling us *what* is illuminated for Anna is consistent with Tolstoy's portrayal of Nikolai Levin's death in *Anna Karenina*. (The narrator's agnosticism is also consistent with how Tolstoy depicts death throughout his oeuvre—as an experience that is incomprehensible from an earthly perspective even though there appears to be something following physical extinction; see, for example, Prince Andrei's death in *War and Peace*, the Master's in "Master and Man," and Ivan Ilich's in the eponymous short story.) The only way that we can determine if Anna sees something true and real during her final moments is if we can find additional evidence in the novel's world that supports this possibility.[53]

There are, in fact, two important scenes containing details somewhat reminiscent of the imagery that communicates Anna's suicide and the idea that it is accompanied by a sudden glimpse into a higher reality. The first is Levin looking at Kitty just before she goes into labor and seeing that "all the wrappings were suddenly removed and the very core of her soul shone in her eyes" (707–8, VII.13, my literal translation). This recalls the second— Mikhailov's realization when he is painting that "great attention and care were needed to remove a wrapping without harming the work itself, and to remove all the wrappings" (474, V.11). The context for both scenes strongly suggests that the birth of a child and of a work of art is the manifestation of a spiritual reality through a material screen. And the consistency between these scenes, which treat two themes that are clearly central to Tolstoy's concerns in the novel—the genesis of art and the raison d'être for family life—supports the insights each describes *(9.1, 9.2)*. The description of

Anna's suicide seems to fit the same pattern, because it also entails what appears to be a supersensory insight into a realm that transcends mundane experience. It is thus possible to read Anna's death as granting her access to a higher truth. (There are comparable metaphysical implications that link Kitty's giving birth and Nikolai Levin's death *[16.2.2]*.)[54] However, it is also possible to argue that the differences between "wrappings removed" and "darkness illumined" are sufficient to undermine parallels among the three scenes, which thus leaves the question of Anna's insight irresolvably ambiguous. There is, moreover, a third possibility that I suggested above. If one chooses to link the passages about the failure of Koznyshev's new book, which begins part VIII, to the description of Anna's reading the book of her life when she dies, which concludes part VII (events that can be seen as *either* textually close or distant), then the possibility that she does not achieve any insight transcending what she already knows becomes more likely *(8.2)*.[55]

Given how often crucial dialogues between characters fail or even fail to occur throughout the novel, it is especially poignant that shortly before her death Anna is given to experience a *false* dialogue with a chance passenger, albeit one that may paradoxically yield a true insight. Anna is caught in the vortex of her despair, which causes her to see everything at the station and in the train compartment in the most negative way. When she concludes that the human condition is all suffering and deception, she asks herself the question, "if you see the truth, what can you do?" Immediately afterward, one of Anna's fellow travelers happens to say to her husband in French: "Man has been given reason in order to rid himself of that which troubles him" (766, VII.31). To Anna this seems like an answer to her thoughts and helps to bring her closer to suicide. It is clear that on one level Anna's omnivorous misery is responsible for transforming this apparently chance remark into a response to her question. But there are other implications to this pseudodialogue as well.

The remark can be seen as embodying a deeply anti-Pauline, indeed anti-Christian message (although one that is ambiguous in the context of the novel as a whole [see *12.6*]). The yielding stance advocated by Saint Paul is, of course, not rational but based on a particular kind of faith, for what everyday logic is there in treating kindly someone who treats you badly? Thus, Anna's embracing the passenger's remark—like the act of suicide itself—can be construed as a measure of her distance from the truth that Levin thinks he discovers at the novel's end, which is explicitly antirational, is based on his personal intuition, and follows his rejecting as deluded another argument for suicide. Anna's reliance on reason also puts her at odds with Tolstoy's consistently negative depiction of reason elsewhere in the novel, as can be seen in his portrayals of those who rely on it most fully—Koznyshev and his academic interlocutors, or the famous doctor who thinks he knows which prescriptions will heal Kitty's broken heart (II.1). Anna's suicide may be foreshadowed by the fact that she herself utters a phrase about reason close to the one she overhears on the train when she tells Dolly that she has decided to use contraception: "Why have I been given reason, if I don't use it so as not to bring unfortunate children into the world?" (638, IV.23).[56]

Furthermore, one of Anna's motivations in committing suicide is to avenge herself on Vronsky for what she believes she has suffered because of him, which means that she usurps a divine prerogative, according to the novel's epigraph *(7)*.[57] This is important, because Anna is the only major character to act vengefully and, therefore, egotistically in the novel. Levin's forcing Vasenka to leave his estate because of the emotional turmoil that Vasenka caused him, which can also be seen as a form of vengeance, is very minor in comparison, especially because Vasenka himself laughs it off. And although Karenin initially wants to avenge himself on Anna, his desire appears to dissipate without issue when he falls under Countess Lydia Ivanovna's sway and the obscure machinations of the false clairvoyant Landau. Thus, Anna's sin may be not just that she commits suicide but that she does this *in order* to hurt Vronsky.

Despite this, it is also possible to interpret Anna's reaction to the passenger's remark as correct and insightful. Given who Anna is and the situation in which she now finds herself, what choice does she have other than suicide? By this point in her life she appears checkmated.[58] Karenin has refused to grant her a divorce, and she of course cannot return to him now that Countess Lydia Ivanovna guides his life. Even if he were to change his mind about a divorce and Anna were free to marry Vronsky, it is unclear if society would ever accept her because of how far she has gone in overturning her circle's norms for women (even Princess Betsy, who once said that Anna sees things too tragically, cuts Anna after she returns from Italy). Moreover, Anna cannot forget the wrongs that she has done to her former family any more than she can forget the pain she has suffered at the hands of Karenin and others. Anna's ostracism creates an insuperable barrier between her and Vronsky, who will not give up his interests outside the home and who is bitter because of her attempts to keep him by her side. Anna has lost her son and can never get him back from his father. She has failed to become closely attached to her daughter by Vronsky. The corollary of Anna's relativized view of things is the isolation that follows from it, which is an idea that she feels strongly during her final journey near the end of the novel: "Is it really possible to tell someone else what one feels?" (760, VII.29). Given the ties she has broken and her inability to form new ones, how can she stop feeling vulnerable as she sees Vronsky's ardor cool and stubbornness increase? Indeed, at this point it is not clear if Vronsky *could* overcome his antipathy toward her because of her possessiveness, jealousy, and the number and depth of the quarrels they have had.

And if Anna were to leave Vronsky, where would she go? Is it possible to imagine her living alone, or being taken in by friends, as her aunt Princess Varvara is, or going abroad by herself? What else could she do but depend on the largesse of a husband or a lover? The way Anna was married off by her other aunt may indicate that she had no property of her own (*13.5.6*), and she certainly depends on Karenin's money later. After all, *Anna Karenina* is not a novel by Dostoevsky, in which a female character who is at rope's end can throw herself on the mercy of a virtual stranger or become a prostitute. Neither are there any signs that Anna could try to redefine herself and become an "emancipated woman" à la Chernyshevsky's *What Is to Be Done?* (although the status of women in society is broached more than once in the novel in connection with Varenka and at Oblonsky's dinner when Levin and Kitty meet [see *16.2.1*]). It seems quite impossible that a woman with Anna's background could seek any kind of employment in her world, despite her dabbling at writing a book for children (*8.1*).

It is also implausible that she could change enough to repent her adultery, embrace selfless Christianity, and ask her husband for mercy or disappear into a religious life. Events like this fall outside the realm of possible behavior in Tolstoy's fictional worlds at this stage in his career. (The situation will change drastically in later works such as "Father Sergius" [1898] and *Resurrection* [1899].) Levin's faith is hardly an example for Anna, because his beliefs are inherently ambiguous, as we have seen; moreover, there is nothing in Levin's personal life to interfere with his turn toward God, as there is in Anna's. Thus, despite the seeming solipsism of Anna's reaction to the pseudodialogue on the train, her conclusion that there is no escape from her quandary except for suicide may be an accurate perception of the degree to which her position has become untenable. This is not to say that Anna *acts* rationally, is marked positively, or is fully in possession of her faculties when she dashes about during her final hours. However, the remarkable *aptness* of the remark Anna hears can be seen as implying that she may have (briefly) grasped the texture of existence in the novel's world, or "the way things are." From this perspective, Anna's quasi-dialogic exchange is of a piece with her fatidic reading of the workman's death at the novel's beginning (see *17*). In other words, Tolstoy's construction of the scene in which she overhears the remark can be interpreted as demonstrating that chance is actually the revealed face of necessity, and that Anna's existence is part of a larger web of signification from which she cannot escape (see *18*).

13.5.5. Anna and Others

Other aspects of Anna's world are affected as strongly by her changing perspectives as are her relations with Vronsky, Karenin, and Seryozha. For example, when Dolly visits Vronsky's estate she notices that Anna quickly masters her confusion over Dolly's unexpected arrival and assumes "that tone of superficial indifference which indicated that the door to the compartment in which she kept her feelings and innermost thoughts was locked" (617, VI.19). We have already seen that this door never really opens between the two women. Dolly also notices that Anna has developed a habit of "narrowing her eyes" or "squinting" (shchuritsia), which Dolly accurately interprets as Anna's attempt "not to see" her life (628, VI.21; see also 619, VI.19).

Another variant of the same practice is Anna's "not listening" to Dolly during an important part of their tête-à-tête because she wants to finish arguments "with which she had so often persuaded herself" (638, VI.23); this obviously also suggests that Anna is speaking primarily to herself. Then, in the next breath, Anna does direct a kind of half-rhetorical question to Dolly, but does not wait for her answer and continues to speak. Dolly reacts in kind. Although Anna's arguments about not wanting to bring unfortunate children into the world were "the same arguments" that had occurred to Dolly earlier, "now she listened to them and could not understand them" (638, VI.23). The scene ends with Dolly's not replying at all to what Anna has said because "[s]he suddenly felt she had become so distant from Anna that there were questions between them which they would never agree on and of which it was better not to speak" (639, VI.23). Later, we are also told that although Dolly "pitied Anna with all her soul while talking with her . . . she was unable to make herself think about her" soon after they part because her thoughts turn to her own home and children (641, VI.24).

Anna's relations with Levin are similar and are established in the one scene in the novel when these two central characters meet. Stiva brings Levin to visit Anna, who strives to win him over and succeeds as much as was possible "with regard to an honest, married man in one evening" (704, VII.12).[59] But despite the fact that she genuinely likes Levin and sees in him some resemblance to Vronsky, as soon as Levin leaves the room Anna forgets him. The narrator explains that this is the way she has unconsciously begun to treat *all* young men, which implies that during her meeting with Levin she was interested more in her own power to awaken love in a chance caller—and thus, presumably, to test by proxy her power to keep Vronsky—than in anything intrinsic to Levin himself. In turn, although Levin was initially quite smitten with Anna, he regrets this feeling as soon as he leaves her, especially his "tender pity" for her (702, VII.11), and realizes that he was entirely mistaken to visit her when he sees Kitty's reaction (703, VII.11).[60]

13.5.6. Anna's Arranged Marriage to Karenin

In trying to understand the movements of Anna's psyche, it is essential to take into account what the narrator says about how she came to marry Karenin. In the same way that Levin's pursuit of marriage, family, and country life are presented as a trajectory that begins in his childhood recollections of his parents' lives, Anna's openness to "an affair of the heart" seems rooted in her past.

This issue is first raised obliquely by Kitty, who during her infatuation with Anna before the ball wishes she could know Anna's "whole romance." This translation preserves the ambiguity in the original Russian "ves' ee roman," which can be translated most plausibly as "her whole love affair" but also as the punning "her whole novel" (73, I.20). The last possibility, with its obvious metaliterary implications of an equation between life and art *(8.6),* is actually echoed later in the compliment by Liza Merkalov that Betsy reports to Anna: "you're a real heroine from a novel [geroinia romana]" (297, III.17). By contrast, following her romanticized fantasy about Anna, Kitty recalls Karenin's "unpoetical appearance," which evokes very accurately a tension that, in fact, determines much of Anna's life.

After Anna leaves Karenin, the narrator briefly sketches how they met:

> During his governorship, Anna's aunt, a rich provincial lady, had brought the already not-so-young man but young governor together with her niece and put him in such a position that he had either to declare himself or to leave town. Alexei Alexandrovich had hesitated for a long time. There were then as many reasons for this step as against it, and there was no decisive reason that could make him abandon his rule: when in doubt, don't. But Anna's aunt insinuated through an acquaintance that he had already compromised the girl and that he was honorbound to propose. He proposed and gave his fiancée and wife all the feeling he was capable of. (507, V.21)

In short, the marriage had a serious flaw built into it from the start, although it remains unspecified what moved Anna's aunt: did she want to get rid of Anna, to make a splendid match, to provide for Anna's future by attaching her to a rising bureaucratic star, to gain a useful connection herself? In any event, this crucial moment in Anna's life is marked by the absence of a normal family structure (a detail that also seems relevant to Stiva's case). The narrator's summary of Anna's marriage also corroborates Stiva's earlier and shorter argument to Anna along the same lines: "I'll begin from the beginning: you married a man twenty years older than yourself. You married without love or not knowing what love is. That was a mistake, let's assume." Anna immediately replies, "A terrible mistake!" (427, IV.21).[61] (A negative judgment of arranged marriages in general that may be relevant to Anna's case appears in the ruminations by Princess Shcherbatsky about Kitty's marriage prospects [44–45, I.12].) We do not know the details of Anna's attitude toward Karenin's proposal, although Stiva's remark suggests it was not entirely positive. It is also possible that the aunt manipulated Anna's thoughts and feelings. The direct consequence this has for Karenin is that he never develops any other "heartfelt relations with people" (507, V.21) and so experiences his "most difficult moment of lonely despair" when Anna leaves him (508, V.22). In turn, this leads to an additional sequence of events with dire consequences for Anna: Karenin becomes especially vulnerable to Countess Lydia Ivanovna's friendship, then becomes immersed in her brand of religiosity, and finally falls under the sway of Landau. For reasons we never learn, Landau then advises Karenin against granting Anna a divorce—something that Karenin might have agreed to on his own and that might have changed Anna's life. This causal chain, which is to some degree also a function of the narrator's focus on a limited set of situations, characters, and events in the novel's present (we also learn very little about Levin's childhood and youth, for example), illustrates why it is frequently impossible to distinguish between literary form and fatidic or characterological determinism in this novel (or in narratives in general [see *18*]).

In contrast to Karenin, who gives the marriage everything he can, Anna is unfulfilled by it, especially after her return from Moscow. The narrator makes this point clearly when the couple is preparing for their first conjugal night: "She undressed and went to the bedroom, but not only was that animation which had simply spurted [tak i bryzgalo] from her eyes and smile when she was in Moscow gone from her face: on the contrary, the fire now seemed extinguished in her or hidden somewhere far away" (112, I.33, my literal translation of *bryzgalo*). What Anna suppresses here is the same life force that first attracts Vronsky at the station and that she shares with her brother. Among other details, the similarity between them is underscored by the narrator's characterizing Stiva with the same verb that he uses for Anna: "spurting with joy" (bryzzhushchee vesel'em; 426, IV.21, my translation). However, Stiva makes few if any attempts to restrain this side of his character.

Anna's animation may have been released for the first time in her life by Vronsky. In addition to various subtle and early indices showing the effect Vronsky has on her, Anna realizes soon after she returns from Moscow that his pursuit of her "constituted the entire interest of her life" (128, II.4). Once her affair with him develops, Anna makes a highly telling remark about Karenin that appears to be one of her entirely relativized judgments of him, but that can also be interpreted as a more complex truth about her marriage. Thinking of how Karenin is viewed by members of society, she claims, "They don't know how he has been stifling my life for eight years, stifling everything that was alive in me, that he never once even thought that I was a living woman who needed love. They don't know how he insulted me at every step and remained pleased with himself" (292, III.16). The point here is not the extent to which Anna indulges in hyperbole to justify her adultery. We can infer from the novel that Karenin would not have done anything *willfully* to hurt Anna during the years preceding her involvement with Vronsky. Indeed, there is evidence that at least from Karenin's perspective their relations were so close that Anna noticed the slightest change in his routine (145–46, II.9). But from the point of view of satisfying her emotionally (and possibly physically), his normal behavior may have had an effect that *did not differ* from a conscious decision to withhold from her the kind of love she needs.[62]

13.5.7. Anna's Moral Sense

To love passionately is not the only imperative Anna feels. When she rationalizes her attraction to Vronsky during and immediately after her return from Moscow, we see that she also has a conscience (see also *15.3*). Indeed, her ethical sense proves to be a constant counterpoint to her love affair.[63] When Karenin tries to warn her about the gossip that her behavior toward Vronsky may cause, she feigns incomprehension but is in fact "surprised . . . at her ability to lie. . . . She felt herself clothed in an impenetrable armour of lies" (145, II.9). After Anna and Vronsky consummate their passion, her reaction is so intense that she can scarcely begin to put it into words. Nevertheless, in addition to "joy" and "horror," she feels deeply "criminal and guilty" (thus echoing the narrator's description of the aftermath as a murder scene) and is oppressed by her overwhelming sense of "shame" (149–50, II.11). When Anna agonizes over the need to reveal her affair to Karenin, the narrator characterizes her state of mind with the following semantically linked terms occurring in the space of one page: "false" (lozhnym), "dishonest" (nechestnym), "lying" (lzhi), "deception" (obmana), "lying" (lzhi), "pain" (bol'), "horrible" (uzhasny), "shame" (styda), "ashamed" (stydno), "hopeless" (bezvykhodnym), "afraid" (strashno), "disgrace" (pozor), "frightening" (strashnye), "disgrace" (pozor) (287, III.15, my translations). In this scene, Anna's emotions stem in part from her fear that Vronsky may already have tired of her. This makes her feel animosity toward him, which shows how early in their affair the seeds of its destruction begin to sprout in her mind (which is not to say that this *alone* brings the destruction about). Other examples of Anna's ethical sense abound in later scenes as well.

Anna is thus caught from the start between contending forces that she cannot deny, resolve, or eliminate—love and passion, on the one hand, and a moral sense, on the other.[64] In turn, the moral dimension of her quandary is the result of a kind of *symbiotic* relationship between her conscience (her "inside") and social pressure (the "outside"), which differs from the usual domination of the "outer" by the "inner" that functions elsewhere in her life. The spontaneous upwelling of her moral sense from "inside" her is manifested in such reactions as the profound grief, revulsion, and disorientation she feels when she first "falls." In this scene, she is moved by a sense of right and wrong that she carries within her, one that appears to lie much deeper than her specific relationship with Vronsky, who is, of course, a coparticipant in her fall but not the sole cause of her ethical response to it. Because we know little of Anna's religious feelings, which she manifests rarely, it remains unclear if her moral revulsion is based on religious faith. On the one hand, she sobs, "My God! Forgive me!" in this scene (149, II.11). On the other, when she appeals to God elsewhere in the novel, or when she simply repeats a conventional phrase of entreaty, we are told that although she never doubted the faith in which she had been raised, the idea of seeking that faith's assistance in dealing with her problems was entirely alien to her (288, III.15). Similarly, it is unclear if Anna's crossing herself and asking God for forgiveness just before she dies transcends the formulaic references she makes earlier (768, VII.31). Whatever the case, Anna's internalized moral sense is also manifested in her inability to reveal to Vronsky or anyone else the pain and guilt that separation from her son usually causes her. (An important exception is the earlier part of the journey to Italy, when she is "unpardonably happy" [463, V.8]; however, this is clearly a temporary and, judging by this phrase, an ambivalent happiness at best.) In all these instances, Anna's inherent moral sense is also in accord with societal norms. Moreover, we repeatedly see her sense of guilt reinforced from the outside via the insults and rebuffs she receives—as when Betsy carefully specifies that Anna should come to visit at a time when there will not be any other guests (541, V.32), or when the woman in the neighboring box at the opera leaves in a huff (546–48, V.33). It is possible to correlate this congruence with the implications of the novel's epigraph, according to which the entire fabric of the way things are may be involved in punishing the sinner who feels guilty *(7)*.

This combination of inner orientation and external "aggravation" of an ethical sense is unique to Anna in the novel. Stiva's dalliances do not bother him because his internal "morality" is almost entirely hedonistic: he sees it as natural and good that a robust man like himself should enjoy all the sensual aspects of life. Because Stiva does not parade his affairs in front of Dolly, which could have resulted in a repetition of the "awkward" scenes that upset him at the beginning of the novel, he is also not subjected to any new, external forms of condemnation of any real significance. Indeed, his buoyant and optimistic nature allows him to translate unhappy moments into jokes, such as when a tycoon intentionally humiliates him by making him wait in an anteroom, to which Stiva responds by trying to figure out a pun based on the man's ethnicity (722, VII.17). No other prominent character in the novel commits transgressions serious enough to be compared to Anna's. Levin's rudeness to Veslovsky is condemned by other characters, but this does not bother Levin for very long, because in the end he relies on his own moral code, according to which his family happiness is the paramount value.

The only possible solution to Anna's problem could have been self-denial combined with moral rectitude.[65] She could have refused to follow the inclinations of her heart and decided to remain loyal to her husband and marriage, rather like Tatiana at the end of Pushkin's classic *Eugene Onegin,* who responds to Onegin's entreaties: "I love you (why pretend?), / But I've been given to another; / I'll be faithful to him all my life" (chap. 8, stanza 47). In part because Pushkin's fictional world glimmers in the distant background of Tolstoy's, it is possible to imagine an interpretation of *Anna Karenina* arguing that one of the novel's main points is the necessity of self-denial.[66] From this perspective, Anna would presumably have had to suppress her attraction to Vronsky and continue to live as best she could by focusing on her child and on members of society not associated with Princess Betsy's fast set. Alternatively, Vronsky would have had to stop pursuing her.

But does the conception of character in Tolstoy's novel allow for free moral choice? Answering this question is complicated by the fact that Anna's case is unique in the novel. Because there are no other characters whose experiences approach the complexity or intensity of Anna's, we have no unequivocal reference points on which to rely when trying to understand or evaluate her case (except for those outside the text, and there is no sure criterion for choosing among them). Indeed, as we have already seen, the novel's dominant pattern of making the self the arbiter of meaning and value undermines the impersonal, universalizing imperatives that the novel proffers but does not consistently support. It is, consequently, difficult to imagine Vronsky stopping his pursuit of Anna during the early months of the affair, because this would have gone against the grain of his set's egotistical and amoral code, which he embodies in a very pure form. Later, he cannot extinguish his love any more easily than she can.

The only possible point of comparison among female characters is Dolly, but she is not confronted with choices whose consequences are as grave as the ones Anna faces. The narrator tells us that Dolly continues to think of Stiva as her husband even after he has deceived her, and although she affects a detached and ironic view of him, she does not put her whole existence on the line because of her disappointment in him. (Indeed, it is even possible that she tolerates his philandering, assuming that she is aware of it.) Dolly does have a short-lived fantasy about an ideal lover during the ride to Vronsky's estate to visit Anna: "'Am I any better? I at least have a husband I love. Not as I'd have wanted to love, but I do love him, and Anna did not love hers. How is she to blame, then? She wants to live. God has put that into our souls. I might very well have done the same.' . . . And Darya Alexandrovna pictured the most passionate and impossible love affairs" (608, VI.16). But this fantasy evaporates even before Dolly leaves the estate with her newly discovered disappointment in Anna's life. In the end, the significance of Dolly's fantasy is to underscore the deeper *differences,* rather than any lasting similarities, between her character and Anna's.

Where are the possible moral turning points during which Anna could have and should have stopped Vronsky and herself? In a sense, they are everywhere and therefore nowhere in particular. Anna's dualistic reaction to Vronsky and to her own attraction to him lasts from their first meeting in Moscow to her death. During the stop on the train to St. Petersburg, Vronsky's answer to Anna that he is following her in order to be near her is "the very thing that her soul desired but that her reason feared" (103, I.30).[67] Anna manages to keep him at arm's length for several months, to the extent that he even begins to despair of ever succeeding in his pursuit. The turning point for Vronsky occurs in Princess Betsy's drawing room when he speaks with Anna about love and sees her reaction: "She strained all the forces of her mind to say what she ought to say; but instead she rested her eyes on him, filled with love, and made no answer" (139–40, II.7). Although Vronsky is greatly heartened by her reaction, this moment is not a turning point *for Anna* as much as it is an *iteration* of her *continuing ambivalence*.

This does not mean that Tolstoy avoids all dramatic peripeties in the lives of his characters, as some readers have claimed. The novel contains a number of highly plotted moments that have major consequences for the participants—Kitty's heartbreak at the ball, Vronsky's horse race, Anna's "fall," her "near death" during childbirth, Vronsky's attempted suicide, Levin's cryptographic exchange with Kitty, Kitty's giving birth, Nikolai's death, Levin's ejection of Veslovsky, Koznyshev and Varenka's diffident courtship, Anna's suicide, Vronsky's departure for the Balkans. Rather, Tolstoy's focus seems to be on showing the destructive consequences of the ongoing *struggle* between ethics and passion in Anna and not on the possibility of resolving it. The ineradicability of this struggle can be read as either confirming or disconfirming the novel's epigraph. That Anna cannot get over her moral suffering and feels she has to take her own life supports the epigraph by confirming her ethical sense and by showing that her revenge against Vronsky is also her own punishment. That Anna is alone in feeling this way undermines the epigraph, as does the possibility that her character may have been her destiny.

13.5.8. Anna's "Doubling"

Another feature of Anna's psyche that raises questions about the extent to which she is free and therefore able to make moral choices is the "doubling" she experiences. If this is a psychological state, it suggests a pathology that is not of her own making and certainly not under her control, because it appears to be a reification of her moral quandary. This is even more the case if she is prey to some kind of spiritual or metaphysical malaise, because if her "soul" is somehow doubled, this would also appear to be a consequence of the struggle going on within her.

The reality of the doubling is first suggested by Vronsky's sense that as soon as Anna begins to speak about her unresolved situation with Karenin, it is as if "she, the real Anna, withdrew somewhere into herself and another woman stepped forward, strange and alien to him, whom he did not love but feared, and who rebuffed him" (189, II.23). Shortly after the narrator dismantles an appeal to God that Anna makes, she herself begins to experience a "new, never experienced state": "She felt that everything was beginning to go double in her soul, as an object sometimes goes double in tired eyes. Sometimes she did not know what she feared, what she desired"

(288, III.15). The context makes it clear that she is tormented by the competing demands of passion and morality, and the image of doubling in her soul implies the irreconcilability of these demands.

However, the fact that the narrator uses the simile of objects doubling before weary eyes—a hermeneutic index that translates an ethical and psychological state into a problem of visual acuity—simultaneously raises the possibility that Anna may not be "seeing" her situation clearly. In other words, if her eyes were not "weary," would her doubled vision stop? And what would a unified vision imply in this case? In general terms, it would presumably be a higher level of abstraction that can include in one category what had been two irreconcilable phenomena at a lower level. The problem with this possibility is that it does not seem realizable in Anna's case.[68] It also goes against the novel's dominant tendency to show "reality" as dependent on the perceiver as well as the difficulty of reconciling different characters' perspectives. Indeed, the reality of Anna's doubling—in the sense that it defines her in her world—is confirmed by how it progresses in her mind. She goes from the repeated feeling of psychological doubling during moments of heightened stress (290, III.15; 293, III.16) to the sense during her illness that she has actually split in two: she tells Karenin, "I'm the same . . . But there is another woman in me, I'm afraid of her—she fell in love with that man, and I wanted to hate you and couldn't forget the other one who was there before. The one who is not me. Now I'm real, I'm whole. I'm dying now" (412, IV.17, ellipses in original). Because this reads as an aggravation of the condition that beset Anna before her illness, it would be implausible to discount it as merely febrile raving.

It may not be possible to decide if Tolstoy intended to evoke the European literary tradition of "the double" in connection with Anna. In addition to E. T. A. Hoffmann, this includes well-known Russian examples such as Gogol's "The Nose," "The Portrait," and "The Overcoat" and Dostoevsky's *The Double, Crime and Punishment,* and others. Tolstoy knew all these works and valued Gogol especially highly, but his opinions about them were quite variable.[69] Nevertheless, a repeated motif in *Anna Karenina* about an evil "spirit" that seems to take possession of Anna lends itself to a "Gothic" interpretation that is in keeping with, if not identical to, aspects of the long and influential tradition of doubles in literature.[70]

It remains unclear, however, whether there is an "authentic" hint of the supernatural associated with the motif or if it is merely a turn of phrase or a parody. Skeptical readings are certainly possible. For example, when Karenin fails to have a frank talk with Anna during the early stages of her affair, he feels "the *spirit of evil and deceit* that possessed her also took possession of him, and he said something to her that was not right at all and not in the tone in which he had wanted to speak" (148–49, II.10, emphasis added). However, Karenin may fail to say what he means simply because his command of language is especially limited, and because language is never the best medium of communication in Tolstoy's world anyway. Later, "feeling in herself the presence of the already familiar *spirit of lying and deceit,* [Anna] at once surrendered to it and began talking without knowing herself what she was going to say. . . . 'You'll spend the night, I hope?' were the first words that the *spirit of deceit* prompted her to say" (204–5, II.27, emphasis added). This too can be explained in mundane terms as another example of the kind of deceptive play with language that the narrator identifies as typically female (see *16.2*). At one point, when Anna's relationship with Vronsky has deteriorated, she is pleased by his brief appeal to tenderness, "But some strange *power of evil* would not allow her to yield to her impulse, as if the conditions of the fight did not allow her to submit" (705, VII.12, emphasis added). It is possible to interpret this as an allusion to the inertia of the relations between them or to the power of memory, both of which are implied by the idea of their "fight" having "conditions." The same kind of interpretation is possible for Anna's thoughts about suicide, which she believes is her only alternative: "death presented itself to her clearly and vividly as the only way to restore the love for her in his heart, to punish him and to be victorious in the struggle that the *evil spirit* lodged in her heart was waging with him" (751, VII.26, emphasis added).

However, it would be an oversimplification to ignore the additional associations that these passages have in the novel and that consist of possible glimpses and hints of the transmundane. Can the "evil spirit" that Anna, Levin, and Karenin feel at various times be related to the theme of fate in the novel, which includes elements such as the terrifying dream of a mysterious peasant that Anna and Vronsky share *(17.1)* and the slippage of time that moves them toward death at an accelerated pace *(13.3)*? And do all these elements have any relation to Mikhailov's "Neoplatonism" or to Levin's sense that he glimpses a higher realm of being when Nikolai dies and when Kitty is giving birth *(9)*? Given the kinds of textual evidence that can be adduced for all these possibilities, the only honest answer has to be a qualified "yes." "Qualified" because there is not, in fact, a prominent "occult," "mystical," or "spiritual" dimension in the novel that can be identified unequivocally (which would also go against the grain of what is known of Tolstoy's own beliefs, even if these lie outside the novel). And "yes" because a force that influences Anna's behavior is reified in a way that is too resonant with familiar cultural types of occult agencies to be simply ignored.

In the end, all these varied details and experiences constitute a persistent whiff of the otherworldly in the novel that hints at other dimensions of being than those dominating its foreground. It would be misleading to put it more strongly. Tolstoy's general tendency to strip the supernatural from matters of faith in this and many other works also forestalls making any more definite or specific arguments about the presence of the otherworldly in Anna's existence. Nevertheless, another consideration that needs to be borne in mind is that there is a kind of binary "logic" to the possibility that characters who are engaged in an unrelenting egotistical struggle are associated with a possibly metaphysical evil that stands in opposition to the Pauline ideal of charitable self-sacrifice, even if this theme is expressed only problematically in the novel.

13.6. Stiva

Although Stiva is a "rounded" character and not a caricature, he is, nevertheless, dominated by a small handful of traits that determine how he sees the world and interacts with others. We first meet him when he wakes up in his study from his delightfully absurdist dream. This already says a great deal about him, because it implies that he slept perfectly well despite his problems with Dolly, who, by contrast, apparently did not sleep at all that night. The dream is also entirely in keeping with Stiva's interests and character because it combines images of a festive dinner, singing, and women. When Stiva does recall his transgression, he first moans out loud but then comes to a paradoxical conclusion: "I'm the guilty one in it all—guilty, and yet not guilty. That's the whole drama" (2, I.1). As the following paragraphs make clear, his sympathy for Dolly's suffering is genuine, but he does not really feel any guilt toward her because he cannot deny his fun-loving, easygoing, "amorous" nature and bachelor tastes. In his view, the one crucial mistake he made when Dolly confronted him with his incriminating letter to the former governess was that instead of trying to deny, dismiss, or explain it he smiled his "habitual, kind and therefore stupid smile." The key hermeneutic detail here is that Stiva did so "involuntarily" and that he thinks of the smile as "reflexes of the brain" (3, I.1). In other words, Stiva removes the onus of adultery from himself because he believes that his actions were spontaneous, instinctual, and natural (which is, in fact, supported by the narrator's specifying that Stiva's "face" smiled). This means that Stiva does not see himself as a free agent, which raises questions about whether or not he can be held responsible according to an impersonal code of ethics like Saint Paul's (of course, this thought never even occurs to Stiva). It is also difficult to fault Stiva for trying to exonerate himself because other characters do so as well, including not only Anna and Karenin but also Kitty and Levin. Moreover, Stiva's reaction to Dolly's suffering is short-lived and episodic. He sympathizes with her when he is with her and even weeps in her presence when he attempts a reconciliation that morning (11, I.4), but the rest of the time he shifts easily into his usual buoyant state, to the extent of thinking of a joke at the clockmaker's expense scant seconds after leaving a distraught and angry Dolly (13, I.4).[71]

Other aspects of Stiva's external life also appear to be reflections of his inborn traits. He subscribes to a liberal newspaper, and the narrator explains that "Stepan Arkadyich chose neither his tendency nor his views, but these tendencies and views came to him themselves, just as he did not choose the shape of a hat or a frock coat, but bought those that were in fashion" (7, I.3). The narrator's comparison is somewhat blurred, because it makes it seem as if Stiva simply imitates what he sees and hears around himself. In fact, however, his motivation appears to come from within and thus controls how he sees the world:

it was not because he found the liberal tendency more sensible, but because it more closely suited his manner of life. The liberal party said that everything was bad in Russia, and indeed Stepan Arkadyich had many debts and decidedly too little money. The liberal party said that marriage was an obsolete institution and was in need of reform, and indeed family life gave Stepan Arkadyich little pleasure. . . . The liberal party said, or, rather, implied, that religion was just a bridle for the barbarous part of the population, and indeed Stepan Arkadyich could not even stand through a short prayer service without aching feet. (7, I.3)

The notion of the self as the arbiter of value also enters inevitably into Stiva's relations with Levin. They have been friends since childhood, but despite their genuine affection for each other, "each of them, while rationally justifying the other's activity, despised it in his heart." In fact, Stiva, like Levin, cannot help thinking that "the life he led was the only real life, and the one his friend led was a mere illusion" (17, I.5). (This is yet another example of how the novel's laconic claims about positive relations between characters are undermined or counterbalanced via detailed descriptions of the ways in which their interests or behavior are actually incommensurable.) When Stiva visits Levin in the country and they argue about who is a real aristocrat, Levin makes a remark about how cheaply some can be bought that Stiva realizes is directed at him as well. Nevertheless, Stiva does not take offense because he focuses not on the *content* of what Levin says but only on what he sees as the appealingly energetic *tone* with which Levin says it (172, II.17), which means that Stiva effectively *recodes* Levin's remarks into his own terms.

Later in the novel, a similar situation emerges when Stiva is discussing with Karenin a certain Count Anichkin, who is Stiva's new superior. Karenin is interested only in the man's administrative "direction." But Stiva's attitude toward the count is also completely a function of his own interests: "I don't know his tendency, but one thing I do know—he's an excellent fellow. . . . We had lunch, and I taught him to make that drink—you know, wine with oranges. It's very refreshing. And remarkably enough, he didn't know it. He liked it very much. No, really, he's a nice fellow" (380, II.8). A few pages later Stiva does the same thing when, during a general conversation about women's rights, he addresses the issue not in the abstract but specifically in relation to the ballerina with whom he is involved and "whom he had had in mind all the while" (389, IV.10; see *16.2.1*).

At times, Stiva's generous bonhomie leads him to formulate hermeneutic indices that say more about his own purview than about the person he is trying to cheer up or the matter he is seeking to describe. On his way to visit Anna with Levin, Stiva summarizes her plans to divorce Karenin and marry Vronsky and concludes with the remark: "Well, and then her situation will be *as definite as mine, as yours*" (695, VII.9, emphasis added). Stiva and Levin obviously have antipodal attitudes toward marriage, but Stiva literally cannot grasp this in his desire to have all those around him be as happy as he is himself. Stiva's personal pleasure also figures as the primary touchstone in his revaluation of his life in Moscow according to the standards of his set in St. Petersburg. He finds it highly attractive that Prince Chechensky has two families, the first legitimate, the second not, and that he takes his eldest son to visit the second family, because it was "useful for the boy's development." Stiva also likes it that "[i]n Petersburg children did not hinder their father's life. . . . Here they understood that a man is obliged to live for himself, as an educated person ought to live." And whereas in Moscow working at a job was "drudgery," in St. Petersburg "there was interest in it. An encounter, a favour, an apt word, an ability to act out various jokes—and a man's career was suddenly made. . . . Such service had some interest in it." As for money, Stiva feels beset by his debts in Moscow, while in St. Petersburg he takes heart from stories about men such as Petrovsky, who, despite the fact that he had "run through five million," continued living in style and was even a "financial director" (729–30, VII.20). Thus, from Stiva's point of view, which the reader is made to share in this passage, the imperial capital's value lies in fostering a carefree, youthful approach to life that is unburdened by practical cares or ethical concerns.

From the point of view of someone like Levin or Dolly, however, what attracts Stiva is simply appalling. There is obviously little common ground between the two perspectives, but it is a noteworthy feature of the novel's ethical ambiguity that even the narrator and Levin are attracted to some aspects of urban dissolution, as when the narrator admires Liza Merkalov's languid beauty or when Levin is seduced by the atmosphere of the English club and falls prey to Anna's carefully modulated charm. Both are atypical reactions, and Levin quickly rejects the entire experience under Kitty's influence. But both reactions still make it difficult to put together an entirely coherent image of urban life because they do not contribute to consistent perspectives onto it.

Stiva's adultery and the moral issues it raises serve as an obvious thematic echo of Anna's story. It is especially notable, therefore, as has been remarked by readers since the novel first appeared, that in the long run Stiva emerges virtually unscathed by the judgments of other characters, to say nothing of his own. Dolly becomes reconciled to his philandering, and Levin, who strongly disapproves of libertinage and most of what Stiva loves best, never ceases to look upon him as a close friend. The narrator also does not condemn Stiva, although he characterizes him frankly at times and can, in fact, be seen as acquiescing in Stiva's self-indulgent albeit well-meaning view of things. For example, when Stiva wakes up and cannot figure out what to do about his problems, the narrator responds with an analytical passage that articulates Stiva's point of view but in terms that Stiva is not likely to have used himself: "There was no answer, except the general answer life gives to all the most complex and insoluble questions. That answer is: one must live for the needs of the day, in other words, become oblivious. To become oblivious in dreams was impossible now, at least till night-time; . . . and so one had to become oblivious in the dream of life. . . . 'We'll see later on,' Stepan Arkadyich said to himself" (4, I.2). The narrator's viewpoint here leaves little room for moral judgment. Instead of an appeal to principles of right and wrong, we have a situational, or entirely relativized, conception of behavior, according to which the best answers to problems will somehow arise by themselves when individuals stop seeking them and simply go on living. The fact that Dolly does something similar in order to deal with her grief (14, I.4) makes it unlikely that Stiva's indulging the "dream of life" is a sign of his unique moral failing.[72]

There is also some resemblance between Stiva's immersion in life and Levin's discovery at the novel's conclusion that he was living correctly (but thinking badly) all along when he was caught up in his daily affairs. As we have seen, Levin's life is not focused primarily on enacting moral edicts but on serving the complex needs of his family and estate. The personal, if not selfish nature of these goals, which also appear to be instinctual because they arise spontaneously, bring Levin closer to Stiva than might otherwise have seemed plausible. This correlation of their goals also blurs somewhat the moral distinction between them and further suggests that wisdom may often (but not always?) lie in submitting to the natural cycles of activity that constitute human existence (see *16.1*).

The number and variety of Stiva's acquaintances are so large—"Half Moscow and Petersburg were relatives or friends of Stepan Arkadyich" (14, I.5)—that it might seem paradoxical to claim that his view of the world is as personal, private, and isolating as that of Levin or Anna. Stiva's popularity makes it appear as if he has managed to bridge the distances that usually separate most other individuals in Tolstoy's world. In fact, however, the narrator makes it clear that everyone responds to Stiva on a visceral but inconsequential level that is the analogue of his own dominant trait of general and superficial sympathy:

> Stepan Arkadyich was not only liked by all who knew him for his kind, cheerful temper and unquestionable honesty, but there was in him, in his handsome, bright appearance, . . . something that physically made an amiable and cheerful impression on the people he met. "Aha! Stiva! Oblonsky! Here he is!" they would almost always say with a joyful smile on meeting him. And if it sometimes happened that talking with him produced no especially joyful effect, a day or two later they would all rejoice again in the same way when they met him. (15, I.5)

We see this side of Stiva's behavior in greater detail during the scenes with Levin in the restaurant. Despite Levin's discomfort with the artificiality of the place and its denizens, the two men have a heart-to-heart talk, during which Levin reveals his resolve to ask for Kitty's hand and Stiva speaks frankly of his "amorous" nature. Stiva's sympathy for Levin during the meal is confirmed by his quick understanding of Levin's feelings and his encouraging remarks to him regarding his chances with Kitty. But as soon as Stiva mentions Vronsky as a rival, Levin's mood sours and he withdraws emotionally from Stiva for the remainder of the meal, to the extent that he even stops listening to him in the end (42, I.11).

Stiva behaves similarly. He enters the conversation more easily than Levin and is perhaps even more frank than Levin in what he reveals about himself, but he is able to withdraw from intimacy with his childhood friend without batting an eye. After Stiva and Levin both realize that the food and wine did not, in fact, draw them closer together and that each "was thinking only of his own things, and they had nothing to do with each other," the narrator comments about how regularly Stiva had felt something similar in the past. His solution is well practiced: he calls for the bill and shifts his focus to someone else. In this case, it is an acquaintance with whom he starts up a conversation about "some actress and the man who kept her." As the narrator explains, this makes Stiva feel "relieved and rested after talking with Levin, who always caused him too much mental and spiritual strain" (42, I.11).

This example shows that Stiva is very much prey to the moment, which does not allow him to achieve any kind of durational contact with others, or with truths that transcend the given situation and that are not already part of his character. One could say that his genial openness toward everyone, which is stressed more than once by the narrator (e.g., 17, I.5), reflects a kind of inborn goodness and generosity of spirit to which Levin aspires and that is a minor version of what Saint Paul advocates. Stiva has, in fact, elicited far more good feeling among his fellow human beings than Levin has, although much of it could be judged as shallow. However, in the end, Stiva's mostly sensual motivations, even if tempered by a kind of unreflecting general decency and good fellowship, put him more at odds with the moral problems that trouble Levin and Anna than in harmony with them (even if their "instinctual" motivations are comparable).

Stiva's paradoxical status in *Anna Karenina* as an appealing libertine is also reflected in a major hermeneutic index that appears in his remarks to Levin about the relation between individuals and their worlds. Stiva's remark is important because it applies to many of the experiences that characters have throughout the novel. However, what he says also lends itself to antithetical interpretations, and it is not clear if these are to be celebrated or deplored. At the end of their dinner in the restaurant, Stiva points out that Levin is very "consistent" (*tsel'nyi* can also be translated as "whole," "entire," "integral" in this context, but it does not mean "wholesome," as Pevear and Volokhonsky translate it):

That is your virtue and your defect. You have a consistent [tsel'nyi] character, and you want all of life to be made up of consistent [tsel'nykh] phenomena, but that doesn't happen. So you despise the activity of public service because you want things always to correspond to their aim, and that doesn't happen. You also want the activity of the individual man always to have an aim, that love and family life always be one. And that doesn't happen. All the variety, all the charm, all the beauty of life are made up of light and shade. (42, I.11)

Stiva's diagnosis of Levin and his accusation against him are both accurate and wrongheaded, both in principle and in practice. Levin does want the outside world to coincide with his inner world, but in this he is no different from all the other characters in the novel, including Stiva himself, who wants everything to be happy and easy and who is saddened when it is not. Moreover, the idealism of characters (which blurs the distinction between inside and outside) makes them see the world in their own terms anyway, even if this is not quite the same as consistency between desire and fulfillment. Stiva is also accurate in how he describes life as a nonhomogeneous mass of light and shade, because this implies noncoincidence both within and among individuals, and this is, in fact, how the world in the novel is portrayed. The varieties of perspectives in *Anna Karenina* as well as Anna's own "doubling" support this view.

What remains unclear, however, is whether or not a mix of "light and shade" is really a good thing.[73] Although Stiva's positive evaluation accords with the prevalence of relativized perspectives in the novel, Levin's constant search for an absolute anchor in his life and his seeming discovery of a spiritual truth at the novel's end imply a desire for holism that is atypical of the mundane existence that most characters lead. Despite the problems inherent in the faith Levin discovers, by the novel's conclusion he does experience a major new form of (at least partial) coincidence between desire and fulfillment. This can be taken as an argument against Stiva's positive evaluation of the inescapably motley nature of existence.

But Levin's experiences also suggest the opposite conclusion. After his marriage, he feels that he needs his writing project so that his new life will not be "so uniformly bright" (*odnoobrazno svetla,* or "monotonously bright"). By contrast, before the marriage he had needed his work so that his life would not be "too bleak" (*mrachna,* or "dark") (483, V.15). One could argue as well that Levin's realization that he will not be able to communicate his faith to Kitty or to change his behavior also supports Stiva's view of noncoincidence as the characteristic of human existence. The narrator makes a similar comment about Vronsky's search for an occupation: "He soon felt that the realization of his desire had given him only a grain of the mountain of happiness he had expected. It showed him the eternal error people make in imagining that happiness is the realization of desires" (465, V.8).

Stiva's image of "light and shade" is possibly reevoked later in the novel during an important scene that is colored by an even greater ambivalence. When Dolly is going for a walk with Vronsky on his estate, he suddenly asks her to help him persuade Anna to seek a divorce from Karenin. In response,

"Darya Alexandrovna looked with questioning timidity at his energetic face, which kept moving into sunlit gaps in the shade of the lindens, then was darkened again by the shade" (625, VI.21). In addition to its function as a deftly caught realistic detail, the play of light and shade seems an especially appropriate association for Vronsky at this stage in his life since he and Anna are the most striking example in the novel of individuals whose desires are *not* fulfilled. But the quandary in which they find themselves is of course entirely untouched by the "variety," "charm," and "beauty of life" that Stiva celebrates. What Anna and Vronsky want instead is precisely a version of the holistic family existence that Levin also seeks. (However, Anna will never be able to achieve this state even if she is divorced from Karenin because she realizes that he will not let her have her son, Seryozha.)

13.6.1. To Judge or Not to Judge Stiva?

Even if the characters and the narrator do not condemn Stiva, it is possible that he can be judged by someone else—namely, the reader. But how can we determine if this is something that is elicited by specific features of the text as opposed to being projected onto it by a reader who happens to be so inclined? The distinction between these two kinds of judgments will not always be clear in any event, because what constitutes a textual prod to evaluation (or a hermeneutic index that requires not only interpretation but also *judgment* according to some criterion of right and wrong) can itself be subject to debate. Nevertheless, it is possible to argue that specific techniques in particular works are designed to elicit specific reactions from the reader.[74]

13.6.2. The Example of Turgenev's Hunter's Sketches

An example that can serve as a useful contrast to *Anna Karenina* in this regard is Ivan Turgenev's practice in his *Hunter's Sketches*. Moral judgment on social-political grounds became an essential facet of the critical response to this collection beginning with the separate publication of the first sketch, "Khor and Kalinych," in 1847. Leading contemporary writers and critics such as Vissarion Belinskii, Aleksandr Herzen, Pavel Annenkov, and Nikolai Nekrasov saw it and the later pieces as presenting truthful, sympathetic portraits of real Russian peasant types, as well as accurate depictions of their plight at the hands of landowners—in short, of showing serfdom as an irredeemably negative institution. It is also widely believed that the future Emperor Alexander II was so influenced by the *Hunter's Sketches* after they were published in book form in 1852 that he was moved to do away with serfdom—something that Turgenev later liked to think of as the greatest achievement of his life.[75] Nevertheless, there have been readers who claim that the problem of serfdom is not one that concerned Turgenev in the *Sketches* at all.[76] The way in which this discrepancy can be explained sheds useful light on Turgenev's narrative technique and also puts into perspective Tolstoy's method in *Anna Karenina*.

Turgenev's procedure for eliciting the reader's moral judgment emerges clearly in the second of the sketches, "Ermolai and the Miller's Wife." The hunter-narrator is normally a highly opinionated individual who does not hesitate to express either positive or negative judgments about anything. Here, for example, is his description of Ermolai's treatment of wounded game: "I noticed in him more than once unwitting manifestations of a kind of somber ferocity: I didn't like the expression on his face when he finished off a wounded bird with his teeth."[77] The miller in the sketch is described as if he were an ogre: "a tall man with a fat face, the back of his head like a bull's, and a round and big stomach" (26). The Zverkovs (the name is derived from the Russian word *zver'*, or "animal"), to whom Arina, the miller's wife, had belonged as a serf, are described in consistently negative terms: she is "flabby, sentimental, teary and malevolent—a commonplace and difficult creature"; her son is "spoiled and stupid"; and as for her husband, "The appearance of Mr. Zverkov himself did little to predispose one in his favor: out of a broad, almost square face, mousy eyes peered cunningly; . . . thin lips ceaselessly moved and smiled cloyingly" (29). The Zverkovs' cruel behavior toward Arina—whom they punish because she wants to get married, which they fear will make her a bad servant—is of course in keeping with these descriptions. But what about Arina herself? Apart from twice mentioning that he looked upon her "with compassion" (28, 31) and that she is still beautiful (27), the narrator expresses no judgment about her plight or its causes. In fact, near the conclusion of the sketch, Turgenev has his hunter-narrator ask Ermolai an extraordinarily naive question about Arina: "What is she, ill?" to which Ermolai answers, "What health!" implying that her problems are not at all a matter of physical well-being.

This example shows that the *narrator* is Turgenev's primary device in the *Sketches* for manipulating the reader into making the necessary moral judgments that are nowhere articulated *explicitly* in the cycle. The narrator expresses positive and negative evaluations about *everything* that comes into his purview *except* for the institution of serfdom itself. In fact, in "Ermolai and the Miller's Wife" he actually falls silent after Ermolai's sardonic comment "What health!" Instead, he paints a brief landscape, which completes the "nature" frame for the sketch, and then falls asleep. But because the narrator had loaded all the other components of his tale with strong and vivid judgments, his egregious lapse into unconsciousness at this juncture inevitably calls forth the reader's reaction, which is pity for Arina and moral outrage at the system that caused her plight.

It is clear, of course, that any overt condemnation of serfdom by the narrator was out of the question for Turgenev because it would not have passed the censorship in effect in Russia at the time. But the tactic of having the narrator become silent at a crucial point in his tale is also a much more effective way for Turgenev to get his point across because of the way it works on the reader's imagination. Rather than being confronted with an overt and loud condemnation contained in the text, the reader is put into the position of having to make the necessary judgment and condemnation on his own. Turgenev's tactic illustrates well Boris Uspenskii's point that "the compositional structure of a literary work may specifically foresee some responses on the part of the reader, in such a way that the reader's reactions enter into the author's calculations, as if the author were programming those responses into the work."[78] In more general terms, this narrative technique resembles what Lotman called a "minus device" (minus priem) in literary works, which produces its effect precisely by *not* providing what the reader has been conditioned to expect in a given structural location either by cultural codes, generic conventions, or patterns set up by the work itself.[79]

The situation we find in "Khor and Kalinych" is repeated in another sketch, "Raspberry Spring" (see also *5.4*). The hunter-narrator ironizes bitterly at the expense of the landowners in Shumikhino, where the pathetic Stepushka now lives (34–35). He also laments Stepushka's plight but without fixing blame on anyone. The narrator then shifts to the tale that Tuman tells about the self-indulgence and cruelty of an eighteenth-century grandee he had served. But after Tuman finishes with his descriptions of the abuses allowed in the grandee's household, Turgenev has his narrator make only two brief comments: "your master was strict, I see," and "Now this sort of thing isn't done." To this Tuman responds: "Now, of course, it's better" (40). The subject is then dropped. No explicit judgment follows from the narrator; in fact, in a characteristic move, he turns to a description of the natural setting. But the irony the author planted in Tuman's comment about things being better now is revealed by the appearance on the scene of Vlas, another peasant with a tale of woe. Vlas's son has just died, and his master refuses to listen to him, much less adjust his quitrent (41). In typical fashion, the narrator records the peasant's pathetic remarks, even asks how much he has to pay his owner, but otherwise restricts himself to the laconic remark, "My poor Vlas became sad," and then falls into a long silence: "We parted after half an hour" (42). Thus again there is no moral judgment of the landlord by the narrator; this is left to the reader as a consequence of Turgenev's arrangement of the elements in the sketch.

Other sketches by Turgenev that are fashioned in this way include "Lgov," "The Bailiff," "The Office," "Biriuk," "Death," "The Singers," "Petr Petrovich Karataev," and "Living Relics." Turgenev continued to use narrative silences skillfully in his famous later novels as well.

In the case of *Anna Karenina,* we are dealing with moral issues that are different from those related to the institution of serfdom, but the narrator's moral agenda is still clearly a function of how contemporary Russian society is constituted. We have seen that the narrator does not hesitate to *describe* Stiva's actions and thoughts at every turn. The difference from Turgenev is that Tolstoy's narrator *judges* neither Stiva negatively nor anyone else *systematically.* When combined with the ultimately positive attitudes of other characters toward Stiva, this does not allow much, if any, room for the reader to conclude otherwise. Indeed, what sense would it make for the reader to condemn Stiva for his womanizing if Dolly acquiesces in it and all the other characters ignore it? In short, in the world of *Anna Karenina* Stiva is oddly and largely guiltless (even as he dissipates the family's wealth). And the consequence this has for the novel's ethics is to make them inescapably relative.

13.7. Dolly

Any analysis of Dolly has to consider that she is a secondary character with a relatively limited role in the novel, that her existence is restricted almost exclusively to being a mother and much-enduring wife, and that she consequently has few opportunities to interact with anyone outside her immediate circle. Nevertheless, her role in the novel is important for several reasons.[80] As the embodiment of experienced motherhood, Dolly is the leading exemplar of the theme of family life that is sounded in the novel's opening sentence. Anna is obviously a failure in this regard; Kitty and Levin are promising beginners; the senior Shcherbatskys and especially the Lvovs are minor characters; and successful peasant families are seen too briefly and obliquely to serve as leading examples, even though they still have an important function as sympathetic resonators for themes raised in connection with major characters. However, it is highly ironic that Dolly's role as a beacon should be tarnished by Stiva's behavior, which, as she fears, could actually undo all or most of her efforts. Through her overwhelming concern with her children's *moral* upbringing, Dolly also echoes strongly the ethical implications of the novel's epigraph, although, as we have seen, Stiva adds a loud, discordant note here as well.

Dolly is also important because even she can be tempted to contemplate straying from the moral path by personal considerations: "Abstractly, theoretically, she not only justified but even approved of what Anna had done. Weary of the monotony of a moral life, as irreproachably moral women in general often are, she not only excused criminal love from a distance but even envied it. Besides, she loved Anna from the heart" (621, VI.20). Of course, Dolly does not act on her inclinations. But this passage is still significant and surprising because *the narrator* posits a necessary *dialectical* connection between morality and immorality, or between a universal code of behavior and personal needs. The implications of this claim support Stiva's argument to Levin about the motley nature of existence *(13.6)*. The claim also accords with the behavior of several characters who seem inevitably to drift away from the moral resolutions or commitments they make: Karenin cannot maintain his stance of Christian charity, Kitty abandons emulating Varenka, and Levin recognizes the practical limits of his faith. The narrator's claim thus suggests that human nature is inherently inconstant, and possibly and fundamentally incompatible with absolute spiritual values and states of being. In turn, this leads to two very different possibilities: that it is hopeless to apply absolute moral standards to human beings or that morality is still important because although human beings may drift away from it, they can also return to it (see *12.6*).[81]

Because of Dolly's capacity for sympathy, it may also seem at first that she is able to transcend the boundaries of the self to a greater extent than the other characters discussed above. For example, when she sees Kitty's distraught state after Vronsky abandons her, "Dolly, with her motherly, family habit of mind, saw at once that there was woman's work to be done, and she prepared to do it. She took off her hat and, morally rolling up her sleeves, prepared for action" (122–23, II.2). In the scene that follows, she understands Kitty perfectly even though they do not speak openly about the reason for Kitty's misery (125, II.3). Later, Dolly is equally perspicacious when she understands that Levin's pride will not allow him to visit her while Kitty is spending the summer in the country (270, III.10). In all these instances, she clearly is able to grasp the other's viewpoint, even though it differs from her own.

However, upon closer examination, what makes this possible is that Dolly, like the other characters, is moved by a priori loves or antipathies. This is obviously the case in her dealings with her younger sister Kitty. It is also the case with Levin, as we can infer from Dolly's reaction to Vronsky during dinner at his estate: "Darya Alexandrovna found it strange to hear how calmly in the right [Vronsky] was, there at his own table. She remembered Levin, who thought the opposite, being just as resolute in his opinions at his own table. But she loved Levin and was therefore on his side" (633, VI.22). In other words, Dolly here enacts the same kind of value judgment based on prior sympathy rather than inherent merit that Kitty and Levin raise to a fundamental principle at the Oblonskys' dinner *(13.4.1)*.

Because Dolly's visit to Vronsky's estate is the one instance in the novel when we see her away from her home and her family, it becomes a test case for her ability to grasp what is unfamiliar to her. The entire discussion at Vronsky's table, which is about the advantages and duties of being a landowner, is clearly of minor interest to Dolly. What she notes instead is that the discussion actually reflects an "intimate quarrel" between Anna and Vronsky. This can be taken in various ways—as a sign of Dolly's insight with regard to Anna, to whom she still feels indebted, or as Dolly's heightened sensitivity to signs of marital discord that echo her own, or both. However, the continuation of the scene suggests that the second, more personal alternative may be more likely. When all the guests go to play lawn tennis, Dolly disapproves of the flirtatious relations between Anna and Veslovsky, which, no matter how innocently, still evoke the theme of marital infidelity. Dolly also does not think it is natural for grown-ups to "play at a children's game by themselves, without children," which is probably in large measure a function of her own preoccupation with her children (as well as possibly the narrator's veiled comment about those who like the game: Vronsky and Sviyazhsky "played very well and seriously"). Similarly, at the end of the day Dolly feels "as if she were playing in the theatre with actors better than herself" and yearns to return to the familiar reality of her children (634, VI.22). All the worries and difficulties of child rearing on which she had focused during her trip to Vronsky's estate now seem joys to her. Moreover, after returning to Levin's estate she describes how "sweet and touching" Anna and Vronsky are and says this, as the narrator comments, "with perfect sincerity, forgetting the vague sense of dissatisfaction and discomfort that she had experienced there" (642, VI.24). Later, Dolly's attitude toward Anna will change once more, thus demonstrating again the extent to which her views of everything are functions of her frame of mind.

The only other instance of Dolly's attempt to interest herself in someone outside her immediate family circle is her conversation with Karenin about Anna during the dinner party Stiva organizes. Dolly begins by being "firmly convinced of Anna's innocence" and feels herself "growing pale and her lips trembling with wrath at this cold, unfeeling man who so calmly intended to ruin her innocent friend" (392, IV.12). But when Karenin describes his certainty regarding Anna's adultery and confesses his unhappiness to Dolly, the narrator remarks: "He had no need to say it. Darya Alexandrovna understood it as soon as he looked into her face. She felt sorry for him, and her belief in her friend's innocence was shaken" (393, IV.12). Dolly's ability to read Karenin's face is a sure Tolstoyan sign of privileged communication. But the unmediated contact does not last, and the frame of reference that Dolly invokes is inevitably her own past with Stiva. When Karenin says, "it is impossible to live as three," Dolly responds, "'I understand, I understand that very well,' . . . and she bowed her head. She paused, thinking of herself, of her own family grief, and suddenly raised her head energetically and clasped her hands in a pleading gesture" (394, IV.12). Dolly then tells Karenin of Stiva's infidelity and how she was able to forgive him with Anna's help, all of which she intends as an example to Karenin of what he can do as well. Embedded within Dolly's plea, however, is a detail that undermines the relevance of her remarks for Karenin and that simultaneously underscores the extent to which she is caught within her own past. She describes the consequence of Anna's having "saved" her as follows: "And so I live. My children are growing up, my husband comes back to the family, he feels he wasn't right, becomes purer, better" (394, IV.12). Dolly's rosy picture of Stiva may be a temporary, protective self-delusion or a consequence of her enthusiasm for the prospect of "saving" Karenin from abandoning Anna and for instilling in him the Christian virtue of forgiveness. Dolly assesses Stiva much more coldly at other points in the novel, for example, "Had it not been for [her children], she would have remained alone with her thoughts of her husband, who did not love her" (262, III.7).[82] Whatever the case, Karenin's reaction confirms the irrelevance for him of Dolly's proselytizing: he "listened, but her words no longer affected him. In his soul there arose again all the anger of the day when he had decided on divorce" (394, IV.12). Thus, in a pattern that is typical for the novel as a whole, at the very moment when two interlocutors begin to speak of what is most important for each of them, they do not communicate with each other as much as withdraw into themselves. The scene between Dolly and Karenin also makes it difficult to believe that Christian teaching can ameliorate human relations. When Dolly tells Karenin to "[l]ove those who hate you" she does so "shamefacedly," which implies discomfort with the role that she is now assuming. Karenin's response is to smile "contemptuously. He had long known that, but it could not be applied in his case. 'Love those who hate you, but to love those you hate is impossible'" (395, IV.12). Is this Karenin's failing or Saint Paul's?

13.8. Vronsky

Vronsky's life falls into two unequal parts. Initially, he is entirely a creature of his St. Petersburg set's codes of behavior, so that his perspectives are really functions of their values. But the latter part of his affair with Anna forces him to change.

The first time we see him in action is at the Shcherbatskys', shortly after Kitty rejects Levin. Among the narrator's characterizations of Vronsky is one dealing specifically with his inability to imagine alterity: "If he could have heard what her parents said that evening, if he could have taken the family's point of view and learned that Kitty would be unhappy if he did not marry her, he would have been very surprised and would not have believed it. He could not have believed that something which gave such great and good pleasure to him, and above all to her, could be bad. Still less could he have believed that he was obliged to marry her." The degree to which Vronsky's view of Kitty is egotistical is further suggested by the narrator's ironic remark about why Vronsky leaves her house with a "pleasant feeling of purity and freshness": "partly because he had not smoked all evening" (57, I.16). Nevertheless, in his own way, Vronsky does sense that the "secret spiritual bond" existing between him and Kitty has strengthened during the evening in question to the extent that he feels an unfocused desire to do something about it. All this ends as soon as he meets Anna the following morning, which leads him to forget Kitty completely.

Vronsky's a priori distaste for marriage is, in part, a consequence of his not having known real family life (56, I.16; this, however, never stops Levin from yearning for it, even though he was orphaned in childhood). Even more important is that, "according to the general view of the bachelor world in which he lived," husbands and families are "something alien, hostile and, above all, ridiculous" (57, I.16). This view is contiguous with the slippage between what Vronsky feels about his mother and how he behaves toward her. Although he actually dislikes her, the codes of his set and his education in the Corps of Pages require him to feign complete submission and respect (61, I.17).

The first stage of Vronsky's love for Anna is largely narcissistic. After he speaks with her when the train stops during the snowstorm, he settles into his seat and begins to gaze at the other passengers in his compartment "as if they were things." In particular, a hapless young functionary at whom Vronsky looks "as at a lamppost" struggles in vain to assert his humanity in the face of Vronsky's imperturbability. Why does Vronsky behave this way? The narrator explains:

He felt himself a king, not because he thought he had made an impression on Anna—he did not believe that yet—but because *the impression she had made on him* gave him happiness and pride.

What would come of it all, he did not know and did not even consider. He felt that all his hitherto dissipated and dispersed forces were gathered and directed with terrible energy towards one blissful goal. And he was happy in that. (104–5, I.31, emphasis added)

There is some similarity between Vronsky's state on the train and Levin's inability to see anything but his own joy following the Oblonsky dinner party (see *13.4.1*). Both characters "read" the world exclusively in personal terms and fail to grant it any existence independent of their own.[83] However, any comparison of Levin and Vronsky is limited by their very different characters, values, and experience of women and of life. In contrast to Levin's overflowing generosity, Vronsky's fixation on his infatuation is entirely egotistical. This inevitably evokes negative cultural associations, which are also implied by the narrator's description of the effect Vronsky has on the functionary. Thus, if Levin errs by being too generous in assuming that all are like him when he is in love, Vronsky errs by being too selfish when he fails to recognize any connection between himself and others. Each character's attitude toward his rival reflects this difference as well. When Vronsky sees Karenin meet Anna at the St. Petersburg train station, he is offended by the thought that anyone else might presume to love her. But he is not at all flustered by the husband's presence and obvious coldness, and even secures an invitation for their "at homes." Vronsky's singlemindedness of purpose is a kind of inversion of Levin's equally strong reaction when Stiva mentions Vronsky as Levin's rival during their dinner at the restaurant. Levin acts as if his personal feelings are desecrated, and the elation he experiences because of Stiva's encouragement immediately dissipates (he also suddenly feels guilty for having forgotten his brother Nikolai; 39–40, I.11). However, Levin's generosity emerges here as well, because when he has a chance to see Vronsky for the first time immediately after Kitty rejects his proposal, the narrator underscores Levin's curiosity about and positive evaluation of his successful rival (50, I.14).

Snobbery is a defining characteristic of Vronsky's world in general, and he divides people into two "completely opposite sorts." The "inferior sort" consists of "banal, stupid and, above all, ridiculous people who believed that one husband should live with one wife, whom he has married in church, that a girl should be innocent, a woman modest, a man manly, temperate and firm, that one should raise children, earn one's bread, pay one's debts, and other such stupidities." In other words, these are people of Levin's and Kitty's ilk. On the other hand, there are the "real" people to which Vronsky's entire set belongs and who "had, above all, to be elegant, handsome, magnanimous, bold, gay, to give oneself to every passion without blushing and laugh at everything else" (114, I.34). Vronsky also applies this transvaluation to his financial and other affairs, as when he feels compelled to pay immediately a debt incurred by a comrade to a cardsharper, whereas merchants, hotel keepers, and the like can wait indefinitely; or when he feels free to deceive a husband even though he believes that in principle one must be honest toward everyone (304–5, III.20).[84] The negative consequence of Vronsky's attitude is suggested by the possibility that he may have abetted the ruin of his English horse trainer. When Vronsky is tending to his accounts, he places the sum he owes the Englishman in a category of secondary importance and plans to pay only a fraction of the total (303, III.19). Later, we learn that the Englishman has become a drunkard and abandons his family, which Anna takes in (695–96, VII.9). Perhaps the events are linked (see also *8.1*).

Those close to Vronsky, such as his fellow officer Yashvin, mirror the same codes, or "immoral principles," as the narrator characterizes them (176, II.19). Vronsky's mother is initially pleased that he has been having an affair with Anna, because she feels that nothing "gave the ultimate finish to a brilliant young man like a liaison in high society" and because she does not see Anna's adultery as any different from the behavior of other "decent" women in her own circle. Vronsky's older brother cares about the affair only because its intensity has begun to displease the powers that be in St. Petersburg and not because he has any personal interest in its character or morality (174, II.18). His values are also dictated by the hedonistic interests of his set.

The inward turn of Vronsky's feelings prompted by Anna is consistent with what the narrator identifies as his defining characteristic: "Ambition was the old dream of his childhood and youth, a dream which he did not confess even to himself, but which was so strong that even now this passion struggled with his love." In fact, there is an even closer link between

Vronsky's ambition and his liaison with Anna, because, as the narrator explains, the sensation the affair had caused in society and the glamour with which it had invested Vronsky had "pacified for a time the worm of ambition that gnawed at him" (306, III.20). Anna becomes, at least initially and in part, a tool of his vainglory.

Another facet of Vronsky's self-conception is his chivalry. Because Anna has given him her love, he sees her as being "worthy of equal and even greater respect than a lawful wife. He would have let his hand be cut off sooner than allow himself a word or a hint that might insult her or fail to show her that respect which a woman may simply count on" (305, III.20). Vronsky's stance bespeaks a certain nobility of spirit that there is no reason to deny. At the same time, however, it is important to recall the context for this glimpse of Vronsky's attitude toward Anna, which is the narrator's openly ironic description of the entire system of codes according to which Vronsky lives. This includes such digs as that Vronsky is prepared to force anyone who speaks publicly of his affair to "respect the nonexistent honour of the woman he loved" (305, III.20). In other words, even Vronsky's chivalry toward Anna reflects his set's codes, which are treated scornfully by the narrator and serve primarily to perpetuate its members' feelings of unwarranted superiority to all outsiders.

The ultimate inadequacy of Vronsky's codes is also demonstrated by his reaction to Anna's pregnancy, which he recognizes "called for something not wholly defined by the code of rules that guided him in his life." Initially "his heart" prompts him to suggest that she should leave her husband. But then he thinks the matter over and decides that it would be better if she did not leave Karenin, although he also wonders if this "might . . . not be a bad thing?" (305, III.20). I will discuss later other instances when characters experience prompts from their conscience (see *15*). For the present, suffice it to point out that Vronsky's suggestion to Anna is characterized by relative selflessness: her burdens would be eased if she were no longer living under Karenin's roof, and Vronsky's own would be markedly increased. Given this, it is hardly surprising that the voice of Vronsky's conscience quickly fades, that he decides against leaving the army, and that he takes comfort in recalling Anna's remark about not wanting to change her position. He also reestablishes the connection between his affair with Anna and his ambition when he says that because he has her love he cannot envy an old friend's brilliant career (307, III.20).

Vronsky's renewed inward turn is also reaffirmed in the ensuing scene of his drive to a rendezvous with Anna: "Before, too, he had often experienced the joyful awareness of his body, but never had he so loved himself, his own body, as now. He enjoyed feeling that slight pain in his strong leg, enjoyed feeling the movement of his chest muscles as he breathed. That same clear and cold August day which had had such a hopeless effect on Anna, to him seemed stirringly invigorating" (313, III.22). Although Vronsky thinks during the drive that his love for Anna is not only complete but ever increasing, the narrator's remark about Anna's feeling of "hopelessness" shows how one-sided this view is. And when they meet, it becomes obvious that they understand each other and confide in each other only partially at best (see *13.5.3* for Anna's side). On the one hand, Vronsky is infected by Anna's anxiety as soon as he sees her and even before he knows her reason. On the other, as soon as she tells him that she has confessed their affair to her husband, Vronsky's inner thoughts veer sharply away from Anna's concerns. The narrator underscores that she never would have guessed that the first idea to enter his mind is that he will now have to fight a duel with Karenin. What follows is a series of painful mismatches between Anna's hopes and Vronsky's responses. Anna's wish that Vronsky would cut through her problems by urging her to flee with him is not realized. His drawing her onto a side path in the garden to avoid possibly being seen by acquaintances disappoints her. When she gives him Karenin's letter to read, Vronsky's imagination is filled with the impending duel and how he will fire into the air with a cold and proud expression while he awaits the husband's shot; but Anna has no part in Vronsky's imagined scene. Indeed, the thought flashes through his mind that it would be better for him not to be tied down by her at all. After Vronsky finishes the letter, his indecisive mien shatters Anna's last hopes. She realizes that she has nothing left except for his love and then, in an especially painful moment, cannot specify why she feels proud of her position as his lover (314–16, III.22). Vronsky feels pity for her, of course, but at the same time cannot think how to help her, because "he knew that he was to blame for her unhappiness, that he had done something bad" (316, III.22).

When we next encounter Vronsky several months later, his attitude toward Anna has changed greatly. He no longer thinks that he could end their affair if he wanted to, his personal ambitions have receded into the background, and because he does not engage in his old pastimes as much as he used to he increasingly surrenders to his passion, which ties him to Anna more and more strongly (356, IV.2). Nevertheless, their relations do not change, and new barriers arise between them. The narrator stresses that Anna now regularly projects an impossibly elevated opinion onto Vronsky (357, IV.2). She is also constantly jealous, which causes frictions both large and small. A neat illustration of how this frustrates communication between them appears in the scene of Vronsky's ill-fated visit to her house when Karenin is supposed to be gone. Torn between jealousy and a need to speak to Vronsky after a hiatus of several days, Anna interrupts what he says. But when her fears are briefly allayed and she urges him to continue, "he could not immediately recall what he was going to say. These fits of jealousy, which had come over her more and more often lately, horrified him and, no matter how he tried to conceal it, made him cooler towards her, though he knew that the cause of her jealousy was her love for him" (358, IV.3). Vronsky now feels himself to be in the paradoxical position of being farther from happiness than when he was just beginning to pursue Anna. (He is also granted a moment of painful self-awareness when he sees a resemblance between himself and the vacuous foreign prince he has been escorting [355, IV.1].) During the meeting in her home, the one sensation Vronsky shares fully with Anna is terror due to the nightmare about the French-speaking peasant that he had just had as well (361, IV.3). And although one might have thought that the child Anna is expecting would bring them closer together, the narrator ends the chapter stressing Vronsky's inability to "understand the meaning" of the expression on Anna's face when she feels "the stirring of new life inside her" (362, IV.3).

We next see Vronsky by Anna's sickbed when everyone believes she is dying. Vronsky feels crushed by Karenin's magnanimity and by his sense of his own baseness. He also feels that he has never before loved Anna as fully as he does now. The situation is again paradoxical, because although Vronsky feels that he has been changed irrevocably by these new experiences, he has no way of acting upon them and believes he is on the verge of losing Anna forever. His attempt at suicide thus confirms the privacy of his despair and the extent to which he is isolated from everything and everyone around him. (It also foreshadows Anna's frame of mind before her suicide and Vronsky's own isolation when he is leaving for the Balkan war, which can be interpreted as a surrogate form of suicide [780, VIII.51].) The narrator reinforces the solipsism of Vronsky's state by alluding to the vicious circle of thought from which he cannot escape: "he stood motionless with the revolver in his hands and considered. 'Of course,' he said to himself, as if a logical, continuous and clear train of thought had brought him to an unquestionable conclusion. In fact, this 'of course' that he found so convincing was only the consequence of a repetition of exactly the same round of memories and notions that he had already gone through a dozen times within the hour" (417, IV.18). The association of Vronsky's circular thought, which is a tautological hermeneutic index, with an illusory rationality also evokes all the negative judgments of reason that the narrator makes in the novel and foreshadows especially the ambivalent phrase about reason that Anna over-hears shortly before her own suicide (see *13.5.4*).

The inward focus of Vronsky's attempted suicide is also suggested by how he views it in retrospect, which can be interpreted in two divergent al-though not antithetical ways. The key detail is Vronsky's redefinition of himself when he recovers from his wound as "completely free of one part of his grief": "By his act he had washed himself, as it were, of the shame and humiliation he had felt previously. He could think calmly now of Alexei Alexandrovich. He recognized all his magnanimity and no longer felt him-self humiliated" (433, IV.23). In one sense, therefore, Vronsky's attempted suicide is a form of self-punishment for the wrong he had done Karenin. But in its privacy and autotelic nature it preserves Vronsky's solipsistic pridefulness because he does not seek out Karenin to ask for his forgive-ness, and does not explain to anyone why he attempted to take his own life, which could also have been due to his despair over Anna's imminent death. In fact, he specifically asks his sister-in-law to tell everyone that he shot himself accidentally, because "[o]therwise it's too stupid" (433, IV.23).

However, it is also possible to argue that Vronsky's retrospective view resembles the possible consequences of the duel he had fantasized about fighting with Karenin (which is not to say that he is deluded about this dur-ing the moment he pulls the trigger [417, IV.18]). Vronsky imagined that he would have discharged his own pistol into the air and then stood ready to receive Karenin's fire, as a result of which only Vronsky himself could have been injured or killed. Thus, the way Vronsky looks back upon his at-tempted suicide is as if he had, in fact, submitted to being fired upon by Karenin. In either case, Vronsky's conclusion that he has restored the equi-librium between himself and Karenin constitutes a hermeneutic index that implies two overlapping cultural practices. The more general one is the widespread belief in the need to pay with one's own suffering or blood for the wrongs done to another. This idea is inherent in secular conceptions of both justice and vengeance, as well as in the Christian notion of redemp-tion and of Christ as the ultimate Redeemer. (It also underlies Saint Paul's conception of divine vengeance and the image of the evildoer with coals on his head *[7]*.) The narrower cultural practice is the Russian (and European) dueling code, according to which the mere fact that both the challenger and the challenged are *willing* to shed their own *or* their opponent's blood may be sufficient to erase any transgression between them; in this case, it makes no difference who is the victimizer and who the victim.[85] From an anthropological point of view, both cultural beliefs presumably share a common genesis. However, Vronsky's action differs markedly from the model of Christ's "guiltless guilt" because it restores him to his confident self and leaves no lasting effect on anyone except himself: "he fell back into the old rut of his life. He saw the possibility of looking people in the eye without shame and could live under the guidance of his habits" (433, IV.23). Despite the narrator's comment about "the old rut," Vronsky does undergo one significant change when Anna recovers and he sees her again. He gives up a "flattering and dangerous" mission to Tashkent dreamt up for him by Serpukhovskoy that would have satisfied his previous ambition, and leaves for Europe with Anna instead (435, IV.23). Thus, it is not the case that the extraordinary event of Vronsky's attempted suicide dissipates without any issue except for the reestablishment of the past.

When Anna and Vronsky meet for the first time after they recuperate, they recommit themselves to each other passionately. But their rhetoric is punctuated by dissonant notes of estrangement, which they attempt to ignore (434, IV.23). When Anna says there is something "terrible" in their love, Vronsky responds that this will only strengthen it. Anna smiles, but, as the narrator notes, her response is "not to his words but to his enamoured eyes," which means that she may not have fully registered what he said (435, IV.23). Vronsky also makes several comments about Anna's appearance that can be read in antithetical ways: he says that he does not recognize her with her short hair (which had been cut during her illness) and that she reminds him of a "boy," which he further qualifies by adding, "You're so pretty" and "how pale you are!" These remarks indicate either that he (temporarily) sees her in a new light as a consequence of all they recently experienced, or that he is responding to surface changes in her appearance that have little to do with her actual character and their actual relationship (and surface appearances become defining traits for them both shortly thereafter). In either case, the reference to "boy" also evokes the dark role that Anna's son plays in their relationship and her private grief, and suggests that little may have changed for Anna and Vronsky despite the seemingly extraordinary events both experienced.

The differing perceptions that Anna and Vronsky have of her son also constitute indices implying that there is still a fundamental hiatus between them. Anna admits that she cares about nothing now, not even a divorce, but then adds, "Only I don't know what [Karenin will] decide about Seryozha." Vronsky's response is presented in two forms. The first is unspoken and is reported by the narrator: "He simply could not understand how, at this moment of their reunion, she could think about her son, about divorce. Was it not all the same?" Out loud Vronsky says, "Don't talk about it, don't think," which is his veiled attempt to dismiss something that has been crucial for Anna since the beginning of their affair. Vronsky also tries to draw Anna's attention to himself after saying this, but she will not look at him. Instead, her response is to exclaim, "Ah, why didn't I die, it would be better!" and to smile at him through her tears "so as not to upset him," which implies that she conceals more than she communicates (435, IV.23).

The description of Anna and Vronsky's trip focuses on the growing imbalance in their relationship and their tendency to see things in ways that are divergent or entirely different. Whereas Anna revels in her restored health and freedom and idealizes Vronsky ("to possess him fully was a constant joy for her"), he is not completely happy (464–65, V.8). The fact that he has finally gotten what he had long yearned for gave "him only a grain of the mountain of happiness he had expected. . . . He soon felt arise in his soul a desire for desires, an anguish." This leads him to "grasp at every fleeting caprice, taking it for a desire and a goal," which is what leads to his dabbling in painting and collecting art (465, V.8). The narrator's dismissal of Vronsky's artistic pursuits, which includes the hermeneutic index "pleasant delusion" (my translation of "priiatnoe zabluzhdenie" [466, V.9]), underscores the extent to which he is an imitator, and thereby recalls how he always relied on the guidance of his social set's codes of behavior:

He understood all kinds [of art] and could be inspired by one or another; but he could not imagine that one could be utterly ignorant of all the kinds of painting and be inspired directly by what was in one's soul, unconcerned whether what one painted belonged to any particular kind. Since he did not know that, and was inspired not directly by life but indirectly by life already embodied in art, he became inspired very quickly and easily, and arrived as quickly and easily at making what he painted look very much like the kind of art he wanted to imitate. (465–66, V.8)

Vronsky becomes so fond of Italian life during the Middle Ages that "he even began wearing his hat and a wrap thrown over his shoulder in a medieval fashion, which was very becoming to him" (466, V.9). Given the narrator's negative characterization of Vronsky's artistic dilettantism, his style of dress emerges as a form of playacting. Its inauthenticity may thus bear on Vronsky's estranged view of Anna on her sickbed because of her boyish haircut (and enters into the larger network of references to the semiotics of clothing throughout the novel, including Stiva's dress, Levin's wedding shirt, and the Plotinian acts of "uncovering," to which I will return [18]). Similarly, a comment that Mikhailov makes about the falsity of Vronsky's painting also functions as an implicit negative judgment of

Vronsky's love for Anna: Mikhailov equates Vronsky's "toying" with painting to someone's making "a big wax doll and kiss[ing] it"—behavior that
would be offensive to a lover who has a real beloved (478–79, V.13). Vronsky himself unwittingly confirms that his relationship with Anna lacks an
essential core when he becomes disenchanted with his art and simultaneously discovers that his life with Anna in Italy has become "boring." Their
solution is to seek support outside themselves by returning to Russia,
where Anna will go to see her son (thereby reconfirming once again the
boy's divisive significance in their lives) and Vronsky will try his hand at
being a country squire.

In Russia, things deteriorate further for Vronsky and Anna. While they
are still in St. Petersburg, he notices a new mood in her that he cannot
understand: "At one moment she appeared to be in love with him, at another she became cold, irritable and impenetrable." It is a striking example
of Vronsky's blindness that he still has not grasped that Anna is most likely
troubled by her wish to see her son: "Since the day she left Italy, the
thought of seeing him had not ceased to excite her. . . . She had already
been in Petersburg for two days. The thought of her son had never left her
for a moment" (530, V.28). Even her beauty and elegance, which had always attracted Vronsky earlier, now "irritate" him because she refuses to
submit to ostracism by her former circle (543, V.32). Later, when they move
to the country, Vronsky's need to have an occupation leads him first to
making improvements on his estate and then to provincial politics. His
early successes in both fields—Sviyazhsky refers to the hospital Vronsky is
building as "the only quite properly set-up" one in Russia (624, VI.20),
and Vronsky thinks of standing for election himself in the future (663,
VI.31)—clearly reflect some of the old ambitions he had cherished while
still an officer and thought he had abandoned when he refused the post de-
vised for him by Serpukhovskoy. However, although Anna takes an interest in his work on the estate (even though Dolly thinks she acts more like a
guest there than a hostess), she thwarts his activities away from home because she cannot tolerate his independence. And she cannot share in all aspects of his life because of the irregularity of her social position.

At this juncture in the novel Vronsky appears to change in an unexpected way. In his conversation with Dolly he reveals that he values his
work on the estate more than what his former comrades do at court or in
the army. But because the narrator characterizes Vronsky's activities as the
"role" he has chosen (643, VI.25), which is the same word that he used in
connection with Vronsky's artistic pursuits, and because Vronsky openly

announces that he needs an occupation, his assertion about the absolute importance of his new endeavors seems suspect (even though it puts Vronsky partially in Levin's camp; see also *16.3*). However, whether or not Vronsky has found a permanent profession is less important than his suddenly broaching the matter of his heirs. He tells Dolly that he wants the fruits of his labors to be passed on to his children, and asks her to persuade Anna to seek a divorce so that his and Anna's daughter, and any other children they may have, will be legally his rather than Karenin's. Vronsky's concern with children, legitimacy, and inheritance represents a dramatic departure from his views on family life during earlier stages of his affair, as well as a contrast with his continuing inability to understand how important Anna's son is for her.

It is all the more poignant, therefore, that Vronsky's new views on these matters are still entirely personal and are emphatically not shared by Anna. As Dolly discovers to her amazement and horror, Anna does not want more children and has taken steps to prevent having any (637, VI.23). There is also obvious irony in the fact that here too Vronsky's interests and values begin to converge with Levin's. By contrast, Anna's interests increasingly diverge from Kitty's, who is completely immersed in her roles as wife and future mother and can value her husband's pursuits even if she does not understand them (438, V.1).

Vronsky's recollection of Anna after her death and before he leaves for the Balkan war is the final demonstration of how his perceptions of her are functions of his changing emotional states rather than insights into a stable personality:

And he tried to remember her as she had been when he first met her, also at a station, mysterious, enchanting, loving, seeking and giving happiness, and not cruelly vengeful as he remembered her in the last moment. He tried to remember his best moments with her, but those moments were for ever poisoned. He remembered only her triumphant, accomplished threat of totally unnecessary but ineffaceable regret. (780–81, VIII.5)

The narrator here betrays his character's point of view by listing the things Vronsky *cannot* in fact retrieve from memory. Simultaneously, the narrator underscores the beauty and weight of that inaccessible past, which suggests that Anna's alluring nature has an independent value *for him*. Another way to read the passage is as Vronsky's failed attempt to recall the *details* of what he recalls *in general* as happier times. In either case, Vronsky emerges as (partially) divided from himself and from his own past.

13.9. Kitty

When Kitty is at the German spa, she falls under the influence of Varenka and tries to imitate her role as ministering angel to the sick. The consequence is that a Russian artist, Petrov, develops a crush on Kitty, his wife becomes jealous, and the couple quarrels. Kitty thus inadvertently becomes a potential home wrecker, which constitutes a highly ironic (but aesthetically pleasing, because intriguing) echo of Vronsky's and Vasenka Veslovsky's roles, except that Kitty is innocence personified, while they are determined seducers (see *10.2*). Kitty's reaction when Varenka informs her of the effect she has had on the Petrovs is to utter one of the novel's strongest attacks against the possibility of personal change that is also one of the novel's strongest defenses of one's personal nature. She rails against the "pretence" of her attempt to "seem better to people, to myself, to God" and, instead, adjures herself: "Be bad, but at least don't be a liar, a deceiver! . . . I can only live by my heart." This recalls a variety of efforts by other characters, including Levin's attempts to become a better person, as well as the "roles" that Vronsky and some others try to assume. It is noteworthy, therefore, that in this case the narrator supports Kitty's conclusion: "She did not renounce all that she had learned, *but she understood that she had deceived herself in thinking that she could be what she wished to be*" (235–36, II.35, emphasis added). This hermeneutic index makes a very far-reaching claim. At the very least, it posits a considerable degree of psychological determinism and thereby again raises major doubts about how ethical behavior is possible in a world where such determinism rules.[86] There is, of course, very little danger to others from Kitty, who is a gentle and loving character. Whatever fears Petrov's wife has are likely her husband's and her own fault. But Anna, who is also gentle and loving, could not live except by her own heart either, and the results for those around her were very different. Kitty's behavior is thus an especially bold illustration of the potential problems inherent in any defense of a personalized and relativized view of the world.

The relation between human action and religious belief is also a central theme in the descriptions of other characters at the German spa. Mme Stahl's hypocrisy is obvious. However, Varenka's charity is more complex, because it does not appear to reflect a choice that she made as much as a practice into which she grew, initially as Mme Stahl's ward, then as a hybrid between servant and companion (215, II.30; 219–20, II.32). The fit between Varenka's past, her character, and her occupation supports Kitty's claims about the immutability of her own nature and raises questions about the practical utility of the Christian teaching that had attracted her. What good is it if it can be practiced successfully only by those who are born to it? Indeed, the narrator suggests a causal connection between Varenka's charitable behavior and her *lack* of the élan vital that Kitty feels strongly in herself: Varenka "could not be attractive to men because she lacked what Kitty had in over-abundance—the restrained fire of life and an awareness of her attractiveness. She always seemed to be busy doing something that could not be doubted, and therefore it seemed she could not be interested in anything outside it" (215, II.30). Varenka's restraint resurfaces later as a form of characterological determinism when she and Koznyshev fail to act on their attraction for each other.[87]

There are also possible connections between Kitty's situation and the novel's epigraph. Kitty abandons her ministering role in part because of how her father ridicules the Pietism of Mme Stahl, who, he states, "thanks God for everything, for every misfortune—and for the fact that her husband died, she also thanks God. Well, and that's rather funny, because they had a bad life together" (229, II.34). (Whether or not the father's characterization is accurate is less important than recognizing the congruence between his sarcasm and the narrator's negative portrayal of Mme Stahl, as well as of Pietism in the scenes with Countess Lydia Ivanovna, Karenin, and the "clairvoyant" Landau.) A possible interpretation of the prince's caricature of Mme Stahl's theodicy is that it echoes the epigraph on divine punishment, which, in Saint Paul's schema, "backs up" the charitable behavior human beings are supposed to practice. It follows that if a believer assumes human suffering is a consequence of divine punishment, he necessarily has to accept it. This is not identical to the Pietists "thanking" God for suffering, but it is not entirely distinct from it either. (On the other hand, because Mme Stahl is also described by the narrator as an egotistical hypocrite, perhaps she can be seen as the just recipient of divine punishment, which also echoes the epigraph.) This possible textual echo could be interpreted as showing that God's laws are inevitably perverted by self-righteous individuals like Mme Stahl and the other Pietists. Levin comes to a related although more humble conclusion about there being severe limitations to what he and other human beings can know about God *(13.4.4)*. But it is also possible that the textual echo works in the opposite direction, like a "reversible" hermeneutic index *(5.2)*, by undermining the epigraph's message through its association with a series of characters who are marked negatively. Mme Stahl and the Pietists illustrate that the *distance* between the divine (if it exists) and the human may be too great for most humans to bridge.

There is another possible connection between the epigraph and Kitty's experiences at the spa. By ministering to Petrov and his family, she makes a small-scale, conscious effort to act in accordance with the principles of Christian charity (despite the somewhat prideful pleasure she takes in her own role). Although in the end her effort fails through no fault of her own, it is she and Petrov—the relatively innocent parties—who bear the primary brunt of the consequences. By contrast, the wife gets what she wants when she manages to stop Kitty's visits. In other words, the Pauline paradigm is undermined by the fact that selfishness in the form of the wife's jealousy is rewarded, and also by how Kitty responds to the relatively mild rebuff she receives from the wife, which is to forget about turning the other cheek (something Varenka does all the time) and to abandon her charitable work altogether. Given the way Kitty is presented throughout the novel, there is no reason to think that her "failure" to live up to the Christian ideal is meant to reflect negatively *on her*. On the contrary, one could argue that the *teaching* falls short because of the way it goes against her nature. (Tolstoy is clearly not interested in portraying living saints in this novel, as he may have been with Platon Karataev in *War and Peace,* and as he was in a number of later works such as "God Sees the Truth, but Waits," "Alyosha the Pot," and "The Three Hermits.") Thus, the fact that Kitty cannot keep herself "on that level to which she had wished to rise" (236, II.35) does not actually appear to discredit *her*. Kitty has another opportunity to manifest charity later in the novel when she tends to her dying brother-in-law Nikolai Levin. But despite her skill and the narrator's admiration for her, Kitty's behavior in this case is not purely charitable either, because it is entirely in keeping with the principle that value is a function of prior sympathy between individuals (which she discusses with Levin at the Oblonsky dinner party). In other words, Kitty insists on going to Nikolai's side with her husband only because that is her place as his wife. It is worth recalling that earlier Kitty had actually experienced "an irrepressible feeling of disgust" toward Nikolai when she saw him at the German spa because he *reminded* her of Levin. At that time she had still not recovered her emotional balance after rejecting Levin and having her hopes deceived by Vronsky (216, II.30).

13.10. Karenin

Karenin's isolation in his own perspectives is so egregious that it is almost a parody of itself. As the narrator describes it, "To put himself in thought and feeling into another being was a mental act alien to Alexei Alexandrovich.

He regarded this mental act as harmful and dangerous fantasizing" (144, II.8). With the exception of his extraordinary but relatively short-lived forgiveness of Anna and Vronsky, Karenin's approach to life is usually mediated by some aspects of bookish culture (with all the negative associations this carries in *Anna Karenina*). For example, when he attempts to devise an educational program for his son he reads several treatises on what he believes are appropriate subjects, with the result that Seryozha feels that "[h]is father always talked to him . . . as if he were addressing some imaginary boy, one of those that exist in books, but quite unlike him" (525, V.27).

After Karenin learns of Anna's affair, he sees her in two distinct and irreconcilable ways, each of which is a product of the change in his attitude toward her. The first is atypical for the novel because the reader can easily understand it as a transparent instance of projection on the basis of evidence the narrator provides elsewhere. When Anna confesses her affair to Karenin, he concludes that she has "[n]o honour, no heart, no religion — a depraved woman! I always knew it, and always saw it, though I tried to deceive myself out of pity for her." As the narrator puts it, "And indeed it seemed to him that he had always seen it" (279, III.13). The second instance occurs when Karenin forgives Anna on her sickbed: "He suddenly felt that the very thing that had once been the source of his suffering had become the source of his spiritual joy, that what had seemed insoluble when he condemned, reproached and hated, became simple and clear when he forgave and loved" (418–19, IV.19). This is a striking example of self-conscious relativization. As Karenin realizes at this moment, the "same" Anna can be implicated in two diametrically opposed reactions. The precedence given to Karenin's internal states is so strong that Anna can hardly be seen as the only cause of either one. Moreover, neither the narrator nor Karenin concludes that it was inaccurate or wrong for him to "condemn," "reproach," and "hate" but only that doing this made him *miserable*. There is a similar shift in Karenin's attitude toward the Evangelical fervor that moves Countess Lydia Ivanovna. When he is miserable because of society's mocking attitude toward him, "these expressions that had once seemed not exactly unpleasant but unnecessary, now seemed natural and comforting" (510, V.2).

What are we to make of Karenin's change of heart? It may be exemplary while it lasts, but it does not last very long, and it is not experienced by any other character. (The only one who approaches it is Levin, but his conception of the "law of goodness" is also problematic because it does not change his relations with others, which is what the teachings in the New Testament are largely about.) It is certainly possible to argue that Karenin's *happiness* when he forgives Anna marks his Christian stance positively. However, Karenin is also "happy" when he decides that Anna had always been depraved. Immediately before the passage in which Karenin comes to this conclusion, the narrator provides a paragraph-long simile in which Anna's confession fills Karenin with "surprise" and "joy" because it relieves him of the "pity and . . . the doubt and suffering of jealousy that had lately tormented him. He felt like a man who has had a long-aching tooth pulled out" (278–79, III.13).

The narrator's graphic and homely simile is a hermeneutic index that equates what appears to be Karenin's vindictive and self-serving re-action with a familiar, universal, and "natural" procedure for alleviating pain. As a result, it is difficult to fault Karenin for his "misperception" of Anna, which, although inconsistent in terms of what the reader knows of Karenin's earlier view of her, still represents a psychological truth about Karenin himself at a specific moment in his life. In other words, the tooth simile reinforces the novel's relativization and thereby counterbalances any claims that could be made on behalf of Christian charity's supposed moral superiority.

The painful tooth reappears later in the novel with similar associations, but this time it is lodged in Vronsky's mouth. The only thing that makes him forget the "nagging pain in the strong tooth" while waiting to leave for the war in Serbia is his recollection of Anna—not during their best moments together, which he is unable to resurrect, but as "cruelly vengeful," which is how he last saw her before her suicide (780–81, VIII.5). As a result, the image of the painful tooth retains its link to a relativized perception of Anna (in addition to the associations that Vronsky's strong teeth have by themselves with such things as his virility).

It is paradoxical that Karenin's changing views illustrate the kind of *amoral* relativization that Princess Betsy urges on Anna as the only viable stance, or that Stiva describes to Levin as the way things actually are. This is not a reason to conclude that Tolstoy condones vengeful thoughts or openly contradicts the novel's epigraph, but that his conception of human nature is predicated on the impossibility of denying a strictly personal or even solipsistic view of things, which is simply too omnipresent and pow-erful to ignore. Because the Christian ideal is also not supported in the novel by Kitty's rejection of Varenka's model or by Levin's even more im-portant, private, mute, and impotent faith, which is a coda to the entire novel, perhaps we need to conclude that in *Anna Karenina* Christianity is merely one of the variants or subcategories of the larger truth that individ-ual human truth and "reality" are mutable.

13.11. Minor Characters

Even minor characters exist in their own worlds. Consider Seryozha Karenin. Among his friends is his father's hall porter, which is noteworthy all by itself because the boy is alone in having this kind of relationship with a servant of such lowly rank. (We are told that Stiva and his valet, Matvei, understand each other perfectly, that Levin confides in his housekeeper, Agafya Mikhailovna, and that she is particularly fond of philosophy, and that Matrena Filimonovna is Dolly's "best friend," but we see them interacting only as servants and masters, not as friends.) As if to underscore the inevitable uniqueness of Seryozha's perspective, the narrator describes him "peering into the porter's face, which he had studied in the smallest detail, particularly his chin, hanging between grey side-whiskers, *which no one saw except Seryozha,* because he always looked at it from below" (522, V.26, emphasis added). In another nineteenth-century novel, this could simply be another well-observed "realistic" detail. But what kind of "reality" is it that can be seen by only one person? In his other relations Seryozha is guided by the same a priori affection of which Kitty and Levin speak at the Oblonsky dinner, as a result of which he "did not let anyone into his soul without the key of love" (526, V.27). The principle of partiality is also central to Seryozha's education, which is effective only insofar as it accords with his natural inclinations.

The same principle appears to operate during the discussion of education at the Oblonskys' dinner table, where the opinions expressed by the speakers reflect their different personal agendas. This continues even (or especially) when characters are talking about the weighty matter of the "woman question." Each sees these matters differently, so that, for example, when Koznyshev makes a joke, Turovtsyn laughs "especially loudly and gaily, having at last been granted that something funny *which was all he was waiting for as he listened to the conversation*" (387, IV.10, emphasis added; see also *16.2.1*).

Levin's half-brother, Koznyshev, is at home in the world of intellectual abstractions. This inevitably affects his relations with others, as in the case of his failed romance with Varenka, and in how he sees Vronsky at the end of the novel. When he meets Vronsky at the train station on the eve of the latter's departure for Serbia, Koznyshev has the impression that Vronsky makes believe that he has not noticed him. However, "That made no difference to Sergei Ivanovich. He was above keeping any personal accounts with Vronsky. In Sergei Ivanovich's eyes, Vronsky was at that moment an important actor in a great cause, and he considered it his duty to encourage him and show his approval" (779, VIII.5). In other words, Koznyshev redefines Vronsky exclusively as an index of an ideological position that is dear to him and not in terms relevant to Vronsky specifically.

Vasenka Veslovsky embodies a different form of selfishness, one driven by childish blindness to the consequences of his actions and by a gravitation toward whatever is pleasing or entertaining. ("Vasenka" is a diminutive of endearment for the name "Vasilii" and is normally appropriate only for children or intimates.) His behavior at Levin's estate approaches farce. When he goes off to hunt with Stiva and Levin, Vasenka begins by forgetting his wallet and cigars (578, VI.8), then comes close to shooting Levin (579, VI.9), after which he mires the carriage (580, VI.9), breaks a wing off the carriage when he tries to help extract it (581, VI.9), drives too quickly as a result of which they reach their destination too early and a horse is strained (581, VI.10; 596, VI.13), and together with Stiva devours all the provisions so that there is nothing left for Levin (596, VI.13). He also acts as if pretty peasant girls exist only to divert him (590, VI.11) and treats Kitty in the same way (597–98, VI.14). But except for the fact that Stiva's behavior and tastes are somewhat more sophisticated than Vasenka's and that he is not as clumsy, there is little to distinguish the two from the perspective of how their inner motivation dominates their values and relations with the external world. Another minor character who is close to being a caricature because of the narrowness of his self-interests is the lawyer Karenin consults about the divorce and whose deepest response to his distinguished visitor's marital difficulties revolves around how his fat fee will allow him to reupholster his furniture (369, IV.5).

14. Self and Others

14.1. Understanding and Uniting with Others

In describing at length how characters' worlds are largely their own projections and how this isolates them from each other, I inevitably appear to underemphasize the instances of connection, understanding, and feelings of unity that also occur. I would now like to focus on these, and to do so in one section, so that the significance of this feature of the novel will be readily apparent.

Even though more narrative attention and pages are dedicated to what separates individuals than to what unites them, the idea of unity still looms large in *Anna Karenina* because it is marked positively by the characters themselves and by the narrator. The characters demonstrate this in obvious ways, such as by yearning for love, companionship, fulfillment, and recognition by others. The narrator clearly implies that he values unity by opening the novel with a claim about a universal truth that also marks difference negatively, and via related broad generalizations about the human condition at various other points. Finally, the novel ends with Levin's seeming discovery of the universal law of goodness and his claims of solidarity with believers everywhere, which echo the novel's epigraph and the narrator's opening sentence (despite the questions about the validity of Levin's claims).[1] This thematic trend in the novel is clearly important, therefore, even if it does not eliminate the isolation that characters experience or negate the ambiguities inherent in claims about universality such as the narrator and Levin make.

What needs to be determined is the relation between the two opposing trends, or their function vis-à-vis each other. For example, in part V, chapters 14 through 16, the narrator describes Levin and Kitty's life together three months after their wedding, and during the course of ten pages repeats several times how happy Levin is (e.g., 483, V.15). Levin also exclaims, "How good it is for us here together! . . . Precisely why have I been given such happiness?" (485, V.15). But despite this, and despite Levin and Kitty being the exemplary antithesis to Anna and Vronsky, the narrator dedicates most of these pages to anatomizing either how Levin is of two minds about his new life with Kitty—which simultaneously delights and disappoints him—or how his interests diverge from Kitty's. This mixture of light and shadow, which recalls Stiva's characterization of life, is presented by the narrator as entirely natural. He even embodies it in his carefully balanced syntax and lexical repetitions: "This trifling preoccupation of Kitty's . . . was one of [Levin's] disenchantments [razocharovanie]; yet this sweet preoccupation . . . was one of his new enchantments [ocharovanie]. Their quarrels were another disenchantment and enchantment" (481, V.14). Few readers are likely to be troubled by a view of life as consisting of ups and downs, even (or especially) in the case of newlyweds. But the effect of Tolstoy's narrative practice is to diminish the effect of unity by embedding relatively brief references to it within a more ample analysis of distance and difference.

What conditions are necessary for characters to get out of themselves to the extent of understanding others immediately and fully? The majority of instances are the result of preexisting love, although, as we have seen, love does not guarantee automatic or perpetual unanimity, which is always intermittent at best. This implies that *Anna Karenina* is pessimistic about or not very interested in communication between *strangers* and the issue of general societal cohesion. Instead, we return to the principle that value is based in individual perspectives.

Given this, it is hardly surprising that understanding would occur most often between family members who share a complex prehistory of relations, including a private vocabulary that is often nonverbal. An early example is the scene of Stiva and his favorite daughter, Tanya, communicating "at once" and without having to say everything out loud about his quarrel with his wife (9, I.1; however, the fact that Stiva would have a "favorite" child demonstrates simultaneously how partial and biased this instance of cohesion is). The same kind of exchange occurs between Kitty and her mother (46, I.12), Levin and his brother Nikolai (91, I.25; 351, III.32), Dolly and her parents (122, II.2), and Dolly and Kitty (125, II.3). It is hardly random that there would be more examples of such moments in these two positively marked families than in others. Even Princess Betsy, who is Vronsky's cousin, understands perfectly his risqué story about a pair of young officers on the basis of his hints and oblique references, although this is presumably due largely to their having similar interests as members of the same select circle (129, II.5).

Levin is given the strongest sense of unity with another person in the novel when he emerges from his wedding ceremony feeling that Kitty and he "were already one" (458, V.6). Levin feels this even more strongly later when he realizes to his surprise that he no longer knows where he ends and she begins, which reflects the extramundane atmosphere that surrounds some aspects of his relations with Kitty and that I will revisit below: "He understood it by the painful feeling of being split [razdvoenie, or "doubling"] which he experienced at that moment" (482, V.14; see also *13.4.1, 17.2*). (Levin's feeling a loss of unity at this point because of a quarrel with Kitty is another example of Tolstoy partially taking back with one hand what he gave Levin with the other.) Levin's impression is in striking contrast to Anna's sense of doubling *within* her own psyche, which not only underscores the highly problematic nature of her state but also constitutes one of the myriad "situation rhymes" that are the bricks and mortar of the novel's structure.

However, as the narrator indicates, Levin's experience is actually an exception that proves the rule: "Never afterwards did he feel it so strongly" (482, V.14). Why not? There is no question that within the novel's spectrum of marriages Levin and Kitty are very happy—or as happy as someone with Levin's mentality can be, which is an essential caveat. On one level, he comes to count on his sense of unity with Kitty during certain "loving moments" to such an extent that he can almost dispense with language and still be sure that she will understand him, which is always a positive Tolstoyan sign (559, VI.3). Similarly, Kitty feels her husband's invisible presence even when she is away from him, as during her chance meeting with Vronsky at her godmother's (673, VII.1). On another level, the reason for the intermittent and limited nature of Levin's experience of unity is the disjunction between the ideal marriage he had expected before the wedding and the "reality" he experiences after it. The latter actually consists of his misunderstanding Kitty's nest-building instincts, which prompts him to fault *her* for the "idle" life that *he* is leading (485–86, V.15). This puts Levin's sense of unity with Kitty into perspective: although it makes him happy and he values it, it is not all-embracing and cannot satisfy all the deepest needs of his soul. In other words, Levin resembles Vronsky in also discovering that he has "a desire for desires." In Levin's case, these will be partially fulfilled only when he discovers God, which provides him with an inkling of the ultimate unity that he seeks, but that he suspects he will never fully understand and that he knows he cannot fully experience.

Understanding is intertwined with love in *Anna Karenina* even when it is not rooted in kinship or long familiarity. For example, early in the novel Levin can tell from Kitty's expression alone that the man entering the drawing room is Vronsky and that she loves him "as surely as if she had told it to him in words" (50, I.14). When Anna and Vronsky's liaison is just beginning and she asks him why he is traveling to St. Petersburg, he responds with words that repeat exactly what she knew he would say (103, I.30). Because Kitty develops a crush on Anna when they first meet (she will repeat a variant of this later with Varenka), she can read unerringly Anna's elation at her success during the ball. However, it is very telling that in this case Kitty's perspicacity would not have been possible without a degree of *projection* that allows her to understand Anna's behavior as a variant of her own (thus returning us to the novel's dominant, personal mode of perception): "She knew that feeling, knew the signs of it, and she saw them in Anna" (81, I.23). Moments later, Kitty also sees accurately that Anna and Vronsky's "insignificant" ballroom conversation "decided their fate and hers" (81, I.23). In this case, what she understands is, ironically, the distance that separates her from them. Another example of this kind of paradoxical understanding of the chasm between self and other is Anna's reaction to an expression of Vronsky's after their affair has begun: "She understood at once that he had already thought it over to himself. She knew that whatever he might tell her, he would not say everything he thought. And she understood that her last hope had been disappointed" (315, III.22).

If we shift now to affection, love's younger sister, we see that it is also a prerequisite for or intertwined with understanding. This appears to be one of Stiva's dominant characteristics and explains his ease at establishing (superficially) friendly relations with a wide range of individuals.[2] For example, he senses what Levin must be thinking when Levin visits him at his office (16–17, I.5). Similarly, we see on several occasions that Levin's housekeeper, Agafya Mikhailovna, understands him perfectly as well (96, I.27), but she is of course only a minor character. A somewhat more complex example is Levin visiting Dolly on her estate. They "read" each other immediately and without any difficulty because they like each other or, more precisely, because she knows that he sees her as embodying the family life and values that he yearns for, which accords with her own self-image (266, III.9). However, Levin's mood sours, and he breaks off his emotional connection with Dolly as soon as she mentions Kitty to him. Children and family are also the short-lived link between Dolly and a group of peasant women; she finds it very interesting to talk to them because their interests are "so completely identical" to hers (266, III.8). (Levin establishes a similar, albeit also short-lived, rapport with the peasant mowers with whom he works and shares a rustic meal [253–54, III.5].)[3] A related pattern emerges later in the novel when Dolly visits Vronsky's estate and is so taken with his "natural, naïve passion" for the innovations he has introduced that she can put herself in Anna's place and see how Anna could have fallen in love with him. The reason for understanding in this case, however, may be that Dolly recognizes something of herself in Vronsky because his enthusiasm is a variant of her own naive surprise (624, VI.20). Their similar reactions function as both catalyst and vehicle for their friendly relations in the scenes that follow. But as we have seen, Dolly's feelings do not last even for the duration of her brief visit to the estate, and she is happy to get away from its artificiality.

Another variant of affection is Kitty's ability to minister to Nikolai, her moribund brother-in-law, which contrasts sharply with Levin's paralysis, revulsion, and fear. She alone understands the sick man's needs, and he responds to her with touching tenderness. Why does this connection occur between them if this is the first time they have actually met? Because, as the narrator explains, Kitty already has something within her that predisposes her toward a person who is ill—she is a *woman:* "At the sight of the sick man, she felt pity for him. And pity in her woman's soul produced none of the horror and squeamishness it did in her husband, but a need to act" (493, V.18). (We should also recall that Kitty accompanies Levin because she sees this is her *wifely* duty; she felt entirely differently about Nikolai when she saw him earlier in Germany [see *13.9*].) Levin admires and loves Kitty for her dedication, of course, but even though Nikolai is his brother, Levin cannot share her viewpoint.

There are other relations in the novel based on different forms of affection, such as Vronsky and Yashvin's, Karenin and Countess Lydia Ivanovna's, and Levin and Sviyazhsky's. In all these cases, the friendships obviously constitute part of the normal fabric of the characters' lives. But with the possible exception of Karenin and the countess, whose feelings appear to drift from affection to love, the ties do not reach very deeply below the surface. Thus Yashvin never understands or even cares about Vronsky's passion, and Sviyazhsky never allows Levin entry "beyond the reception rooms of his mind" (e.g., 335, III.27).

Instances when a character is able to see another's perspective even though they do not share any positive emotional bond are very rare, and most of those that do occur reflect long prior familiarity. One example is Karenin understanding Anna's emotions during the horse race when he looks at her face: "against his will [he] read on it with horror what he did not want to know" (209, II.28). When Karenin comes into Anna's room seeking Vronsky's letters, he is so upset that he mispronounces the word "experienced" as "experimenced." (The Russian original has him say *pelestradal* for *perestradal,* or "suffled" for "suffered.") Anna is initially amused by his mistake but then feels ashamed by her reaction. The result is that she is briefly jolted out of her now-habitual view of him as an enemy and a source of guilt: "for the first time, momentarily, she felt for him, put herself in his place [pereneslas' v nego] and pitied him" (364, IV.4). This is a classic, small-scale example of Tolstoyan "defamiliarization," but on the level of a fictional character rather than the reader. The precision and deliberate style of Karenin's normal pronunciation makes his mistake stand out because it constitutes a crack in his facade. However, the incident is so short-lived and understated that it is not very plausible to see it as exemplary in any way—as, for example, a figuration of a path the reader might follow in attempting to escape a fixed mentality. On the other hand, the fact that Anna's defamiliarized perception is triggered by mispronunciation also reevokes the idea that there is a connection between the nature of the world and the language in which it is fixed. This is a subject to which I will return *(18)*.

Anna also unexpectedly shares Countess Lydia Ivanovna's perspective when she writes to the countess asking to see Seryozha and is told at first that there will be no answer: "Anna felt herself humiliated, offended, but she saw that from her own point of view Countess Lydia Ivanovna was right" (531, V.29). However, Anna's understanding lasts only until she gets a letter from the countess later that day that she finds so offensive that she stops blaming herself and becomes indignant. By contrast, the countess's initial silence had allowed Anna's imagination free rein, and since she was torn by guilt with regard to her son anyway, she not only felt humbled but could also suffer passively whatever reproaches she *imagined* the countess as making, all of which could be understood as variants of Anna's own.

14.2. The Individual and the Collective

The isolation of characters in the novel can be correlated with the way in which large, impersonal collectives are consistently portrayed in a negative light. Levin feels that he has discovered a universal fraternity of believers by the end of the novel, but he identifies himself as a kind of secret and silent member, one who will not manifest his new convictions in any obvious or overt way. The largest social unit that receives the narrator's or Levin's approbation is the group of peasants that comes together for the collective labor of mowing. However, these scenes are filtered through Levin's consciousness and stress his unique reactions, although some attention is given to the modicum of bonding that the master and peasants feel while they work (and that does not last, of course, after the labor is done, or away from the fields). Levin also encourages peasants on his estate to form a cooperative association called an *artel'* in Russian, but each of these comprises at most a few families, and their success is far from clear (340, III.29). (His brother Nikolai also attempts to form an *artel'*, the success of which seems dubious [88, I.25].) With these exceptions, whatever good appears to come from more than one individual in *Anna Karenina* is limited by the size of a family.

Why is this the case? The answer is suggested by the narrator's description of how individuals who feel they belong to larger groups effectively abrogate their responsibility to act according to their own beliefs, and submit instead to collective norms or group values, with the result that their behavior becomes immoral, perverse, or ridiculous. This inevitably contributes to the problem in the novel of reconciling personal views with collective values, which are the cornerstone of any morality.[4]

Urban, aristocratic society has the most pernicious effect on its members, especially in St. Petersburg. Moscow's mores are presented as less corrupt (which is in keeping with a long Russian cultural tradition that dates from the founding of the northern capital at the beginning of the eighteenth century, a tradition to which Tolstoy himself contributed with *War and Peace*). For example, the Shcherbatskys retain their role as a highly attractive repository of family virtues, especially in Levin's eyes (but also in Vronsky's, Stiva's, and Lvov's, all of whom court or marry the three sisters), despite their being members of Moscow's social elite. They also carry this aura with them when they travel to the German spa, where they immediately occupy a particular place in the local society but without any negative associations (214, II.30).

In Tolstoy's depiction of St. Petersburg society, however, no one seems immune from judgment. At one end of the spectrum, the circle called "the conscience of Petersburg society" (127, II.4), consisting of old, pious, and supposedly moral individuals like Countess Lydia Ivanovna, is tarnished via its association with religious fads and the charlatan Landau. The causal chain of his pernicious influence includes Karenin, who under Landau's direct guidance refuses to grant Anna a divorce, which aggravates her situation. At the other end of the spectrum, we have the dazzling and self-indulgent circle that includes Princess Betsy and that occupies itself with balls, dinners, and other revels. Members of the imperial family also appear to be implicated in this circle's atmosphere of general license. Evidence for this includes carefully planted details such as Anna and Princess Betsy's reaction when Sappho Stolz's new admirer appears in the princess's drawing room. Sappho is a strikingly attractive and immoral young woman who is one of the current darlings of St. Petersburg's fast set and whose name is presumably meant to evoke sexual permissiveness if not actual depravity (thus echoing the two apparently homosexual officers in Vronsky's regiment whom he treats with open disdain [175–76, II.19]). When this admirer enters, the narrator explains that he is such an important guest that despite his youth both Anna and the princess rise to greet him (299, III.18). Given the ladies' social standing and age, it is very probable that the young guest is a member of the imperial family; etiquette would not require either woman to rise for anyone of a lower rank.[5]

Stiva is completely a creature of this culture, except that opprobrium does not stick to him. His home is in Moscow, but he always feels rejuvenated by his trips to St. Petersburg, where, as he sees it, people know how to really live without being burdened by the familial problems and marital obligations that annoy and constrain him at home. The official position that he has at the beginning of the novel, which Levin views with contempt and which the narrator does not attempt to defend or explain, is the nearly automatic reward of his vast network of various friends, acquaintances, and relatives in both cities (14, I.5). The absurdly convoluted name of his new position, which he secures through this network by the novel's end, obviously functions to undermine its validity and to tarnish the entire contemporary urban system that gave rise to it (719, VII.17; see also *11*).

We have already seen that at least initially Vronsky's values are also those of his social circle with regard to issues of civilian life such as marriage, fidelity, debts, and so on. In his regiment, his comrades admire him because he disregards all other interests except theirs, and he responds by feeling that it is "his duty to maintain the established view of himself" (173, II.18). What this means in practice differs little from civilian life and entails matters such as social visits, the theater, horse racing, gambling, carousing, escorting a debauched visiting foreign prince, and having to extricate two young officers from the trouble they got into by pursuing the wife of a civil servant; military training and drills are hardly ever mentioned (in comparison to early drafts, where they figure more prominently).[6] Vronsky's older brother exemplifies an even more extreme version of the nexus between immorality and corporate military values. He personally does not care whether Vronsky's affair with Anna is serious or not, and disapproves of it only because he parrots the views of those whom it was necessary to please (174, II.18). When Vronsky and Anna return from Europe, his brother cannot decide whether Vronsky's affair "was right or wrong until society decided the question; he himself, for his own part, had nothing against it" (528, V.28).

The workings of the government bureaucracy that we see in connection with Karenin also demonstrate the kind of anticommonsensical absurdities that seemingly intelligent individuals will engage in under the pressure of partisan factions and collective interests (285–86, III.14; 317–18, III.23). The chapters dealing with the noblemen's provincial elections have a similar function in the novel. The scenes are often satirical, and the proceedings themselves seem meaningless from Levin's point of view, which dominates the narrative perspective. (At the same time, the relativization of perspectives is maintained, because other characters, including Vronsky and Stiva, are shown to take the proceedings very seriously and to react to them with exultation or despair.) Levin is especially struck by how the normally decent individuals he knows well begin to act grotesquely because of the hidden agendas and unexpected emotions that are induced by the collective proceedings (648–54, VI.27–28, etc.). In the novel's conclusion, the negative descriptions of the volunteers leaving for the Balkan war, which are presented from the perspectives of Koznyshev, Katavasov, and Levin, also undermine the value of another kind of large-scale collective undertaking. Most of the volunteers are unattractive both morally and physically. The scenes about them include subtle negative touches such as Koznyshev's being asked to write a note on behalf of a certain young man who was recommended by Countess Lydia Ivanovna (773, VIII.2). Given that all of her other enthusiasms are tarnished, her unnamed protégé may be as well.

Anna's relation to society is more ambiguous. When Dolly visits her on Vronsky's estate, Anna asks a fundamental question about the extent to which she can be free of societal constraints: "I simply want to live; to cause no evil to anyone but myself. I have that right, haven't I?" (616, VI.19). The answer is apparently "no." Anna's effect on Karenin, her son, Vronsky, his circle, her friends, etc., and the way in which society shuns her, show that she is too thoroughly embedded in a matrix of defining relations with everyone around her for her wish to be fulfilled. It is not clear, however, whether this web of relations is for the better or the worse. Most of the ties Anna has outside her family circle prove to be relatively superficial. Nevertheless, because Anna has transgressed against deeply rooted social customs and religious teachings, the opprobrium she feels from society can perhaps be interpreted as a justified form of punishment. But this interpretation can also be questioned because society is itself hardly the embodiment of virtue. Among many other passages, this point emerges from Vronsky's conversation with his sister-in-law when she says that she feels constrained by social norms not to attempt to "rehabilitate" Anna; to this Vronsky replies that Anna is no worse than hundreds of other women who continue to be received by society (529, V.28).

14.3. Collective Coercion and the Reification of Evil

On several occasions in the novel, Karenin feels coerced by a force with fatidic and malevolent overtones that appears to be a reification of flawed cultural norms (see *12.5*). As we have seen, after he undergoes his spiritual crisis at Anna's sickbed and discovers the "good spiritual force" that guides his soul, he also senses that there is "another force, crude and equally powerful, if not more so, that guided his life, and that this force would not give him the humble peace he desired" (419, IV.19). This force is clearly associated with society's mocking attitude toward him, but whenever it is mentioned, it seems to transcend the individuals who manifest it. Thus Karenin sees Princess Betsy as "an embodiment of that crude force which was to guide his life in the eyes of the world and which prevented him from giving himself to his feeling of love and forgiveness" (423, IV.19). Similar references to a "crude, mysterious force" (425, IV.20) and a "powerful, crude force" (432, IV.22) appear in connection with Karenin's feeling that he must change his charitable stance toward his wife and grant her a divorce. Under these circumstances, and because this "force" appears to be opposed to Karenin's Christian feelings, it would be unreasonable to dismiss entirely the possibility that the "force" may be related to some kind of transmundane evil.

This would be a more far-fetched interpretation were it not for a related detail that appears later in connection with Levin, when he finds himself at his philosophical dead end and senses the existence of an "evil power" in his life that is "the latest result of age-long labours of human thought" (789, VIII.9). In other words, this "evil power" is related to a *collective* human effort. Anna's experiences provide some support for this interpretation as well. A moment before she tells Vronsky about her horrifying dream, as a result of which he feels the "same horror filling his soul," she confesses that she feels trapped by society's condemnation and that she expects these constraints will be "untied" or "resolved" (*razviazhetsia*) by her imminent death (361, IV.3). Anna may be wrong about her actual death, but this sequence of details creates a suggestive association between the societal constraints she feels and her fatidic outlook, which does culminate in her suicide. Thus, although Anna's threatening dream is not the same as the reified evil that Karenin and Levin sense, the tentative connection between evil and the collective persists.

15. The Inner Voice and Conscience

The difficulty characters have with communicating in *Anna Karenina*—which defines their relations on a "horizontal," or experiential, plane—is also manifested on a "vertical" axis that connects the characters' conscious behavior to the deepest recesses of their own psyches and perhaps to something else. At some important point in their lives, virtually all the major characters, as well as some of the minor ones, hear an inner voice or feel some other comparable prompt telling them that what they are doing is false and wrong or that something else is true and right. This resembles the workings of conscience (a designation the narrator uses himself at times), which by long cultural tradition, as well as for reasons intrinsic to *Anna Karenina,* may reflect a link between the individual and the transcendent, or at least the transindividual. However, because characters usually do not listen to their prompts, they in fact reproduce *within* themselves the alienation that typifies the relations *among* them.

That characters usually ignore the imperatives they feel complicates but does not eliminate the thematic significance of conscience in *Anna Karenina.* For one thing, these inner voices address the morality of the characters' behavior and thus provoke questions about the connections between the characters' lives, the general theme of ethics in the novel, and its epigraph. For another, because the prompts arise spontaneously and differ from each other in their "messages," they resurrect the problem of the characters' isolation within their personal value systems. Nevertheless, the existence of a kind of moral substratum or superstructure that appears in characters' minds in the form of individualized conceptions of good and evil raises the possibility that all the characters may be linked in some essential fashion. This inference is supported by similarities in how the prompts are described, which includes lexical repetitions, and by the correlations that can be made between the prompts and other details in the novel. In short, the consistency in narrative technique and abstract message suggests that the prompts may be manifestations of a hidden force in the novel's fictional world.

But it is also important to note that some of the prompts may be no more than characters registering something purely mundane, such as normative views held by other members of society (see also *14.2, 14.3*). For example, we see from the start that Karenin is unimaginative and unobservant. Thus, when he is debating whether or not to warn Anna that her nascent relation with Vronsky is beginning to draw attention, and we read that "some voice said to him . . . that if others had noticed it, it meant there was something" (143, II.8), the likeliest interpretation is that he has finally noticed some of what has been happening between his wife and her lover. A similar example is Vronsky's reaction to his mother's and brother's attempts to interfere in his affair with Anna: "He was angry with everybody for their interference precisely because in his soul he felt that they, all of them, were right" (183, II.21). However, other prompts cannot be explained in this way quite as readily.

15.1. Stiva

The first example we see is Stiva debating whether or not to try to make it up with Dolly. "And his inner voice told him [vnutrennii golos govoril emu] that he should not go, that there could be nothing here but falseness, that to rectify, to repair, their relations was impossible, because it was impossible to make her attractive and arousing of love again or to make him an old man incapable of love" (9, I.3; in the original Russian, the word *fal'sh*, or "falseness," is repeated two more times in the same paragraph). Thus, Stiva's inner voice articulates a divergent or contradictory message that cannot be reduced to any simple position. On the one hand, the voice is ethical because it urges Stiva not to compound through falsehood the wrong he has already done; in principle, this could be seen as having universal validity. On the other hand, the reason why Stiva does not want to lie is strictly personal—he cannot deny his essential sensuality. The result is a deterministic, personal ethics that is really an anti-ethics, because it makes being true to one's self, rather than to some transpersonal norm, the highest value. From one perspective, therefore, Stiva's inner, particularizing voice can be seen as putting him at odds with the universal ethical standards implied in the novel's epigraph and in the narrator's first sentence. However, from another perspective, if we assume that the prompt is concerned with the truth of Stiva's nature (and the truth about Stiva is that he will *not* change after he patches things up with Dolly), then on an *abstract* level Stiva is in harmony with the Bible and the narrator in the sense that they all express Truth. But this is a very awkward conclusion to maintain, because Stiva's truth puts him at odds with Christian teaching in general and with Saint Paul's conception of sensuality in particular. It is also possible to hypothesize that if Stiva's inner voice reflects a transcendent reality, then his sensuality—or the way he is constituted—emerges as part of a larger design in which he is an unwitting participant, which means (as he himself claims) that he cannot be held responsible for his actions. This again raises the theme of determinism in the novel, which is incompatible with ethics as it is usually understood.[1]

We also need to consider the possibility that Stiva's "inner voice" is merely a metaphor for his reluctance to deal with Dolly. However, this is unlikely because of the way the narrator characterizes the voice when it speaks again, assuming that it is the same in both cases. Stiva is planning to try to persuade Karenin to grant Anna a divorce when, to his surprise, he feels an unaccustomed timidity: "It was so unexpected and strange a feeling that Stepan Arkadyich did not believe it was the voice of his conscience [golos sovesti], telling him that what he intended to do was bad. Stepan Arkadyich made an effort and conquered the timidity that had come over him" (429, IV.22). The narrator's comment is a major hermeneutic index implying that there is some sort of moral force independent of Stiva that attempts but fails to influence him; we can infer as well that it has acted very rarely in his life. Two major issues remain unclear, however—the origin of Stiva's "conscience" (is it metaphysical, cultural, psychological?) and why his plan to persuade his brother-in-law to grant Anna a divorce should be so "bad" that his conscience would interfere. We do not see similar interference when Stiva talks about his normal philandering, for example. Perhaps the difference is that now Stiva is urging *someone else* to commit an act that can be construed as immoral because it involves *lying*. We are told early in the novel that honesty toward himself (3, I.2) and honesty in dealing with others are dominant traits of his character (15, I.5). As the narrator explains, in order to satisfy the requirements for a divorce and simultaneously to protect Anna, whom he has just forgiven, Karenin will have to "take upon himself an accusation of fictitious adultery" rather than let her acknowledge her own guilt. Does Stiva know or expect that Karenin will have to do this? There is no indication in the text that he does. In his conversation with Karenin, all Stiva refers to is that a divorce is possible if neither party intends to remarry (431, IV.22).[2] Apart from being his possible reference to Russian laws of the time, this also happens to be an allusion to one of Saint Paul's dicta in the context of his general condemnation of divorce in 1 Corinthians 7:11. Perhaps the falsehood is that Stiva knows that Anna would marry Vronsky after being divorced from Karenin. In any event, it is still striking that Stiva is able to overcome the voice's prompt. This may make it seem as if he is free to act immorally. However, since this is how he acts all the time anyway, one could also argue that his immoral behavior is predetermined (by his character or some other agency).

15.2. Levin

Of all the characters, Levin is the most concerned with trying to become a better person. There is some evidence that he succeeds, as when he remains chaste during the winter following his rejection by Kitty. But on the whole, his (relatively modest) success is usually overshadowed by personal motivations that are not ethical in any general sense.

Levin also feels moral prompts at times. When he learns that his brother, Nikolai, is in Moscow, he feels torn: "in his soul there struggled the desire to forget just then about his unfortunate brother, and the consciousness that to do so would be wrong" (26–27, I.8). The nature of this struggle is clarified during a very telling moment when Stiva informs Levin that Vronsky appears to be a serious rival for Kitty's hand. Upon hearing this unwelcome news, Levin scowls gloomily and "at once remembered his brother Nikolai and how mean he was to have forgotten about him" (40, I.11). In short, Levin's moral turn toward a brother in need, which is an expression of selfless, charitable love, is prompted by Levin's resentment that there is a complication in and possible rebuff to his love for Kitty, which is romantic, personal, and therefore "selfish." Had Levin not heard of Vronsky and not felt that Kitty's having a suitor tarnishes his courtship or implies rejection, he might have suppressed his sense of obligation toward Nikolai. Levin had in fact made this point to Stiva moments earlier when he said that he is so happy at the thought of marrying Kitty that he has become "mean" by forgetting about Nikolai; he also adds what is likely a self-serving projection when he says, "It seems to me that he's happy, too" (39, I.10).

The way Levin's conscience and more abstract sense of good and evil are eclipsed by his personal and "selfish" feelings can also be seen in the description of his state three months after Kitty rejected his proposal: "In his past . . . there were actions he recognized as bad, for which his conscience ought to have tormented him; yet the memory of the bad actions tormented him far less than these insignificant but shameful memories [of his failed proposal]" (151, II.12). Only when Levin's feelings of shame and injury fade with the arrival of spring, and he feels "firm and calm" when thinking about Kitty (165, II.15), is he able to respond positively to the moral imperative he feels with regard to his brother. This is dramatized in a scene when Levin hears approaching sledge bells and is *initially* upset at the prospect that it might be Nikolai because "the presence of his brother might spoil this happy spring mood of his." But "[t]hen he became ashamed of this feeling, and at once opened, as it were, his inner embrace and with tender joy now expected and wished it to be his brother" (159, II.14). On another occasion involving his half-brother, Koznyshev, who is not sick and in need like Nikolai, Levin does not hesitate to assert the importance of personal over general value. Levin feels thoroughly guilty about leaving Koznyshev alone for days on end, but decides that he has to mow with the peasants as a form of therapy: "'I need physical movement, otherwise my character definitely deteriorates,' he thought, and he decided to mow no matter how awkward it was in front of his brother and the peasants" (248, III.4). Levin's motivation is ethical, but he paradoxically and typically chooses what is good for him rather than someone else.

During the church rituals prior to his wedding, Levin experiences something similar to what Stiva feels when he is about to broach the issue of divorce at Karenin's. Levin is still an unbeliever at this point in his life, so the preparations make him feel "awkwardness and shame at doing what he himself did not understand and therefore, as his inner voice [vnutrennii golos] kept telling him, something false and bad" (439, V.1). Levin's judgment implies that morality is a function of personal truth, which, although in keeping with the novel's negative portrayal of all intellectual systems or social collectives *(14.2)*, is still striking given that the context is Tolstoy's depiction of Russian Orthodoxy. Levin's inner voice also resembles Stiva's, because by reminding Levin of what he already knows, it functions as an analogue of the spontaneous, instinctual behavior that is usually treated positively by the narrator. (There is at least one possible exception to this, however. On the eve of Levin's wedding, "some voice" suddenly instills doubts in him about whether or not he knows Kitty's true feelings for him [444, V.2]. Although Kitty allays Levin's fears, it is possible to see his doubts as foreshadowing the distance between them that persists after their marriage.)

This complex of associations is also at the heart of Levin's spiritual awakening at the end of the novel, where references to the soul as a touchstone for higher truth appear a number of times and in a way that resembles the inner voices described above (see also *13.4.4*). After Levin discovers God and the law of goodness that he believes is the one indubitable sign of God's existence for all humankind, he is described as feeling "in his soul the presence of an infallible judge" (791, VIII.10) and "not ceasing joyfully to hear [slyshat'] the fullness of his heart" (812, VIII.18). At another point when he is pondering his new illumination, he is described as not thinking anymore but "as if only listening to the mysterious voices [tainstvennye golosa] that spoke joyfully and anxiously about something among themselves" (800, VIII.13). These are not described as inner voices, but the fact that Levin's new faith is repeatedly and inevitably associated with his "soul" suggests that we are dealing with the same semantic field (804, VIII.14; 813, VIII.18; 815, 817, VIII.19).

An important facet of Levin's illumination is that it is triggered by one peasant's comment about another one named Plato, which is presumably an index of wisdom and authority, as it was also in *War and Peace* (see *13.4.4*). However, there is some irony in the fact that we do not actually *see* this Plato, which means that Levin is deprived of direct contact with the source of wisdom. (By contrast, the effect that Platon Karataev has on Pierre Bezukhov is holistic, is achieved via all the senses, and is largely independent of language.) Although Levin reacts to his new belief in God as to a revolution in his worldview, he still concludes that what he has discovered is actually something he has always known, even if he had never realized it. Revelation is thus *redefinition* rather than the influx of something completely new. When Levin reexamines his life from the perspective of his new state, he decides that he readily believed the injunction to love one's neighbor when he was a child because he was told "what was in my soul." He also concludes that although as an adult he was *living* well, he was not *thinking* properly (796, 797, VIII.12). The consequence of Levin's retrospective reinterpretation of his past is that he is marked by at least a degree of determinism; as he puts it, "I have freed myself from deception, I have recognized the master" (796, VIII.12, my literal translation). He repeats this idea when he stresses his *passivity* in relation to his revelation: he says that he does not so much "unite myself" (ne soediniaius') with the rest of humankind "as I am united, whether I will or no [voleiu-nevoleiu soedinen], with others in one community of believers" (815, VIII.19). In other words, God's design is everywhere hidden in plain view.

There is also a cognitive dimension to Levin's determinism that resembles the private perceptions of the characters in the novel. Levin understands what he has discovered not as something "new" but as an iteration of something "old." Thus, although Levin thanks God for the revelation he receives, he understands it in terms of ideas and images that he draws from his own past experience that he now reinterprets as divinely inspired. This makes his revelation fundamentally ambiguous because it becomes impossible for an outsider (such as the reader) to distinguish between divine inspiration and Levin's projections, especially because of the dominance of the latter throughout the novel *(13.4)*.

Levin's faith thus resembles the cognitive schema that all the characters enact, whereby they create the worlds they inhabit. In fact, this appears to be the meaning of the novel's remarkable last lines, in which Levin claims that "my whole life, regardless of all that may happen to me, every minute of it, is not only not meaningless, as it was before, but has the unquestionable meaning [smysl] of the good which it is in my power to put into it [vlozhit' v nee]!" This statement is notable both for what it says and what it does not say. Levin does not claim that he will be able to *act morally*, but that he will be able to *interpret in moral terms* the events in his life that had seemed meaningless before. His faith emerges as a matter of *semiotic recoding* and not of existential *praxis* because it is the new context of his belief in God and goodness that makes it possible for him to assign a specific meaning to the events in his life that could otherwise be given "arbitrary" significance. Furthermore, Levin does not claim any freedom of action—in fact, a few lines earlier he explicitly acknowledges his impotence before his own characterological traits—except for the freedom of reinterpretation.

Another way of putting this is that Levin's experiences suggest a disjunction between ethical *thought* and ethical *behavior*. Although perhaps unable to change what he does, he can still think in ethical terms. This opens up the possibility that the world in the novel is dualistic in the sense that characters may be determined in how they behave, but have some degree of freedom in how they think. (Tolstoy's narrator expounds a similar view in *War and Peace*, book III, part I, chapter 1: "There are two sides to the life of every man: the personal life, which is free to the degree that its interests are abstract, and the elemental life of the swarm, in which he ineluctably follows the laws decreed for him. . . . Consciously man lives for himself, but unconsciously he serves as an instrument for the accomplishment of the historical, social ends of mankind.")[3] Another possibility is that God gave everyone a *personal* sense of right and wrong, which makes the exercise of moral judgment into an activity that is determined on one level and relativized on another (and which is, in other terms, the recognition of *difference* at the root of human communication and experience). A conception such as this is troubling, however, because it suggests that God might punish evildoers for something they cannot help doing and according to an ethical system they do not recognize.

Levin's final ruminations leave unexamined these important aspects of the relation of freedom to determinism, or how conscience can be efficacious. In other words, he does not address the question of how an individual's thoughts are related to action in a world determined by God— that is, how he has the freedom to rethink events but not to change himself, or how his discovery that he unwittingly obeyed God's law in the past can be reconciled with the freedom he had to think badly at the same time, which is what he feels had misled him (796–97, VIII.12). From a skeptical perspective, the fact that Levin ignores such issues could be interpreted as his attempt to *rationalize* his inability to change for the better; the echoes between Levin's experiences and Karenin's support this interpretation. There is no way of telling on the basis of the novel if Tolstoy or his narrator was aware of this problem.

But perhaps by virtue of their rationality these questions about discrepancies are the wrong kind to ask in the context of Levin's intuitions, which are explicitly *ecstatic* by nature. Levin himself feels this very strongly, as we can see in a hermeneutic index that eschews any connection between ethical behavior and ratiocination: "Whether he was acting well or badly he did not know, and not only would not start proving it now [ne tol'ko ne stal by dokazyvat'] but even avoided talking or thinking about it" (791, VIII.10). As in all such cases in Tolstoy, there is an obvious paradox in trying to understand the relation between a character's bias against language and reason and a reader's desire to make sense of the text in which this bias is articulated. Moreover, an important part of Levin's illumination is his realization that human beings are too distant and different from God to be able to fathom Him or His world fully. This functions as Levin's "loophole" for avoiding some of the hardest questions that swirl around any theodicy: "Creation . . . existence . . . The devil and sin . . . evil . . . The Redeemer" are all issues about which he knows "nothing, and can know nothing" (799, VIII.13). However, none of these limitations with regard to what is knowable has any effect on Levin's conviction regarding God's role in human existence (which is echoed by some of his other experiences, as well as those of the artist Mikhailov).

15.3. Anna

Anna's intermittent torment over her affair results in numerous stirrings of her conscience, of course, even though these are not all labeled "inner voices." For example, shortly after meeting Vronsky at the train station, Anna feels uncomfortable about the two hundred rubles that he gave to the dead worker's family because she senses "there was something in it that concerned her, and of a sort that should not have been" (74, I.20). This can be interpreted as Anna's sense that Vronsky's gesture was designed in part to catch her attention. It is less likely that Anna projects this impression, because at the station she is described as throwing a "ball of coquetry" to Vronsky and then choosing not to continue in the same vein (63, I.18). Anna also leaves Moscow in a hurry because she doubts herself and feels excited when she thinks about Vronsky (98, I.28). (This is one of the early signs of temporal acceleration in the Anna-Vronsky plotline *[13.3]*.)

When she is on the train to St. Petersburg, Anna suddenly feels "ashamed" (the word is repeated seven times in a dozen lines), and her inner voice identifies Vronsky as the cause of her feelings (100, I.29). Later, when she catches sight of her husband, an "unpleasant feeling gnawed at her heart," and she feels "dissatisfaction" with herself. This is an "old, familiar feeling" for Anna, "similar to that state of pretence she experienced in her relations with her husband; but previously she had not noticed it, while now she was clearly and painfully aware of it" (104, I.30). This description suggests that her vague and unfocused moral prompt ("unpleasant" and "gnawed at her heart" are value judgments) is a kind of amplification of something already present on a lower level of her consciousness. Her reaction thus resembles Stiva's to the prospect of patching up his marriage with Dolly. Just as he has to pretend he has feelings that he has lost and behave in a way that goes against his nature, so Anna finds herself having to feign the kind of loving relations with Karenin that she now believes never actually existed (perhaps because of the lingering consequences of the coerced nature of their marriage [see *13.5.6*]). Anna's sensation of doubling also needs to be considered in this context, because the fact that she recognizes a split in herself can be seen as a reification of the voice of conscience *(13.5.8)*. A variant of this is Anna's sadness at the prospect of Dolly's leaving Vronsky's estate, because she knows that, "with Dolly's departure, there would be no one to stir up in her soul those feelings that had been aroused in her at this meeting. To stir up those feelings was painful for her; but she knew all the same that that was the best part of her soul and that it was quickly being overgrown in the life she led" (642, VI.24). Anna's reference to a good "part" of her soul, and to the feeling that this part is losing out to an implied bad one, echoes her anguished remarks about feeling that she was split into two women, one good and the other evil.

Despite experiencing moral prompts like the other characters, Anna differs from them as well because her conscience does not simply reaffirm the predilections or appetites that dominate her personality. She is unable to resist her attraction to Vronsky, but she never ceases to feel that she has sinned by indulging it. This feeling is stilled only during the relatively brief period when she recovers from her illness and travels to Italy. Taken together with her desire to avenge herself on Vronsky, Anna's sense of guilt constitutes the clearest link between the implications of the novel's epigraph and the body of the novel. But conversely, when considered in the context of the novel as a whole, Anna's experiences emerge as merely one of the possible variants of how moral prompts function. From this perspective, her sense of guilt, which grows in amplitude, may be as much a part of her nature as is Stiva's self-indulgence.

15.4. Kitty

"'It's a pity, a pity, but what to do? It's not my fault,' she kept saying to herself; yet her inner voice [vnutrennii golos] was saying something else" (55, I.15). This is Kitty worrying at the beginning of the novel about whether or not she had led Levin on and was right to reject his proposal of marriage. Subsequent events demonstrate, of course, how misguided she was to lay her hopes on Vronsky. But why does her inner voice say that she *is* to blame, especially because she is inexperienced and trusting and Vronsky is irresponsibly attentive to her? Does her inner voice resemble Stiva's and Levin's in simply reconfirming dominant truths about herself? Or is it more like Anna's emerging sense of guilt, which displaces the formerly dominant aspects of her character?

The answer appears to be in keeping with Kitty's later decision that she cannot "become" Varenka—that is, that she is like Stiva and Levin in having a fixed character. Just before Levin arrives to propose, Kitty compares her suitors (which is how she and her mother naively view Vronsky as well). It is easy and pleasant for her to think of Levin, but "in her recollections of Vronsky there was an admixture of something awkward . . . as if there were some falseness [fal'sh']—not in him . . . but in herself" (47, I.13). It is not possible to say what exactly made Kitty reject Levin that evening in anticipation of Vronsky's proposal, but presumably it included such considerations as Levin's being a familiar family friend whereas Vronsky was a dazzling newcomer from St. Petersburg, her mother's preference for Vronsky, the fact that Levin had been away for a long time and left the field open to Vronsky, and the advantages for the novel's plots of having young love thwarted. Be that as it may, it turns out that Kitty's inner voice after she rejects Levin repeats a truth she already knew on some level of her consciousness.

There is an additional link between Kitty's thoughts about Vronsky before Levin arrives and the experiences of the other characters. The key concept here is again "falsehood." We already encountered it in connection with Stiva's reluctance to patch up his marriage to Dolly, in Levin's reaction to participating in religious rituals, in Vronsky's reaction to his affair with Anna (184, II.21), and in other related details such as Dolly's impression of Anna and Vronsky's household in general (634, VI.22). Kitty is like all these characters in the sense that she experiences internal prompts regarding what is true and false in relation to an issue that is important for *her* specifically—namely, her suitors. But at the same time, the fact that Kitty and the other characters all have reactions that are *ethical* implies that there may also be a connection between them and a larger network of truth and falsehood woven into the fabric of the novel.

This is suggested by a feeling like conscience that Kitty has when Levin confesses his wild jealousy of Vasenka Veslovsky because of the way he had "dared" to look at her: "In the depths of her soul she found that there had been something of the sort, . . . but she dared not confess it even to herself, much less venture to tell it to him" (573, VI.7). In the ensuing scenes, the only ones who are incensed by Levin's showing Vasenka the door are Kitty's mother and Stiva, but Stiva's anger does not last. Even Vasenka appears to sense that he had gone a bit too far when Levin tells him to leave (602, VI.15). Thus, despite there being a range of reactions, there is some (not always conscious) agreement among different characters who belong to one loose but not exclusive set about the immorality of Vasenka's behavior.

15.5. Vronsky

Vronsky also has experiences like the promptings of a conscience, albeit considerably less frequently than Anna. They are not labeled "inner voices," but their description implies that they may belong to the same category. For example, on the eve of the horse race, we are told that ever since he began his affair he is occasionally overcome by a "feeling of loathing for something—whether for Alexei Alexandrovich, or for himself, or for the whole world, he did not quite know. But he always drove this strange feeling away" (184, II.21). If this is like the experiences of the other characters, is it an expression of an essential truth about him or about good and evil? The answer appears a few lines later when Vronsky realizes "for the first time" that "it was necessary to stop this lie [lozh']." Thus, his realization probably applies to his having to conceal his relations with Anna and perhaps to his being party to the fictitious relations between Anna and Karenin.

But is it also possible that Vronsky is revolted by his own immorality? An indication that this may be the case, even if only on a barely conscious level, is the narrator's pointed and elaborate description of Seryozha as a moral compass that shows both Vronsky and Anna how far they had strayed off course, which is something that "they knew but did not want to know." We are told that Vronsky's feeling of "loathing" is awakened by the child's presence (186, II.22), which links the boy to the less focused "loathing" Vronsky feels a few pages earlier. Consequently, it is possible to see Vronsky's spontaneous negative reactions as revealing not only his genuine distaste for deception but also his link to the novel's ambiguous moral superstructure. A related example is when Vronsky hears from Anna that she is pregnant, and his "heart" urges "him to demand that she leave her husband" (305, III.20). Although Vronsky does not immediately overcome this prompt the way the other characters do theirs, he soon begins to doubt its wisdom and practicality. He also does not succeed in eliminating all the falsehood from his affair with Anna, either at an early or at a late stage. Indeed, he will come to see their relations as authentic and as thwarted by the lies of others, which relegates the moral prompts he experiences earlier to a kind of ineffectual limbo.

15.6. Conscience, Ethics, and Relativization

The above argument about the possibility of seeing *personal* judgments as reflecting an ethical system that *transcends* the individual might look as if I am trying to have relativization both ways. On the one hand, when describing how individual characters see the world, I stress their isolation from each other with regard to issues that are important to them personally; on the other, I suggest that the characters' private conceptions of what is good or bad can be seen as reflecting a universal ethical imperative in the novel's fictional world. In other words, the common element in the prompts that characters feel is a desire to avoid *falsehood,* but this is refracted through their personal definitions of what is true and false. The question that arises, therefore, is, how can the apparently disconnected and autoteleological motivations of individuals also be part of some transcendent telos, or at least significant pattern? One could argue that this is impossible and that

Tolstoy shows unique behavior well, but fails to subsume it under larger, overarching truths and generalizations. From this perspective, the abstract opposition between good and evil is no more than the inescapable condition of *difference,* and thus of value, that underlies all aspects of human existence and that could be found in any narrative (or utterance).

However, we can infer a possible solution to this problem from the narrator's description of how Vronsky brings his financial affairs into order: "Every man, knowing to the smallest detail all the complexity of the conditions surrounding him, involuntarily assumes that the complexity of these conditions and the difficulty of comprehending them are only his personal, accidental peculiarity [lichnaia, sluchainaia osobennost'], and never thinks that others are surrounded by the same complexity as he is. So it seemed to Vronsky" (302, III.19). This statement can be interpreted as a hermeneutic index with far-reaching implications: that uniqueness is a universal delusion because there is a much greater degree of commonality among individuals, at least with regard to the abstract texture of their lives, than might otherwise seem to be the case; and that, consequently, there are at least two levels of "reality," the personal and the general, with the second perhaps being "truer" than the first. It is therefore possible to read this index as supporting the interpretation I suggested above of the relation between personal and universal ethics. However, it is also possible to argue that the narrator's comment is only about the kind of prosaic and mundane activity that Vronsky carries out in this scene and not about life in general. After all, his bringing his affairs into order is not one of the pivotal events in the novel, so there is no reason to overinterpret the remark the narrator makes about it. The narrator also describes Vronsky's procedure in apportioning his payments as immoral. In the final analysis, however, the reason for inferring that the narrator's generalization may be more rather than less widely applicable to the novel as a whole is that this accords better with his other arguments of an essentialist nature (see *16*), and with the interest shown in universals and large truths by the narrator and Levin (which does not eliminate the discrepancies between these universals and the novel's details). Indirect evidence supporting this inference can also be found in an early draft of the passage in question. In addition to the first sentence in the above quotation, which is identical in the draft, the narrator adds illustrations of how different characters misread each other's situations in accordance with the abstract principle of underestimating the complexities that others face. Thus, Vronsky is described as envying the easy lives of Petritsky and his brother, while they are described as envying his wealth, connections, and freedom to indulge any whim.[4] These illustrations broaden the significance of the narrator's generalization from Vronsky and his monetary and amorous concerns to human behavior more generally. However, the fact that Tolstoy cut these details from the novel means that, for all we know, he may have changed his mind about them, which, in turn, indicates that they cannot be used to prove anything conclusive about the final text.

16. Essentialism

Another kind of unity evoked in *Anna Karenina* is essentialism, which takes two forms. The first is the claim made by the narrator and several characters that some categories of human beings—especially women and peasants—are defined by unalterable traits. (The "situation rhymes" among different characters also imply the interchangeability and therefore the universality of certain human traits.) The text does not always support these generalizations, but there are enough of them to constitute an argument—albeit not a proof—for the existence of transpersonal truths, and to imply that the world is more structured than might seem to be the case if we judge only by the perceptions of individual characters. This is obviously an important consideration in the context of the novel's allusions to God, divine law, good and evil, fate, and the like. However, as in the case of characters' feelings of unity with others, which tend to be overshadowed by descriptions of how they are isolated from each other, the claims for essentialism occupy relatively little textual space even though they carry considerable hermeneutic weight. And as in the case of the unclear relation between personal and universal ethics, the nexus between individual behavior and supposedly universal essentialist traits is difficult to trace, in part because it is not something with which the narrator concerns himself outside the moments when he asserts its existence.

The second form of essentialism is manifested in the link between human beings and nature. Some of the narrator's descriptions, and the attitudes of several characters, imply that human existence in proximity to or in harmony with nature and natural processes is most fulfilling and best. In other words, there is something in human behavior and values that is fixed, that is not simply a product of culture, and that reflects an ordering principle that encompasses the seemingly disparate worlds of nature and humankind.[1]

16.1. Nature and Humankind

The character who embodies this link most fully is Levin. One of the most elaborate passages confirming his harmony with nature begins with the narrator's description of spring's arrival following the winter when Kitty rejects Levin's proposal. The narrator directly correlates the seasonal change, which he describes as bringing "joy to plants, animals and people alike" (152, II.12), with Levin's determination to overcome his past disappointments and to redefine his life without Kitty. However, given how the rest of this scene develops, there is a curious discrepancy between the harmony Levin experiences and what he wants. Levin never entirely overcomes his love for Kitty, and by the end of the summer reconfirms it when he glimpses her in a carriage at dawn. Thus, although the narrator shares in Levin's ecstatic mood when spring arrives, the harmony between Levin and nature is falsely prophetic or inaccurate about the future course of his life, which turns out more positively than he had dreamt (although he does claim later that he always felt his marriage to Kitty was preordained [see *17.2*]).

An additional link between nature and things human is suggested by the narrator's correlating changes in weather with the Russian Easter church calendar—Lent, Easter Monday, Krasnaya Gorka (the week after Easter). Moreover, his closely observed and highly knowledgeable observations are couched in rhythmically organized language, which adds a correlation between nature and the human mode of expression.[2] This is further augmented by the narrator's inclusion of human, animal, and vegetable agents in an anaphoric structure, and by his personifying verbs applied to the animal world. In the example that follows, I intentionally betray English word order, and Pevear and Volokhonsky's fine translation, in order to preserve some of the structure of the original Russian: "the bright sun rose and quickly ate up the thin ice covering the water . . . Greened the old grass and sprouting needles of new grass, swelled the buds . . . buzzed the newly hatched bee . . . trilled invisible larks . . . wept the peewit . . . flew with their spring honking the cranes and geese . . . lowed in the meadow . . . the cattle, played the bow-legged lambs, ran the fleet-footed children, chattered by the pond the many voices of women, knocked in the yards the peasants' axes . . . came the real spring" (153, II.12). Immediately following this variegated chorus, the narrative shifts to Levin striding across his estate and culminates in the hermeneutic index that he is "like a tree in spring" because he does not yet know what he will do first. (The mirror image of this form of harmony between man and nature can be seen in the description of how steadily increasing physical pain and suffering—or the "natural" deterioration of the body—make Levin's brother, Nikolai, "look at death as the satisfaction of his desires, as happiness" [503, V.20].)[3]

Throughout the novel, nature also functions regularly as an evaluative touchstone for other characters. For example, heartily singing peasant women who approach Levin after having finished their labors are likened to a "thundercloud of merriment" (275, III.12). Kitty expects and wants to live in the country after marrying Levin because she realizes its importance for him; after settling there she is compared to a bird weaving her nest as she prepares for motherhood (486, V.15). Dolly believes strongly in the benefits of country life for her children. The engrossing discussion about child rearing that she has with peasant women is an additional sign of her heart clearly being in the right place. By contrast, Anna's life on Vronsky's estate serves to foreground the *unnaturalness* of her situation rather than her wish to remedy it. The fact that she shocks Dolly by implying that she uses contraception confirms the extent to which she is out of synchrony with the natural order. Similarly, urban visitors to the country such as Stiva, Koznyshev, and Vasenka Veslovsky see it as a source of entertainment or relaxation rather than as a place where one lives and works, as a result of which they emerge as flawed or lacking something. (For example, Levin mows with his peasants all day and experiences transcendent moments of timelessness, whereas Koznyshev says he is pleased with his day as well because he has solved two chess problems [258, III.6].) As these examples make clear, virtuous "country" necessarily implies its antithesis—flawed "city."

16.2. Women

Within gender essentialism, women receive the most comments from the narrator, and one prominent topic is their supposed penchant for indirection or duplicity. When Kitty's parents discuss her marriage prospects, the narrator characterizes the mother's reservations about Levin as "that way women have of sidestepping the question" (43, I.12). Similarly, when Anna thinks about the kinds of relations she will have with her son if she leaves Karenin, she becomes so frightened that, "like a woman, [she] tried only to calm herself with false reasonings and words, so that everything would remain as before" (190, II.23). Later, Anna drafts a note to Vronsky in which she writes, "I have informed my husband," and then sits for a long time, unable to continue; she is troubled by the frank nature of her admission, which is "so coarse, so unfeminine" (291, III.15). Even when there is nothing terrible to deny, Anna is still presented as enjoying duplicity with Princess Betsy. The two have been alluding to Anna's affair with Vronsky, which prompts the narrator to explain: "This playing with words, this concealment of the secret, held great charm for Anna, as for all women. It was not the need for concealment, not the purpose of the concealment, but the very process of concealment that fascinated her" (296, III.17). Given the importance of Truth in the novel and for Tolstoy in general, and his distrust of language as an adequate vehicle for Truth *(11),* these narrative comments define a fundamental form of corruption that is presumably shared by all women.

However, it would be a gross oversimplification to claim that Tolstoy is simply a misogynist, because there are important moments in the novel that qualify or complicate these unflattering generalizations about women. Dolly is very frank and perspicacious when speaking with Levin about his failed proposal to Kitty, and explains Kitty's behavior in such a way that at least one form of women's duplicity emerges in a somewhat different light. Dolly says that the existing form of courtship puts young women at a disadvantage and forces them into uncertainty. She explains that a man is free to visit a young woman's home as he pleases and to weigh his decision as long as he likes until he is certain of his choice. What men cannot understand, however, is that young women, with their "feminine, maidenly modesty," remain in a state of suspense during courtship. They know men only from a distance, are obliged to take everything on trust, and, as a result, may not have a clear sense of whom they want or even what to say when confronted with a proposal of marriage (270, III.10; all of this clearly also bears on Karenin's "courtship" of Anna). The paradoxical consequence of Dolly's explanation about why Kitty refused Levin, and how this means nothing in the long run, is that the experiences of young women may be necessarily related to the predilection for evasive language shown by older women as different as Anna and Betsy, and could be the result of either inborn traits or social conventions that are asymmetrical in how they apply to the sexes.

Another complication of the narrator's generalizations about women is that there are male characters who also show a penchant for avoiding the truth, although not necessarily via deceptive language. When Karenin confronts Anna with his suspicions, he fears having them confirmed so much that "he was now ready to believe anything" (213, II.29). Levin's acquaintance Sviyazhsky is also characterized repeatedly as becoming frightened and changing the subject whenever a discussion approaches any private matter of fundamental importance (333, III.27). Vronsky's code of behavior allows him to deceive a husband, as the narrator explains, and Stiva is quite prepared to say anything that will smooth over an awkward situation. On the other hand, there is also at least one minor female character who is forthright in her use of language. Princess Miagky's remarks in social gatherings are always noticed, even though they are not always to the point, because they were "simple things that made sense. . . . In the society in which she lived, such words produced the impression of a most witty joke" (135, II.6). This is presumably an example of the exception proving the rule. However, another way of interpreting the narrator's comment is that what he presents as a female weakness contaminates the upper reaches of urban society as a whole.

The novel also contains a number of essentialist remarks about women that are meant to be highly complimentary. One category has to do with women's instincts. These need to be understood in the context of the novel's general celebration of elemental, nonrational, "natural" life, rather than as an attempt to debase women by associating them with the "primitive"; in Tolstoy's Rousseauistic fictional world, urban "civilization" is always marked negatively. Kitty's nest building is one prime example. The true nature of "women's work" also emerges in connection with Kitty's prompting her mother for reminiscences about her own courtship: "Kitty felt a special charm in being able to talk with her mother as an equal about these most important things in a woman's life" (555, VI.2). Similarly, Kitty's pregnancy is characterized as "the greatest event in a woman's life" (707, VII.13), which echoes the significance of the discussion Dolly has with a group of peasant women about children. By contrast, Anna's abandonment of her son and her decision not to have any more children puts her at odds with the conception of women that the narrator articulates and that Dolly and Kitty embody. This contributes to the tragic irony of her adulterous affair, which is her attempt to experience the kind of love and life that underlies the novel's essentialist generalizations about women (with their dedication to families and children), but that she was unable to experience fully with Karenin.

Kitty's future role as an exemplary mother is also foreshadowed by what turns out to be her essentialist ability to nurture and comfort Nikolai, her dying brother-in-law. As the narrator describes it, she takes his hand and begins "talking to him with that unoffending and sympathetic animation peculiar only to women" (492, V.17). (But this "spontaneous" behavior appears to have been guided by Kitty's [essentialist?] loyalty to her husband because she was repulsed by Nikolai in Soden. Whatever wisdom she may have about the great mysteries of existence may thus be colored by contingency, and may be more limited than Levin's reactions imply [see also *13.9*].) Levin recognizes Kitty's instinctual gift, but broadens its significance to include spirituality. He concludes that men in general and philosophers in particular have a discursive and abstract understanding of death that is not even "a hundredth part of what his wife and Agafya Mikhailovna knew about it." Different as these two women are, "Both unquestionably knew what life was and what death was." Although Levin believes that neither one could have understood the ultimate questions that trouble him, he concludes that both share with millions of other "people" an automatic and profound understanding of death that is revealed by their ability to help the dying and not to fear them (496, V.19). His reference here to "people" (liudei) is somewhat confusing, because it implies that he has extended his conclusion about a spiritual instinct from the two women to humankind in general (while presumably excluding the "many great masculine minds" that represent urban civilization and its defects).

Levin's inclusive remark thus implies another kind of essentialism, one that women can share with men, and that foreshadows the "proof through numbers" argument he invokes at the novel's conclusion to buttress his new faith in God and the law of goodness: the fact that millions of human beings believe the same thing warrants his doing so as well *(13.4.4)*. While his brother is dying, Levin does not yet possess this faith. But he shows a predisposition toward, and an understanding of, a spiritual reality when he concludes that Kitty's and Agafya Mikhailovna's behavior around Nikolai is not simply "instinctive, animal, unreasoning," because both women insist on the greater importance of spiritual over physical care, which is manifested for them in the rituals of communion and anointing (497, V.19). It is unclear, however, how Levin's conclusion can be reconciled with his contentions that Kitty and the housekeeper could not understand the questions that trouble him and that they act spontaneously.

There are also smaller comments that posit female essentialism even though they do not specify its nature in any detail. On the evening when Levin comes to propose to her, Kitty "experienced a feeling similar to that of a young man before battle" (46, I.13), which implies a gender-specific experience like a rite of passage. At the train station in Moscow, Anna tells a certain Ivan Petrovich that hers is "merely a woman's" viewpoint, but we never learn what she is referring to (62, I.18). Anna also invokes privileged female understanding when she tells Dolly that "as a woman" she understands her pain (70, I.19). In turn, Dolly refers to "pride" as the main obstacle men face when trying to understand the situation in which women find themselves during courtship, and contrasts this with another feeling that "only women know" but that she does not name (270, III.10). At the ball, Anna throws a "fleeting feminine glance" at Kitty's dress (79, I.22). The narrator also comments that although there is a sharp distinction between Levin and Vronsky from a male point of view, Anna "as a woman . . . saw what they had in common, for which Kitty, too, had loved them both" (704, VII.12).

16.2.1. The "Woman Question"

The most focused discussion of women in the novel takes place around the Oblonskys' dinner table.[4] However, because the narrator does not participate, and because the different opinions expressed are not resolved or reconciled in any way, the question of what the status of women should be in general is left hanging. One point of view is articulated at some length by the character Pestsov, who speaks in favor of women's education and condemns their lack of rights. He goes so far as to use the word "enslavement" (poraboshchenie) in reference to women, and compares their status to that of "negroes" in the United States prior to emancipation. Pestsov also argues that inequality between the sexes in marriage is a consequence of the fact that the infidelity of a husband and a wife is punished unequally both by law and by public opinion (391, IV.12). Koznyshev agrees with Pestsov's general position but quibbles over his use of the word "rights," instead of which he prefers "obligations" (388, IV.10). And Karenin objects to Pestsov's last point and makes the rather enigmatic but still essentialist remark that the reasons for the inequality "are in the very essence of things" (391, IV.12). However, Pestsov's greatest opponent is Prince Shcherbatsky, who jokingly invokes biological determinism to ridicule the idea that women want social, political, and economic rights that they do not have.

It is clearly possible to see this entire discussion as bearing on Anna. Specifically, it foreshadows her situation later in the novel when she herself is struck by the fact that Vronsky can live as he wishes in contemporary Russian society whereas she has no rights. She concludes that her beauty is the only tool she has to keep him (666, VI.32). One could argue that Anna's conclusion is a resounding confirmation of Pestsov's generalization (and a hermeneutic index equating women and American slaves) and thus the heart of the novel's critique of the dependent status of women in Russia in the 1870s. But this argument holds only if one chooses to weigh Pestsov's views more heavily than those of the other characters involved in the discussion. And the problem with this choice is that there does not seem to be a textual warrant for doing so. Pestsov's views are not foregrounded in any way or echoed elsewhere in the novel; and he is too minor for his views to be taken more seriously than those of other, more important characters.

Furthermore, although the discussion during the Oblonsky dinner is seemingly about abstract issues pertaining to women in general, it is typical of the novel's perspectivalism that a number of the characters actually conceal specific personal concerns behind their remarks, as a result of which the real focus of the discussion is more diffuse than might appear at first. Thus, as we have seen, Stiva's defense of Pestsov's position on women's rights is motivated specifically by his affair with the ballerina Chibisova (389, IV.10), which is hardly an "enlightened" stance with regard to women. Dolly guesses as much, which prompts her irritated comment that any young woman should always be able to find women's work in a family, which of course implies that this is what she sees as a woman's proper place.[5] Kitty also takes the discussion entirely personally by "not being interested in it at all" due to the burgeoning relationship between her and Levin. This is all the more noteworthy because Kitty had often thought of the difficult life that her friend Varenka leads, and had feared a similar future for herself if she did not succeed in marrying, which effectively confirms her support for the importance of fixed traditional roles for women.

Levin is implicated in this process of relativization even more strongly. He initially sides with Dolly's view, but then shifts to Kitty's simply because he loves her and immediately makes her fears his own. He also completely redefines Pestsov's advanced sociopolitical arguments for women's emancipation by taking his cue from Kitty's "fear of spinsterhood and humiliation," which denotes traditional notions of patriarchy and domesticity (397, IV.13). By contrast, Turovtsyn follows the discussion about women only because he is waiting for a pretext to burst out laughing at the first witticism that anyone utters (387, IV.10). His actual relation to the specific issue is entirely tangential: Kitty praises him for his kindness and "heart of gold" because he spent three weeks helping Dolly when her children were ill with scarlet fever (390, IV.11). But later Dolly thinks that he may have helped her because he was in love with her (608, VI.16), which relativizes his involvement with the question of what is "women's work" even more.

All these centrifugal views circling around the "woman question" are also inevitably colored by the way in which the speakers are themselves marked in the novel. In addition to Pestsov being too minor to warrant evaluation by the narrator, both Karenin and Koznyshev have already been shown as effete characters with unfortunate predilections for abstraction, which raises the possibility that their views on women are similarly flawed. As usual, Stiva's concerns are entirely personal, and so are Turovtsyn's.

Thus, there does not appear to be any extrapersonal criterion according to which their opinion can be evaluated. And what about the views of Prince Shcherbatsky, Dolly, Kitty, and Levin? They are the novel's most favored characters, and with them essentialism and a "patriarchal" viewpoint reign supreme. (Earlier in the novel, Dolly does acknowledge to Anna that the way she was raised by her mother made her not only "innocent" but also "stupid" [68, I.19]. However, Dolly does not draw any larger conclusions from this beyond explaining her naïveté with regard to Stiva's infidelity.) The harmony between these characters and the narrator's essentialist claims suggests that both identify one of the dominants of human nature in the novel, or at least one of the dominant ways in which human nature is understood in its world.

16.2.2. Women's Wisdom, Narrative Structure, and Male Insight

Given what the narrator says about the inborn ability women have to understand mysteries of existence such as death, it is possible to read several major moments in the novel as embodying the "female point of view." For example, the narrator assumes a kind of *implicit* female understanding of the relation between life and death when he chooses to announce Kitty's pregnancy immediately after Nikolai dies in the only chapter in the entire novel that has its own title, "Death" (505, V.20). This pointed way of juxtaposing life and death suggests that the two events may be linked. Of course, Kitty's whole being as a pregnant woman tending to a dying man can be seen as a response to death, because birth balances death on the physical and spiritual levels of existence.

The importance of this relation in the novel is indicated by how often Levin juxtaposes and equates his son's imminent birth and his brother's death: "No sooner had the one mystery of death been accomplished before his eyes, and gone unfathomed, than another arose, equally unfathomed, which called to love and life" (505, V.20). "He knew and felt only that what was being accomplished was similar to what had been accomplished a year ago . . . on the deathbed of his brother Nikolai. But that had been grief and this was joy. But that grief and this joy were equally outside all ordinary circumstances of life, were like holes in this ordinary life, through which something higher showed" (713, VII.14). And when Kitty gives birth, "In her face there was the same change from earthly to unearthly that occurs in the faces of the dead; but there it is a farewell, here it was a meeting" (717, VII.16).

Why does Levin articulate hermeneutic indices that link birth and death? His answer is not altogether surprising within the tradition of religiously informed worldviews and hinges on his inkling about occult knowledge. When he contemplates both events or, in other words, tries to relate them to each other and himself, he feels that his soul ascends to heights it had never reached before, to where reason cannot follow, and to the very limits of understanding (713, VII.14). This is in stark contrast to how he felt earlier by his brother's deathbed, when he envied "the knowledge that the dying man now had but that he could not have" (501, V.20). In other words, it is through the ability to relate the two polar events in human existence that Levin comes closest to grasping some kind of unity that transcends life and death. This inference is supported by Kitty's intuition that not only is her infant son capable of recognizing her and an old family servant, but that he "knew and understood everything, knew and understood much else that no one knew and which she, his mother, had herself learned and begun to understand only thanks to him" (783, VIII.6). Kitty's view echoes the kind of belief expressed in William Wordsworth's famous "Ode: Intimations of Immortality from Recollections of Early Childhood":

> Our birth is but a sleep and a forgetting:
> The Soul that rises with us, our life's Star,
> Hath had elsewhere its setting,
> And cometh from afar.[6]

Because Levin draws parallels between birth and death, Kitty's view functions as a likely answer to his longing for the knowledge that he imagines his dying brother has. Levin's parallels also serve as a plausible template for the connection that the reader can make between the birth of Levin's son and Anna's death because of the image of a flame that they share (see *8.2*). It is paradoxical that the narrator's essentialist claims about women are thus weakened, though not negated, by the possibility that both he and a favored character—as well as the reader—are able to see liminal events as a woman might. Perhaps this is a reason to recall that the narrator is not identical to the implied author in the novel (despite the difficulty of distinguishing between them), and that the function of higher levels of abstraction is to resolve paradoxes at lower levels of experience.

16.3. Men

The essentialist claims about men in the novel are fewer in number and more general than those about women, and fit the traditional pattern of complementing "patriarchal" generalizations about women. All this implies that Tolstoy did not see men as driven by predetermined traits to the same extent that women are. One trait that he does invoke appears in the comment that Prince Shcherbatsky was "like all fathers . . . especially scrupulous about the honour and purity of his daughters" (44, I.12). Another is suggested by the remark that Levin, "like all men, involuntarily pictured [family life] . . . only as the enjoyment of love. . . . like all men, he had forgotten that [his wife] also needed to work" (480, V.14). Levin's implied male need to have independent interests even after he is married—his estate and treatise on the relations of peasants to the land—resembles Vronsky's casting about for various occupations after he begins to live with Anna. In both cases, this leads to different degrees of friction: Levin resents that he cannot work diligently because of Kitty's sweet constraints on his life, and Vronsky's need to have an occupation independent of his love causes him to resent Anna's feelings of insecurity (see, for example, his insistence on his "male independence" [645, VI.25]). The narrator's likening Vronsky's search for an occupation to the way "a hungry animal" will seize anything in the hopes of finding food contains a hermeneutic index implying that his need is instinctual, essential, and thus excusable; this adds to the tragic incommensurability of his and Anna's situations (465, V.8). Perhaps even Stiva's philandering is an extreme variant of the male need for a degree of independence. The narrator explains that no matter how much Stiva tries "to be a solicitous father and husband, he never could *remember* that he had a wife and children. He had a bachelor's tastes, and they alone guided him" (260, III.7, emphasis added). (That Stiva could "forget" something like this is not only humorous but also a hermeneutic index that takes some of the onus off his misdeeds by making them nonvolitional.) Levin obviously does not share Stiva's "tastes" and differs markedly from him in other respects as well. Nevertheless, it is worth recalling that despite Levin's yearning for family life, he still finds something missing when he is (otherwise) happily married, and is satisfied only when he discovers a (private) spiritual reality.

16.4. Peasants

Levin's daily contacts with peasants on his estate lead him to conclude that they have a fixed character unlike that of any other labor force in Europe. He makes this the basis of his treatise on agriculture, in which he considers the Russian peasant "as an absolute given in farming, like climate and soil," and argues that "all propositions in the science of farming ought to be deduced not from the givens of soil and climate alone, but also from the known, immutable character of the worker" (152, II.12). Levin's point of view is highly reductive because it does not distinguish between "character" and "labor": peasants are the work they do, and their work defines them fully. From a Rousseauistic perspective a hermeneutic index that likens people to soil and climate might seem positive; from another point of view, however, it can be seen as demeaning. Other traits that peasants might have are either nonexistent or not important in this context (although Levin does have a somewhat more "rounded" view of peasants as human beings on a number of other occasions).[7]

Levin comes to his views about the Russian peasantry only after failing to impose his own innovative techniques and practices on them. His somewhat contradictory realization is that the peasants ruin all of his initiatives not because they wish him any ill, but because they want to work in a way they find pleasant, and because his interests are not only "foreign and incomprehensible to them, but fatally opposed to their own most just interests" (322, III.24). Levin's preoccupation with labor also dominates his perception of a wealthy peasant's household when he is on his way to a hunt. The members of this large and healthy family are presented as a harmonious and effective labor force even when they are seen at a meal (III.25). As Levin puts it, what he and other landowners were trying to impose was "the European way," which did not consider the Russian peasants' "own instincts" (338, III.28). All of Levin's readings in political economy demonstrate that the supposedly universal laws deduced by writers of varying ideological persuasions in Europe have nothing to do with the Russian situation. The failure of European methods in Russia is thus due to the intractability of the peasants, which is "rooted in the spirit of the people." Levin's objections to the growth of capitalism in Russia, including especially the railroads, also stem from his primary focus on agricultural labor (484, V.15). However, apart from recognizing the peasants' conservatism, and alluding to the Russian "mission" of having to occupy vast empty territories, which somehow helps define the peasants' "spirit," Levin does not specify what the uniquely Russian traits are (342, III.29).

It is worth noting that there is at least one contradiction of Levin's ideas within the novel, which appears in the description of how Vronsky runs his estate. When Levin visits Sviyazhsky and discusses farming with the other landowners who are there, he discovers that they all operate their estates at a loss (333, III.27). This is, in fact, Levin's primary reason for wanting to abandon the foreign methods on which they all rely. By contrast, when Vronsky moves to his estate after returning from Italy, he appears to be successful where Levin and the others fail. The narrator tells us that Vronsky's "affairs . . . went splendidly. Despite the enormous amount of money that the hospital, the machines, the cows ordered from Switzerland and many other things had cost him, he was certain that he was not wasting but increasing his fortune" (643, VI.25). We are also told that he combined the most conservative business practices with a desire to introduce the most advanced technology and innovations—whatever was "still unknown in Russia and capable of causing amazement" (644, VI.25). This is the exact opposite of Levin's nativist inclinations, and it is not clear how the success of Vronsky's practices can be reconciled with them, or with the failures of the other landowners. Perhaps the phrase that Vronsky "*was certain* that he was not wasting but increasing his fortune" (emphasis added) is actually a loophole implying that he merely imagined his success. This possibility is supported by a landowner at the noblemen's elections who tells Levin that Vronsky's approach always leads to a loss (657, VI.29). There is also some oblique and ironic support for this possibility in the narrator's description of how Levin sees his own agricultural innovations in a similarly ambiguous way. In the space of one page, the narrator begins four paragraphs with the word "True" when describing how Levin's plans *fail* to take hold: "True, in the cattle-yard things went no better than before," "True, Fyodor Rezunov's company did not cross-plough their land before sowing," and so on. This litany culminates with the narrator's remark that "despite all that, Levin thought that things had got going" and that he would succeed in the end (340–41, III.29); similarly, a few pages later we are told that "the practical side of the farming was going excellently, *or at least it seemed so to Levin*" (343, III.30, emphasis added).

This apparent contradiction between Levin's and Vronsky's approaches to agriculture, on the one hand, and possibly between what they believed and what they achieved, on the other, raises a series of questions: is Levin's essentialism valid, did Tolstoy agree with it, and how rigorously did he think it through in relation to the fictional world in the novel? However, because Levin's ideas are described at much greater length than is Vronsky's approach to agriculture, Levin's remain dominant in terms of the novel's overarching themes and values. On the other hand, the narrator also undermines Levin's ideas more than once through relativization. As a result of such comments, Levin's conception of the Russian peasant, and his conclusion about what is "true" for Russia, can be seen as a variant of the way characters relativize all truth throughout the novel.

16.5. Essentialism and the Problem of Freedom

Essentialism is obviously not easily reconciled with freedom or contingency. If, as the narrator claims and several characters confirm, courtship, marriage, and children are the most important foci of any woman's life, then the life of a particular woman is presumably only a variant of this universal plot that is ingrained within her. There will be room for freedom of choice and for chance in her existence only with regard to particulars. However, because Tolstoy's conception of essentialism differs for men and women, whatever holds true for a female may not apply to a male character (except for the "female perspective" on life and death that Levin experiences [see *16.2.2*]). A similar conclusion is that whatever may be central to the life of a peasant, whose existence is largely defined by the seasonal cycle of agricultural labor, will not apply to the mistress and especially to the master of the estate. Because of these large-scale variations, one cannot simply generalize from the lives of peasants (who are the most constrained) to that of gentry women or men (who are the least constrained) when trying to understand the extent to which freedom and chance play a role in a human existence in *Anna Karenina.* The quantities and kinds of textual evidence that we are given about different characters, and the types of characters that we encounter, also vary too much for anything resembling a balanced comparison to be possible.

16.5.1. Levin

However, we can get a sense of what the *maximal* degree of freedom in human existence may be by focusing on a male character of the gentry class, especially one who is conscious of freedom as an issue. (Determining the role of *chance* in the life of a fictional character is complicated for theoretical reasons that I will consider below *[18]*.) Of all the characters, Levin is the most concerned with trying to become a better person, which necessarily implies that he believes he is free to do so. But the results of his efforts are mixed at best.

On the way home following his rejection by Kitty, Levin makes several resolutions to improve: he wants to live for the present and to give up fanciful hopes such as marriage, to resist lust, to monitor closely and help his brother Nikolai, and to be more frugal (92–93, I.26). However, these resolutions are somewhat undermined by Levin's realization when he settles into his domestic routine that "he was himself and did not want to be otherwise. He only wanted to be better than he had been before" (92, I.26). Thus, Levin's formulation of his goal is somewhat ambivalent and recalls other similar moments in the novel when a character either creates what already exists (Mikhailov's removing layers of dross from the ideal image embodied in his painting), or resolves to be what he or she is anyway (Kitty at the German spa, Stiva on all occasions, Koznyshev after deciding not to marry Varenka), or discovers that he has always lived according to an admired principle (Levin and the divine law of goodness at the end of the novel). When he walks into his study, Levin undergoes a rapid emotional oscillation that neatly frames the problem he faces. First, all the familiar objects seem to say to him that he will never change; but then "another voice in his soul" insists that he should not submit to the past and that it is possible to do whatever one wants with oneself (93, I.26).

What does happen to Levin? On the one hand, despite his resolve not to be wasteful, and despite the fact that he lives alone, he heats his entire old house because the idea of family life that it represents is too important for him to be able to abandon it. Similarly, when spring comes, he realizes that he did not in fact carry out many of the plans he had set himself during the winter, although we are not told exactly what these were and if they differ from the ones he made following his rejection by Kitty (152, I.12). On the other hand, Levin concludes that he did accomplish what he considers most important: he had lived "a pure life," which implies that he did not succumb to sexual temptations (although it is not specified what hypothetical opportunities he could have had—peasant women like his creator in his youth? someone else?). Levin also takes pleasure in how he managed to help his brother go abroad for treatment. Taken together, this mix of successes and (moderate?) failures constitutes what could be considered a kind of "realistic" middle ground, where a character does show his moral freedom to improve himself somewhat according to criteria he values, but without embracing any really new form of behavior.

Although this is the most plausible surface interpretation of Levin's efforts, it is also possible to conclude that there is a countercurrent of narrative irony at his expense. This stems from the fact that in the continuation of the *same* paragraph in which Levin thinks of his successes, we are told for the first time about the "immutable character of the worker." This juxtaposition of Levin's view of the Russian peasantry, with whom he identifies to a significant extent when he says he is also one of the "people" (806, VIII.15; 810, VIII.16), and his perception of himself as capable of change, raises questions about both: perhaps Levin is as misguided about peasant immutability as he is about his own mutability? An argument in favor of this possibility is that Levin himself admires the rich peasant who, together with his family, has broken out of the communal pattern of life that still characterizes the largely faceless mass of peasants on Levin's estate even after the reforms he has introduced (III.25). (Despite the rich peasant's exceptional success, and as if echoing Levin's essentialist views, the narrator does not bother to give the peasant's name.) It is also noteworthy that the rich peasant is not at all averse to various agricultural "innovations" (325, III.25), which is at odds with Levin's view of peasants as inflexibly conservative. (This peasant is clearly atypical, but does this mean that he is the exception that proves or disproves Levin's "rule" about peasant character?)

Another moment that sheds light on Levin's freedom to act morally involves his brother. Hearing an unexpected visitor approaching the manor house, Levin realizes that it could be Nikolai, and his initial reaction is to recoil. But then Levin feels ashamed of himself and "at once opened, as it were, his inner embrace and with tender joy now expected and wished it to be his brother" (159, II.14). Here Levin appears to overcome a moment of selfish weakness and *chooses* to behave lovingly. The fact that it is Stiva who has arrived does not diminish the significance of Levin's spiritual gesture; unless, of course, one again decides to interpret his character as fixed in the sense of being permanently inclined toward charitable behavior (but only toward people who are already members of his inner circle; as we have seen, he repeatedly makes it a *principle* not to take an interest in others). The problem with the latter interpretation is that there is no easy way out of it, which makes the question—is Levin free to act morally?—impossible to answer.

In the rest of the novel a distinction arises between Levin's *abstract* belief that he can act freely and/or morally and his *experience* that freedom lies only in recognizing the necessity of which he is a part. For example, during the mowing scene, which is a "quintessentialist" peasant activity in this novel, Levin's work goes badly when he consciously tries to do his best, but well when he stops trying and feels that "some external force moved him" (256, III.5). Similarly, it is paradoxical that close contacts with the peasants make Levin yearn to give up his "burdensome, idle, artificial and individual life," as he thinks of it, and to follow the "pure" and "lovely" life of peasant communal labor (275, III.12). The paradox lies in his being moved to make a *conscious* effort to join the *unconscious* life led by peasants that he considers to be admirable and moral. This is of course the usual quandary of anyone with a postlapsarian longing for a prelapsarian past. But Levin's particular moral imperative proves entirely specious, because shortly after feeling it and deciding that his life has changed as a result, Levin glimpses Kitty on the road at night, abandons "with disgust" his dreams of marrying a peasant woman, and reconfirms his love for Kitty (277, III.12). This does not mean that he has chosen to be immoral, but simply that old, determinate characterological traits either die hard or do not die at all (which puts into question the possibility of freely chosen action).

Another comparable instance is Levin's fantasy that he could be the catalyst for worldwide prosperity because of his revolutionary ideas about restructuring the workings of his estate based on the immutability of peasant character (344, III.30). However, not long after his marriage he confesses to Kitty that although he still wishes he were a better person, he has ceased pursuing his reforms with any zeal, and carries them out mechanically because he is absorbed by his love for her (560, VI.3).

Levin's outlook becomes more resigned in general following his betrothal. At one point during the preparations for the wedding, which include having to confront complex and troubling religious questions, Levin feels especially elated and joyous, and explains this in terms of a hermeneutic index that entails finding happiness in submitting to the will of others: he "said that he was as happy as a dog that has been taught to jump through a hoop and, having finally understood and done what was demanded of it, squeals, wags its tail, and leaps in rapture" (442, V.1). When Levin goes to the noblemen's elections, he brings with him an attitude of a priori deference to whatever transcends his ken: "Levin had changed greatly since his marriage; he was patient, and if he did not understand why it was all arranged that way, he said to himself that he could not judge without knowing everything, that it probably had to be that way, and he tried not to be indignant" (646, VI.26). Levin's reluctance to judge (which he betrays to an extent at the elections) again evokes the novel's epigraph, and suggests that its emphasis may be less on acknowledging *divine omnipotence* than on recognizing that *human ignorance* necessitates a nonjudgmental stance. The same implication is present in Levin's recollection near the end of the novel, after he has had his religious awakening, of the episode in the Russian Primary Chronicle about how the ancestors of the Russians appealed to Varangian princes to come and rule over them: "We joyfully promise full obedience. All labours, all humiliations, all sacrifices we take upon ourselves, but we will not judge or decide" (810, VIII.16). Here Levin celebrates a kind of passive submissiveness based on ignorance of ultimate goals that recalls Tolstoy's remarks in the epilogues to *War and Peace* (or the conception of a slavish and deceived humanity posited by the Grand Inquisitor in Dostoevsky's *Brothers Karamazov*). The difference in *Anna Karenina* is that Levin wants each human being to act in accordance with the law of goodness that is revealed to each individually, even though he still implicitly equates being "freed from deception" with having "found the master" (796, VIII.12). Moreover, as we have seen, in the novel's final lines Levin reveals that this action is semiotic, a matter of understanding, and not pragmatic, or a matter of action (see also *13.4.4, 15.2*).

16.5.2. Other Characters

We have also seen other major characters act as if driven by personal traits they cannot deny. Anna cannot resist Vronsky because he offers her the love and passion she needs and never experienced with Karenin. Kitty abandons Varenka as a role model because abnegation is not in her nature. Levin describes his brother, Nikolai, in similar terms (which, moreover, also reflect back onto him): "He was not to blame for having been born with an irrepressible character and a mind somehow constrained. But he had always wanted to be good" (85, I.24). This exculpatory remark posits a separation between *action* and *thought* that echoes Levin's own dualism at the end of the novel. It suggests that character is destiny on the level of praxis but not on the level of theory. Thus, ethics are relegated to the realm of private wishes that cannot be (easily? ever?) fulfilled. As we have seen, indirect evidence that Tolstoy could have entertained such a division in *Anna Karenina* can also be found in part 2 of the epilogue to *War and Peace,* where he argued that necessity rules over all aspects of human existence except for *consciousness,* which is the locus of freedom.

In *Anna Karenina,* variations of this idea are repeated by characters at different ends of the social spectrum. Given Levin's respect for the "conservative" nature of the Russian peasant, it is consistent that someone from their midst—in this case, his steward—would react fatalistically to his master's innovative plans (which is also highly ironic under the circumstances). The steward does not understand that Levin believes he is trying to instill in the peasants a kind of enhanced version of their own essential traits. After Levin explains again what he wants, the man's expression seems to say, "That's all very well, but it's as God grants" (156, II.13).

The near-courtship of Koznyshev and Varenka reenacts the same abstract opposition. The two wander off while gathering mushrooms, but he remains silent, although the moment is ripe for him to propose. Then, in a rare instance of direct commentary about an action that a character has not even carried out yet, the narrator states: "It would have been better for Varenka to remain silent. After a silence it would have been easier to say what they wanted to say than after talking about mushrooms." But Varenka cannot hear or comply with the narrator's warning and is unable to resist speaking: "against her own will, as if inadvertently, Varenka said: 'So you didn't find any?'" (564, VI.5). Her remark disappoints Koznyshev, who thinks of trying to return the conversation to a more appropriate topic; but, instead, "as if against his will, after being silent for a while, he commented on her last words" (564, VI.5). A few lines later, Koznyshev speaks about mushrooms again, and the moment for a marriage proposal is lost forever. Each character thus appears to be caught between conflicting motivations. On a more superficial level, each is almost fully convinced that marriage is the right choice. However, on a deeper level, which is first betrayed by their hesitation and equivocations, and then by their evasive remarks about mushrooms, each appears to resist a commitment that would radically change their lives. In other words, each believes that he or she wants to change, and feels free to do so, but cannot; each is free in thought but not in behavior. The reason why may be that both lack an élan vital, or, more accurately, do not possess enough of it. This is suggested by the fact that although Varenka had initially thought of marriage to Koznyshev as "the height of happiness" in comparison to her previous life, and then felt "hurt and ashamed" at the outcome, she also "had a sense of relief" when the moment passed (565, VI.5). (Levin would not have felt this way if Kitty had turned him down a second time at the Oblonsky dinner.) Her reaction recalls her placid behavior and compliant character in the scenes at the German spa. As for Koznyshev, after reviewing all the reasons he had formulated in favor of marriage, he concludes that he had erred in his feelings for Varenka and that he cannot be unfaithful to the memory of a woman who had died long before. In this context, the Romantic cliché of attachment to the dead rather than the living reconfirms Koznyshev's spiritual sterility. The entire scene also functions as another illustration of how difficult it is for characters to get out of themselves to the extent of being able to communicate freely about a matter that seems to be of the utmost importance to both.[8]

Additional confirmation of Varenka's and Koznyshev's inability to change can be found in the narrator's likening them to pupils who had failed an examination in school and who either had to remain in the same class or be expelled (566, VI.6). This simile is a hermeneutic index that does not bode well for the possibility of learning what one does not already know. By contrast, half a page later, we see Levin reviewing Latin and arithmetic with one of Dolly's sons in preparation for school, or pursuing what is apparently a successful program of education (567, VI.6). Whatever other resonances this detail may have, its contrast with Koznyshev's and Varenka's "failure" suggests the finality of their inability to change.

17. Fate

In addition to the behavior of characters, and statements by them and by the narrator, what other kind of evidence can there be in a novel for the existence of forces or laws that rule over the given fictional world? A related question is, how can a reader verify a character's, or even the narrator's, claims about the existence of forces or laws that transcend the individual? Surely not by turning *first* to one's own experience of life, or to other evidence and arguments from *outside* the text, which may have nothing at all to do with the sui generis world created within it. In fact, the answer to both questions is based on either authority or recurrence, which are actually different sides of the same coin because recurrence can itself easily become authoritative.

Authority of the most straightforward kind entails the manifestation in a text of a consciousness superior to the narrator's. From a narratological perspective, there is an "implied author" in every written story, because no matter what kind of narrator is ostensibly telling it, both he and his act (or his voice) are always someone else's construct. The truth of this claim is more obvious in the case of a novel narrated from the third person than it is in an autobiography. But even if someone is telling his own life story there can never be complete coincidence between that person and the consciousness manifested in the language of the story. The vagaries of memory, the elusiveness of language itself, and changes wrought in the memoirist by the acts of reflection and expression inherent in writing about oneself—all inevitably cause "slippage" between the autobiographer and the subjectivity he projects and portrays.[1]

In novels like Tolstoy's that have an omniscient narrator, it is often difficult or impossible to distinguish between the narrator's consciousness and that of an implied author. This narrative technique also makes it both tempting and perilous to assume a connection between what the narrator says and the ideas of Lev Nikolaevich Tolstoy himself. We have already seen that the narrator's ex cathedra pronouncements throughout *Anna Karenina* are rarely fully supported by textual details, even though the narrator is not "unreliable" in any traditional sense, such as being intentionally deceptive. This kind of discrepancy could be interpreted as showing that the novel's implied author is ambivalent about various important matters that may seem clear or self-evident to his narrator. However, this conclusion says nothing more or different about the novel than does pointing out the discrepancy in the first place. Any connection between this aspect of the novel and Lev Nikolaevich Tolstoy remains entirely speculative (which does not mean that it is uninteresting or pointless).

In *Anna Karenina* an important form of authority is located elsewhere. There are several sets of images in the work that are repeated with such frequency that they do not seem to be products of chance (although it must be acknowledged that this possibility cannot be ruled out entirely for all of them). These repetitions inevitably attract the reader's attention, and the possibility of linking some of them to other important textual elements increases their significance even more. Because the recurring details cannot be attached to any identifiable consciousness in the novel (even the narrator does not call attention to them at the same time that they appear within his discursive field), they seem to escape the limitations inherent in individual perspectives. This is an important conclusion in the context of a novel that is much concerned with relativization. As a result, the networks of images can be seen as part of the very *texture* of the narrative, and thus as the manifestation of a level of meaning in the novel's fictional world that transcends individual characters at the same time that it is related to them. In general, as well as in the case of *Anna Karenina,* it can be difficult or impossible to tell whether or not this kind of meaning was put into the work by the historical author consciously or unconsciously. It can also be unclear if the meaning is more a function of a reader's ingenuity—or perversity—than of unconscious "channeling" through the author. This is where hermeneutic indices are especially illuminating, because whatever the meaning may be will depend entirely on the particular work in question.

I will discuss below the way in which some recurrent imagery can be connected with the theme of fate. But I would like to point out as well that despite the novel's tight weave, I do not see it as a collection of allegories and symbols, and do not believe that all of its imagery can be plausibly related to weighty themes. One example is mushrooms, references to which appear to cluster around the theme of courtship, and which might seem to be marked because they are a more important part of gastronomic life in Russia than in some other cultures. At the Oblonsky dinner, Kitty is described as trying to pierce a mushroom with a fork shortly before Levin's courtship finally succeeds (384, IV.9; note that this detail appears in connection with references to bears [see *17.2*]). By contrast, Koznyshev and

Varenka's courtship disintegrates while mushroom hunting. Varenka is also described earlier as wearing a hat like a mushroom (218, II.31).[2] But Levin's housekeeper, Agafya Mikhailovna, sprains her wrist when she falls down the stairs with a jar of freshly pickled mushrooms, which seems unrelated to the preceding references. In this case, the only possible (and rather un-likely) connection may be to the old peasant mower's stooping to pick up mushrooms as "a treat" for his "old woman" in the middle of his work when Levin is mowing near him (255, III.5). Consequently, mushrooms can be seen as a sign of domesticity, but there does not seem to be any con-vincing reason in *Anna Karenina* to read more into them than that. Never-theless, as in the case of any repetition, this one also contributes to the ab-stract sense of the work's unity, which, because it is a formal trait, also inevitably affects the work's ultimate meanings (see *18*).

17.1. Anna

Two of the most important hermeneutic indices in the novel are Anna's famous characterization of the death of the railway watchman as "A bad omen" (Durnoe predznamenovanie) and Stiva's immediate response: "What nonsense!" (Kakie pustiaki!) (65, I.18). Anna's brief remark is a major interpretive claim with metaphysical implications, which, if correct, po-tentially transforms the entire world in the novel into a semioticized realm where nothing is random. That she does die under a train, and that she and Vronsky share the same bizarre dream that can be linked to the watch-man's death, implies that her fear of a bad omen may have been justified. Or is Stiva's outright dismissal right? Can Anna and Vronsky's dream be read in purely secular and psychological terms as an unconscious echo of a traumatic event that marks their meeting, one that Vronsky quickly ex-ploits to produce an impression on Anna? In this context, how significant is it that Anna's other dream prophecy—that she will die in childbirth—is *not* borne out (362, IV.3)? How can we decide who is right?[3]

We can do so only by examining how meanings develop in the novel. Whereas the accident at the station involves a watchman who is killed on iron tracks by a train that is backing up, Anna's dream centers on a small, frightening peasant with an unruly beard who fumbles with something in a sack and rapidly speaks a series of French phrases about having to "beat the iron, pound it, knead it" (361, IV.3). By themselves, these two sets of details do not constitute unequivocal parallels between the accident and the dream. There is also no indication that Anna "reads" the accident at the station through the prism of her dream; it is possible that she saw the watchman's death as inherently fatidic.

However, the dream and the accident *do* emerge as linked at the end of a series of other details that also gain in importance as they accumulate. Near the novel's conclusion, the narrator reveals that Anna's terrifying nightmare "had come to her repeatedly even before her liaison [sviaz'] with Vronsky." In this context, the word *sviaz'* (which can also mean "affair") probably implies physical consummation, which first occurred a year after Anna and Vronsky met; but it could also indicate Anna's first contacts with Vronsky or some point in between their first meeting and the consummation. In any event, she is especially frightened by the fact that although the peasant in the nightmare does not pay any attention to her, he does something dreadful over her by working on the iron (752, VII.26). This can be linked to something that Anna glimpses during her final train trip—a dirty, ugly peasant wearing a cap who is examining the wheels of her car and who *reminds* her of her nightmare (765, VII.31). Shortly thereafter, a freight train approaches, she *recalls* the accident on the day she first met Vronsky, "and realized what she must do" (768, VII.31). Finally, after she allows herself to fall under the train, feels its enormous mass hit her, and utters a prayer for forgiveness, we read the following sentence, which unites the entire preceding sequence of references to dreams and workmen: "A little muzhik, muttering to himself, was working over some iron" (768, VII.31). It is clear that this sequence tells us something about Anna's own fatidic outlook. But does it also say anything about a fateful force or pattern in her world that is independent of her mind? Because Anna's consciousness is in the process of being extinguished in the last two sentences of part VII, the narrative may no longer be based exclusively on her point of view. For this reason, the sentence about the peasant, and the final one about the candle, could be interpreted as having the (relative) authority of the narrator behind them, and not simply as expressions of Anna's viewpoint. This enhances the possibility that Anna's recurring dream and her comment about a bad omen *are* fatidic in the novel's own terms. However, the opposite argument can also be made. Because the narrator usually does not contradict characters elsewhere in the novel, it is possible that he is still merely echoing Anna's fading point of view at the time of her death (see also *8.2, 13.5.4*).

Another set of images relevant to interpreting Anna's case involves shadows.[4] When the train carrying her and Vronsky to St. Petersburg stops during the snowstorm, which can obviously be read as an "objective correlative" of their developing passion, the narrator mentions in his description of Anna's purview as she stands on the platform that "[t]he stooping shadow of a man slipped under her feet, and the sounds of a hammer on iron could be heard" (102, I.30). This is my literal rendering of the Russian original, which evokes both the dead watchman—and his implied work—at the train station in Moscow, as well as the peasant in Anna's dream who works "iron" in a mysterious way. This syncretic image thus appears to "follow" Anna on her trip. And because there is no evidence that she actually notices the shadow (one assumes that she might have recoiled if she had because of its association with the watchman's death not long before), it is possible to conclude that the shadow is not simply her delusion but a portentous element in her world.

Anna also does not know about the association that erstwhile friends make between her and a shadow, which is again something only the reader can connect to a larger pattern. Just before Anna arrives for a gathering at Princess Betsy's, several guests gossip about her and her husband. They remark that Anna has changed a great deal since her trip to Moscow, because "she's brought a shadow with her—Alexei Vronsky." This leads to banter regarding a supposed story by "Grimm" about a man who lost his shadow, and ends with a remark by "Anna's friend" that "women with a shadow generally end badly."[5] "'Button your lip' [Tipun vam na iazyk, literally, "A murrain (or pip) on your tongue," i.e., "Hold your tongue"], Princess Miagky suddenly said, hearing these words" (135, II.6). The phrase the princess utters is a traditional Russian saying used to express disapproval of an unhappy eventuality to which someone thoughtlessly refers. Thus, although it is a colloquial expression, it echoes a distant origin in (mildly) occult popular beliefs. It would of course be far-fetched to suggest that this lost magical aura is resurrected by Princess Miagky's remark, but it would also be reductive to deny the slight fatidic flavor of the entire exchange.

One of the most important arguments against Anna's dream being merely a projection of her fears is that Vronsky also experiences it (and Pierre's two vatic dreams in *War and Peace* are indirect evidence that Tolstoy was capable of conceiving dreams in "occult" terms).[6] It is possible to argue that the reason for this coincidence is that both have an unconscious response to a traumatic event that accompanies their meeting. But this kind of interpretation is based on a conception of psychological causality (and of probability) that is not invoked overtly in the text. (Recall Levin's skepticism during the philosophical discussion of the relation of sensory data to consciousness [*13.1*].) It also sidesteps the ways the narrative underscores the significance of the coincidence via echoes with other major moments in the novel. One is Vronsky feeling "the same horror filling his soul" as Anna does when she describes her dream to him, which is interpreted by a servant within the dream as foretelling her death in childbirth (361, IV.3). The only other times Vronsky feels anything like this is when Anna almost dies in childbirth and he tries to commit suicide, and later when he learns of Anna's actual death, as we can infer from his mother's description (778, VIII.4). His reaction to Anna's dream is thus marked by associations with death, both Anna's and his own, which enhance the fatidic flavor of the dream he shares with her. Moreover, Vronsky tries to dismiss the significance of what Anna is saying by repeating three times "what nonsense" (kakoi vzdor), but, as the narrator notes, Vronsky does this without any conviction in his voice. This can be read as Vronsky's perfectly mundane attempt to deny something unpleasant. But if this is so, he also comes close to repeating Stiva's response, "What nonsense!" (Kakie pustiaki), to Anna's remark about the omen. Is this merely a coincidence? Or is the repetition significant?

What makes it difficult to dismiss these details is Anna's reason for breaking off her frightening conversation about the dream: "But suddenly she stopped. The expression on her face changed instantly. Terror and anxiety suddenly gave way to an expression of quiet, serious and blissful attention. He could not understand the meaning of this change. She had felt the stirring of new life inside her" (362, V.3). It is highly ironic and typical that Vronsky does not understand what has just happened to Anna. More important, however, is that Anna's mental shift from death to birth echoes the "female understanding" of existence that the narrator celebrates elsewhere in the novel and that Levin and the reader are given to glimpse as well *(16.2.2)*. Specifically, Anna's moving from one thought to the other recalls how Kitty's pregnancy is announced immediately after Nikolai Levin dies. It also recalls that it is possible to juxtapose the image of a candle that is extinguished when Anna dies and the flame that appears when Levin's son is born *(8.2)*. In both these major moments the relation between life and death is simultaneously one of difference and continuity—radical difference on the physical level of existence, and possible continuity on the spiritual. These metaphysical implications, which have additional resonances and implications that I will consider below, also add weight to the possibility that the dream "coincidence" was fateful.

Other details are more ambiguous, even in light of this possibility. It is difficult to say if Anna's reference to the "strange, terrible fate" that both Karenin and Vronsky are named Alexei (411, IV.17), and Vronsky's conclusion that there is something "terrible" in their love (435, IV.23), are more than examples of the relativized perceptions of the world that I discussed above. If that is what they are, then they are as true and false as any other perspectives, in the sense that although they may define the *individual's* world (or at least part of the individual *couple's* world), they are largely irrelevant to anyone *else,* such as Levin and Kitty. Similarly, there does not seem to be any way to decide on the basis of the details themselves if Anna's repeated references to death—anticipating that things will end "horribly" for her (427, IV.21), fearing that she will want to kill herself (705, VII.12), regretting that she did not die in childbirth (745, VII.24), and experiencing the terror of death (752, VII.26)—are part of her self-fulfilling prophecy, or a darkling awareness of a transpersonal fate.

Another ambiguous detail is the Frenchman Landau. Karenin and Countess Lydia Ivanovna seek his guidance on whether or not Karenin should grant Anna a divorce, so her fate is literally in Landau's hands, as Princess Miagky tells Stiva (732, VII.20). In the end, Karenin refuses to divorce Anna, and Stiva infers that this stems from "what the Frenchman had said in his real or feigned sleep" (739, VII.22). Because this refusal helps to push Anna toward suicide, and because it stems from feigned clairvoyance, there may be a connection here with Anna's own fatidic dreams. This interpretation can be taken even farther, to the limits of plausibility, by connecting Landau's national origin to the language that the peasant inexplicably mutters in the dream. But even if these fateful connections seem unlikely, Landau retains his significance in the novel's *plot* via the causal links and thematic echoes that ensnare Anna.

17.2. Levin

Another approach to this question is to see if there are fatidic recurrences in parts of the novel that do not seem to be connected with Anna and Vronsky. As it happens, Levin makes precisely such an interpretive claim when he says to Kitty after they have received her parents' blessing for their marriage that "I never hoped, but in my soul I was always sure. . . . I believe it was predestined"; implying that she agrees, Kitty responds "And I?" (406, IV.16). On the face of it, this seems a rather far-fetched claim, and one cannot help being skeptical about it, at least initially. We can recall Levin's doubts about whether or not Kitty really loves him when he dashes to her side on the eve of their wedding (445, V.2). However, references to fate *do* accompany Levin's courtship of Kitty from the start (and, like Anna, he makes his remark about fate at the inception of an affair of the heart that will define the rest of his life). The narrator tells us early in the novel that Levin nearly falls in love with Kitty's two older sisters until he realizes which one "he had really been destined" to love (22, I.6). During their dinner together, Stiva tells Levin that Dolly has "a gift of foresight [predviden'ia]," especially with regard to marriages, and that she is certain that Kitty will be his wife. Levin is ecstatic, of course, and describes what he feels for Kitty in terms of "some external force taking possession of me" (38, I.10). (This description is echoed later in the novel during another epiphanic moment in Levin's life—his achievement of timeless bliss while mowing—when he feels that "some external force moved him" [256, III.5].) But one could also argue that these "insights" are merely instances of wishful thinking or purely figurative expressions.[7]

A different possibility is suggested by the resemblance between Levin's interpretive claim and Mikhailov's reaction to the stained sketch *(8.4)*. Both believe that they retrospectively discover an ideal unity in what may have seemed a contingent event. Moreover, because Mikhailov's experience evokes a Neoplatonic model, perhaps Levin's remark about predestination can be seen in the same way. But it is also possible to take Levin's remark in the opposite way—as illustrating the (perhaps unavoidable) human propensity to project causality retroactively.[8]

More important, therefore, is an unusual motif attached to Levin and Kitty that also has an intriguing connection to the Vronsky-Anna-Karenin plotline and that may be read as evidence of fatidic patterning in all these characters' lives. Immediately after making his remark to Kitty about predestination, Levin prepares to confess to her about his sexual past and his indifference to religion when they are interrupted by Mlle Linon, Kitty's old French governess, who comes to congratulate her favorite pupil. The only reason this interruption is at all noteworthy is that Mlle Linon is also the first person (other than two servants) whom Levin encounters when he enters the house to ask for Kitty's hand that morning (404, IV.15). Why frame Levin's arrival at the Shcherbatskys' and his avowal about predestination with Mlle Linon, whom we have not seen for some four hundred pages? The answer may simply be, why not? She lives in the house and is excited by her pupil's engagement—it is natural or plausibly "realistic" for her to be around. On the other hand, something else starts to emerge if we recall the circumstances when we last saw her. Levin spoke with Mlle Linon at the ice-skating rink at Kitty's behest when he came to Moscow to ask for Kitty's hand. "*Tiny bear* has grown up!" Mlle Linon says to him about Kitty, reminding him of an old joke he supposedly told the Shcherbatsky sisters that was based on an English story (30, I.9). The narrator explains that Levin does not recall having done so, but that Mlle Linon has been fond of this joke for a decade.

Be that as it may, it is striking that the image of a bear reappears in various avatars throughout the text at junctures when Levin is thinking of Kitty after she rejects him.[9] When he goes bird hunting with Stiva, Levin at first appreciates Stiva's tact in not mentioning Kitty because he still cannot think about her without pain. Then, during a lull in the hunt, the narrator describes the night sky and how Levin tries to discern in it the stars of the constellation Great Bear (164, II.15; in Russian the constellation is Medveditsa—Ursa Major or Greater *She* Bear). This leads to a veritable cascade of references to interrelated celestial bodies that appear to inscribe Levin's love for Kitty symbolically in the heavens. The Greater She Bear is mentioned two more times in the same short paragraph, together with three references to the planet Venus, which of course evokes the Roman goddess of love. There is also one reference to "somber Arcturus" (mrachnyi Arkturus), which augments the connection between stars and bears because Arcturus means "bear watcher" in Greek. Given this, it is especially interesting to note that the narrator uses the same epithet "somber" or "gloomy" (mrachnyi, mrachno) in relation to Levin several more times in the pages that follow (166, 167, II.16; 171, II.17), which serves to link him to the "somber" "bear-watching" star. (It may also be worth noting that Arcturus is in the constellation Boötes, which means "plowman" in Greek and which can perhaps be connected to Levin via his endeavors on his estate.) All these romantically charged references to celestial bears seem to culminate in Levin's "suddenly and unexpectedly" asking Stiva about Kitty for the first time a few moments *after* he searches the sky (165, II.15).[10]

Later in the novel, when Stiva stops by Levin's hotel room to invite him to the all-important dinner party at which Levin will finally be accepted by Kitty, he is measuring a fresh bearskin; "A fine thing! A she-bear?" Stiva asks (375, IV.7; three additional references to bears appear within a page of Stiva's remark as a continuation of the conversation about the hunt). At the dinner, bears are mentioned four more times in the space of fourteen lines, all in connection with Levin's hunting, and Kitty takes a special interest in this (384, IV.9).[11] Just prior to the wedding, during his bachelor dinner, Levin is kidded by his half-brother and a hunting chum about how his wife will not allow him to go on bear hunts after he is married (443, V.2; bears, including a she-bear, are mentioned a total of four times in the span of the following page). It may be noteworthy that these bears appear specifically in connection with Levin's eagerness to have his freedom constrained by marriage to Kitty.

After this, bears do not reappear again in relation to Kitty and Levin, but stars do. It is not certain if a connection can be made between them and the celestial bodies Levin observes during the hunt with Stiva, but this is a possibility. A few pages before the novel's end, when Levin is in the throes of his newly discovered faith in God, he looks at the night sky and sees the Milky Way, as well as several "bright stars" that remain unnamed but that he thinks of as having been "thrown by some unerring hand," and a "bright planet" (815–16, VIII.19).[12] He also refers to astronomy and heavenly bodies in general when he thinks about his reliance on the idea of goodness that is the cornerstone of his faith, although his emphasis on relativization in this scene tends to undermine any special privilege that the sky may have *(13.4.4)*. Finally, Kitty peers into his face "by the light of the stars" as she wonders if he is upset (816, VIII.19). If we choose to link these passages to the one about the hunt, which is possible but not necessary, the fact that Levin correlates the stars and the sky with his new faith can be interpreted as his having become partially aware of the face of Providence that is manifested as fatidic recurrence elsewhere in the novel.

A possibly related detail is the narrator's pointedly symbolic comment about the sky earlier in the novel—just before Levin sees Kitty passing by in a carriage on the country road: "The bleak moment came that usually precedes dawn, the full victory of light over darkness" (277, III.12). The encounter makes Levin realize that he loves only Kitty, and he dismisses all his previous fantasies about marrying a peasant woman. (Perhaps there are also links among Kitty, the "mother-of-pearl shell" of clouds that Levin sees [276, III.12], and Venus, which appears during the hunt with Stiva [164–65, II.15].) That the sky in this instance is associated with otherworldliness in Levin's mind, which is neither negated nor supported by the narrator, emerges from the description of dawn approaching: "The sky had turned blue and radiant, and with the same tenderness, yet also with the same inaccessibility, it returned his questioning look" (278, III.12). To some extent, this sky recalls the one Prince Andrei sees over Austerlitz in *War and Peace*. The difference is that in *Anna Karenina* there is even less certainty about the sky being the locus of a transcendent that can be grasped by a human being.

17.3. Fatidic Connections between Anna's and Levin's Plots

What does any of this have to do with the Anna-Vronsky plot? It turns out that bear hunting is the central link between what can be seen as a fatidic pattern in Levin's life and an analogous one in Vronsky's and Anna's lives.

After his affair with Anna has begun, Vronsky is asked to guide a visiting foreign prince through all the Russian national amusements, which include bear hunts and spending "the whole night in a display of Russian bravado" (354–55, IV.1). This association of bears with "Russianness" is not a leftover from the cold war, but a national symbol with roots in ancient Russian pagan beliefs, which are still preserved in the taboo name for the animal: *medved'* in Russian means "he who knows [how to find] honey." Thus, the foreign prince was in fact exposed to a facet of the Russian national spirit via the bear hunt. In this light, Levin's repeated association with bear hunting can perhaps also be seen as an especially authentic form of "Russianness," one that contrasts with the foreign prince and Vronsky's ethnic "tourism." Levin's Russianness has been stressed in other ways before—via his belief in the "essence" of the Russian peasant, his preference for life in the country rather than the city, his conclusion that Europe has nothing to teach Russia about how to solve its problems, and his identification with the "people."

The bear-hunting motif then takes an odd twist in Vronsky's life. After leaving the foreign prince, he returns to his apartment to find a note from Anna telling him when he can visit her in her home without running into Karenin. Vronsky lies down to rest, and images of the preceding days become "confused and joined with the thought of Anna and the muzhik tracker [or "beater," obkladchik] who had played an important role in the bear hunt." Vronsky then falls asleep, presumably as a consequence of the nocturnal "Russian bravado" following the bear hunt. But when he awakens he realizes that he has had a frightening dream that is partially rooted in impressions of the hunt: "The muzhik tracker, I think, small, dirty, with a dishevelled beard, was bending down and doing something, and he suddenly said some strange words in French" (355, IV.2). At this point, Vronsky is unaware of the resemblance of his dream to Anna's and, as we have seen, dismisses his in a way that nearly recapitulates Stiva's reaction to Anna's remark about an omen. Under the circumstances, this near repetition (and what Vronsky says shortly thereafter when he hears Anna's description of her dream) can be interpreted as shedding an ironic retroactive light on Stiva's overly quick dismissal of what turns out to be a pattern of meaning in the novel that is considerably more complicated than seemed at first glance. Vronsky also realizes that because he fell asleep he is now late for his rendezvous with Anna, and he tries to compensate by rushing to her house. This leads to the momentous event of his practically bumping into Karenin, which is something that Anna had striven to avoid. In other words, her destructive plot is moved forward, and not because she projects anything onto her life.[13]

Thus, Vronsky's dream is the point of intersection of several important themes in the novel. Because it blends elements of Anna's dream with Levin's bear motif, it establishes a link between the two that seems to be fatidic in terms relevant to both Anna's and Levin's plotlines. (In fact, when Levin is measuring a she-bear skin in the hotel and Stiva invites him to dinner, a peasant hunter, Arkhip, is present as well, which establishes an additional connection to the peasant tracker or beater who figures in Vronsky's hunt with the foreign prince as well as in his dream.) Because Vronsky's dream delays him and leads to the encounter with Karenin, who had made it a condition that Vronsky should never come to his house, it aggravates Anna's and everyone else's situations. As a direct consequence, Karenin begins to investigate a divorce, which leads not to Anna's freedom but to her deepening sense of hopelessness and entrapment. Finally, because the dream-filled sleep makes Vronsky late, it also forces him to rush, which feeds into the consistent acceleration of his and Anna's life lines in comparison to Kitty and Levin's *(13.3)*. (The motif of a dreamlike stupor may also link the horse race in which Vronsky inadvertently breaks Frou-Frou's back and the dreams shared by Anna and Vronsky: after an earlier race ends, an officer sits on his horse as if awakened from "a deep sleep" [193, II.24], and Anna walks "as if in a dream" after Vronsky falls [211, II.29].)

To sum up: the significance of the various recurrences described above lies primarily in the *patterns* they constitute, and the significance of the patterns is dictated by the claims about *fate* made by the two major characters in the novel. Moreover, the hermeneutic indices about fate in Anna's and Levin's remarks are also in harmony with the novel's epigraph, with Mikhailov's intuitions about the origin of art, and with Levin's conclusions about the presence of God in the world. This constitutes a significant and authoritative level of consistency in the novel that would be difficult to dismiss even if it is not conclusive proof that fate operates in the novel. As usual, however, Stiva falls out of the pattern, and it is unclear if anything like fate operates in the lives of Dolly and other characters.[14]

There is less certainty with regard to the specific *symbolic* significance of images such as hunting, bears, stars, and the like.[15] For example, my suggestion regarding the "Russianness" of bears does not incorporate the fact that Levin avidly seeks to kill the animals. Although there is no "ecocritical" onus attached to hunting in *Anna Karenina*, Levin does want to be a "guardian" of the land and of the kind of life he inherited from his parents and grandparents. This is not an aim that would seem to be advanced by killing bears, especially females (unless one assumes that a landowner needs to control their population at sustainable levels, or to reduce their population to protect his livestock). Similarly, what is the significance of the fact that Levin is urged by a friend to go bear hunting in "Tver" Province (444, V.2); that Princess Betsy's surname is "Tverskaia," which is a female genitive formation from the toponym "Tver'"; and that her servant wears a cape made of bearskin? One could try to generate possible explanations of the princess's connections to Levin or Kitty via bears, but these are unlikely to be very convincing. A possible example would be that the reference to the servant's cape appears in the context of Karenin's noticing the concealed joy in everyone's eyes because of his marital difficulties, "as if they were getting somebody married" (420, IV.19). Whatever connection this may have to the theme of Levin and Kitty's marriage is highly tentative and is probably best left unpursued. (But by the same token, because this novel, like any complex verbal work of art, is a circumscribed and structured verbal universe, all lexical repetitions in it inevitably call attention to themselves and are examples of Jakobson's poetic function.)

Are we justified, therefore, in concluding that fate operates in *Anna Karenina*? I would say "yes," even if this claim is not as certain as that Nikolai dies or that Kitty gives birth to a son. In fact, I would try to communicate the impression of fate's presence in the novel as something that "flickers," apparently there one moment but not necessarily the next; there is, of course, no iron determinism in *Anna Karenina*.

As I fully realize, it is easy to equate textual patterning with fate, and this ease is suspicious because all fictions are patterned to varying degrees. On the other hand, the conclusion that textual patterning is fatidic is also surprisingly difficult or impossible to disprove in a novel that itself *thematizes* fate by having major characters interpret events as fateful. Dismantling the fatidic implications of patterning in a novel such as this would require one of two procedures. The first would entail going outside the text and relying on one's own sense of what life is like (assuming that one does not believe in fate). And this would involve saying that because I do not believe there are fatidic patterns in my life, there cannot be any in anyone else's, be they real people or fictional characters. The pointlessness of this procedure is obvious (even though it is commonly practiced [see 2]). The second way to disprove the fatidic implications of patterning would be to demonstrate, somehow, that a given detail, such as Mlle Linon's association of Kitty with a story about bears, is not and cannot be related to other textual elements, such as Levin's being associated with Arcturus or Ursa

Major. This would seem to be a singularly fruitless task in the case of a work like *Anna Karenina,* which generations of readers have successfully mined for patterns of signification, and which presents overtly a conception of artistic structure that is predicated on the interrelations of parts and on the relational nature of meaning (*8.4, 8.5, 9.1, 10.2, 10.3,* and this despite the novel's insistence on the relativity of perception and understanding *[13]*). As the actual texture of imagery in *Anna Karenina* makes clear, patterning that has fatidic significance is not simply a matter of linear plot structure because meaning also arises from textual elements that are related "spatially" throughout the work. (In fact, it is the latter that play the crucial role in making narrative into *art* [see the introduction and *4*].)

This argument can also be rephrased in the following way: if the *form* of *Anna Karenina* is the countless echoes and linkages among its constituent details, then this form is the "lens" that the novel provides us to see and understand the conception of life in it. We cannot fully know the world in any text from an ideological, philosophical, psychological, or formal vantage point outside the text, for to try to do so would be to split form from content. This is the case even though we cannot understand the world in a text without being aware of the extratextual reality implied by language. What Jakobson called the "referential function" of language is an inherent feature of all utterances, and is what enables us to understand phrases such as "bear hunt" without Tolstoy's having to define or describe the creature or the process in the novel.[16] But although the reader has an a priori knowledge of the words, semantic fields, objects, and concepts defined by a particular culture (or cultures) and brings this knowledge automatically to the act of reading, the specific *inflections* that words and concepts receive in a given work are the result of the *formal relations* among all the elements—words, phrases, scenes, higher semantic formations—that constitute the work. Thus, "bear hunting" in *Anna Karenina* is marked by the specific associations this activity acquires in *this* novel, which sets it off from the "same" activity described anywhere else.

18. Literary Form, Fate, Freedom, Chance

I would like to give another illustration of the restrictive effect that literary form has on interpretation by focusing on the relation between literary form and the concepts of freedom and chance. Because it has been claimed in recent years that freedom, contingency, and the general randomness of life are Tolstoy's main concerns in *Anna Karenina,* I thought it would be useful to follow a discussion of fate in the novel with a discussion of the difficulty of demonstrating fate's *absence* from it. But first I would like to sketch some of the general considerations relevant to this issue.[1]

The existence of freedom is one of the most common and unquestioned assumptions of our times, especially in modern liberal Western societies (and I am being intentionally agnostic about whether or not this belief is correct). From conceptions of human nature to the principles of ethical behavior, and from the constitution of the state to sexual practices and choice of life path, everything is underlain by faith in the possibility, indeed, the imperative, of existential self-fulfillment and self-creation.

A related conviction about the role of chance in human existence is equally widespread. That things simply happen, without any ultimate necessity or reason, is inherent in many contemporary systems of belief, especially among academic intellectuals, and embraces everything from humankind's place in the cosmos, to the processes of evolution, to the minutiae of daily existence. There are obviously countercurrents to these dominant beliefs that are predicated on various forms of causality or determinism, but they do not disprove the larger generalizations.

It is hardly surprising, therefore, that a belief in the role of freedom and chance in human existence would also be reflected in literature, both from the point of view of writers who thematize freedom and chance, and from the point of view of readers who believe that both must exist in literature as they do in life. However, this transference of beliefs from life to literature is highly problematic, because chance and freedom are usually incompatible with literary form, especially the kind of form we find in Tolstoy.

Explanations for this state of affairs are suggested by several of Lotman's formulations about randomness or contingency in life as compared to literature. One of his seminal observations is that "[w]hat is asystemic in life is reflected in art as polysystemic."[2] In other words, in a highly organized literary work, the *illusion* of freedom from systematicity is achieved, paradoxically, via polyvalence—via the relation of a particular detail to many textual series. Thus, a detail that can be related to six thematic contexts in a novel, for example, will seem less fixed and more free than a detail that can be related to only two. What also follows from this is that there will always be a limited (although possibly large) number of relations between a detail and other elements in a structured utterance like a literary work, which means that genuine asystematicity in literature is not possible. Lotman also states that everything that is "noticeable in an artistic text is inevitably perceived as meaningful, as carrying a specific semantic load" (195). This is another way of saying that readers will search for connections among details that will allow them to fit whatever they focus on into a system of meaningful relations via the process of the hermeneutic circle (see 5.4). Why do readers behave this way? In the end, because this is a cultural norm. As Lotman puts it: "The listener is inclined to believe that all the elements in a work of art are the result of the poet's designing actions insofar as he knows that there is a certain design in them but does not yet know what that design is" (195).[3]

One could argue that the inertia of cultural practices implicit in this formulation is precisely what an author could try to thwart via techniques that disrupt the reader's ability to discern textual designs. But this possibility is difficult to reconcile with the even more fundamental principle of the relational nature of linguistic meaning. Thus, claiming that a detail in a text is free or present in it by chance would require denying that it has any meaning beyond its limited and localized one because the particular detail is unrelated and cannot be related in any significant way to any other detail; it is merely "noise." This is clearly not the way that an elaborately structured novel such as *Anna Karenina* actually works if we take as evidence the history of the novel's interpretations, which are always arguments about *which* details should be related to each other and *how*.

Indeed, one wonders what an instance of freely chosen action or a chance event would look like in a work of art that is sufficiently coherent to be recognized as a work. The reader who believes that such an action or event exists would have to be able to demonstrate that there are no links— be they semantic, thematic, acoustic, rhythmic, or structural—between any chosen textual detail and anything else in the given text. For if there were one such link, then the free or contingent nature of the detail would be put into question by the textual association it has. Even if some utterance is "embedded" in a text only mechanically, there is a potential relation between it and its context. Lotman has argued that "[a] statue thrown onto grass can create a new artistic effect as a consequence of the appearance of a relation between the grass and the marble" (99). Only if a given work advances the argument (via hermeneutic indices or other means) that hidden connections do not underlie seemingly independent details should a possibility such as this be entertained by the reader.

I conclude, therefore, that claims regarding instances of seeming freedom or chance in Tolstoy's works are more expressions of readers' own beliefs and worldviews than of insights into the character of Tolstoy's complex verbal weaves. However, although formal and, thus, "deterministic" patterns emerge everywhere in Tolstoy's works, the complexity and intricacy of the resulting series and networks are so great that one never gets the impression of dealing with mechanical predictability. The virtual impossibility that any reader could hold all of the permutations simultaneously in mind (much less discover all of them), when combined with the patterning that does emerge more and less clearly from the works, provides the kind of play between clarity and endlessly receding depths of meaning that appear to be one of the hallmarks of all great art.

I would like to end by illustrating this argument with the example of a detail that may seem to support the view that Tolstoy celebrates life's lack of structure in *Anna Karenina.* When Levin is getting dressed for his wedding with Stiva's help, he discovers that his servant has not prepared a clean shirt for him. A frantic search ensues before one is finally secured, and Levin is late for the church ceremony. What does this event mean? Does it illustrate the unpredictability of life? Is it gratuitous in the sense that it is unrelated to any larger issue? Is it a sign, therefore, of Tolstoy's wish to communicate a view of life as free and contingent, where things merely happen without signifying anything beyond themselves, because life is inherently "messy"?[4] We can try to respond to these far-reaching questions on the basis of various textual data dealing with large issues such as character, fate, God, social conventions, and so on. But how can we answer these questions with regard to the episode of the wedding shirt itself? The answer lies in seeing if it is isolated within the text, or if it has connections with other details.

One connection is suggested by Stiva's reaction to Levin's quandary. "Then you'll wear mine," Stiva says, generously offering one of his own shirts, and adds, "things *will shape up* [obrazuetsia]" (448, V.3, emphasis added). For the reader who remembers the novel's opening scenes, Stiva's remark evokes another servant and shirt and the same expression of encouragement. In the earlier scene, Stiva's faithful valet, Matvei, uses the word *obrazuetsia* (which Stiva likes so much that he repeats it, and which Matvei got from Matryona Filimonovna, the nanny and Dolly's closest ally [261, III.7]) to calm his master before proceeding to dress him in a shirt gathered up like a "horse collar" (5–6, I.2). Stiva's reassuring remark to Levin thus functions as a hermeneutic index that will prompt the reader to juxtapose two scenes. And given that the earlier scene centers on Stiva's marital difficulties, a highly ironic echo is created between it and Levin's imminent marriage via the possibility that Levin might put on one of Stiva's shirts. This irony is confirmed by Levin's discovering that Stiva's shirt does *not* fit him: it proves to be "impossibly wide and short" (449, V.3), which can be taken as an additional sign of the differences between Levin's and Stiva's approaches to marriage and much else besides. The earlier reference to a "horse collar" is also simultaneously telling and ambivalent. In addition to being simply descriptive, it may be seen as echoing Levin's *welcoming* the prospect of losing his independence, which he acknowledges during his bachelor dinner on the eve of the wedding, as well as Stiva's *regret* at having lost his. In short, the event of the misplaced wedding shirt can be interpreted as Tolstoy's realizing and toying with metaphors or proverbs that center on the idea "if the shirt fits, wear it." The dictionary by Dal' lists several that could be relevant to Levin: "Svoia rubashka k telu blizhe" (Your own shirt is closest to your body), "Svoia rubakha, svoi prostor, svoia i tesnota" (In your own shirt you've got your own freedom and your own constraints), "Veru peremenit'—ne rubashku pereodet'" (Changing your faith isn't like changing your shirt).[5]

Another context relevant for understanding the function of the episode with Levin's shirt is the general confusion that reigns throughout the wedding ceremony. Levin does not understand the priest's instructions about how he has to take Kitty's hand and is corrected repeatedly before he finally catches on (451, V.4); Kitty and Levin guess incorrectly several times what they have to do with the rings and have to be instructed by the priest; when they try to exchange rings, they again do it improperly "two times," as a result of which three people have to set it right (453, V.4); the crown-bearers get tangled up in the train of Kitty's wedding dress and bump into the newlyweds (458, V.7). Are all these minor glitches simply "realistic" examples of the meaningless small events that constitute the actual texture and meaning of life? (Although one should also always ask, *whose* life?) Well, perhaps, although the consistency of the pattern suggests otherwise. A more plausible reading of the function of the awkwardnesses during the ceremony is the *contrast* between these external ritual actions and what is happening within Levin's and Kitty's souls. In fact, Levin is struck by the expression of "innocent truthfulness" on Kitty's face "in spite of" her elaborate dress, veil, flowers, and grooming (450, V.4). And if this opposition is considered to be a plausible context for the confusion with the shirt, then it is possible to see the church ritual as reflecting the much larger opposition between artifice and authenticity, or between "civilized" urban life and the life in the country that Levin embodies.

These kinds of associations can be extended. It may also be that the mishap with the shirt is relevant to "the semiotics of clothing" in the novel. This would include things such as Karenin's evocation of the biblical edict about not pursuing vengeance by giving up one's "shirt" to the one who has taken your "caftan" (432, IV.22); Vronsky's wearing a hat and cloak in "medieval fashion" (466, V.9); Dolly's reaction to the style of dress at Vronsky's estate and Anna's great concern with remaining attractive in his eyes (629, VI.22); the negative effect that uniforms have on the behavior of participants in the noblemen's elections (649, VI.27); and Levin's using the metaphor of inadequate clothing when he ponders the inability of science to provide answers to the basic questions about existence (786, VII.8). The connections that can be made between scenes such as these and the episode with Levin's shirt would appear to interdict the claim that the shirt episode is simply an example of the random messiness of existence. In fact, following Spinoza, we can say that in this case "a thing is called contingent only because of a defect in our knowledge."[6]

Conclusion

In his classic history of Russian literature, Prince Dmitry Sviatopolk-Mirsky characterizes the end of *Anna Karenina* as "a no-thoroughfare, a path gradually losing itself before the steps of the wayfarer."[1] With some exceptions, the map of readings of the novel that I have sketched above produces a similar impression. Almost everything that seems important in it can be interpreted in two or three, or even more divergent or antithetical ways. And because of the extensive networks of relations among the novel's constituent elements—characters, situations, imagery—these different possible interpretations extend across the entire work, thereby complicating or interdicting partial readings of themes and issues considered in isolation. Despite this, the novel's ambivalences and ambiguities do not lead to incoherence, because they refer to a restricted array of issues and because they recur throughout the work.

The one paradoxically consistent feature of the novel is that all the characters are largely locked into their own minds, which results in a plurality of perspectives that thwarts other forms of consistency. Even when characters temporarily achieve rapport with someone else, out of sympathy like Stiva with various characters, or like Karenin by Anna's sickbed, or when they fall in love, like the two couples in the novel, they still eventually drift apart and stop sharing what is most important for them.

This feature of the novelistic world has major consequences for other issues that are also central to it. A primary one is ethics. All of the characters are concerned with concepts of right and wrong and how these apply to their behavior in both everyday and extraordinary situations. But because these concerns are refracted through the individual characters' personal views of existence, the values that emerge are usually relativized in the sense that they reflect the characters' personalities and local interests rather than principles that transcend them. The same is true of the spontaneous moral prompts that characters feel throughout the novel. As a result, there is a major explanatory gap between the values of individual characters and the absolutist ethics invoked by the epigraph and by the narrator in his ex cathedra pronouncements. Karenin's case illustrates this problem especially clearly. He appeals to the Bible more than anyone else, but his negatively marked character undermines the teachings he invokes. Similarly, despite Karenin's difference from Levin in almost all respects, the new faith Levin discovers at the novel's conclusion, which functions as a coda to the entire ethical theme in the work, is undermined, at least partially, because it is based on the same kinds of intuitions that also characterize Karenin's beliefs.

The one striking exception to this pattern is Anna. Her sense of guilt, her suffering, and her death can be seen as punishment for her transgressions against social and religious moral edicts, including the Pauline prohibition against vengeance. However, the apparent justice of Anna's end according to these criteria is counterbalanced by other important indices pertaining to her distorted courtship and marriage, and to her character. In fact, Tolstoy's conception of character as destiny, which is manifested to varying degrees by individuals as different as Anna, Karenin, Stiva, Levin, and Kitty, makes it uncertain that the freedom necessary for self-denial and moral choice actually exists in his fictional world.

This impression is augmented by the possibility of reading the novel as embodying a fateful worldview. Textual patterns pertaining to dreams, to temporal indicators, and to recurring imagery can be related to the lives of the two major couples in ways that suggest they may be in thrall to an occult transmundane agency of which they may also be darkly aware. Levin's intuitions about the mysteries of birth and death, and his sense that women have privileged knowledge of these liminal events, further support a "fatidic" reading of the novel by positing a realm that transcends, but that may still impinge, on the earthly. However, the absence of such patterns or intuitions from the lives of other characters, and the fact that textual patterning is inevitable in any verbal work of art, introduce uncertainty into any attempt to explain the novel simply in metaphysical terms. Similarly, the narrator's essentialist claims about women, peasants, and life in harmony with nature support the interpretation that the novel portrays a reality that transcends individuals. But behavior by characters that contradicts the claims undermines the idea that essentialism is real.

The theme of art in *Anna Karenina* points in two related directions. Some of Mikhailov's intuitions imply that his paintings originate in a transcendent realm; and recurring imagery suggests that this realm may also be behind Kitty's transfiguration when she is about to give birth. But the different ways in which individuals usually perceive works of art throughout the novel, which parallels the way mundane communication also often fails in it, has the effect of dissipating the metaphysical implications associated with Mikhailov's creativity. At the same time, the relativized perceptions of art and of other kinds of texts do parallel the ways in which characters manifest their own values and perceive their own worlds.

The apparent inescapability of personal perspectives in *Anna Karenina* inevitably affects how social life is portrayed in it. The brotherhood of believers that Levin invokes at the novel's conclusion is an intellectual abstraction that actually foregrounds how all groupings larger than the family or peasant "artel" tend to be associated with immorality. With the exception of some ephemeral assemblages that are marked positively or negatively, most permanent institutions and groupings associated with elite contemporary, and especially urban, culture are marked as negative and effete because they influence individuals to abrogate personal judgment. This recapitulates the problem of how to reconcile personal views with collective values in the novel, which would seem to be the cornerstone of any morality.

As this brief summary shows, *Anna Karenina* can be seen as an array of readings that contradict and diverge from each other, and that cluster around an opposition between personal truths and universal truth. It does not seem possible to resolve this difference by accepting only one or the other kind of truth because there are too many examples of each in the novel for either to be dispensable. In this light, it is worth recalling that the novel itself ends on a similarly paradoxical note when Levin realizes that it is futile for a limited human being like himself to try to understand the divine order of things beyond the commandment to do good, which he takes to mean continuing to live in the way he always has. There are moments in the novel when the narrator also seems to become aware of this inescapable predicament, as when he identifies, criticizes, and excuses Karenin's facile faith, all at the same time. The ways in which the opposing and divergent readings intercalate in the novel suggest an analogy with the relation between the hemispheres of the human brain. Even if the left is the primary locus of language and temporal processing, and the right of visual and spatial perception, it is their mutual correlation, and ultimate untranslatability into each other's terms, that define the world in which we exist.

This is of course not the end of what can be said about *Anna Karenina*. I fully expect there to be counterarguments about readings that I either did not mention or that I do not accept as belonging on my "map," about what are plausible as opposed to implausible interpretations, and about what are determinate and indeterminate meanings. But I do not expect to be persuaded that the idea of a map of possible readings has to be abandoned as a methodological goal, either for this novel or for any other.

This is also not the end of what can be said about the novel in another sense. *Anna Karenina* is the name for a particular kind of verbal phenomenon that is an array of possible readings, and not for anything more or less fixed than this. I would argue, therefore, that *Anna Karenina* conceived in this way is the inevitable point of departure for any approach that is not concerned primarily with this novel's inherent configuration of meanings. In other words, no matter what a reader's ultimate interest in *Anna Karenina* may be—its relation to Tolstoy's biography, to the evolution of his art, to the Russian cultural context, to the European novel, to the "woman question," to Darwinism, psychoanalysis, Marxism, neocolonialism, tropological deconstruction, the stylistics of punctuation, etc.—this ultimate interest cannot be pursued without first grasping the novel's map of possible readings. The reason is that interpreting *Anna Karenina* from any of these perspectives means trying to relate to *this* novel all those specific concepts about which one cares sufficiently to make them one's primary focus, and one cannot profitably relate something concrete to something vague—to something one has not tried to see as clearly as possible. I realize that this argument does not entirely avoid tautology because it presupposes the methodology presented in the first part of this book. But whether or not the methodology is satisfactory cannot be argued any further here, and is best judged by the map of readings that constitutes its second part.

Notes

Works Cited

Index

Notes

Introduction

1. As I hope this book will demonstrate, the method that I advocate and that grows out of the Russian tradition bears no relation to the following characterization of (mostly French) structuralism by Rivkin and Ryan: "Structuralists saw signs as windows to a trans-empirical world of crystalline order, of identities of form that maintained themselves over time and outside history, of codes of meaning that seemed exempt from the differences entailed by the contingencies of living examples" (334).

2. See Delbanco for a similar characterization of the academic field of English: "It regards the idea of progress as a pernicious myth, but never have there been so many critics so sure that they represent so much progress over their predecessors" (38).

3. Lotman, *Struktura khudozhestvennogo teksta* 89.

4. For an example of this position and my arguments against it, see 5.5.

5. See Striedter for a balanced summary of this problem (34–35). See also Jürgen Habermas's critique of Jacques Derrida, in which Habermas argues for abandoning a conception of context as open-ended and for returning to what Jakobson and the Czech Structuralists saw as the normative constraints on interpretation resulting from formal relations in particular kinds of texts (summarized by Norris 57–58).

6. This bears some relation to both Roman Ingarden's and Felix Vodička's different conceptions of the extent to which the "potential of the [literary] artifact is describable" (Striedter 130–31). In my focus on "immanent" structures of meaning I am closer to Ingarden than to Vodička's more historicized approach.

7. However, for a notable step in this direction, see Brooks's analysis of the relation between novelistic plotting and the psychology of desire.

8. Parts of the argument below appeared in my articles "Alterity, Hermeneutic Indices, and the Limits of Interpretation" and "Biology, Semiosis, and Cultural Difference in Lotman's Semiosphere."

9. Quoted in Tooby and Cosmides 67, following Werner Heisenberg.

10. For a similar conclusion in relation to reading, see Attridge: "To be other is necessarily to be other to"; and alterity is "premised on a *relation*"; thus, "[a]n entity without this relation would simply not impinge on me; and as far as I was concerned, it would be nonexistent" (22).

11. For a characterization of this discipline, see Shweder.

12. Lotman, *Kul'tura i vzryv* 54.

13. Geertz, "From the Native's Point of View" 132.

14. Helms 707.

15. Landrine 745.

16. Gĩtĩtĩ 6.

17. Geertz, "From the Native's Point of View" 134. Haney makes a similar point when he argues that "the structure of the reader's interpretive relationship to a literary text has affinities with a person's ethical relationships to others" (38).

18. My approach thus bears only a vague resemblance to some of E. D. Hirsch's well-known arguments in *Validity in Interpretation*. For example, I agree that there is a useful distinction between the meaning that inheres in a work and what readers can do with it (Hirsch's "meaning" and "significance," 8), but I disagree that we can recover authorial intention (or "will," 27, 96) or that plural meanings are impossible (45). I do find it interesting and potentially useful, however, at least to consider statements that authors make about their intentions and to see how they relate to their texts.

19. Williams 169–70; Lewis B9; see also Farber and Sherry.

20. For a recent overview of some of these trends, see Morgan.

21. Derrida, Letter, 11 Feb. 1993: 44.

22. Derrida, Letter, 25 Mar. 1993: 65.

23. Wolin 66, emphasis in original; see also Sheehan, Reply.

24. De Man 181.

25. De Man's partisans acknowledge freely the a priori philosophical positions (one could call them "biases") that motivate his readings of particular works. For example, Culler speaks of de Man's general attempt "to undo totalizing metaphors, myths of immediacy, organic unity, and presence and combat their fascinations" ("Paul de Man's Contribution" 271). Similarly, Latimer describes the "ultimate question of de Man's work" as "the irreparable separation of consciousness from Being, or even more insistently, the separation of expression from the intuition of plenitude." As a consequence of this, de Man "pressures" writers such as Coleridge, Yeats, Hölderlin, and the Russian Symbolists "until they renounce their theological claims and admit poetry's inevitable enslavement to the merely human and temporal" (Latimer 184).

26. Miller characterizes de Man's theory of "reading" (which in Miller's view implies all human acts and not just reading words) as fundamentally "ethical" in the special sense that human beings cannot avoid trying to make sense of their worlds even though this effort must fail, because there is no way to reach a secure ground for knowledge outside language (58–59). Miller's conception of ethical

reading is the same: "I am unable, finally, to know whether in this experience [of being compelled by the law of the ethics of reading] I am subject to a linguistic necessity or to an ontological one" (127). However, in my view, Miller's and de Man's conception of the human linguistic condition is just one of many that have arisen in different cultures; thus, to apply their conception to all human activity everywhere is to risk a homogenization that is *unethical* according to Kant's "categorical imperative" (see *1*). Miller does try to allow for the possibility of difference by saying that his ethical imperative "is always the same but always different, unique, idiomatic" (127). However, Booth reports a conversation with Miller about this point that reconfirms Miller's view that the indeterminacy of moral instruction from literature is always the same (9).

27. Lentricchia 64.

28. Jakobson, "The Speech Event" 78.

29. Striedter 93.

30. For a detailed exposition and illustration of this conception of "literariness," see, for example, Lotman's *Struktura khudozhestvennogo teksta* (The structure of the artistic text).

31. Mikhail Bakhtin, who constitutes an independent theoretical line, is, of course, the one exception and remains highly influential in non-Slavic circles. It is interesting to note that the attitude toward some aspects of the Slavic tradition in some parts of Europe is different. In Italy, for example, the last book Lotman published during his life, *Kul'tura i vzryv* (Culture and explosion, 1992), was translated into Italian in 1993 and immediately cited by specialists *outside* the Slavic field; see also the overview by M. de Mikiel. Lotman's death in 1993 had relatively little resonance in the United States; by contrast, commemorative conferences on Lotman were held in Italy and Spain in 1994 and 1995, respectively. There are also some signs of new interest in his work in the United States, as evidenced by two conferences: "The Works of Yury Lotman in an Interdisciplinary Context: Impact and Applicability," held in 1999 at the University of Michigan, Ann Arbor, which included both Slavists and non-Slavists from fields such as anthropology, history, and political science, and "Slavic Theory Today: Between History and System" at Yale University in 2002, which included discussions of Lotman among others.

1. An Ethical Argument for Recognizing Textual Alterity

1. The argument in the following sections is an expanded version of my article "Alterity, Hermeneutic Indices, and the Limits of Interpretation."

2. For an overview of contemporary approaches to the relation between ethics and literary study, see Buell. When speaking of ethics, a distinction needs to be made between the conception of self developed in modern Western societies (or those influenced by them) and those in other parts of the world, which can differ markedly and which have been the subject of scrutiny in the field of

"cultural psychology"; see the introduction to this volume and my "Biology, Semiosis, and Cultural Difference in Lotman's Semiosphere." But since my focus is on the characteristic features of *Western* literature and culture, generalizations about the self as discrete and unique remain valid.

3. Mohanty 117 n9, 116. It is, in fact, ironic that ethnographic evidence about widely differing conceptions of personhood in "Third World" cultures shows that Mohanty's use of Kant's conception of the self to defend multiculturalism actually recapitulates the kind of Western cultural bias against which Mohanty argues. See the introduction to this volume.

4. Haney, following Gadamer, makes a similar argument: reading a work of literature resembles an ethical response to another person because of the relative autonomy of the literary work, which resists our attempts to understand it in terms and for reasons other than its own and which is a consequence of its form (38–39). Attridge also locates the "otherness of a work" that motivates an ethical response to it in how its language is arranged or in its form (26).

5. See Bakhtin, "Formy vremeni i khronotopa v romane"; and Holquist, *Dialogism* 152, 155.

6. For a similar argument, see Attridge 26. The Peirce quotation is from Booth 226.

7. For similar positions, see Attridge, who argues that even if we know nothing about the author we still have to read a work on the assumption that it was authored and respect it as such (25); Booth, who develops the idea that the reader is obligated to treat the text as a "friend" (201ff.); and Hirsch, *The Aims of Interpretation* 90. There is, of course, an important distinction between *understanding* and *accepting* another's utterance, because as Wolfe points out, "all points of view are *not* equally valid precisely because they have material *effects* whose benefits and drawbacks are distributed asymmetrically in the social field" (62).

2. A Psychological Argument for Recognizing Textual Alterity

1. Flavell 48–50, 155, 270–74, 408.

2. Vygotsky, *Thought and Language* 187.

3. Bruner 73, 132. It should be noted that Vygotsky criticizes Piaget's deterministic theory in chapter 2 of *Thought and Language;* for an analysis of differences between them, see Holquist, *Dialogism* 78–80.

4. Edelman 115, 149.

5. Edelman 150, 129.

6. Edelman 150.

7. Sacks 42.

8. This idea is omnipresent in Bakhtin's thought; for an example, see his "Slovo v romane," esp. 90ff. Clark and Holquist give a concise characterization of Bakhtin's psychology (206–7). See also Holquist for a discussion that anticipates

mine (*Dialogism* 78–81). Of some relevance here is Lacan's theory of the linguistic basis of the self. However, his conception of "a subject constituted in relation to an Other it cannot know and oriented toward an object it can never possess" points in a direction opposite to Bakhtin's; see Clark 453.

3. Alterity and Semiotics

1. For a brief overview, see Todorov, "Sign." Jakobson quotes with admiration Peirce's definition of meaning as "the translation of a sign into another system of signs" ("A Few Remarks" 35); see also Eco, *A Theory of Semiotics* 17, 48, 49, 61, 66, etc.

2. For a chain of possible influences linking the linguistic theory of Lev Iakubinsky and the developmental psychology of Vygotsky (and through him Bruner), see Holquist, *Dialogism* 57–58. For Vygotsky's familiarity with theories developed by the Russian Formalists, see Kozulin xi–lxi, esp. xiii; see also Vygotsky's *The Psychology of Art*.

3. Lotman, "Tekst v tekste" 153.

4. Lotman, "Fenomen kul'tury" 36.

5. Todorov, *The Conquest of America* 157.

6. Lotman, "Ritorika" 168, emphasis added.

7. Lotman, "Kul'tura kak sub"ekt i sama-sebe ob"ekt" 371.

4. Jakobson's "Metalingual Function" and Alterity

1. Jakobson, "Closing Statement" 353–58.

2. Waugh 145.

3. See the analogous distinction made by Sergei Kartsevskii about formal and semantic values of words, quoted in Holquist, *Dialogism* 168.

4. Jakobson, "Closing Statement" 357.

5. Waugh 148.

6. Jakobson, "Closing Statement" 356; see also Jakobson, "Metalanguage."

7. There is also some evidence that these features of human communication may be rooted in the basic structure of all animal communication, which consists of "simultaneous" or "sequential" messages or a combination of the two; see Caplan et al. 1488.

8. Jakobson, "Two Aspects" 119, 122, 123–25.

9. On Bakhtin's views, see Morson and Emerson 129–30, 429, 430; see also Bakhtin, "Formy vremeni i khronotopa v romane" 400–403; Gadamer 368–69, 385–88, 472; Jauss. For a related discussion that also incorporates Emmanuel Levinas's ideas, see Haney 39–40, 43–44.

10. Iser, of course, distinguishes between reading and dialogue as well. See, for example, his *Act of Reading* or the brief overview in "Interaction."

5. Hermeneutic Indices, or Guides to Textual Alterity

1. For related concepts, see Todorov, who concludes that texts invariably provide "meta-exegetic" guides for their own "consumption" ("Reading as Construction" 76–78); Schor redefines Peirce's term *interpretant* and applies it to the first-person narrator or main protagonist in fiction, whom she sees as being an authorial means of telling the reader something important about how the idea of interpretation is conceived in that work; similarly, Prince finds that many narratives contain "reading interludes" that perform "some of the reading operations that a given reader may perform" and a "metalinguistic commentary on some of the words and phrases" of which the texts are composed (230, 232). A similar idea figures in Brooke-Rose, who includes a list of "thirty indices, all partaking of both the action and hermeneutic codes," in a short story by Washington Irving that allow the reader to understand what a character cannot (106–9). Frank speaks of *Crime and Punishment* as containing "a hermeneutic of its interpretation" (*Dostoevsky* 103, 115). See also Geertz for the analogous conclusion from anthropology that "societies, like lives, contain their own interpretations. One has only to learn how to gain access to them" ("Notes" 453).

2. Jakobson, "The Speech Event" 76.

3. Turgenev, *Ottsy i deti* 195, emphasis added; I have modified the Matlaw translation (Turgenev, *Fathers and Sons* 1). One *desiatina* equals 2.7 acres.

4. Pushkin 234.

5. Dostoevsky, *Crime and Punishment* 511.

6. See, for example, "Kurbskii, A."; Slavinskii; Tverskoi.

7. Bely 1–2.

8. See chapter 3 in my book *Andrei Bely*.

9. Melville 163–70 (chap. 42, "The Whiteness of the Whale").

10. Melville 12.

11. Nabokov, *Lolita* 9, 283. See also my *Nabokov's Otherworld* 160–86.

12. For more on this kind of connection in myth, see Toporov 481–82 n54.

13. Jakobson also speaks of "equational predication" as an equivalent of metalanguage in expressions such as "a bachelor is an unmarried man" ("Two Aspects" 122).

14. Padel 33–34.

15. My interest in the *plurality* of interpretation resembles Roland Barthes's argument in *S/Z* that "to interpret a text is not to give it a (more or less justified, more or less free) meaning, but on the contrary to appreciate what *plural* constitutes it" (5). Barthes's focus on "connotation as a function of sequence and agglomeration" (8) also bears some resemblance to Jakobson's "poetic function." And I sympathize with Barthes's interest in inferring "codes" relevant to a given work (9). However, Barthes's conception of meaning as fluid and indeterminable and as unrelated to probability, possibility, narrative structure, and "holism" (6) differs from mine, as does his actual analytic procedure.

16. By contrast, Iser claims that "whatever regulates this meaning [that results from the reader's negotiation of the "gaps" between textual segments] cannot itself be determinate, for . . . there is no *tertium comparationis*" (*The Act of Reading* 196). Ingarden influenced Vodička, who in turn influenced Iser (and Jauss); for a discussion, see Striedter 123–32, 231–34; Galan 152–54. Iser gives his view of Ingarden in *Prospecting* 285–86n8.

17. Turgenev, *Zapiski okhotnika* 35.

18. Lotman, *Struktura khudozhestvennogo teksta* 178.

19. Lotman, "Ustnaia rech'" 186.

20. Lotman, "Ustnaia rech'" 187.

21. For the first, see Fish, "Why No One's Afraid" and Iser, "Talk like Whales." See Rorty, Eco, "Interpretation and History," and Culler, "In Defence," all in Eco et al. 23–43, 89–108, 109–24. For an analysis of analogous discussions in the context of Russian Formalism, Czech Structuralism, and German reception theory, see Striedter 69–71.

22. Rorty; Fish, "Why No One's Afraid" and "Interpreting the *Variorum*."

23. Iser, *The Act of Reading* and "Interaction"; Eco et al.

24. Fish, "Why No One's Afraid" 7.

25. In "Change," Fish tries to account for change by arguing that it occurs in communities that already presuppose its possibilities in particular directions (148). But this remains unconvincing for situations that entail a massive influx of new information, because there is a vast difference between the potential for change and its realization. For example, if we believe Chomsky, we are all programmed to be able to learn all languages, but how many of us actually do learn more than a few at best?

26. Jakobson, "Metalanguage" 92.

27. Lotman, "Fenomen kul'tury" 36; Lotman, "O semiosfere" 19.

28. It is important to acknowledge that Fish of course realizes that "if determinate and indeterminate . . . are conventional categories *within* a system of intelligibility, then those who are implicated in the system will 'see,' in the sense of producing, determinacies and indeterminacies, but everything they see will be at once constructed (as opposed to being simply 'found') and constrained (as opposed to being simply invented)" ("Why No One's Afraid" 12). However, the distinctions that Fish collapses here are fundamental and lead to vastly different conceptions of selves, reading, the literary work of art, and literary history.

29. Padel 12.

30. Padel 21–23.

31. Rorty 103.

32. Rorty 106.

33. Rorty 107, 108; see also Collini 12.

34. Culler, "In Defence" 114, 115. Dimock also argues for limitless contextualization of works of literature, as a result of which they are infinitely variable. She does not speak about literary form, however, and does not appear to recognize any

criteria that would distinguish between an informed or competent reading (even in a linguistic sense) and a completely arbitrary one.

35. See, for example, Lotman, "Fenomen kul'tury" 45; and Lotman, "Tekst v tekste" 153.

7. Early Signals

1. English quotations are from the translation of *Anna Karenina* by Richard Pevear and Larissa Volokhonsky. I checked these against the Russian original— Lev N. Tolstoi, *Anna Karenina. Sobranie sochinenii v dvadtsati tomakh. Tom vos'moi. Tom deviatyi.* All references to this generally excellent translation, which I have modified very rarely (and usually silently), and to the Russian original are given in the text in the following order: page, part, chapter; thus, 462, V.2 means page 462 in the English translation, which is in part V, chapter 2 of the novel. I have consulted the revised Russian edition of the novel edited by Zhdanov and Zaidenshnur and published in the Literaturnye Pamiatniki series but refer to it only once, in a note to *13.6,* when it makes some difference for interpreting Stiva's behavior. A useful description of this edition, and a table containing English translations of the most notable changes in the text, can be found in Turner, *A Karenina Companion* 53–97.

2. See Eikhenbaum, *Lev Tolstoi* 171–72. The fact that Tolstoy did not signal the connection with Schopenhauer's *The World as Will and Representation,* and that in the published version of the novel he quotes the standard Slavonic translation of the passage from Romans, suggests that the association of the epigraph with Schopenhauer became transparent and may be irrelevant to interpreting the novel. On the other hand, there are allusions and overt references to Schopenhauer elsewhere in *Anna Karenina* (see the discussion in *12.3,* note 5). See Eikhenbaum, *Lev Tolstoi* 127–47; Gusev 271ff.; and Turner, *A Karenina Companion* for detailed discussions of Tolstoy's work on the novel.

3. Mandelker raises similar questions and identifies echoes of the epigraph in contemporary English novels that Tolstoy admired (44–47). However, it is not, in fact, unclear if the epigraph was drawn from the Old or New Testament, with their different conceptions of divine retribution (Mandelker 45), because the final Slavonic wording of the epigraph is clearly from Romans. Gol'shtein tries to read the novel in terms of the allusion to Deuteronomy. Ermilov relies on an article by Eikhenbaum about Schopenhauer's influence on Tolstoy and concludes that the epigraph's original meaning supports the interpretation that Anna is not judged and condemned in the novel (357). However, Ermilov paradoxically also acknowledges that there is ample evidence in the text for both condemning and vindicating Anna (356), which is by itself a plausible conclusion.

4. Meyer 1162. There are no significant differences between the Russian or Slavonic translations of the Bible that Tolstoy presumably used and the King James version that I cite above.

5. Meyer 1162–63.

6. Jackson stresses that the epigraph also sounds the "major theme of love and reconciliation" that is developed in the novel ("The Ambivalent Beginning" 346). The Russian Symbolist writer Dmitrii Merezhkovskii dismissed the novel's Christian epigraph as superficial and saw Anna as "moving toward establishing a new identity in a state of consecrated flesh" that was thwarted by Christianity (cited by Sorokin 232).

7. By relying on Tolstoy's later religious writings, Gustafson concludes that the epigraph does not, in fact, imply a God who "punishes sin," because "sin returns" as the errant individual's suffering and punishment (147). It is unclear how this can be reconciled with Saint Paul or how it is relevant to Stiva and his ilk, whose sins do not, in fact, "return" to them. Gustafson also points out Tolstoy's later commitment to divorcing the Gospels from the Old Testament and from Saint Paul and suggests that Tolstoy used the epigraph *ironically* (190). Although the numerous questions raised by the epigraph do demonstrate the difficulty of seeing it as a simple précis of the novel, I will suggest below that there are reasons for understanding the epigraph in terms of a fundamental ambivalence inherent in the novel.

8. This distinction was certainly not perceived by all readers. For example, the writer Nikolai Leskov reported that when the novel was being serialized in the 1870s many of his acquaintances felt that Anna must be forgiven (quoted in Ishchuk 138–39). Similarly, the early-twentieth-century émigré writer Mark Aldanov questions the epigraph's validity because it does not appear to apply to Stiva, Betsy, and others. Aldanov concludes that the epigraph may demonstrate Tolstoy's inability to make his fictional world subservient to his moral idea, a view similar to what Berlin and his followers would repeat later in the century and that I discuss below (quoted in Eikhenbaum, *Lev Tolstoi* 164–65).

9. Eikhenbaum sees this as the meaning of the epigraph and the explanation for Anna's suffering and death (*Lev Tolstoi* 172–73). Orwin argues that Anna "is worse than Betsy and the others only because, unlike them, she makes moral judgments about herself" (178). However, this would seem to relativize ethics and punishment as well as to diverge from the epigraph. Kujundzic discusses the epigraph's implications in detail and concludes that Anna suffers and dies because she refuses to submit to the process of pardoning that plays a central role in the novel, a process that "has the power to restore the initial imbalance and repetitively supply guilt with its resolution" (70). This interpretation bears some resemblance to feminist and Socialist Realist readings of Anna as a rebel against injustice (see note 10 below and section *8* note 7). However, the repetition of pardoning in the novel does not have to be seen only in negative and poststructuralist terms as a sign of the act's emptiness; it can also be interpreted as reflecting the widespread theme of guilt and contrition in the novel and the need for forgiveness that Saint Paul taught.

10. Eikhenbaum tries to "solve" the problem of the epigraph by relying on an event from 1907, or approximately thirty years after the completion of *Anna*

Karenina (*Lev Tolstoi* 167–73). One of Tolstoy's sons-in-law reported to him an interpretation of the epigraph proposed by the writer Vikentii Veresaev. This prompted Tolstoy to comment that although he admired Veresaev's ingenuity, his original intent was to suggest that the consequence of the evil that people do is their suffering, which comes to them not from others but from God, and that this is what Anna experienced (167). On this basis, Eikhenbaum concludes rather arbitrarily that the epigraph is not meant to apply to the novel as a whole but only to Anna and Vronsky, whose evil actions lead to their suffering (169); specifically, Anna perishes because her passion leads to her struggle with Vronsky (172–73). Eikhenbaum also denies that the ethical problem facing Anna has any relevance for Stiva and Betsy, which neglects the thematic echoes and formal parallels among all three. Khrapchenko provides a representative Soviet reading by secularizing the epigraph into a general appeal to eternal laws of morality that are not directed primarily at Anna (188–90). For an overview of feminist perspectives of Anna and other interpretations of Anna's death in relation to the epigraph, see Mandelker 38–43, 46–47.

11. Orwin suggests that the epigraph differs from the first sentence because the epigraph lies outside the text and thus "provides a standard for judging events and characters"; the first sentence, by contrast, articulates the "necessary imperfection of life" that is the focus of novels in general (179–80). However, the epigraph's assumption of human imperfection can also be seen as paralleling the novel's opening. And the fact that Tolstoy intentionally juxtaposed a biblical passage with his novel forces us to at least entertain the possibility that there are relations of *similarity* and *difference* between them.

12. Because of his reliance on Bakhtin's distinction between monologic and dialogic discourses, Morson assigns a radically undialogical character to this sentence and then ascribes it to Tolstoy's (unrealizable) wish to make statements that are "completely non-novelistic, that is, both nonfictive and nondialogized" (*Hidden* 19). This faults Tolstoy in terms of categories and values that do not necessarily apply to him or to his novel. A less mediated approach would be to examine the relation between the claims Tolstoy's narrator makes in such passages and what actually happens in the novel.

13. This presumably reflects Tolstoy's well-known remark to his wife that the central theme of *Anna Karenina* is the "family," whereas that of *War and Peace* is the "people" (*L. N. Tolstoi v vospominaniakh sovremennikov* 149).

14. Jackson reads this passage similarly ("The Ambivalent Beginning" 348).

15. Schultze provides lists of unhappy and happy marriages in the novel, including very minor ones, and finds that there are many more of the former than of the latter (100–102).

16. Gustafson 44, Stenbock-Fermor 83, and Jackson, "The Ambivalent Beginning" 348–49 make a similar point.

17. Nabokov's parody of the novel's first sentence in the opening lines of *Ada* suggests that he may have come to a similar conclusion, which reflects his own

predilection for uniqueness: "All happy families are more or less dissimilar; all unhappy ones are more or less alike." However, Orwin argues that Anna's unhappiness and that of her family "will be unique . . . precisely because she has turned her back on moral law" (181).

18. Stenbock-Fermor makes the same point (83). The Maudes' English translation does not preserve these insistent repetitions, whereas Pevear and Volokhonsky keep most of them. Nabokov describes the "ponderous and solemn repetition . . . [as] tolling . . . for doomed family life" ("Anna Karenin" 210).

19. Among other candidates for "errors" is Levin's sister, who, as McLean perceptively notes "rather implausibly" does not come either to Levin's wedding or to Nikolai's funeral (which is not actually shown in the novel, however) ("Truth in Dying" 131). Stenbock-Fermor interprets the valet's and the nanny's siding with Stiva as their willingness to dismiss his sins as minor in order to preserve peace in the family (83–84). This does not explain why the nanny is on Stiva's side, however, or why she and the valet did not try to mollify Dolly instead (although the valet's behavior might reflect the "double standard" of the time, according to which a man's adultery is only a venial sin).

20. Parker is committed to an "anti-foundational ethics" that leads him to see *Anna Karenina* as an ethically significant novel because it consistently resists the reader's tendency to see the world in it "in terms of simple categorical operations"; only by "*dissolving* his moral certainties" can Tolstoy "portray so inwardly the Romantic-expressive values represented by the new vitality in Anna" (111, 119). It is not clear how one can claim that this was Tolstoy's design rather than evidence of his ambivalence.

21. A discussion of various possible textual meanings such as I have just attempted has terminological and expressive implications for the entire project I am trying to carry out. The mere fact of verbalizing a meaning that is possible, even if unlikely, can give it more weight than it might have or actually deserve. But because there is no way to *quantify* probabilities in situations like this, the only alternative is to use *qualifiers* such as "more likely," "less probable," and so on. These are not entirely satisfactory, however, because they are coarse-grained: they cannot communicate in a nuanced way the probability of the assertions to which they are attached; another way of saying this is that such probabilities can be conceived only in general terms. Nevertheless, these are all we have, and they are better than nothing. Even though they introduce an additional level of ambiguity into literary analysis (one person's "implausible" is another's "somewhat unlikely"), they do allow a more accurate response to a work than would claims that focus only on "presence" or "absence."

22. On this point, see Wasiolek 131, and especially Orwin 157–60, 178.

23. Berlin 24. See, for example, Veresaev 109, and Orwin 3–12 for an overview of this critical tradition. See also note 8 above.

24. Quoted by Christian, *Tolstoy* 177. Herman also sees the novel as affirming two irreconcilable truths (23).

8. Reading Readings, and Art about Art

1. Šilbajoris points out that in Tolstoy's novels there is a "hierarchy of response to art," with painting coming first, then music, and lastly literature (153). Šilbajoris speculates that Tolstoy may have been moved to "avoid the potential absurdity of writing words about words" or that the Russian society Tolstoy depicted did not read much fiction. However, one could also argue that there is considerable linguistic self-consciousness in the novel (see below in this section and *11*).

2. By contrast, Khrapchenko interprets Anna's book for children simply as a sign of her giftedness (183).

3. Herman reads this scene as a model of the kind of communication Tolstoy sought to have with his reader (20). However, the unique nature of this moment, which, in fact, pointedly excludes the reader (see *13.4.1*), and the varieties of miscommunication in the novel make it difficult to privilege this scene over others.

4. See Gustafson for a detailed and insightful reading of this episode that focuses on the "emblematic" significance of the movements of Anna's psyche and whatever it engages (304–9). Mandelker, in keeping with her feminist reading of *Anna Karenina,* concludes that the English novel "leads Anna into adultery" by stimulating desires in her that cannot be fulfilled except via "a liaison with the male protagonist" (135). Šilbajoris sees Anna's reading about "English happiness" as an ironic foreshadowing of her own misery on Vronsky's Anglophilic estate later in the novel (156–57).

5. By contrast, Herman interprets the scene as a successful act of reading, because Anna is "seduced" by the characters' desires in the English novel (19).

6. Stenbock-Fermor discusses candles in connection with Anna (chap. 4).

7. By contrast, Mandelker reads Anna's death in feminist and mythic terms as a liberation from constraints imposed by a male-dominated society (162). This partially resembles Khrapchenko's Soviet argument, that Anna is heroic because she seeks a true and pure life in contrast to the lies and hypocrisy that surround her (173). Ermilov sees Anna's self-love as the decisive reason for her death (381). Orwin interprets Anna's wish to draw back from the rails at the last moment as a sign that a "spiritual" choice remains possible for her (186).

8. Gustafson sees the subject of the painting as the opposition between egotism and selflessness, which is the "emblem" of the novel's main theme (142–43).

9. Mandelker makes the same point (113).

10. Mandelker notes these and other, less plausible similarities that depend on characters being portrayed as if via paintings that are described verbally (116–20).

11. Despite the fact that Tolstoy rejected sophisticated works like *Anna Karenina* in *What Is Art?* and wrote the treatise some twenty years after *Anna Karenina,* Mandelker considers Mikhailov's paintings from its perspective (110). She concludes that *Pilate's Admonition* is the least successful because of the education required to understand it, that the boys fishing is more successful because of its accessible simplicity, and that the portrait of Anna is the most successful because of

the transformative effect it supposedly has on Levin. It is unclear how this interpretation can be coordinated with Levin's subsequent regret, under Kitty's influence, for feeling any sympathy for Anna or with the other instances of semiotic indeterminacy in the novel.

12. Evdokimova makes a similar point and emphasizes the artist's creative response to the "accidental" ("The Drawing" 41; see also Evdokimova, "Protsess" 16–24). The incident with the sketch also bears on Morson's repeated argument that it is wrong to read events in the first part of *Anna Karenina* as "foreshadowing" those in its final part, because Tolstoy could not have known about the war in the Balkans that he mentions in part VIII when he began to serialize the novel (*Hidden* 160–61). Morson believes this biographical fact demonstrates that there can be no "structure tying everything together," no "closure," and no "satisfying resolution to all themes" in the novel. He concludes that Tolstoy waged "war" in *Anna Karenina* on "foreshadowing, structure, and closure" in order "to present a written artifact [as] still being written, and so closer to lived experience" in its preservation of contingency and freedom (*Narrative and Freedom* 171). However, Mikhailov's work on the sketch can be seen as a model of the process of artistic creation that is also embodied in the *form* of *Anna Karenina,* because both show how an unforeseen element entering an artist's purview is incorporated via *relations* into what had been set down before, which can also be modified to accommodate the new. Thus, the Balkan War exists in meaningful relations with themes and plot elements such as Levin's consistent opposition to collective action, his insistence on a personal definition of value, Koznyshev's effete intellectual interests, high society's fads (Countess Lydia Ivanovna shifts her enthusiasm from Pietism to Serb heroism), the beekeeper's deference to the tsar as yet another sign of the peasantry's passivity (VIII.15), and much else besides (see also *10.3*). Indeed, Nabokov finds Vronsky's departure for the Balkans so well integrated into the plot that it is "too easy, too pat" ("Anna Karenin" 145). *Anna Karenina* can also be read as presenting the exact opposite interpretation of the relation between art and life that Morson proposes (see *17, 18*).

13. Mandelker finds an antecedent for this contrast in Lessing's *Laocöon* (108).

14. See, for example, Jakobson, "On Realism in Art."

15. Mandelker identifies Lessing's *Laocöon* as an antecedent for some of Levin's ideas about art in this scene. However, she does not discuss the problem of reception or the nature of artistic form and suggests that Tolstoy is concerned with art's "theurgic potential" (105–7). Šilbajoris points out the similarities of Levin's views with Tolstoy's in *What Is Art?* (146–48).

16. The term was coined by the nineteenth-century Russian writer and thinker Nikolai Chernyshevksii (quoted in Kovalev 28). Gromov discusses the development of this stylistic trait in Tolstoy's art. See Skaftymov for a discussion of Tolstoy's conception of character as changeable and of psychology as fluid (144–45).

17. However, see Gustafson, who argues that there are parallels between Tolstoy's narrative form and epistemology (292).

9. Art and Metaphysics

1. Terras invokes Plotinus in connection with Mikhailov, specifically, his example of a "beautiful image of a god or hero liberated by a sculptor from the prison of a crude marble block" (13); Terras further underscores that this liberation is never complete in Plotinus's scheme, and the artist's inner vision is never fully realized in matter (228). This also accords with Mikhailov's experience, because we last see him when he is continuing to work on *Pilate's Admonition*. By contrast, Babaev's Soviet perspective is that Mikhailov is a materialist and an atheist ("Siuzhet i kompozitsiia" 176). Šilbajoris points out several parallels between Mikhailov's views and the ones Tolstoy expressed in the late treatise *What Is Art?* (1898) but does not discuss metaphysics (152–53). Contrary to Mandelker's suggestion, Plotinus's metaphysical aesthetics are irreconcilable with Morson's approach to the novel (109; see also section *8* note 12).

2. Lotman, *Struktura khudozhestvennogo teksta* 195.

3. On the other hand, at an early stage of work on the novel, Tolstoy referred to it as an "obligation which has been set upon me by some higher power" (quoted in Stenbock-Fermor 11).

4. The metaphysically inclined nineteenth-century Russian poet Afanasii Fet, a close friend of Tolstoy, saw the scene of the birth in similar terms, as a "hole into the spiritual world, into Nirvana" (quoted in Eikhenbaum, *Lev Tolstoi* 184); Eikhenbaum also analyzes the influence of lyric poetry on the novel (*Lev Tolstoi* 174–85).

10. The Formal Implications of the Novel's Conception of Art

1. Schultze finds that segments from the dominant plotlines dealing with Anna and Levin are often paired and related in terms of contrast, comparison, and irony (22–23). She describes other large-scale structural features in her chapter 1.

2. Jakobson, "Two Aspects" 129, 132–33. Frank argues that the form of much modern literature puts units of meaning into relationships with each other that are not contiguous, as a result of which their significance does not emerge when they are "read consecutively" but only when "the entire pattern of internal references can be apprehended as a unity" ("Spatial Form" 13).

3. Pevear and Volokhonsky identify the model in their translation of *Anna Karenina* (831 n21).

4. Gustafson also speaks of contiguity and similarity as linking principles in Tolstoy's art (as well as "intensity"). However, he derives this from the "psychology of empiricism" and does not consider Jakobson's arguments that the "poetic function" and relations of contiguity and similarity are universal principles of linguistic and artistic structuring (and are thus not distinctive features of Tolstoy's art alone) (290–91). Catteau examines meanings that arise as a result of several juxtapositions of details in the novel but without mentioning Jakobson or the universality of the kind of phenomenon he illustrates. Cornillot carries out a similar

analysis of juxtapositions that he calls "contrapuntal." Jakobson mentions Anna's red handbag in the scene of her suicide (768, VII.31) as an example of a realist author's fondness for "synecdochic details" that appear as a function of metonymic shifts among contiguous elements ("Two Aspects" 130). It is important to realize, however, that this handbag is also clearly part of a network of metaphoric relations pertaining to Anna's affair with Vronsky, because it first appears at the beginning of her train trip home from Moscow (99, I.29). For more on the history of the formulation and "cultural diffusion" of Jakobson's ideas (as well as comments on Anna's handbag), see McLean, "Jakobson's Metaphor/Metonymy Polarity." The symbolism of Anna's handbag is also analyzed by Knapp, "The Estates."

5. Christian borrows this term from J. M. Meier and applies it to *War and Peace* (*Tolstoy* 132). For several additional examples of a relation that is widespread throughout the novel, see Stenbock-Fermor, who identifies interesting parallels between the first railroad scene in the novel (I.17–18) and the last (VIII.4–5) (73).

6. Schultze also notes a series of triangular relationships (145). Curtis sees *Anna Karenina* as occupying a unique place in Tolstoy's oeuvre, because it relies on metaphoric relations in contrast to the dominance of metonymic ones in his earlier works, including *War and Peace* (111, 119). In my view, this distinction is debatable, as is Curtis's suggestion that metaphoric relations appear in *Anna Karenina* because of Dostoevsky's influence.

7. Bayley, *Tolstoy and the Novel* 217–19, and Wasiolek 141 note the parallels and comment that the novel's drafts show that Tolstoy created them deliberately. Sorokin quotes the Russian Symbolist writer Dmitrii Merezhkovskii (1865–1941) on the parallels and notes that he was the first to point them out (217). Eikhenbaum, among others, makes the point that the horse's fate foreshadows Anna's and discusses the French play from which Tolstoy borrowed the horse's name (*Lev Tolstoi* 188–90).

8. Critics have interpreted the horse race to blame either Anna or Vronsky; for a list of representatives of both positions, see Mandelker 208 n30.

9. See Lotman on how literature functions as a generator of meaning ("Mozg—tekst—kul'tura" 27).

10. In *Narrative and Freedom,* Morson interprets the novel as a celebration of the "prosaic" aspects of existence and of life's complete openness. This may be the result of his understanding structure primarily in terms of linearity, plot, or the syntagmatic axis and his exclusion of the myriad situation rhymes or metaphoric relations of *simultaneous similarity* and *difference* that are also essential features of its artistic structure; for example, "In *War and Peace* and *Anna Karenina,* there are numerous incidents that occupy a great deal of space but lead nowhere. Nothing follows from them, and from the point of view of 'the plot' they might just as well not have happened. Order and chanciness are both present" (159; see also *10* and *18*).

11. Both letters quoted in Tolstoy, *Anna Karenina,* trans. Maude and Maude 753–54, emphasis added. I have modified the translations on the basis of the Russian

originals in Tolstoi, *Pis'ma* 467–68. See Stenbock-Fermor for diagrams and discussions of the novel's "architecture" (99–101).

12. Tolstoy, *Anna Karenina*, trans. Maude and Maude 750, with an additional passage from Tolstoi, *Pis'ma* 433–34, emphasis added. Jackson suggests a connection between Tolstoy's aesthetic program expressed here and the theme of family unity sounded in the novel's first line ("The Ambivalent Beginning" 348–49; see also 7). Orwin interprets Tolstoy's remarks about linking ideas in terms of his religious beliefs and how art can express them (204–5).

13. Stenbock-Fermor pursues Tolstoy's reference to "architecture" and describes a series of scenes that are arranged as "diptychs" and "triptychs" (103ff.). In "The Estates," Knapp argues that it is possible to understand the oblique form of communication that Tolstoy employs via the unsignaled "linkages" among various details in the novel. See Feuer for numerous additional examples of structural and thematic echoes in the novel.

11. The Problem of Language

1. For example, see Weir for a general discussion of the theme of language in the novel. See also Gibian; Knapp, "Tue-la!"

2. There are some minor variations in the name in different Russian editions of the novel. In their translation of *Anna Karenina,* Pevear and Volokhonsky acknowledge the parodic dimension of the name and note that it conflates the names of two existing institutions (836 n19).

3. Ginzburg calls attention to such moments as examples of the "disjunction" between the situation of a husband greeting a wife returning from a trip and his bureaucratic inability to express feeling (292).

4. Similarly, Ginzburg points out that Stiva's deft orchestration of conversations at the beginning of the dinner party in his home is reminiscent of the "conversational machine" that Anna Scherer starts in her salon at the beginning of *War and Peace* (vol. 1, pt. 1, chap. 2) (300–301). One of the functions of each of the scenes is to underscore the empty artificiality of society chatter.

12. Absolutism: Claims about Universal Truth and Morality

1. Riffaterre makes a related argument (based on C. S. Peirce) about "narrative truth" being "born of tautology" or of "repetition and equivalences adhering to a single rule" (7, 14ff.). Similarly, Todorov speaks of "verisimilitude" being achieved in a text via the use of a consistent internal rhetorical strategy that the reader is meant to take as references to reality ("Introduction au vraisemblable" 95).

2. Pevear and Volokhonsky in Dostoevsky, *The Brothers Karamazov* 780 n7.

3. By contrast, Christian chooses one side and argues that what interested Tolstoy was not absolute categories of justice but individuals and their sense of right and wrong (*Tolstoy* 174).

4. Nabokov concludes that a distinctive feature of Tolstoy's style in the novel is his use of metaphors and similes for ethical purposes ("Anna Karenin" 202–3).

5. *Predstavlenie* is the usual Russian translation of the German *Vorstellung* in the title of Schopenhauer's famous treatise *Die Welt als Wille und Vorstellung* (*Mir kak volia i predstavlenie,* The world as will and idea/representation). Tolstoy's interest in Schopenhauer's philosophy while he was writing *Anna Karenina* is well documented (see Eikhenbaum, *Lev Tolstoi* 171–72ff.) and is reflected in Levin's overt reference to it, including his attempt to substitute "love" for "will" (788, VIII.9). It is possible, therefore, that there is a specifically Schopenhauerian flavor to the term *predstavleniia* in the passages dealing with Karenin's facile faith. Schultze surveys Schopenhauerian themes in the novel, which include the conception of sexuality, the appeal of suicide, and sleep as an escape (78–79). Orwin analyzes in detail aspects of Schopenhauer's influence on Tolstoy and *Anna Karenina,* especially with regard to morality (150–65ff.). See also Turner for an overview of various influences on Tolstoy (*A Karenina Companion* 99–122).

6. By contrast, Gustafson appears to conflate the two phases in Karenin's spiritual life and concludes that his forgiveness was "flawed by his false position," which is that he cannot "act on his forgiveness" and is guided by the opinions of others (127).

7. Wasiolek sees this as "the force of society" with Betsy as "its embodiment" (145).

8. By contrast, Holquist sees Karenin and all the other characters as gripped by impersonal social and economic forces that function the way fate used to in various pre-nineteenth-century conceptions of existence ("The Supernatural"). In my view, this overemphasizes the role of the "outside" in the asymmetric relation between a character and his world and underemphasizes the transmundane forces also evoked in the novel.

9. In a draft (Tolstoi, *Polnoe sobranie sochinenii,* vol. 20, pt. 2, 433), Karenin is said to reread this chapter often and quotes two additional passages from it: verse 27, "Soedinen li ty s zhenoi—ne ishchi razvoda, ostalsia li bez zheny—ne ishchi zheny" (Art thou bound unto a wife? seek not to be loosed. Art thou loosed from a wife? seek not a wife), and the last part of verse 28, "Takovye, t. e., zhenatye, budut imet' skorb' po ploti, a mne vas zhal'" (such [i.e., those who marry] shall have trouble in the flesh: but I spare you). These quotations differ slightly from the biblical text.

10. In a draft, Karenin reads in Saint Mark that if a husband divorces a wife for a reason other than adultery and marries another, then he commits adultery; as a result, Karenin concludes, "Stalo byt', razvod dopushchen" (Therefore, divorce is permitted) (Tolstoi, *Polnoe sobranie sochinenii,* vol. 20, pt. 2, 330).

11. Orwin also notes that Varenka cannot be an exemplary character because she lacks the physical vitality that Tolstoy sees as necessary in addition to spirituality (196–97).

12. This complicates somewhat Wasiolek's conclusion that "Kitty's and Levin's union is uncontaminated by sex," which is true only relative to Anna and Vronsky (153). See also Gutkin.

13. Evans interprets Anna as the embodiment of sexual passion and its threats to social order (12, 14, 81). She also reads Anna as Tolstoy's "fictionalized version of his own needs and his own projections about women," and goes so far as to suggest that the novel's popularity with male critics may be due to their sharing Tolstoy's "fantasies about women and female sexuality" (82–83).

14. If this is the narrator's view of Liza, then he appears to enact the tension between beauty and morality that Orwin identifies as a major new development in Tolstoy's art in *Anna Karenina* (150). It is possible to read this tension, and the narrator's comparable ambivalence about Anna, as interdicting a consistent view of ethics in the novel.

13. Relativity: Characters as Arbiters of Meaning and Value

1. Lotman, *Struktura khudozhestvennogo teksta* 327, 333.

2. Striedter 34–35; he borrows the term *multiple interpretability* from the Russian Formalist Viktor Shklovskii.

3. Lukács 75–76. See also Bakhtin's related characterization of novels in terms of "heteroglossia" and "polyphony" ("Slovo v romane" ["Discourse in the Novel"]).

4. Flaubert 230. Nabokov makes the same point ("Anna Karenin" 143). By contrast, Wachtel concludes that the novel's epigraph shows Tolstoy's "presence" in the text, which thus departs from Flaubert's model (111).

5. Quotation from A. D. Obolensky's "Dve vstrechi s L. N. Tolstym," quoted in Gusev 299. Eikhenbaum agrees with the conclusion of Konstantin Leont'ev (a nineteenth-century Russian writer and thinker) that *Anna Karenina* is characterized by an "objective" narrative style, especially in comparison to *War and Peace,* and ascribes this to the influence of Pushkin's prose (*Lev Tolstoi* 157–58). Jackson argues that Tolstoy's "objective," "non-judgmental" narrative style is an aesthetic embodiment of the epigraph's ethical injunction not to judge ("The Ambivalent Beginning" 346–47). Gornaia demonstrates on the basis of drafts of the novel how Tolstoy worked to remove narrative comments about characters (189–92).

6. Stenbock-Fermor discusses train imagery in the novel and Tolstoy's distaste for railroads in general as emblems of contemporary material civilization (65–74). See also Bethea 77–79.

7. Bakhtin, *Problemy poetiki Dostoevskogo.*

8. Bakhtin himself makes this point in *Problemy poetiki Dostoevskogo* (81–84). See Emerson for a general discussion of Bakhtin's conception of Tolstoy and its limitations ("The Tolstoy Connection"). Kurrik stresses the extent to which "the singular, autonomous, and monological individual . . . dominates" *Anna Karenina*

(102) and how characters not only lack "knowledge of the other" but also lack the "drive to know the other" (107).

9. Ginzburg makes a similar generalization about Tolstoy's portrayal of dialogue: he combines "extreme conversational determinism, or the conversation's actual, empirical connection to a given situation, and *disjunction,* or the indirect relationship that obtains between a situational utterance and its ulterior personal motive. There is a dual conditionality (both external and internal) in Tolstoian dialogue that is the source of the poetics of submerged dialogue that extends from Chekhov to our own day" (291). Ginzburg further states that the "individual's need to realize his own personality, to realize his own potentialities and capacities, stands as the principal impetus behind all the other motives of his speech" (286). Orwin also notes that characters in *Anna Karenina* "may communicate indirectly . . . [but] remain fundamentally isolated from one another"; she explains this via Tolstoy's belief at the time that humans are separated by their bodies (208–9). For a brief overview of this point, see Schultze 134–35.

10. Indirect confirmation of this point can be found in Holquist, who uses "dialogue" as a synonym or metaphor for different kinds of relations, such as those between two physical bodies in motion, between figure and ground or plot and story, and between different kinds of "manifold possibilities" (*Dialogism* 20, 114, 181). As additional evidence, see also Lotman's successful conflation of Bakhtin and semiotics in essays such as "O semiosfere," "Fenomen kul'tury," and "Mozg—tekst—kul'tura."

11. See, for example, Jakobson's entirely relativized conception of the term in "On Realism in Art" and Wellek's and McLean's ("Realism") discussions of its history.

12. These everyday definitions of "realism" and "idealism" (as distinct from more strictly philosophical ones) are drawn from *Webster's Seventh New Collegiate Dictionary* (712–13, 413).

13. Kupreianova accents the relation differently when she generalizes about Tolstoy's entire career and concludes that the mutual influence between perceiver and perceived implied by the concept of a "feedback loop" in cybernetics explains his artistic practice (180–81). Thus, the "subjective prisms" in Tolstoy not only underscore the individuality of characters' perceptions but also bring out facets of objective reality. Skaftymov also stresses that the movements of characters' psyches occur in response to external stimuli (148–49). Gustafson provides an illuminating analysis of how the reader is made to see scenes and psyches in the novel (257–64); he also concludes that the aim of Tolstoy's techniques is to allow the reader to feel "present" in a variegated world (263) and "at-one" with a character or event (264). Orwin discusses Tolstoy's objections to subjectivism and, in the context of her analysis of his reading of Rousseau and Schopenhauer, concludes that Tolstoy believed in the reality of the outside world, which is known via the senses (157–58). However, she also notes that Tolstoy's increasing subjectivism in the 1870s anticipated

the "open subjectivism and symbolism" of the Silver Age of Russian literature (i.e., roughly 1895–1920) (208).

14. Tolstoy, *Anna Karenina,* trans. Pevear and Volokhonsky 820 n14.

15. Herman makes a similar point about Kitty, Levin, and other characters but speaks of their self-centeredness in terms of "passion" (9–10). Bayley makes this point about Anna and Vronsky ("Anna Karenina" 22; see also Bayley, *Tolstoy and the Novel* 220–23). Ermilov also finds that characters in the novel are often alienated from each other and blames this on the growth of capitalism in Russia (384–85).

16. Gustafson also sees Kitty and Levin as being "shown mostly in moments of disagreement" (46).

17. Christian, *Tolstoy* 194–95; Stenbock-Fermor 59–60. Gornaia speaks of "intersecting characteristics" (202–3), and although she notes that Anna's and the narrator's evaluations "do not always coincide," she concludes that this enhances the reader's understanding of Karenin (203 n21).

18. Lotman, *Struktura khudozhestvennogo teksta* 53, 57–60.

19. Nabokov, *Pnin* 130 and "Anna Karenin" 195–97; Alexandrov, "Relative Time."

20. In "The Passage of Time," Christian views the temporal discrepancies as errors. Batereau discusses various aspects of time in the novel. Aucouturier analyzes the way time is structured in the novel. Schultze seeks to eliminate the temporal discrepancies (24–25). Orwin points out how Vronsky's and Levin's estates are also temporally marked (182).

21. Tolstoi, "Predislovie k sochineniiam Giui de Mopassana" 264 (emphasis added).

22. Among others, Ivan Turgenev expressed distaste for Levin's "egoism" (quoted in Eikhenbaum, *Lev Tolstoi* 178–79). Similarly, Christian speaks of Levin's "blundering egoism" (*Tolstoy* 175). Bayley also notes that Levin's feelings are his alone and that his surroundings change with his moods ("Anna Karenina" 24–25; see also Bayley, *Tolstoy and the Novel* 206–7).

23. By contrast, Gustafson does not see Levin's ecstatic state as undermined by his blindness toward others (364–65).

24. Plato 28–32 (189C–193E). See also Gutkin's discussion of this and other allusions to Plato in the novel, especially the opposition between fleshly and spiritual love, and Orvin, "Zhanr platonovykh dialogov," who distinguishes how Tolstoy adapted some of Plato's ideas and his dialogic form.

25. In their translation of *Anna Karenina,* Pevear and Volokhonsky gloss "Capuan" as meaning "inactive" in Tolstoy's private vocabulary (832 n28); "sybaritic" is a more accurate translation.

26. As Maria Torgovnick puts it, by the end of the novel "lack of communication has become a way of life for Kitty and her husband" (quoted in Mandelker 56). For another overview of Levin and Kitty's mixture of understanding and misunderstanding, see Turner, "Blood" 132–34.

27. In "Truth in Dying," McLean provides an illuminating analysis of the function of Levin's two brothers as contrasts that show his traits and his well-ordered life to best advantage.

28. Blackmur simplifies Levin's relations with Nikolai to a monochromatic, purely positive "new and compassionate judgment" under the impact of Kitty's rejection (130–31). For another discussion of Levin's mixed relations with Nikolai and Koznyshev, see Turner, "Blood" 130–32.

29. See Gusev 160–90, 199–204ff. There are inevitably other divergences between Tolstoy's fictional characters and their real prototypes, including Tolstoy himself. In "Truth in Dying," McLean provides a judicious analysis of Nikolai Levin's death in the novel from the point of view of its relation to Tolstoy's actual experiences of the deaths of his two brothers.

30. In his *Diary of a Writer,* Dostoevsky was especially incensed by Levin's indifference to the war in the Balkans (quoted by Wilson 306–7), although he also praised very highly other aspects of the novel, especially the scene of Karenin's forgiving Anna and Vronsky by her sickbed (quoted in the Maudes' translation of *Anna Karenina* 759–61). A different plausible interpretation of Levin's self-interest is given by Ermilov, who argues that scenes such as Levin mowing with the peasants show how his personal interest can become transformed into a collective one, which is one of Tolstoy's central themes in the novel, even if it is not fully realized (420–22, 434–35).

31. Gutkin also notes that all meetings between Stiva and Levin follow this pattern (88).

32. Stenbock-Fermor notes that the scenes of Levin's confession and marriage are additional sympathetic foreshadowings of his "conversion" (118).

33. Herman makes a similar point (13–14). By contrast, and in keeping with her emphasis on ekphrasis in the novel, Mandelker identifies Levin's looking at Anna's portrait as the spiritual turning point in his life (182). It should be noted, however, that immediately afterward Levin concludes that visiting Anna and feeling pity for her was a mistake. Stenbock-Fermor notes the parallel that Levin is also "blinded" by the love in Kitty's eyes when she approaches him on the morning of their betrothal (60), which suggests a link between Levin's conceptions of divine and romantic love (404, IV.15).

34. Ginzburg interprets the relation between Levin's contemplating suicide, on the one hand, and his spontaneous, deep involvement in family matters, on the other, as a "discrepancy" and "inconsistency" that results from Tolstoy's projection of his own experience into the novel. This allows Tolstoy to "assert the full extent of his ideological hero's freedom and responsibility" by weakening "the system of his motivations at precisely those points where the issue concerns his loftiest moral experience" (344). In other words, the inconsistency in Levin's character shows that it is not determined, and this can be correlated with his free choice of moral behavior. However, as I argue, because Levin chooses his heart over his head, it is difficult to see his behavior as genuinely ethical.

35. Stenbock-Fermor points out this phraseological echo (53). This echo also supports the different reading of the exchange between Levin and his housekeeper suggested by Ermilov: that Levin's personal motivation in restructuring his estate turns out to be in harmony with the collective goals and needs of the peasants as expressed in the work of the *artel'*; thus, Levin's motivation, which may seem a- or immoral (because it is selfish), turns out to be part of a larger design that is moral (435–36).

36. Many readers are unconvinced by Levin's "conversion," including Dostoevsky (cited in Stenbock-Fermor 61), Veresaev 78–79, and Shklovskii 380 (although his views may be functions of the Soviet ideology constraining his reading of the novel). By contrast, Orwin interprets Levin as embodying the division between nature and culture that had become important for Tolstoy in *Anna Karenina* and that requires human beings to "insert" morality into their lives, which would not otherwise manifest it (149). Although this is how Levin imagines he will live henceforth (VIII.19), my discussion below and elsewhere (see *17.2*) raises questions about the extent to which Levin is free.

37. Orwin concludes that Levin's faith is genuine and that he consciously acts morally (167).

38. By contrast, Orwin reads Levin's way of seeing the sky as Tolstoy's demonstrating the "moral power of subjective insight" that nature by itself does not have (203). See also Orvin, "Psikhologiia very."

39. Gustafson concludes that Levin overcomes his desire to master life and uncovers his loving "divine self," in contrast to Anna's egotism (142–43).

40. The privacy and incommunicability of Levin's beliefs suggest that he has not escaped from the limitations of the self by the novel's end. For the opposite conclusion, albeit not based on Levin's final thoughts and actions, see Morson, *Narrative and Freedom* 268–69.

41. Gustafson locates Anna's sin in her choosing to pursue personal happiness regardless of others (130–31). As I suggested above (*13.4*), this is also Levin's primary motivation, although he obviously does not hurt anyone to the extent she does. I. N. Uspenskii provides a Soviet reading of Anna as a heroic rebel and a moral beacon against the norms of nineteenth-century Russian society (228; see also Kuleshov 182–83). For a summary of different views of Anna as victim or victimizer, see Konick, who concludes that she victimizes others because of a neurotic need for absolute love and domination (48).

42. Evans, among others, also notes this characterization of Anna but interprets the vitality as a sign of her physicality (7–8).

43. There is a critical tradition of interpreting Anna as responsible for her own fate. See Jackson, who notes that Anna "seeks out and creates her own reality, or realm, to play out her drama" ("Chance and Design" 40). David Sloane provides a variant interpretation of Anna as "writing" her own tragic fate, on the model of a literary work, by projecting her fears onto the world (quoted in Šilbajoris 156–57). Similarly, Morson characterizes Anna as projecting a tragic and romantic fate for

herself and as behaving in a way that aggravates her condition, all against a Tolstoyan background that counters Anna's fixation (*Narrative and Freedom* 72–81). However, these interpretations do not take into account either the extent to which all characters see the world and interact with it in their own terms, or the "impersonal" fatidic elements in the novel (see *17*).

44. Others who see Anna as dishonest in this scene include Evans 27 and Morson, "Prosaics" 7. Gustafson interprets Anna's behavior similarly and concludes that she does not make Stiva face up to his guilt just as she does not accept her own initially (120). By contrast, Mandelker claims that Anna "enters the novel as a Victorian stereotype of the Angel of the House" (151).

45. This statement is supplied with a footnote in the Maudes' translation of the novel (173), explaining that in Russia only the *innocent* party could apply for a divorce. Although this is useful to know and is clearly relevant to Anna's quandary in general, it does not seem to be the primary issue that concerns Anna at this point, which is more the dynamics of a guilty conscience than legalisms.

46. Evans sees Anna as guilty of wounding Vronsky "fatally" in the end in addition to destroying her own family (36).

47. Evans sees Vronsky as more "a creature of [Anna's] own projected needs and desires than he was ever a creature of flesh" (40).

48. One might also claim, as Denis de Rougement does, that for complex cultural reasons descriptions of "happy love" actually have no history in the Western literary tradition and that this is manifested in Anna's story. However, the reasons for unhappy love that emerge from Tolstoy's novel are unrelated to the vast generalizations about the legacy of dualistic beliefs that interest Rougement.

49. Ishchuk calls attention to echoes of the novel's epigraph in a related, later scene when Anna questions how she can be guilty of her transgression, which she sees as inevitable (116–17; see 635, VI.33). Shklovskii, in conformity with Soviet codes, constricts the range of reasons for Anna's suicide by claiming that she is guilty of wanting to have her love for Vronsky and society's acceptance at the same time (*Lev Tolstoi* 370). This resembles Veresaev's argument that Anna errs by not yielding fully to her love for Vronsky because she fears society's opprobrium (148–49). Orwin argues that in Tolstoy's conception of the division between nature and morality, which he developed under Schopenhauer's influence, Anna's natural vitality and needs do not excuse her sins; ethical behavior is possible only through free human choice (158–59). However, because the possibility of freedom in the novel is open to debate (see *7.6, 17*), so is Anna's guilt.

50. Joan Grossman contrasts the shallow discourse and easy communication in Princess Betsy's salon with Anna's and Vronsky's inability to communicate effectively with each other when alone (128). However, a degree of alienation also characterizes the relations among all of the other characters, including Kitty and Levin.

51. Wasiolek insists that Anna does not really miss her son and that her love for Vronsky is stronger (145–46). He also argues that Anna does not really want a divorce from Karenin, because marriage to Vronsky and a normal life with him

would jeopardize her destructive hold on him. This is a plausible interpretation, but Anna's motives are also more contradictory and multifarious.

52. Wasiolek sees a fundamental mismatch between Anna's insatiable love and possessiveness and Vronsky's constitutional inability to satisfy her (147). Similarly, Nabokov locates the failure of Anna's affair in its carnality and egotism (in contrast to Levin's love) ("Anna Karenin" 147). Kupreianova discusses Anna's abrasive relations with Vronsky in terms of their embodying Schopenhauer's conflictive will (105). However, Anna's behavior is also clearly distorted by her unsettled social position, and she idealizes Vronsky much of the time.

53. Leont'ev criticizes the image of the extinguished candle and interprets it as foreclosing any possibility of immortality (59–61). Morson, in keeping with his overarching thesis about life as open and unstructured, concludes that the "true terror" of Anna's final moments is caused by her recognizing other possibilities in her life that she could have followed and that are now lost forever (*Narrative and Freedom* 79).

54. Stenbock-Fermor inclines toward this interpretation (50–51), as does Nabokov, who links Anna's "soulbirth" (i.e., death) with Kitty's "childbirth" ("Anna Karenin" 165, 180). The parallel between the two was also noted early by Tolstoy's friend, the poet Afanasii Fet, in a letter from 12 April 1877 (excerpt quoted in Tolstoy, *Anna Karenina,* trans. Maude and Maude 751).

55. Stenbock-Fermor also links the scene of Anna reading the English novel on her way back to St. Petersburg and her suicide via the recurring image of a "little red handbag" (47–48).

56. Stenbock-Fermor points out the similarity between the two remarks (49–50).

57. Schultze lists the numerous different interpretations of Anna's guilt, which range from denying it to explaining it in social, religious, and psychological terms (10–11).

58. Thorlby sees Anna similarly—as caught in "tragic inevitability" (22).

59. Mandelker points out that Levin's visit parodies the traditional novelistic plot of men visiting a brothel after dinner (something that is, of course, inconceivable from Levin's perspective at this point in his life) (111). Ishchuk finds an echo of the epigraph in Anna's remark to Levin that only someone who has suffered what she has is in a position to understand and forgive her (117; see 701, VII.10).

60. Khrapchenko does not consider Levin's change of heart and interprets the meeting in terms of Levin's sympathy for Anna (186). Mandelker concludes that Levin's sympathy for Anna, which is elicited initially by Mikhailov's masterful portrait of her, "is the beginning of true faith on Lyovin's part" (113) and "initiates" his spiritual conversion (115). It is unclear how this can be reconciled with Levin's subsequent suicidal thoughts or with his own impression that his spiritual rebirth is triggered by a peasant's chance comment (see *13.4.4*). By contrast, Wachtel sees Anna's portrait as a sign of her "apostasy" (109).

61. Mandelker underscores how little we know of Anna's past before we meet her but then states that we "never learn the precise circumstances of Anna's courtship by Karenin" (125–26, 127). By virtue of her commitment to understanding *Anna Karenina* in terms of its relation to the (primarily English) nineteenth-century novel, Mandelker also argues that Tolstoy does not provide Anna's past history because he "intended his reader to write Anna's story according to the intertext of the Victorian novel that she reads" (127). However, given the narrator's comments about the novel Anna reads on the train, "in opposition" to the Victorian novel seems as likely an alternative. Thorlby also sees the arranged marriage as mitigating somewhat Anna's guilt toward Karenin (41). Nabokov characterizes Anna's aunt simply and thus rather implausibly as "well-meaning" ("Anna Karenin" 144).

62. The past history of Anna's marriage, the incongruence of Anna's and Karenin's characters, and Vronsky's attractiveness (cf. Kitty) all complicate Morson's conclusion that Anna teaches herself to dislike Karenin ("Prosaics" 8). Nabokov finds that "the Karenin marriage, lacking as it does true affinity between its partners, is as sinful as Anna's love affair is to be" ("Anna Karenin" 188). Veresaev sees Anna as having betrayed due to fear the fullness of the love that she could have experienced with Vronsky (148–49).

63. By contrast, Gustafson finds that Anna does not fully accept her guilt (127).

64. Feuer makes a similar point about Anna and Stiva: "Honesty makes Stiva and Anna acknowledge their faults, but the conviction that they cannot go against their innermost nature tells them that they are not to blame" (350). Evans has a diverging perspective and sees Anna as the "guilty party in a wrecked marriage and several wrecked lives . . . [because] she was unable to control and discipline her passions and her inclinations" (35).

65. This is the argument advanced by Orwin (166, 170).

66. Eikhenbaum discusses in detail the effect that Tolstoy's reading of Pushkin's prose had on *Anna Karenina* (*Lev Tolstoi* 147–60). Eikhenbaum also sees Anna as enacting the "tragedy of betrayal" rather than the "tragedy of loyalty" that characterizes Pushkin's Tatiana (154). See also Gornaia.

67. Orwin sees this as the turning point when Anna allows herself to be tempted by Vronsky and when she "shuts out" her conscience (166, 177–78); Orwin does acknowledge that Anna frequently hears her conscience later as well (185). However, the snowstorm could also be interpreted in the opposite way—as an image of the undeniable power of the passion that overcomes reason and ethics.

68. Mandelker discusses Anna's doubling in terms of the impossibility for a woman to achieve psychic holism in a social system that oppresses women (157–60). Rancour-Laferriere invokes psychoanalytic conceptions of narcissism and masochism to explain Anna's experiences and behavior.

69. See the relevant entries in Lomunov.

70. See Hruska for a study of some Gothic elements in early Tolstoy.

71. That Stiva's attitude toward his betrayal of Dolly used to be more serious

is suggested by a phrase that was omitted from the Pevear and Volokhonsky translation (as well as from various Russian editions) and that was restored by Zhdanov and Zaidenshnur in the Literaturnye Pamiatniki edition of *Anna Karenina*: "He could not feel sorry now for what he had felt sorry for six years ago, when he had first been unfaithful to her" (9; 3, I.2).

72. It is worth noting that there is a possible although rather unlikely secondary meaning to the narrator's remarks that is implied by his use of the metaphor "dream of life." This could, in principle, be taken as invoking a Gnostic conception of existence, because if mundane life is a "dream," it follows that the true waking state, or "reality," lies elsewhere, perhaps in an ideal, transcendent realm. The problem with this interpretation is that the dualism of the Gnostic worldview cannot be reconciled with Christianity or coordinated with the world Tolstoy creates in the novel. (Moreover, although Gnosticism was known earlier, most of the important textual discoveries pertaining to it were made in the twentieth century.) Not only do we find various biblical references scattered throughout the text, we also have Levin's discovery of divine goodness in *this* world as well as the novel's celebration of marriage, children, dancing, food, country life, and much else that is antithetical to Gnosticism's exclusive orientation toward the immaterial world of spirit.

73. See Orwin's discussion of the parallels between Stiva's ideas and Tolstoy's, but with the significant difference that Stiva is amoral (149, 166–67, 176).

74. Kovarsky argues that Tolstoy's artistic design in *Anna Karenina* first draws the reader into identifying with the morally flawed characters Stiva and Anna and then confronts the reader with having to recognize and transcend his own sinfulness via a process of moral education (73). It is unclear, however, who or what can be seen as the model for this process in the novel.

75. Turgenev, *Zapiski okhotnika* 537–38, 540–41; Schapiro 65–66. This moral dimension of the *Hunter's Sketches* is also acknowledged by most twentieth-century readers. The present discussion is based on my paper "Narrative Silences in Turgenev," Third World Congress for Soviet and East European Studies, Washington, D.C., 3 November 1985.

76. For example, Leonid Grossman argues that serfdom as a sociopolitical problem was not a theme that interested Turgenev in the *Sketches*. Ripp claims it is wrong to see the political element in the collection as being "unambiguously present. The work is not simply an expression of a liberal credo; rather it projects the wish to be such an expression, and for all the ideological points Turgenev makes, he is ultimately most concerned with the difficulty of commanding any ideology at all in mid-nineteenth-century Russia" (75). The dominant form of evidence for this in Ripp's view is the "narrator's efforts at self-effacement [in the *Sketches*, which] are so extreme that they end up calling attention to themselves: the narrator's intricate devices for locating himself offstage constitute a thundering announcement of his hovering presence" (79). The conclusion Ripp draws is that the narrator's refusal or inability to express moral outrage against serfdom is evidence

for Turgenev's belief that it was impossible to have political opinions, much less undertake political action, in the intellectual climate of mid-nineteenth-century Russia (83, 86). Both Grossman and Ripp ultimately search for Turgenev's meanings in his words alone and approach them assuming that an author's ideas are entirely immanent in his works. The problem with this approach is that it ignores the techniques authors use to draw *readers* into *creating* a work's meaning, as I illustrate below.

77. Turgenev, *Zapiski okhotnika* 25. Subsequent page references will be given in the text. Translations are mine.

78. Boris Uspenskii 169.

79. Lotman, *Struktura khudozhestvennogo teksta* 66–67.

80. Evans suggests that Dolly is the novel's "real heroine" because she comes to terms with Stiva's failings in a way that Anna never achieves with Vronsky and because Dolly is the "most morally assertive character in the novel" (73, 78, 84). Morson shares the view that Dolly is the heroine ("Prosaics" 4). By contrast, Khrapchenko finds that Tolstoy does not fully succeed in making Dolly exemplary and that Anna remains more appealing (185).

81. In diary entries composed in 1898, or some twenty years after completing *Anna Karenina,* Tolstoy underscored the fluidity of human nature and how the changeability of human beings is the guarantor of morality: "The human being flows, and all possibilities lie within him: he was stupid, then became wise, was evil, then became kind, and vice versa. In this lies human greatness. And because of this we should not judge human beings. Which one? . . . You've judged him, and he's already something else" (quoted in Skaftymov 143, 156–57, my translation). This conception seems applicable in varying degrees to Anna, Stiva, and Karenin, all of whom drift from and are drawn back to morality.

82. Moments like this make Dolly more complex, or inconsistent, than the assessment by Mandelker that Dolly's "heroic endurance" as a mother is actually "exposed as being sustained by the same dangerous bourgeois delusions of romantic love that drive Anna Karenin's passion" (55).

83. Bayley makes the same point (*Tolstoy and the Novel* 225; "Anna Karenina" 25).

84. Details such as these are part of Tolstoy's arsenal for discrediting Vronsky (which does not mean that he is entirely without redeeming features). However, in a famously perverse argument, the nineteenth-century writer and thinker Konstantin Leont'ev, who was Tolstoy's contemporary, contends that Vronsky is preferable to Levin as a real human being because Vronsky is strong, reliable, and restrained, while Levin is an ineffectual dreamer (3–4, 56).

85. Nabokov also discusses Vronsky's attempted suicide in terms of dueling but specifies that if the injured party is killed in a duel, then he is avenged by his opponent's (supposed) remorse ("Anna Karenin" 174).

86. Morson reads Kitty's rather selfish or self-protective decision to cut off contact with the Petrovs in the opposite way, as showing that she learns how to defer to

others, or make herself *"the minor character in someone else's story"* (*Narrative and Freedom* 74). Morson also interprets Kitty's decision in this scene as reenacting her ability to see Levin's point of view when she rejects his proposal. However, given that Kitty feels "ecstasy" and "happiness" when she refuses Levin (48, I.13), it is questionable that she can see his viewpoint, or that she cares about it then, any more than she can imagine a diminished future role for herself in the Petrovs' story.

87. Veresaev, among others, sees Varenka similarly (84–85).

14. Self and Others

1. Stenbock-Fermor argues that at the end of the novel Levin's family becomes the core of a larger social unit, including relatives, servants, and employees, bound by collective goals and positive relations not seen elsewhere in the novel (84).

2. Similarly, in "Prosaics," Emerson speaks of Stiva as a "facilitator" and a "mediator" (153) and as one who tries "to bring relief" to others (157); although it should be added that he is not always successful.

3. Goscilo-Kostin notes the resemblance of the food in this scene to an act of "communion" between master and laborers (485).

4. Jahn sees the railroad in the novel as an emblem of the social and interprets Anna in this light as "the tragic victim of human nature which calls both for the unhindered expression of the individual and the antithetical acknowledgment of the ultimate dependence of the individual on the social" (8).

5. An early draft of the novel contains more detailed references to a "Highness" ("Vysochestvo"—a term reserved for members of the imperial family) who is present at a party that Anna attends at the Rolandakis, which is a precursor of the scenes at Princess Betsy's (Tolstoi, *Polnoe sobranie sochinenii,* vol. 20, pt. 2, 301, 302). See also Pevear and Volokhonsky's translation of *Anna Karenina,* which confirms this supposition on the basis of different evidence (826 n17).

6. Tolstoy, *Polnoe sobranie sochinenii,* vol. 20, pt. 2, 312–13.

15. The Inner Voice and Conscience

1. Orwin sees Stiva as a sensualist who lacks the "moral freedom" that would allow him "to make moral choices among competing influences" (176–77).

2. However, Stenbock-Fermor suggests the possibility that Stiva was well aware of what was common knowledge in Russia at the time (93).

3. Tolstoy, *War and Peace* 732.

4. Tolstoi, *Polnoe sobranie sochinenii,* vol. 20, pt. 2, 310.

16. Essentialism

1. By contrast, Orwin makes the argument, based on her analysis of Tolstoy's response to Schopenhauer and the latter's polemic with Rousseau, that in *Anna*

Karenina Tolstoy dramatizes the "tension" between nature and the "higher reason" in human beings that is the source of morality (170). Consequently, morality does not originate directly in nature, but is the product of human culture and individual choice and can be at odds with human happiness (171).

2. See Schultze for an analysis of the structure of other lexical repetitions in the novel (57–76). Gornaia makes some useful observations about the narrator's rhythmic, laconic style when describing several tense moments in Anna's life later in the novel (196–97).

3. The spring sequence appears to contradict Orwin's argument based on the scene of Levin spending the night on a haystack (III.12) that there is a split between him and nature, between what it is and how he perceives it (163–64). In fact, Levin's connection with spring renewal recalls Prince Andrei's encounters with the symbolic oak tree in *War and Peace* (bk. 2, pt. 3, chaps. 1 and 3). Veresaev makes a similar point about Nikolai's death and natural processes (168).

4. Eikhenbaum discusses in detail the origins of characters' remarks in contemporary European and Russian polemics and in Tolstoy's own thinking on the subject (*Lev Tolstoi* 110–26, esp. 124–26). See also Babaev for the novel's reception from various points of view by contemporary journalists (*Lev Tolstoi* 107–80).

5. In a draft, Dolly does not infer that Stiva is thinking about Chibisova. Dolly is also in favor of "women's rights," but only because she wishes that she were better educated for her children's sake and more independent so that she could sell by herself the forest on her inherited estate (Tolstoi, *Polnoe sobranie sochinenii,* vol. 20, pt. 2, 344–45). However, the personal reasons that characters have for their opinions about this matter appear in the draft as well, which implies that the contingent nature of ideological positions was always part of Tolstoy's design.

6. Wordsworth 151.

7. Because Orwin sees morality as separate from nature in *Anna Karenina,* she interprets the peasants as being "*in* . . . [but] not entirely *of* nature" and argues that the labor that characterizes them is a manifestation of "God in their souls" (148). As evidence for the peasants' "non-natural" morality Orwin adduces the initially Platonic relations between a young peasant, Ivan Parmenov, and his wife, as well as "Platon's" practice of "living for the soul," which is what triggers Levin's epiphany and "conversion" (148–49). Although this argument is suggestive, the portrayal of peasants in the novel seems more blurred. Ivan Parmenov's "virtue" appears to be due not to choice but to his youth and naïveté, which is how his father characterizes him (274, III.2). Platon's behavior is unselfish; but the other peasants try to cheat Levin even though they like him (273, II.2). They also deeply mistrust him and prefer outmoded forms of labor (340–41, III.29), which confirms that they are fixed in their ways and thus possibly not inclined toward the freedom of choice necessary for ethical behavior.

8. By contrast, Mandelker concludes that Varenka *rejects* Koznyshev and that her action foreshadows Tolstoy's later view that equality between the sexes can be achieved only when the power relations "typical of nineteenth-century bourgeois

marriage" are overcome (178). This feminist interpretation underemphasizes Varenka's fervent interest in Koznyshev's proposal ("To be the wife of a man like Koznyshev, after her situation with Mme Stahl, seemed to her the height of happiness" [565, VI.5]), and neglects Kitty's role in the novel: Kitty's attitude toward marriage is more important than Varenka's. Stenbock-Fermor does not see Varenka and Koznyshev as "examples to be followed" (109).

17. Fate

1. For a similar view, see Eakin 17.

2. Mandelker discusses at length the Russian folkloric associations of mushrooms and attempts to decipher Varenka and Koznyshev's failed courtship in these terms (169–77). However, the diffuse associations of mushrooms in the novel make this procedure uncertain.

3. Christian, *Tolstoy* 204, and Šilbajoris 144–45 are among many interpreters who see Anna's life as gripped by an inevitability as inexorable as fate. Leont'ev 73, and Eikhenbaum, *Lev Tolstoi* 187–88 see the linked dreams as prophetic (and Eikhenbaum finds that they echo Schopenhauer). A different argument is presented by Jackson, who discerns fate in elements of Anna's character and in how it makes chance elements "group themselves into coherent design" ("Chance and Design" 34). By contrast, Holquist in "The Supernatural as Social Force" argues that in general all the characters in the novel are caught by social and economic forces that have replaced supernatural ones in the nineteenth-century novel. Morson claims that Anna's mistake about dying in childbirth proves the falsity of omens in the novel in general (*Narrative and Freedom* 75–76).

4. Anna's red bag accompanies her on trains and has also been interpreted symbolically; see, for example, Knapp, who summarizes the interpretations that Jakobson and others gave this detail ("The Estates" 91–93, 97–98 n24).

5. Pevear and Volokhonsky point out in their notes to their translation of the novel that the brothers Grimm did not write a story on this theme, but that it could be a reference to Adalbert Chamisso or Hans Christian Andersen (823 n10). See also E. Babaev's notes in Tolstoi, *Anna Karenina* (Moscow: Khudozhestvennaia literatura), 9:483–84. Mandelker discusses this issue in detail in the context of her argument about the possibility of reading the novel in terms of myth or fate (148–51). She also discusses additional shadow imagery in connection with Anna and Vronsky (151–54).

6. Gustafson interprets each dream as the character's conscience (310–11). He does not discuss fate or that Anna had the dream before her liaison with Vronsky. Stenbock-Fermor cites V. A. Zhdanov's conclusion based on his study of the novel's drafts that Anna and Vronsky had the same dream before Tolstoy introduced the accident at the train station; this conclusion suggests that he tried to underscore the dream's import (66). Wasiolek interprets the peasant in the dream as a "symbol of the remorseless, impersonal power of sex" and concludes that Anna

is doomed by the sexual passion in her love for Vronsky (153). He also suggests a psychoanalytic explanation for Anna's self-destructive behavior, which is that of a child abandoned by "the father because of the intervening and hateful mother" (157). Morson mentions Vronsky's dream in passing but does not explore its implications (*Narrative and Freedom* 76). Nabokov discusses the two "nightmares" and their evolution in some detail and sees them as having "dreadful prophetic implications": the peasant's French is a "symbol of artificial life," and he is a "symbol of [Anna's] sin, filthy and soul-stunting sin" ("Anna Karenin" 175–77, 178–82, 186–87). In "A Text within a Text" and "Simvolika zheleza," Lönnqvist perceptively discusses complexes of imagery appearing in Anna's and Vronsky's dreams.

7. Morson interprets Kitty's impression that the day Levin proposes will be a fateful one as disproving her (and all) fatidic expectation because she will accept Levin only later (*Narrative and Freedom* 74). However, Levin's conclusion at the end of the novel about the distance between the human and the divine allows for the possibility that fateful intuitions can be true in general even if inaccurate in their specifics. Similarly, Anna is wrong when she dreams that she will die in childbirth, but the candle imagery accompanying her death may evoke the flame that appears when Levin's son is born, thus still linking her death with a different birth.

8. See Lotman for a related discussion of historiography (*Kul'tura i vzryv* 33–34).

9. Schultze 112 and Mandelker 167 make some of the same connections. Lönnqvist (Lennkvist) analyzes in detail many of the references to bears and to related imagery connected with Levin's courtship and marriage. Mandelker also points out the possible biographical pun that "Behrs" was the maiden name of Tolstoy's wife (which, of course, works only in Mlle Linon's initial remark in English).

10. Perhaps this is also why Tolstoy has Venus rising rather than setting, which the Maudes identify as an astronomical error in their translation of *Anna Karenina* (150 n5).

11. Ginzburg provides an illuminating reading of this scene in terms of Levin's new, growing connection with Kitty and of Stiva's abetting it (302–3).

12. Orwin agrees with Kupreianova's interpretation of this scene as a possible illustration of Kant's linking the stars above human beings and the moral law within them in the *Critique of Pure Reason* (206–7).

13. By contrast, Wasiolek sees this event as evidence that Anna authors her own fate by rejecting "what might be solutions to her terrible situation" and by seeking "the death she finally embraces" (143).

14. Morson argues that Tolstoy restricts fateful patterning only to Anna's consciousness, that she chooses "to fulfill what she takes to be an omen," and that "[l]ife as Tolstoy imagines it does not fit a pattern" (*Narrative and Freedom* 78). Because *Anna Karenina* is filled with networks of interrelated details of which the characters are unaware, that the narrator does not underscore, and that can be correlated with the characters' fatidic interpretations of their own lives, it is virtually

impossible to deny that fate operates within the novel (even if this does not un-equivocally prove its existence; see, for example, Nabokov on details such as the discussion of spiritualism at the Shcherbatskys and its "return" via Landau's in-structions to Karenin about denying Anna a divorce ["Anna Karenin" 224]). An-other way of saying this is that Morson's argument focuses primarily on the novel's syntagmatic axis and on patterning and form in terms of plot, whereas the richly developed paradigmatic relations among textual elements are at least as important and are certainly not linked exclusively to Anna's consciousness.

15. However, see Lönnqvist's ingenious examination of the folkloric associa-tions of bears, dreams, and related imagery in the novel ("A Text within a Text" and "Simvolika zheleza").

16. Jakobson, "Closing Statement."

18. Literary Form, Fate, Freedom, Chance

1. Morson argues that Tolstoy's absolutist authorial pronouncements in the novel are undermined by virtue of their inescapable dialogicity, that there are lov-ingly described but "irrelevant" details in the text that have no other function than to illustrate the unstructured nature of existence, and that there is no overarching plot that gives meaning to all the details of which characters' lives consist. In gen-eral, Morson criticizes thinkers he considers "semiotic totalitarians," or those who "presume that to understand a cultural fact is to show its place in a system that can at least in principle explain everything . . . [and who assume] that all apparently accidental or random facts are really signs of some underlying order, to which this special hermeneutic or semiotic system provides the key." To these thinkers Mor-son opposes his idea of "prosaics," according to which "the fundamental state of the world is mess" ("Prosaics" 1). Morson transfers his view of life to literature and enlists Tolstoy as a supposedly great exemplar of prosaics. Parts of my argument against this view that follow are derived from my article "Khudozhestvennaia forma, svoboda, sluchainost'."

2. Lotman, *Struktura khudozhestvennogo teksta* 96; all translations are mine. Subsequent page references will be given in the text. Morson notes that Lessing's *Laocöon* can be read as implying that "narratives, insofar as they rely on structure, are predisposed to convey a sense of fatalism, determinism, or otherwise closed time" (*Narrative and Freedom* 8, see also 33). However, Morson does not find this conclusion applicable to Tolstoy, perhaps because he understands "structure" as "plot" or as a single pattern that "makes everything fit" (38–39). As I argue above, plot is only one type of structuring in *Anna Karenina,* and "spatial" relations among textual elements create a play of meanings rather than a rigid pattern like a puzzle in which all pieces interlock.

3. See Attridge for a similar argument from different principles now current in the United States (25, 26).

4. This is my recollection of Professor Gary Saul Morson's comments about the episode with Levin's shirt after a lecture presented to the Slavic Department at Yale University in the later 1980s.

5. Dal', *Tolkovyi slovar'* 4:107.

6. Spinoza 107. In her insightful analysis of dialogue in Tolstoy's works, Ginzburg points out two scenes in which chance events appear to increase the impression of verisimilitude (304). The first is a sparrow flying onto the Levins' veranda where Kitty and others are making jam, and the second is a wasp flying into Levin's apiary where Dolly and others are eating honey. In each case, the unexpected event elicits responses from the characters that take place just as "in life." However, Ginzburg's examples show a number of structural parallels that undermine the seemingly accidental nature of the events (especially given the necessarily limited verbal scope of a fictional world, even one as long as *Anna Karenina*). For additional structural parallels that have the same effect, see Schultze on heat, electricity, rings, and toothaches (111–13), trains (120–21), telegrams (125–26), and swimming (127). LeBlanc surveys recurring images of sex and eating in the novel (9–19).

Conclusion

1. Mirsky 275.

Works Cited

Achebe, Chinua. "The Madman." *Girls at War and Other Stories*. Garden City, NY: Doubleday, 1973. 1–10.

Alexandrov, Vladimir E. "Alterity, Hermeneutic Indices, and the Limits of Interpretation." *Elementa: Journal of Slavic Studies and Comparative Cultural Semiotics* 4.2 (1998): 97–120. See http://www.tandf.co.uk/journals.

———. *Andrei Bely: The Major Symbolist Fiction*. Cambridge, MA: Harvard University Press, 1985.

———. "Biology, Semiosis, and Cultural Difference in Lotman's Semiosphere." *Comparative Literature* 52.4 (2000): 339–62.

———. "Khudozhestvennaia forma, svoboda, sluchainost'." *Slavica Tergestina, 4, Nasledie Iu. M. Lotmana: Nastoiashchee i budushchee*. Edited by M. C. Pesenti et al. Trieste: Lint, 1996. 101–12.

———. *Nabokov's Otherworld*. Princeton, NJ: Princeton University Press, 1991.

———. "Relative Time in *Anna Karenina*." *Russian Review* 41.2 (1982): 159–68.

Arnold, Matthew. "The Study of Poetry." 1880. *Literary Criticism: An Introductory Reader*. Edited by Lionel Trilling. New York: Holt, Rinehart and Winston, 1970. 231–51.

Attridge, Derek. "Innovation, Literature, Ethics." *PMLA* 114 (1999): 20–31.

Aucouturier, Michel. "Le Calendrier du roman." *Cahiers Léon Tolstoï. Anna Karénine* 1 (1984): 45–51.

Babaev, Eduard G. *Lev Tolstoi i russkaia zhurnalistika ego epokhi*. Moscow: Izdatel'stvo moskovskogo universiteta, 1993.

———. "Siuzhet i kompozitsiia romana *Anna Karenina*." Blagoi et al. 150–80.

Bakhtin, Mikhail. "Discourse in the Novel." 1934–35. *The Dialogic Imagination*. Edited by Michael Holquist. Translated by Caryl Emerson and Michael Holquist. Austin: University of Texas Press, 1981. 259–422.

———. "Formy vremeni i khronotopa v romane. Ocherki po istoricheskoi poetike." *Voprosy literatury i estetiki. Issledovaniia rasnykh let*. Moscow: Khudozhestvennaia literatura, 1975. 234–407.

———. *Problemy poetiki Dostoevskogo*. 4th ed. Moscow: Sovetskaia Rossiia, 1979.

———. "Slovo v romane." *Voprosy literatury i estetiki: Issledovaniia raznykh let*. Moscow: Khudozhestvennaia literatura, 1975. 72–233.

Barthes, Roland. "The Death of the Author." *Image, Music, Text.* Edited and translated by Stephen Heath. New York: Hill and Wang, 1977. 142–48.

――――. *S/Z.* Translated by Richard Miller. New York: Hill and Wang. 1974.

Batereau, Brigitte. "Zeit in Lev Tolstojs *Anna Karenina.*" *Die Welt der Slaven* 16.1 (1971): 1–19.

Bayley, John. "Anna Karenina." Bloom 7–32.

――――. *Tolstoy and the Novel.* New York: Viking, 1966.

Bely, Andrei. *Petersburg.* Translated, annotated, and introduced by Robert A. Maguire and John E. Malmstad. Bloomington: Indiana University Press, 1978.

Berlin, Isaiah. "The Hedgehog and the Fox." *Russian Thinkers.* Edited by Henry Hardy and Aileen Kelly. New York: Penguin, 1978. 22–81.

Bethea, David M. *The Shape of Apocalypse in Modern Russian Fiction.* Princeton, NJ: Princeton University Press, 1989.

Bibliia. Knigi Sviashchennogo Pisaniia Vetkhago i Novago Zaveta. Rpt. n.d. Warsaw: B. Götze, 1939.

Blackmur, R. P. "The Dialectic of Incarnation: Tolstoy's *Anna Karenina.*" *Tolstoy: A Collection of Critical Essays.* Edited by Ralph E. Matlaw. Englewood Cliffs, NJ: Prentice-Hall, 1967. 127–45.

Blagoi, D. D., et al., eds. *Tolstoi- khudozhnik. Sbornik statei.* Moscow: AN SSSR, 1961.

Bloom, Harold, ed. *Leo Tolstoy's* Anna Karenina. New York: Chelsea, 1987.

Booth, Wayne. *The Company We Keep: An Ethics of Fiction.* Berkeley: University of California Press, 1988.

Brooke-Rose, Christine. *A Rhetoric of the Unreal: Studies in Narrative and Structure, Especially of the Fantastic.* Cambridge: Cambridge University Press, 1981.

Brooks, Peter. *Reading for the Plot: Design and Intention in Narrative.* New York: Vintage, 1985.

Bruner, Jerome. *Actual Minds, Possible Worlds.* Cambridge, MA: Harvard University Press, 1986.

Buell, Lawrence. "Introduction: In Pursuit of Ethics." *PMLA* 114 (1999): 7–19.

Caplan, David, et al. "Language and Communication: Animal Communication." *Fundamental Neuroscience.* Edited by Michael J. Zigmond et al. New York: Academic Press, 1999. 1487–93.

Catteau, Jacques. "Le 'Réel' métaphorique." *Cahiers Léon Tolstoï. Anna Karénine* 1 (1984): 16–24.

Christian, R. F. "The Passage of Time in *Anna Karenina.*" *Slavonic and East European Review* (Jan. 1967): 207–10.

――――. *Tolstoy: A Critical Introduction.* Cambridge: Cambridge University Press, 1969.

Clark, Katerina, and Michael Holquist. *Mikhail Bakhtin.* Cambridge, MA: Harvard University Press, 1984.

Clark, Michael P. "Lacan, Jacques." Groden and Kreiswirth 450–54.

Collini, Stefan. "Introduction: Interpretation Terminable and Interminable." Eco et al. 1–22.

Cornillot, François. "L'Ecriture contrapuntique." *Cahiers Léon Tolstoï. Anna Karénine* 1 (1984): 25–32.

"Coyote and White-Tailed Buck." Narrative told by Samuel M. Watters. *Nez Perce Oral Narratives*. Recorded, transcribed, and translated by Haruo Aoki and Deward E. Walker Jr. Berkeley: University of California Press, n.d. [1988]. 98–100.

Culler, Jonathan. "In Defence of Overinterpretation." Eco et al. 109–24.

———. "Paul de Man's Contribution to Literary Criticism and Theory." *The Future of Literary Theory*. Edited by Ralph Cohen. New York: Routledge, 1989. 268–79.

Curtis, James M. "Metaphor Is to Dostoevskii as Metonymy Is to Tolstoi." *Slavic Review* 61.1 (2002): 109–27.

Dal', Vladimir. *Tolkovyi slovar' zhivogo velikorusskogo iazyka*. Vol. 4. 1882. Rpt. Moscow: Khudozhestvennaia literatura, 1935.

Delbanco, Andrew. "The Decline and Fall of Literature." *New York Review of Books* 4 Nov. 1999: 32–38.

De Man, Paul. "The Rhetoric of Temporality." *Interpretation: Theory and Practice*. Edited by Charles Singleton. Baltimore, MD: Johns Hopkins University Press, 1969. 173–209.

De Mikiel, M. "O vospriiatii rabot Iu. M. Lotmana v Italii." *Lotmanovskii sbornik I*. Moscow: ITs-Garant, 1995. 294–306.

Derrida, Jacques. Letter to the Editors. *New York Review of Books* 11 Feb. 1993: 44–45.

———. Letter to the Editors. *New York Review of Books* 25 Mar. 1993: 65.

Dimock, Wai Chee. "A Theory of Resonance." *PMLA* 112 (1997): 1060–71.

Dostoevsky, Fyodor. *The Brothers Karamazov*. Translated and annotated by Richard Pevear and Larissa Volokhonsky. New York: Vintage, 1991.

———. *Crime and Punishment*. Translated and annotated by Richard Pevear and Larissa Volokhonsky. New York: Vintage, 1992.

Eakin, Paul J. *Fictions in Autobiography: Studies in the Art of Self-Invention*. Princeton, NJ: Princeton University Press, 1985.

Eco, Umberto. "Interpretation and History." Eco et al. 23–43.

———. *The Open Work*. Translated by Anna Cancogni. Cambridge, MA: Harvard University Press, 1989.

———. *A Theory of Semiotics*. Bloomington: Indiana University Press, 1979.

Eco, Umberto, Richard Rorty, Jonathan Culler, and Christine Brooke-Rose. *Interpretation and Overinterpretation*. Edited by Stefan Collini. Cambridge: Cambridge University Press, 1992.

Edelman, Gerald M. *Bright Air, Brilliant Fire: On the Matter of the Mind*. New York: Basic Books, 1992.

Eikhenbaum, Boris. "How Gogol's 'Overcoat' Is Made." 1918. *Gogol from the Twentieth Century: Eleven Essays.* Edited and translated by Robert A. Maguire. Princeton, NJ: Princeton University Press, 1974. 267–91.

————. *Lev Tolstoi: Semidesiatye gody.* 2nd ed. Leningrad: Khudozhestvennaia literatura, 1974.

Emerson, Caryl. "Prosaics in *Anna Karenina:* Pro and Con." *Tolstoy Studies Journal* 8 (1995–96): 150–76.

————. "The Tolstoy Connection in Bakhtin." *PMLA* 100 (1985): 68–80.

Ermilov, Vladimir V. *Tolstoi romanist.* Moscow: Khudozhestvennaia literatura, 1965.

Evans, Mary. *Reflecting on* Anna Karenina. London: Routledge, 1989.

Evdokimova, Svetlana. "The Drawing and the Grease Spot: Creativity and Interpretation in *Anna Karenina.*" *Tolstoy Studies Journal* 8 (1995–96): 33–45.

————. "Protsess khudozhestvennogo tvorchestva i avtorksii tekst." *Avtor i tekst.* Edited by V. M. Markovich and Wolf Schmidt. St. Petersburg: Izdatel'stvo S.-Peterburgskogo gosudarstvennogo universiteta, 1996. 9–24.

Farber, Daniel A., and Suzanne Sherry. *Beyond All Reason: The Radical Assault on Truth in American Law.* New York: Oxford University Press, 1997.

Feuer, Kathryn B. "Stiva." *Russian Literature and American Critics: In Honor of Deming Brown.* Edited by Kenneth N. Brostrom. Ann Arbor: University of Michigan, Department of Slavic Languages and Literatures, 1984. 347–56.

Fish, Stanley. "Change." *Doing What Comes Naturally: Change, Rhetoric, and the Practice of Theory in Literature and Legal Studies.* Durham, NC: Duke University Press, 1989. 140–60.

————. "Interpreting the *Variorum.*" *Reader-Response Criticism: From Formalism to Post-Structuralism.* Edited by Jane P. Tompkins. Baltimore, MD: Johns Hopkins University Press, 1980. 164–84.

————. "Why No One's Afraid of Wolfgang Iser." Review of *The Act of Reading* by Wolfgang Iser. *Diacritics* 11 (1981): 2–13.

Flaubert, Gustave. *The Letters of Gustave Flaubert 1830–1857.* Selected, edited, and translated by Francis Steegmuller. Cambridge, MA: Harvard University Press, 1980.

Flavell, John H. *The Developmental Psychology of Jean Piaget.* With a foreword by Jean Piaget. New York: Van Nostrand Reinhold, 1963.

Frank, Joseph. *Dostoevsky: The Miraculous Years, 1865–1871.* Princeton, NJ: Princeton University Press, 1995.

————. "Spatial Form in Modern Literature." *The Widening Gyre: Crisis and Mastery in Modern Literature.* Bloomington: Indiana University Press, 1963. 3–62.

Gadamer, Hans-Georg. *Truth and Method.* Translation revised by Joel Weinsheimer and Donald G. Marshall. 2nd rev. ed. New York: Crossroad, 1989.

Galan, František W. *Historic Structures: The Prague School Project, 1928–1946.* Austin: University of Texas Press, 1985.

Geertz, Clifford. "'From the Native's Point of View': On the Nature of Anthropological Understanding." 1974. *Culture Theory: Essays on Mind, Self, and Emotion.* Edited by Richard A. Shweder and Robert A. LeVine. Cambridge: Cambridge University Press, 1984. 123–36.

―――――. "Notes on the Balinese Cockfight." *The Interpretation of Cultures: Selected Essays.* New York: Basic Books, 1973. 412–53.

Gibian, George. "Two Kinds of Understanding and the Narrator's Voice in *Anna Karenina.*" *Anna Karenina* by Leo Tolstoy. Edited by George Gibian. New York: Norton, 1970. 813–22.

Ginzburg, Lydia. *On Psychological Prose.* Edited and translated by Judson Rosengrant. Princeton, NJ: Princeton University Press, 1991.

Gîtîtî, Gîtahi. "African Theory and Criticism." Groden and Kreiswirth 5–9.

Goldberger, Nancy Rule, and Jody Bennet Veroff, eds. *The Culture and Psychology Reader.* New York: New York University Press, 1995.

Gol'shtein, Pavel. *Roman L. N. Tolstogo* Anna Karenina *v svete epigrafa iz moiseeva vtorozakoniia.* Jerusalem: Hebrew University, 1990.

Gornaia, V. "Iz nabliudenii nad stilem romana *Anna Karenina.*" Blagoi et al. 181–206.

Goscilo-Kostin, Helena. "Tolstoyan Fare: Credo à la Carte." *Slavic and East European Review* 62.4 (1984): 481–95.

Greenblatt, Stephen. *Shakespearean Negotiations: The Circulation of Social Energy in Renaissance England.* Berkeley: University of California Press, 1988.

Groden, Michael, and Martin Kreiswirth, eds. *The Johns Hopkins Guide to Literary Theory and Criticism.* Baltimore, MD: Johns Hopkins University Press, 1994.

Gromov, Pavel. *O stile L'va Tolstogo. Stanovlenie "dialektiki dushi."* Leningrad: Khudozhestvennaia literatura, 1971.

Grossman, Joan Delaney. "'Words, Idle Words': Discourse and Communication in *Anna Karenina.*" McLean, *In the Shade* 115–29.

Grossman, Leonid. "Rannii zhanr Turgeneva." 1919. *Turgenev: Etiudy o Turgeneve — Teatr Turgeneva.* Moscow: N.p., 1928. 38–63.

Gusev, N. N. *Lev Nikolaevich Tolstoi: Materialy k biografii s 1870 po 1881 god.* Moscow: AN SSSR, 1963.

Gustafson, Richard F. *Leo Tolstoy: Resident and Stranger. A Study in Fiction and Theology.* Princeton, NJ: Princeton University Press, 1986.

Gutkin, Irina. "The Dichotomy between Flesh and Spirit: Plato's *Symposium* in *Anna Karenina.*" McLean, *In the Shade* 84–99.

Haney, David P. "Aesthetics and Ethics in Gadamer, Levinas and Romanticism: Problems of Phronesis and Techne." *PMLA* 114 (1999): 32–45.

Helms, Janet E. "Why Is There No Study of Cultural Equivalence in Standardized Cognitive Ability Testing?" Goldberger and Veroff 674–719.

Herman, David. "Allowable Passions in *Anna Karenina.*" *Tolstoy Studies Journal* 8 (1995–96): 5–32.

Hirsch, E. D. *The Aims of Interpretation.* Chicago: University of Chicago Press, 1978.

————. *Validity in Interpretation*. New Haven, CT: Yale University Press, 1967.

Holquist, Michael. *Dialogism: Bakhtin and His World*. New York: Routledge, 1990.

————. "The Supernatural as Social Force in *Anna Karenina*." *The Supernatural in Slavic and Baltic Literature: Essays in Honor of Victor Terras*. Edited by Amy Mandelker and Roberta Reeder. Columbus, OH: Slavica, 1988. 176–90.

Hruska, Anne. "Ghosts in the Garden: Anne Radcliffe and Tolstoy's *Childhood, Boyhood, Youth*." *Tolstoy Studies Journal* 9 (1997): 1–10.

Ingarden, Roman. *The Cognition of the Literary Work of Art*. Translated by Ruth Ann Crowly and Kenneth Olson. Evanston, IL: Northwestern University Press, 1973.

————. *The Literary Work of Art: An Investigation on the Borderlines of Ontology, Logic, and the Theory of Literature*. Translated by George G. Grabowicz. Evanston, IL: Northwestern University Press, 1973.

Ishchuk, Gennadii N. *Lev Tolstoi. Dialog s chitatelem*. Moscow: Kniga, 1984.

Iser, Wolfgang. *The Act of Reading: A Theory of Aesthetic Response*. Baltimore, MD: Johns Hopkins University Press, 1978.

————. "Interaction between Text and Reader." Suleiman and Crosman 106–19.

————. *Prospecting: From Reader Response to Literary Anthropology*. Baltimore, MD: Johns Hopkins University Press, 1989.

————. "Talk like Whales: A Reply to Stanley Fish." *Diacritics* 11 (1981): 82–87.

Jackson, Robert L. "The Ambivalent Beginning of *Anna Karenina*." *Semantic Analysis of Literary Texts: To Honour Jan van der Eng on the Occasion of His 65th Birthday*. Edited by Eric de Haard et al. Amsterdam: Elsevier, 1990. 345–52.

————. "Chance and Design in *Anna Karenina*." *The Disciplines of Criticism: Essays in Literary Theory, Interpretation and History*. Edited by Peter Demetz et al. New Haven, CT: Yale University Press, 1968. 315–29.

Jahn, Gary R. "The Image of the Railroad in *Anna Karenina*." *Slavic and East European Journal* 25.2 (1981): 1–10.

Jakobson, Roman. "Closing Statement: Linguistics and Poetics." *Style in Language*. Edited by Thomas A. Sebeok. Cambridge, MA: MIT Press, 1960. 350–77.

————. "A Few Remarks on Peirce, Pathfinder in the Science of Language." Jakobson, *The Framework of Language* 31–38.

————. *The Framework of Language*. Michigan Studies in the Humanities, Horace H. Rackham School of Graduate Studies. Ann Arbor: University of Michigan, 1980.

————. "Metalanguage as a Linguistic Problem." Jakobson, *The Framework of Language* 81–92.

————. *On Language*. Edited by Linda R. Waugh and Monique Monville-Burston. Cambridge, MA: Harvard University Press, 1990.

————. "On Realism in Art." 1921. *Language in Literature*. Cambridge, MA: Harvard University Press, 1987. 19–27.

_____. "The Speech Event and the Functions of Language." Jakobson, *On Language* 69–79.

_____. "Two Aspects of Language and Two Types of Aphasic Disturbances." 1956. Jakobson, *On Language* 115–33.

Jauss, Hans Robert. *Question and Answer: Forms of Dialogic Understanding*. Edited, translated, and with a foreword by Michael Hays. Minneapolis: University of Minnesota Press, 1989.

Khrapchenko, Boris. *Lev Tolstoi kak khudozhnik*. 4th ed. Moscow: Khudozhestvennaia literatura, 1978.

Knapp, Liza. "The Estates of Pokrovskoe and Vozdvizhenskoe: Tolstoy's Labyrinth of Linkings in *Anna Karenina*." *Tolstoy Studies Journal* 8 (1995–96): 81–98.

_____. "'Tue-la! Tue-la!': Death Sentences, Words, and Inner Monologues in Tolstoy's *Anna Karenina* and 'Three More Deaths.'" *Tolstoy Studies Journal* 11 (1999): 1–19.

Konick, Willis. "Tolstoy's Underground Woman: A Study of *Anna Karenina*." Bloom 45–61.

Kovalev, Vladislav. *Poetika L'va Tolstogo*. Moscow: Izdatel'stvo moskovskogo universiteta, 1983.

Kovarsky, Gina. "Mimesis and Moral Education in *Anna Karenina*." *Tolstoy Studies Journal* 8 (1995–96): 61–80.

Kozulin, Alex. "Vygotsky in Context." Vygotsky, *Thought and Language* xi–lxi.

Kujundzic, Dragan. "Pardoning Woman in *Anna Karenina*." *Tolstoy Studies Journal* 6 (1993): 65–85.

Kuleshov, Fedor I. *N. Tolstoi. Iz lektsii po russkoi literature XIX v.* Minsk: Izdatel'stvo belorusskogo gosudarstvennogo universiteta, 1978.

Kupreianova, Elizaveta N. *Estetika Tolstogo*. Moscow-Leningrad: Nauka, 1966.

K[urbskii], A. *Russkii rabochii u amerikanskogo plantatora. Vestnik evropy* June, July, Aug., and Sept. 1873, Oct. and Nov. 1874.

Kurrik, Maire Jaanus. "Tolstoy's *Anna Karenina:* The Self's Negativity." Bloom 97–110.

Landrine, Hope. "Clinical Implications of Cultural Differences: The Referential versus the Indexical Self." Goldberger and Veroff 744–66.

Latimer, Dan. "Paul de Man." *Contemporary Critical Theory*. Edited by Dan Latimer. New York: Harcourt Brace Jovanovich, 1989. 184–85.

LeBlanc, Ronald. "Unpalatable Pleasures: Tolstoy, Food, and Sex." *Tolstoy Studies Journal* 6 (1993): 1–32.

L. N. Tolstoi v vospominaniiakh sovremennikov. I. Moscow: Goslitizdat, 1955.

Lennkvist [Lönnqvist], Barbara. "'Medvezhii' motiv i simvolika neba v romane *Anna Karenina*." *Scando-Slavica* 41 (1995): 115–30.

Lentricchia, Frank. "Last Will and Testament of an Ex–Literary Critic." *Lingua Franca* 6.6 (1996): 59–67.

Leont'ev, Konstantin. *Analiz, stil' i veianie. O romanakh gr. L. N. Tolstogo. Kriticheskii etiud.* 1912. Rpt. Providence, RI: Brown University Press, 1965.

Lewis, Neil A. "For Black Scholars Wedded to Prism of Race, New and Separate Goals." *New York Times* 5 May 1997: B9.

Lomunov, K. N., ed. *Lev Tolstoi ob iskusstve i literature.* Moscow: Sovetskii pisatel', 1958.

Lönnqvist, Barbara. "Simvolika zheleza v romane *Anna Karenina.*" *Celebrating Creativity: Essays in Honor of Jostein Børtnes.* Bergen, Norway: University of Bergen, 1977. 97–107.

———. "A Text within a Text: The Dream in *Anna Karenina.*" *Scando-Slavica* 44 (1998): 75–83.

Lotman, Iurii. *Besedy o russkoi kul'ture: Byt i traditsii russkogo dvorianstva (XVIII—nachalo XIX veka).* St. Petersburg: Iskusstvo—SPB, 1994.

———. "Fenomen kul'tury." *Izbrannye stat'i: Tom I* 34–45.

———. *Izbrannye stat'i: Tom I, Stat'i po semiotike i tipologii kul'tury.* Tallinn: Aleksandra, 1992.

———. *Izbrannye stat'i: Tom III.* Tallinn: Aleksandra, 1993.

———. *Kul'tura i vzryv.* Moscow: Gnozis, 1992.

——— "Kul'tura kak sub"ekt i sama-sebe ob"ekt." *Izbrannye stat'i: Tom III* 368–75.

———. "Mozg—tekst—kul'tura." *Izbrannye stat'i: Tom I* 25–33.

———. "O semiosfere." *Izbrannye stat'i: Tom I* 11–24.

———. "Ritorika." *Izbrannye stat'i: Tom I* 167–83.

———. *Struktura khudozhestvennogo teksta.* 1970. Rpt. Providence, RI: Brown University Press, 1971.

———. "Tekst v tekste." *Izbrannye stat'i: Tom I* 148–60.

———. "Ustnaia rech' v istoriko-kul'turnoi perspektive." *Izbrannye stat'i: Tom I* 184–90.

Lotman, Yurii. *The Structure of the Artistic Text.* Translated by Ronald Vroon and Gail Vroon. Ann Arbor: University of Michigan, Department of Slavic Languages and Literatures, 1977.

Lukács, Georg. *The Theory of the Novel.* Translated by Anna Bostock. Cambridge, MA: MIT Press, 1971.

Lyotard, Jean-François. *The Postmodern Condition.* Minneapolis: University of Minnesota Press, 1984.

Mandelker, Amy. *Framing* Anna Karenina: *Tolstoy, the Woman Question, and the Victorian Novel.* Columbus: Ohio State University Press, 1993.

McLean, Hugh, ed. *In the Shade of the Giant: Essays on Tolstoy.* Berkeley: University of California Press, 1989.

———. "Jakobson's Metaphor/Metonymy Polarity: A Retrospective Glance." *Roman Jakobson: Texts, Documents, Studies.* Edited by Henry Baran and Sergej Gindin et al. Moscow: Rossiiskii gosudarstvennyi gumanitarnyi universitet, 1999. 725–32.

———. "Realism." *Handbook of Russian Literature.* Edited by Victor Terras. New Haven, CT: Yale University Press, 1985. 363–67.

_____. "Truth in Dying." McLean, *In the Shade* 130–57.

Melville, Herman. *Moby-Dick*. Edited by Harrison Hayford and Hershel Parker. New York: Norton, 1967.

Meyer, Paul W. "Romans." *Harper's Bible Commentary*. Edited by James L. Mays et al. San Francisco: Harper and Row, 1988.

Miller, J. Hillis. *The Ethics of Reading: Kant, de Man, Eliot, Trollope, James and Benjamin*. New York: Columbia University Press, 1987.

Mirsky, D. S. *A History of Russian Literature from Its Beginnings to 1900*. Edited by Francis J. Whitfield. New York: Vintage, 1958.

Mohanty, Satya P. "Epilogue. Colonial Legacies, Multicultural Futures: Relativism, Objectivity, and the Challenge of Otherness." *PMLA* 110 (1995): 108–18.

Morgan, Edmund S. "Back to Basics." Review of *Serving the Word: Literalism in America from the Pulpit to the Bench* by Vincent Crapanzano. *New York Review of Books* 20 July 2000: 47–49.

Morson, Gary Saul. *Hidden in Plain View: Narrative and Creative Potentials in War and Peace*. Stanford, CA: Stanford University Press, 1987.

_____. *Narrative and Freedom: The Shadows of Time*. New Haven, CT: Yale University Press, 1994.

_____. "Prosaics and *Anna Karenina*." *Tolstoy Studies Journal* 1 (1988): 1–12.

Morson, Gary Saul, and Caryl Emerson. *Mikhail Bakhtin: Creation of a Prosaics*. Stanford, CA: Stanford University Press, 1990.

Nabokov, Vladimir. *Ada or Ardor: A Family Chronicle*. New York: Vintage, 1969.

_____. "Anna Karenin." *Lectures on Russian Literature*. Edited by Fredson Bowers. New York: Harcourt Brace Jovanovich/Bruccoli Clark, 1981. 137–236.

_____. *Lolita*. New York: Vintage International, 1989.

_____. *Pnin*. New York: Vintage International, 1989.

Norris, Christopher. *What's Wrong with Postmodernism: Critical Theory and the Ends of Philosophy*. Baltimore, MD: Johns Hopkins University Press, 1990.

Orvin [Orwin], Donna. "Psikhologiia very v *Anne Kareninoi* i v *Brat'iakh Karamazovykh*." *Mir filologii*. Moscow: Nasledie, 2000. 235–45.

_____. "Zhanr Platonovykh dialogov i tvorchestvo Tolstogo." *Russkaia Literatura* 1 (2002): 38–45.

Orwin, Donna Tussing. *Tolstoy's Art and Thought, 1847–1880*. Princeton, NJ: Princeton University Press, 1993.

Padel, Ruth. *In and Out of the Mind: Greek Images of the Tragic Self*. Princeton, NJ: Princeton University Press, 1992.

Parker, David. *Ethics, Theory and the Novel*. Cambridge: Cambridge University Press, 1994.

Plato. The Symposium *and* The Phaedrus: *Plato's Erotic Dialogues*. Translated with an introduction and commentaries by William S. Cobb. Albany: State University of New York Press, 1993.

Prince, Gerald. "Notes on the Text as Reader." Suleiman and Crosman 225–40.

Pushkin, Aleksandr. *Eugene Onegin.* Translated with a commentary by Vladimir Nabokov. Vol. 1. Princeton, NJ: Princeton University Press, 1975.

Rancour-Laferriere, Daniel. "Anna's Adultery: Distal Sociobiology vs. Proximate Psychoanalysis." *Tolstoy Studies Journal* 6 (1993): 33–46.

Riffaterre, Michael. *Fictional Truth.* Baltimore, MD: Johns Hopkins University Press, 1990.

Ripp, Victor. "Ideology in Turgenev's *Notes of a Hunter:* The First Three Sketches." *Slavic Review* 38.1 (1979): 75–88.

Rivkin, Julie, and Michael Ryan. "Introduction: The Class of 1968—Post-Structuralism *par lui-même.*" *Literary Theory: An Anthology.* Edited by Julie Rivkin and Michael Ryan. Oxford: Blackwell, 1998. 333–57.

Rorty, Richard. "The Pragmatist's Progress." Eco et al. 89–108.

Rougement, Denis de. *Love in the Western World.* Translated by Montgomery Belgion. Rpt. New York: Fawcett, 1956.

Sacks, Oliver. "Making up the Mind." Review of *Bright Air, Brilliant Fire: On the Matter of the Mind* by Gerald M. Edelman. *New York Review of Books* 8 Apr. 1993: 42–49.

Schapiro, Leonard. *Turgenev: His Life and Times.* Cambridge, MA: Harvard University Press, 1978.

Schor, Naomi. "Fiction as Interpretation/Interpretation as Fiction." Suleiman and Crosman 165–82.

Schultze, Sydney. *The Structure of* Anna Karenina. Ann Arbor, MI: Ardis, 1982.

Shakespeare, William. *The Tragedy of Hamlet, Prince of Denmark.* Edited by Louis B. Wright et al. New York: Washington Square Press, 1963.

———. *The Tragedy of King Lear.* Edited by Russell Fraser. New York: New American Library, 1963.

Sheehan, Thomas. "A Normal Nazi." *New York Review of Books* 14 Jan. 1993: 30–35.

———. Reply. *New York Review of Books* 22 Apr. 1993: 69.

Shklovskii, Viktor. "Iskusstvo, kak priem." 1917. *Teoriia prozy.* Moscow: N.p., 1929. 7–23.

———. *Lev Tolstoi.* 2nd ed. Moscow: Molodaia gvardiia, 1967.

Shweder, Richard A. "Cultural Psychology: What Is It?" *Cultural Psychology: Essays on Comparative Human Development.* Edited by James W. Stigler, Richard A. Shweder, and Gilbert Herdt. Cambridge: Cambridge University Press, 1990. 1–43.

Šilbajoris, Rimvydas. *Tolstoy's Aesthetics and His Art.* Columbus, OH: Slavica, 1990.

Skaftymov, Aleksandr P. "Idei i formy v tvorchestve L. Tolstogo." *Nravstvennye iskaniia russkikh pisatelei.* Moscow: Khudozhestvennaia literatura, 1972. 134–64.

Slavinskii, Nikolai E. *Pis'ma ob Amerike i russkikh pereselentsakh.* St. Petersburg: Merkuliev, 1873.

Sloane, David A. "Pushkin's Legacy in *Anna Karenina*." *Tolstoy Studies Journal* 4 (1991): 1–23.

Sorokin, Boris. *Tolstoy in Prerevolutionary Russian Criticism*. Oxford, OH: Miami University Press, 1979.

Spinoza, Benedict. The Ethics *and Other Texts*. Translated by Edwin Curley. Princeton, NJ: Princeton University Press, 1994.

Stenbock-Fermor, Elisabeth. *The Architecture of* Anna Karenina: *A History of Its Structure, Writing and Message*. Lisse: Peter de Ridder Press, 1975.

Striedter, Jurij. *Literary Structure, Evolution and Value: Russian Formalism and Czech Structuralism Reconsidered*. Cambridge, MA: Harvard University Press, 1989.

Suleiman, Susan R., and Inge Crosman, eds. *The Reader in the Text: Essays on Audience and Interpretation*. Princeton, NJ: Princeton University Press, 1980.

Terras, Victor. *Belinskij and Russian Literary Criticism: The Heritage of Organic Aesthetics*. Madison: University of Wisconsin Press, 1974.

Thorlby, Anthony. *Leo Tolstoy:* Anna Karenina. Cambridge: Cambridge University Press, 1987.

Todorov, Tzvetan. *The Conquest of America*. Translated by Richard Hower. New York: Harper, 1984.

———. "Introduction au vraisemblable." *Poétique de la prose*. Paris: Editions du Seuil, 1971. 92–99.

———. "Reading as Construction." Suleiman and Crosman 67–82.

——— "Sign." *Encyclopedic Dictionary of the Sciences of Language* by Oswald Ducrot and Tzvetan Todorov. Translated by Catherine Porter. Baltimore, MD: Johns Hopkins University Press, 1979. 99–106.

Tolstoi, Lev N. *Anna Karenina. Sobranie sochinenii v dvadtsati tomakh. Tom vos'moi. Tom deviatyi*. Moscow: Khudozhestvennaia literatura, 1963.

———. *Anna Karenina*. Literaturnye Pamiatniki. Edited by V. A. Zhdanov and E. E. Zaidenshnur. Moscow: Nauka, 1970.

———. *Pis'ma. 1845–1886 gg. Sobranie sochinenii v dvadsati tomakh. Tom semnadtsatyi*. Moscow: Khudozhestvennaia literatura, 1965.

———. *Polnoe sobranie sochinenii*. Vol. 20. Edited by V. G. Chertkov et al. Moscow: Khudozhestvennaia literatura, 1939.

———. "Predislovie k sochineniiam Giui de Mopassana." *Sobranie sochinenii v dvadsati tomakh. Tom piatnadtsatyi*. Moscow: Khudozhestvennaia literatura, 1964. 247–71.

Tolstoy, Leo. *Anna Karenina*. Translated by Louise Maude and Aylmer Maude, rev. George Gibian. 2nd ed. New York: Norton, 1970.

———. *Anna Karenina*. Translated by Richard Pevear and Larissa Volokhonsky. New York: Viking Penguin, 2001.

———. *War and Peace*. Translated by Ann Dunnigan. New York: Signet, 1968.

Tooby, John, and Leda Cosmides. "The Psychological Foundations of Cultures." *The Adapted Mind: Evolutionary Psychology and the Generation of Culture*.

Edited by Jerome H. Barkow, Leda Cosmides, and John Tooby. New York: Oxford University Press, 1992. 19–136.

Toporov, V. N. "Prostranstvo i tekst." *Iz rabot moskovskogo semioticheskogo kruga.* Edited by T. M. Nikolaeva. Moscow: Iazyki russkoi kul'tury, 1997. 455–515.

Turgenev, Ivan. *Fathers and Sons.* Translated by Ralph Matlaw. New York: Norton, 1966.

———. *Ottsy i deti. Polnoe sobranie sochinenii i pisem. Tom vos'moi.* Moscow-Leningrad: Nauka, 1964. 193–402.

———. *Zapiski okhotnika. Polnoe sobranie sochinenii i pisem. Tom chetvertyi.* Moscow-Leningrad: Nauka, 1963.

Turner, C. J. G. "Blood Is Thicker than Champagne: The Bonds of Kinship and the Marriage-Bond in *Anna Karenina.*" *Lev Tolstoy and the Concept of Brotherhood.* Ottawa: Legas, 1996. 128–41.

———. *A Karenina Companion.* Waterloo, Ontario: Wilfrid Laurier University Press, 1993.

Tverskoi, Petr A. [Petr A. Dement'ev]. *Desiat' let v Amerike, iz lichnykh vospominanii. Vestnik evropy* Jan., Feb., Mar., Apr., and May 1893; "Moia zhizn' v Amerike." *Vestnik evropy* Jan. 1894.

Uspenskii, Boris. *Poetika kompozitsii.* Moscow: Iskusstvo, 1970.

Uspenskii, I. N. "Roman *Anna Karenina.*" *Tvorchestvo Tolstogo. Sbornik statei.* Edited by M. B. Khrapchenko et al. Moscow: AN SSSR, 1954. 201–78.

Veresaev, Vikentii V. [Smidovich]. *Zhivaia zhizn'. I. O Dostoevskom i L've Tolstom.* Moscow: Kushnerev, 1911.

Vodička, Felix. "Response to Verbal Art." *Semiotics of Art: Prague School Contributions.* Edited by Ladislav Matejka and Irwin R. Titunik. Cambridge, MA: MIT Press, 1976. 197–208.

Vygotsky, Lev. *The Psychology of Art.* Cambridge, MA: MIT Press, 1971.

———. *Thought and Language.* Translated by Alex Kozulin. Cambridge, MA: MIT Press, 1986.

Wachtel, Andrew. "Death and Resurrection in *Anna Karenina.*" McLean, *In the Shade* 100–114.

Wasiolek, Edward. *Tolstoy's Major Fiction.* Chicago: University of Chicago Press, 1978.

Watt, Ian. *The Rise of the Novel.* Berkeley: University of California Press, 1957.

Waugh, Linda R. "The Poetic Function and the Nature of Language." *Verbal Art, Verbal Sign, Verbal Time* by Roman Jakobson. Edited by Krystyna Pomorska and Stephen Rudy. Oxford: Basil Blackwell, 1985. 143–68.

Weir, Justin. "Anna Incommunicada: Language and Consciousness in *Anna Karenina.*" *Tolstoy Studies Journal* 8 (1995–96): 99–111.

Wellek, René. "The Concept of Realism in Literary Scholarship." *Concepts of Criticism.* Edited by Stephen J. Nichols. New Haven, CT: Yale University Press, 1963. 222–55.

Williams, Patricia J. *The Alchemy of Race and Rights*. Cambridge, MA: Harvard University Press, 1991.

Wilson, A. N. *Tolstoy*. New York: Fawcett Columbine, 1988.

Wolfe, Cary. "In Search of Post-Humanist Theory: The Second-Order Cybernetics of Maturana and Varela." *Cultural Critique* 30 (1995): 58–75.

Wolin, Richard. Reply to Letter of Jacques Derrida. *New York Review of Books* 25 Mar. 1993: 66.

Wordsworth, William. "Ode: Intimations of Immortality from Recollections of Early Childhood." *The Norton Anthology of English Literature*. Vol. 2. Edited by M. H. Abrams et al. New York: Norton, 1968. 149–54.

Zurbuchen, Mary Sabina. *The Language of Balinese Shadow Theater*. Princeton, NJ: Princeton University Press, 1987.

Index

Achebe, Chinua, 43–44, 45
Agafya Mikhailovna, 162–63, 236, 262
Aldanov, Mark, 309n8
Alexander II, 208
alterity, cognizing, 11, 29–31, 33
Andersen, Hans Christian, 330n5
Anna, 69–71, 76–79, 80–85, 98, 99, 108,
    110, 114–15, 122, 128, 129, 130, 135, *13.3*,
    13.5, 13.8, 226, 229–30, 236–38, 241–
    42, *15.3,* 254, 259–63, 267, *17.3,* 294,
    296, 322n43, 328n4 *(14)*, 330n3, 330n6,
    330n7, 331n13, 331n14; death of, *8.2,*
    13.5.4, 200, *17.1;* and Frou-Frou, 102–
    3, 315n7; Mikhailov's compared to
    Tolstoy's, 84; red handbag of, 315n4,
    324n55, 330n4. *See also* horse race
Anna Karenina, form of, *10;* language in, *11,*
    147; overviews of critical responses to,
    73–74, 93, 290, 329n4
Annenkov, Pavel, 208
aphasia, 36. *See also* Jakobson, Roman
Arnold, Matthew, 18
Attridge, Derek, 302n10, 304n4, 304n6,
    304n7, 332n3
authority: fictional, *12.1;* textual, 54, 58–59

Babaev, Eduard, 329n4
Bakhtin, Mikhail, 13, 27, 30–31, 36, 136, 158,
    159, 303n31, 310n12, 318n3, 319n10
Balkan war, 225, 241, 313n12, 321n30
Barthes, Roland, 27, 306n15
Bayley, John, 320n22, 327n83
bears, 283–84, *17.3*
Belinskii, Vissarion, 208
Bely, Andrei, 41, 42, 47, 112

Berlin, Isaiah, 73–74, 309n8
Bethea, David, 318n6
Betsy, Princess, 69–70, 110, 132, 144, 180–
    81, 189, 196, 230, 242
Blackmur, R. P., 321n28
Booth, Wayne, 303n26, 304n7 *(1)*
brain, 33, 297
Brooke-Rose, Christine, 306n1
Brooks, Peter, 301n7
Bruner, Jerome, 29, 30
Buell, Lawrence, 303n2
bureaucracy, government, 241

Catteau, Jacques, 314n4 *(10)*
celestial bodies, 284–85, 331n10. *See also* sky
Chamisso, Adalbert, 330n5
chance, 85–86, 92–93, 191, *18,* 315n10
characters, descriptions of, 89, 137, 138, 145,
    154, 178, 243–44, 313n16
charity, Christian, 68, 122–23, *12.6,* 148–49,
    154, 170, 188, 214–15, 226–28, 230. *See
    also* Saint Paul
Chekhov, Anton, 53, 74, 319n9
Chernyshevsky, Nikolai, 190, 313n16
children, 132, 166–67, 184–85, 187, 220, 225,
    236, 261, 265–66. *See also* Seryozha
Christ, 221–22
Christian, R. F., 316n3 *(12),* 320n20, 320n22,
    330n3; and "situation rhymes," 98
clothing, semiotics of, 223, *18,* 292–93, 294,
    333n4. *See also* wedding
coercion, collective, *14.2, 14.3*
conscience, *15*
consciousness: biological basis of, 29; and
    dialogue, 32, 33, 57

contingency, and artistic form, 90, 92–93, *18. See also* chance
Cord, 77, 217
Cornillot, François, 314n4 *(10)*
critical race theory, 16
criticism, academic literary, 3–7, 13, 14, 16, 21–22, 30
"crude force," *12.5*, 242
Culler, Jonathan, 54, 58–59, 302n25
cultural contexts, 11–13, 26, 46, 47, 52, 53
culture, and misunderstanding, 59
cultures, non-Western, 11–13
Curtis, James, 315n6
Czech Structuralism, 21, 301n5

Darwin, Charles, 164
deconstruction, 8, 18, 73
defamiliarization, 46, 109, 155, 237–38
Delbanco, Andrew, 301n2
De Man, Paul, 17–18, 302n25, 302n26
De Rougement, Denis, 323n48
Derrida, Jacques, 16–17, 28, 58, 301n5
De Saussure, Ferdinand, 32
determinism, 226, *15, 16.5.2*, 288, 292
dialogue, 136, 188, 190–91, 319n9
Dilthey, Wilhelm, 51
Dimock, Wai Chee, 307n34
divorce, 323n45, 323n51, 328n2 *(15)*
Dolly, 71, 75–76, 77, 116, 132, 158, 172–74, 184–85, 191, 197, 201–2, 204, 207–8, *13.7*, 225, 236–37, 251, 259–65, 283, 294, 327n82, 329n5
Dostoevsky, Fyodor, 41, 45, 48, 52–53, 69, 89, 113, 136, 190, 273, 306n1, 321n30, 322n36
doubling, 150, *13.5.8*, 207, 225, 235, 251
dreams, 82, 200, 220, 242, 278–82, 286–87, 330n3, 330n6
dueling, 219, 221–22, 327n85

Eakin, Paul J., 330n1
Eco, Umberto, 23, 32, 51, 54–55, 57–58
Edelman, Gerald, 29–30
Eikhenbaum, Boris, 18, 67, 308n2, 309n9, 309n10, 314n4 *(9)*, 315n7, 317n5, 318n5, 325n66, 329n4, 330n3
Einstein, Albert, 11, 168

Emerson, Caryl, 318n8, 328n2 *(14)*
emotion, 9–10
epigraph, 67–70, 82, 121–22, 179, 185, 189, 198, 212, 227, 233, 252, 273, 308n3, 309n7, 309n10, 310n11, 318n5, 324n59. *See also* vengeance
Ermilov, Vladimir, 308n3, 312n7, 320n15, 321n30, 322n35
essentialism, 151, 237, *16*, 286
ethics, 137–38, 144, 146, 162, *13.5.7, 13.5.8*, 204, 211, 212, 217, 226, 243–44, *15*, 253, 295–96, 311n20, 322n35, 326n74, 327n81; and literary study, 25–28, 33, 302n26, 303n2
Europe, 268
evaluation, literary, 19
Evans, Mary, 318n13, 322n42, 323n44, 323n46, 323n47, 325n64, 327n80
Evdokimova, Svetlana, 313n12
evil, *14.3*

faith, nature of, *12.3, 12.7, 13.4.4*, 190; self-deception and, *12.3*
falsehood, sense of, 253, 254
family, theme of, 70–71, *12.7*, 187, 208, 211, 215, 236, 239, 268, 310n13
fate, 82, 92, 171–72, 177, 200, 258, *17, 18*, 296, 322n43, 330n3, 330n7, 331n13, 331n14, 332n2
feminism, 309n9, 310n10, 312n4, 318n13, 330n8
Fet, Afanasii, 314n4 *(9)*, 324n54
Feuer, Kathryn B., 316n13, 325n64
first sentence, 70–71, 180, 233, 310n11
Fish, Stanley, 54, 56–57, 307n25, 307n28
Flaubert, Gustave, 48, 135
form, literary, 21, 46, 81, 88, 90, *8.6, 10*, 193, 226, *16.2.2*, 277, 289, *18*, 313n12, 315n10, 332n14 *(17)*, 332n2, 333n6
Frank, Joseph, 95, 306n1, 314n2 *(10)*
freedom, 68–69, 196–97, 198, *13.5.8*, 201–2, *16.5, 18*, 321n34, 328n1 *(15)*, 329n7
Freud, Sigmund, 64, 73

Gadamer, Hans-Georg, 36, 304n4
Geertz, Clifford, 12, 14–15, 57, 306n1
geocentrism, 168

Ginzburg, Lydia, 316n3 *(11)*, 316n4, 319n9, 321n34, 331n11, 333n6
gnosticism, 170, 326n72
God, 67–70, 130, 137, 168, 173, 187, 190, 195, 227, 247–50
Gogol, Nikolai, 52, 107, 155, 199
Gornaia, V., 318n5, 320n17, 325n66, 329n2
Goscilo-Kostin, Helena, 328n3 *(14)*
gothic, 199, 325n70
Greenblatt, Stephen, 13
Gromov, Pavel, 313n16
Grossman, Joan, 323n50
Grossman, Leonid, 326n76
Gustafson, Richard, 309n7, 312n4, 312n8, 313n17, 314n4 *(10)*, 317n6, 319n13, 320n16, 320n23, 322n39, 322n41, 323n44, 325n63, 330n6
Gutkin, Irina, 320n24, 321n31

Habermas, Jürgen, 301n5
Haney, David, 302n17, 304n4 *(1)*, 305n9
Heidegger, Martin, 16, 58
Herman, David, 311n24, 312n3, 312n5, 320n15, 321n33
hermeneutic circle, 14–15, 51, 57
hermeneutic indices: and critical reception of literary works, 54, 65; defined and characteristics of, 38, 44–45, 50–51, 53–54, 64, 227; illustrated, 39–44, 64; inherent or projected, 54–59; and the novel, 53, 54; utility of, 48, 50, 63
Herzen, Aleksandr, 208
Hirsch, E. D., 302n18, 304n7 *(1)*
Hoffman, E. T. A., 199
Holquist, Michael, 304n3 *(2)*, 304n8, 305n2 *(3)*, 317n8, 319n10, 330n3
holy foolishness, 169
horse race, 143, 287, 315n7. *See also* Anna, and Frou-Frou
Hruska, Anne, 325n70
humor, 111, 116–17, 232

idealism, 119–20, 136–37
immortality, 266
inconsistencies, 72–73, 74, 92, 111, 133, 180, 206–7, 254–55, 268–69, 272, 276–77

indeterminacies, 70, 82, 85, 99, 101, 103–4, 106, 114, 117–18, 137–38, 146, 154, 160, 164–65, 166, 169, 170, 227, 248–49, 250, 254–56, 268, 277, 281–82, 295–97, 298
Ingarden, Roman, 51, 301n6, 307n16
intention, authorial, 15
interpretation, circularity of, 3, 7, 10; consensus about, 66; limits of, 8, 9, 11, 15, 18, 19, 48, 49–50, 51; mediation of, 10, 11; novelty of, 3–6, 8; plurality of, 8, 9
Iser, Wolfgang, 37, 51, 54, 56, 57, 305n10, 306n16
Ishchuk, Gennadii, 323n49, 324n59
Ivanov, A. A., 97
Ivanovna, Countess Lydia, 76, 125, 128, 164, 165, 174, 176, 189, 238, 241, 282

Jackson, Robert, 309n6, 310n14, 316n12, 318n5, 322n43, 330n3
Jahn, Gary R., 328n4 *(14)*
Jakobson, Roman, 4, 5, 20–21, 32, 34–37, 38, 39, 44–45, 50, 53, 54, 55, 64, 71, 95–96, 105–6, 136, 288, 289, 301n5, 305n1 *(3)*, 306n13, 306n15, 314n4 *(10)*, 319n11, 332n16; and functions of language, 34–35, 55, 71; and language acquisition, 57; and metalingual function, 35–36, 44–45, 50, 57, 64. *See also* poetic function
Jauss, Hans-Robert, 36

Kafka, Franz, 112
Kant, Immanuel, 25–26, 28, 58, 154, 302n26, 304n3, 331n12
Karenin, 69, 76, 85, 93, 108, 115, *12.3–12.7*, 165, 167, 175–76, 178, *13.5.6*, 199–200, 213–14, 218, 219, *13.10*, 232, 237–38, 241, 242, 245–46, 254, 260, 263, 264, 281, 282, 286, 288, 294, 295–96, 317n5, 317n9, 317n10
Kartsevskii, Sergei, 305n3 *(4)*
Khomiakov, Aleksei, 169
Khrapchenko, Boris, 310n10, 312n2, 312n7, 324n60, 327n80
Kitty, 77, 80, 84, 93–94, 98, 109, 116, 117,

Kitty *(continued)*
  131, *13.3, 13.4.1,* 152–53, 162, 163–64,
  169–70, 179, 187, 188, 189, 192, 212,
  215, 217, *13.9,* 234–35, 236, 237, 246,
  247, *15.4,* 259–62, 264, *16.2.2,* 272,
  273, 281, *17.2,* 293–94, 313n11, 327n86,
  329n8, 331n7; and Petrov, situation
  rhymes for, *10.2*
Knapp, Liza, 316n13, 330n4
Konick, Willis, 322n41
Kovarsky, Gina, 326n74
Koznyshev, 79–80, 81, 90–91, 107, 122, 131,
  137, 143, 152–56, 188, 231–32, 247, 259,
  263, 264, 274–75, 329n8
Kujundzic, Dragan, 309n9
Kupreianova, Elizaveta, 319n13, 324n52
Kurrik, Maire Jaanus, 318n8

Lacan, Jacques, 305n8
Landau, 189, 193, 282, 332n14
language: acquisition of, 36, 57; mediation
  of, 55–56, *11,* 250, 259–61, 289; owner-
  ship of, 28. *See also* Jakobson, Roman
Latimer, Dan, 302n25
LeBlanc, Ronald, 333n6
Lentricchia, Frank, vii, 15, 18
Leont'ev, Konstantin, 318n5, 324n53,
  327n84, 330n3
Lermontov, Mikhail, 139, 140
Leskov, Nikolai, 309n8
Lessing, Gotthold Ephraim, 332n2
Levin, 77, 80, 81–82, 84, 88–91, 93–94, 97,
  98, 99, 108–9, 120–21, 124, 128–29, 131,
  137, *13.3, 13.4.1–13.4.4,* 179, 187, 189,
  191–92, 202–8, 212–13, 216, 225, 234–35,
  238–39, 241, 242, *15.2,* 252–53, *16.1,* 262,
  263, *16.2.2,* 267, 268–69, *16.5.1,* 280,
  17.2, 17.3, 292–94, 296, 313n11, 317n5,
  321n30, 322n36, 329n3, 330n7, 333n4
Linon, Mlle, 283, 288, 331n9
literariness, 20–21, 34–35, 55–56, 74
literature, assumptions about, 13
Lomunov, K. N., 325n69
Lönnqvist, Barbara, 331n6, 331n9, 332n15
Lotman, Yurii, vii, 4, 6, 11, 20, 32, 33, 52, 53,
  54, 59, 134, 139, 210, 290–91, 292,
  303n31, 315n9, 319n10, 331n8

Lúkacs, Georg, 134–35
Lyotard, Jean-François, 13

Mandelker, Amy, 308n3, 310n10, 312n4,
  312n7, 312n10, 312n11, 313n13, 313n15,
  314n1 *(9),* 321n33, 323n44, 324n59,
  324n60, 325n61, 325n68, 327n82,
  329n8, 330n2, 330n5, 331n9
mapping, geological, 49–50
Mark, Saint, 317n10
Márquez, Gabriel Garcia, 112
Matvei, 72, 292–93
McLean, Hugh, 311n19, 319n11, 321n27, 321n29
meaning: literary, 20–21, 35, 86, 135; plausibility of, 20
"meaning," meaning of, 32, 33, 38
meanings, map of, 48, 49–50, 51, 53, 54, 64,
  101, 104, 114
mediation, problem of, 11, 13, 15, 16, 18, 53–
  54, 55–59
Merezhkovskii, Dmitrii, 309n6, 315n7
Merkalova, Liza, 133, 180, 192
metaphor, 21, 47–48
metaphor and metonymy, *10.1,* 315n6
Metrov, 158–59
Miagky, Princess, 261, 280
Mikhailov, *8.3, 8.4, 9.1,* 93, 95–97, 162, 187,
  200, 223–24, 271, 283, 296, 312n11,
  314n1 *(9)*
Miller, J. Hillis, 302n26
Mirsky, D. S., 295
Moby-Dick, 35, 42, 45, 46
Mohanty, Satya, 25–26, 304n3
Morson, Gary Saul, 310n12, 313n12, 314n1
  (9), 315n10, 322n40, 322n43, 322n44,
  324n53, 325n62, 327n80, 327n86,
  330n3, 331n6, 331n7, 331n14, 332n1,
  332n2, 333n4
Moscow-Tartu School, 21
mowing scene, Levin's, 143–44
Mukařovský, Jan, 46
multiculturalism, 25–28
mushrooms, 277–78, 230n2

Nabokov, Vladimir, 42, 53, 141, 310n17,
  311n18, 313n12, 317n4, 318n4, 324n52,
  324n54, 325n61, 327n85, 331n6, 332n14

names, personal, 11, 12
narrator, role of, *12.2, 12.3,* 132–33, *13.1, 13.2,* 144, 176–77, 178, 193, 209–11, 212, 225, 265, 276–77, 279, 318n5
nature, 116, 135, *16.1,* 261, 329n3
nature, human, *12.6,* 257, *16.1,* 327n81
Nekrasov, Nikolai, 208
Neoplatonism, 92, 94, 200
neopragmatism, 54
Nez Percé oral narrative, 42–43
Nikolai, 80, 151–53, 188, 228, 237, 239, 246–47, 258–59, 261–62, *16.2.2,* 272, 274, 281, 329n3
Nirvana, 314n4 *(9)*
Nordston, Countess, 118
novel, different viewpoints in, 134–35, *13.2,* 207

Obolensky, A. D., 318n5
Old Testament, 67
orality, 53, 67
"orature," 13
Orwin, Donna, 309n9, 310n11, 311n17, 311n22, 312n7, 316n12, 317n5, 317n11, 318n14, 319n9, 319n13, 320n24, 322n36, 322n37, 322n38, 323n49, 325n65, 325n67, 326n73, 328n1 *(15),* 328n1 *(16),* 329n3, 329n7, 331n12
"overstanding," 58–59

Padel, Ruth, 57
Parker, David, 311n20
passivity, 273
patriarchal viewpoint, 265, 267
Paul, Saint, *12.6,* 166, 188, 206, 245; I Corinthians, 122, *12.7,* 169, 245; Romans, 67–69, 84, 121–22, 148–49, 162, 170, 179, 221, 228, 308n2, 309n7
peasants, 236, 238, 259, *16.4,* 271–72, 274, 329n7
Peirce, Charles Sanders, 27, 32, 306n1
perception, relativization of, 72–73, 83–85, 113–14, 124–26, *12.6,* 132–33, *13,* 243–44, *15,* 264, 269, 275, 281, 286–87, 295–96, 319n13, 322n43
peripeties, 198
Pestsov, 263, 264

Petrov, 226, 228
philology, classical, 47, 57
Piaget, Jean, 29, 30, 304n3
Plato, 150, 161
Platon, 162, 163, 248, 329n7
Plotinus, 92–93, 314n1 *(9)*
PMLA, 4–5, 7
poetic function, 20–21, 34–35, 97–98, 106, 136, 288, 314n4 *(10),* 332n2. *See also* Jakobson, Roman
poetry, 314n4 *(9)*
political correctness, 26–27
poststructuralism, 6, 16–18, 19–20, 22, 309n9
Prince, Gerald, 306n1
psychology: ancient Greek, 57; cognitive, 29, 30; cultural, 11–13
Pushkin, Aleksandr, 40–41, 46, 47–48, 196, 318n5, 325n66

Rachinskii, Sergei, 104–5
Rancour-Laferriere, Daniel, 325n68
reader, role of, 50, 51, 79, 91, 98, 99, 101, 103–4, 130–31, *13.2,* 208, 211, 277, 288, 326n74, 326n76
reading: default assumptions about, 65; depictions of, *8;* and dialogue, 36–37
realism, 136–37
reality, spiritual, 200–201, 243, *16.2.2,* 314n4 *(9),* 324n54
reason, 188–89, 220–21
religious fundamentalism, 16
revelation, as redefinition, 248, 249
Revelation, of Saint John the Divine, 166
Riffaterre, Michael, 316n1 *(12)*
Ripp, Victor, 326n76
Rorty, Richard, 54, 57–58
Rousseau, Jean-Jacques, 261, 268
Russian Formalism, 21, 46, 88, 305n2 *(3)*
Russianness, 286, 287

Sacks, Oliver, 30
Sappho Stolz, 239–40
Schapiro, Leonard, 326n75
Schopenhauer, Arthur, 67, 77, 126, 129, 161, 308n2, 317n5, 324n52, 330n3
Schor, Naomi, 306n1

Schultze, Sydney, 310n15, 314n1 (10), 315n6, 324n57, 329n2, 331n9, 333n6
selfhood, conceptions of, 11–13, 32, 33
semantic fields, 35, 36, 45–46
serfdom, 208–9
Seryozha, 114, 168, 176, 177–78, 181–82, 222–23, 231, 254. See also children
sex, 12.7, 239–40, 318n13, 330n6, 333n6
shadows, 279–80, 330n5
Shakespeare, William, 47, 89, 165
Shcherbatsky, Prince, 107–8, 109, 263, 267
Sheehan Thomas, 16–17
Shklovsky, Viktor, 46, 318n2, 322n36, 323n49
Šilbajoris, Rimvydas, 312n1, 312n4, 313n15, 314n1 (9), 330n3
similarity and contiguity, 21, 36, 38. See also poetic function
Skaftymov, Aleksandr P., 313n16, 319n13
sky, 168, 284–85. See also celestial bodies
Sloane, David, 322n43
snowstorm, 279–80, 325n67
Socialist Realism, 8, 15–16, 309n9
solipsism, 119–20, 145, 155–56, 177, 190, 220
Sorokin, Princess, 185–86
Spinoza, Benedict, 294
Stahl, Mme, 109, 226–27
Stenbock-Fermor, Elisabeth, 311n19, 312n6, 315n5, 316n11, 316n13, 318n6, 321n32, 321n33, 322n35, 324n54-n56, 328n1 (14), 328n2 (15), 330n8
Stiva, 64, 69–76, 107–8, 109, 115–16, 117, 144, 156–58, 172–74, 193, 194, 196, 13.6, 211–12, 214, 236, 240, 15.1, 251, 252, 264, 267, 278, 283, 284, 292–93, 308n1, 325n71, 326n73, 328n2 (14), 328n1 (15), 328n2 (15)
St. Petersburg, 239–40
Strakhov, Nikolai, 105
stream of consciousness, 129, 186
Striedter, Jurij, 21, 134, 307n16, 307n21
structuralism, 3, 8, 21–22, 301n1
style, 71–72, 121–22, 195, 234, 258, 311n18, 329n2
subtext, 51–52
suicide, 220, 221. See also Anna, death of

supernatural, the, 199–200. See also reality, spiritual
Sviyazhsky, 148, 237, 260

teeth, 230, 333n6
terminology, problem of, 20, 311n21
Terras, Victor, 314n1
textual patterning, and fate, 287, 288–89
Thorlby, Anthony, 324n58, 325n61
time: conceptions of, 12, 13, 320n20; lacunae in, 98; relative, 72, 98, 103, 13.3, 200, 251
Todorov, Tzvetan, 32–33, 305n1 (3), 306n1, 316n1 (12)
Tolstoy, Leo, 28, 53, 144, 154, 199, 200–201, 247, 260, 276, 277, 310n13, 314n3 (9), 321n29, 326n73, 327n81, 331n9; about Anna Karenina, 10.3, 135; "Alyosha the Pot," 228; "The Death of Ivan Ilich," 80, 187; "Father Sergius," 190; "God Sees the Truth, but Waits," 228; "Kreutzer Sonata," 132; "Master and Man," 187; Resurrection, 190; "Three Deaths," 48; "The Three Hermits," 228; War and Peace, 46, 70, 73, 74, 80, 95, 112–13, 135, 149, 159, 162, 168, 171, 187, 228, 239, 248, 249, 273, 274, 280, 285, 316n2 (11), 318n5, 329n3; What is Art?, 85, 312n11
Toporov, V. N., 306n12
Torgovnick, Maria, 320n26
trains, 135, 268, 278, 315n5, 318n6, 333n6
translation, 32, 35, 36, 40
Turgenev, Ivan, 39–40, 48, 51–52, 89, 13.6.2, 320n22
Turner, C. J. G., 317n5, 320n26, 321n28
Turovtsyn, 264
Tynianov, Yurii, 46

United States, Russian views of, 41
unity, 14.1, 257, 16, 266, 278, 328n1 (14)
universals, human, 13, 14
urban culture, 158, 239–40, 259, 261, 294. See also St. Petersburg
Uspenskii, Boris, 210
Uspenskii, I. N., 322n41

value, literary, 52–53
value, relativization of, 146, 196, 202. *See also* perception, relativization of
Varenka, 107, 131, 226–27, 274–75, 329n8, 330n2
Vasenka Veslovsky, 157, 189, 232, 253
vengeance, 67–70, 82, 122, 185, 189, 221, 230. *See also* epigraph
Veresaev, Vikentii, 310n10, 311n23, 322n36, 323n49, 325n62, 328n87, 329n3
viewpoints, in narrative, *13.2*
Vodička, Felix, 51, 301n6, 307n16
Vronsky, 69, 71, 76, 77, 82–83, 86–87, 92–94, 98, 103, 110–11, 114–15, 122–23, 135, *13.3, 13.5,* 193, 197–98, 207–8, 213, *13.8,* 230–32, 240, *15.3,* 252, 253, *15.5,* 255–56, 260–61, 263, 267, 269, 278–82, *17.3,* 294, 327n84; brother of, 240
Vygotsky, Lev, 29, 30, 304n3 *(2)*

Wachtel, Andrew, 318n4, 324n60
Wasiolek, Edward, 311n22, 317n7, 318n12, 323n51, 323n52, 330n6, 331n13
Watt, Ian, 134
wedding, 292–94. *See also* clothing, semiotics of
Weir, Justin, 316n1 *(11)*
Wellek, René, 319n10
wisdom, women's, 261–62, *16.2.2,* 281
Wolfe, Cary, 304n7
Wolin, Richard, 16–17
woman question, 190, 231, *16.2,* 329n5
Wordsworth, William, 17, 266

Yashvin, 132, 237

Zhdanov, V. A., 330n6
Zurbuchen, Mary Sabina, 13